INTEGRATING WOMEN INTO SECOND TEMPLE HISTORY

INTEGRATING WOMEN INTO SECOND TEMPLE HISTORY

TAL ILAN

HENDRICKSON
PUBLISHERS

Hendrickson Publishers, Inc.
P. O. Box 3473
Peabody, Massachusetts 01961–3473

INTEGRATING WOMEN INTO SECOND TEMPLE HISTORY, by Tal
Ilan. © 1999 J. C. B. Mohr (Paul Siebeck). All rights reserved. Hendrickson
Publishers' edition reprinted by arrangement with:

J. C. B. Mohr (Paul Siebeck), P. O. Box 2040, D–72010 Tübingen.

First Printing — October 2001

Printed in the United States of America

Library of Congress Cataloging-in-Publication Data

Ilan, Tal.
    Integrating women into Second Temple history / Tal Ilan.
        p. cm. — (Texts and studies in ancient Judaism, ISSN 0721–8753; 76)
    Includes bibliographical references and index.
    ISBN 1–56563–547–7 (paper)
    1. Women in Judaism—History. 2. Judaism—History—Post-exilic
period, 586 B.C.–210 A.D. 3. Jewish women—Historiography.
4. Women in rabbinical literature. 5. Rabbinical literature—History
and criticism. I. Title. II. Texte und Studien zum antiken Judentum; 76.

BM729.W6 I42 2001
296'.082'09014—dc21

                                            2001024813

Dedicated
To my friend
Judith Romney Wegner

Preface

This book is a third in a trilogy on Jewish women of the Second Temple and rabbinic periods. The first book, my Ph.D. dissertation, published in 1995 (*Jewish Women in Greco-Roman Palestine: An Inquiry into Image and Status*) was a rather traditional study of women in the settings in which we would expect to find them—the home, the marriage institution and in bed. When that study was completed I realized that women's role in history should hardly be confined to these restricted domains, since women were part of the rest of history too—social, political, economic, intellectual and religious. My second book (*Yours and Mine are Hers: Retrieving Women's History from Rabbinic Literature*) was a methodological study, suggesting criteria which could uncover women's presence and historical significance in documents and settings of the rabbinic corpus in which one would initially assume their absence. Much data on women in unexpected circumstances began to unfold before my eyes in that quest.

That study also sent me on another expedition into the same and other texts and territories, with the hope of finding more traces and more evidence of women's roles in the main political events of the period, and of the way their presence shaped these events. I began this quest in a number of articles published over the last six years, some of which I have collected, reworked and updated here. Half of this book is a collection of such studies. The other half consists of new studies completed specifically for this volume. I have called this book "Integrating Women into Second Temple History" under the inspiration of the title of Shulamit Magnus' article "Out of the Ghetto: Integrating the Study of Jewish Women into the Study of 'The Jews'," *Judaism* 39 (1990) 28-36. There, on p. 31, Magnus wrote: "The sources for the study of Jewish women ... are largely the sources we already have. What will change is the questions we will ask of them." I hope this book is an attempt to fulfill this vision. With its completion, the next frontier is to write a text-book history of the Second Temple period in which men and women will be equally represented. Such a project, however, lies in the distant future.

Many have contributed to the completion of this volume. First and foremost I must thank my friend and advisor, Prof. Judith Romney Wegner, who always reads my work before it is published and whose linguistic and professional comments are invaluable. Her attentive reading and understanding are unparalleled. When she fails to understand me I know I must rewrite the entire piece. When she suggests a correction, I know she is right. It is for this reason that I have decided to dedicate this book to her.

Chapters of this book I discussed with or were read by colleagues prior to publication. These include my teacher and mentor Prof. Daniel R. Schwartz and Prof. Hannah M. Cotton, Prof. Anna Belfer-Cohen, all of the Hebrew University, Prof. Bernadette Brooten of Brandeis University and Dr. Ada Yardeni. I have profited much from their comments and suggestions. The final product, of course, is entirely my own responsibility.

The suggestion to produce this collection was put to me several years ago by Prof. M. Hengel of the University of Tübingen whose constant support of my work has been a source of great inspiration. Prof. P. Schäfer of the Freie Universität in Berlin, whose friendship and good opinion of my work I treasure, generously seconded it. Herr Georg Siebeck of J.C.B. Mohr (Paul Siebeck) of Tübingen has proved a perfect publisher—careful, generous, patient. This second cooperation between us is proof thereof.

Five chapters of this book were published previously under the following titles:

Chapter 1: "The Attraction of Aristocratic Jewish Women to Pharisaism," *Harvard Theological Review* 88 (1995) 1-33.

Chapter 3: "Josephus and Nicolaus on Women," in *Geschichte-Tradition-Reflexion: Festschrift für Martin Hengel zum 70. Geburtstag*, eds. H. Cancik, H. Lichtenberger and P. Schäfer (Tübingen: J. C. B. Mohr, 1996) 221-62.

Chapter 8: "Julia Crispina Daughter of Berenicianus, A Herodian Princess in the Babatha Archive: A Case Study in Historical Identification," *The Jewish Quarterly Review* 82 (1992) 361-81.

Chapter 9: "Premarital Cohabitation in Ancient Judaea: The Evidence of the Babatha Archive and the Mishnah," *Harvard Theological Review* 86 (1993) 247-64.

Chapter 10: "Notes and Observation on a Newly Published Divorce Bill from the Judaean Desert," *Harvard Theological Review* 89 (1996) 195-202.

I thank these journals and publications for the permission to reprint them here.

For translations from the classics, I used the Leob Classical Library, unless stated otherwise. Translations from the Bible are usually from the Revised Standard Version. Translations of rabbinic literature are my own.

Jerusalem, February 1999   Tal Ilan

Table of Contents

Abbreviations

AJS	Association of Jewish Studies
BA	Biblical Archaeologist
BASOR	Bulletin of the American Schools of Oriental Research
CBQ	Catholic Biblical Quarterly
CII	Corpvs Inscriptionvm Iudaicarvm
CPJ	Corpus Papyrorum Judaicarum
HTR	Harvard Theological Review
HUCA	Hebrew Union College Annual
IAA	Israel Antiquities Authority
IEJ	Israel Exploration Journal
JBL	Journal of Biblical Literature
JJS	Journal of Jewish Studies
JQR	Jewish Quarterly Review
JRS	Journal of Roman Studies
JSJ	Journal for the Study of Judaism
JSOT	Journal for the Study of the Old Testament
JSP	Journal for the Study of the Pseudepigrapha
JSQ	Jewish Studies Quarterly
LSJ	A Greek English Lexicon (eds. H. G. Liddell, R. Scott and H. St. Jones; 1940⁹)
PEFQS	Palestine Exploration Fund Quarterly Statement
PEQ	Palestine Exploration Quarterly
RB	Revue Biblique
REJ	Revue des Études Juif
RQ	Revue Qumrân
SBL	Society of Biblical Literature
VT	Vetus Testamentum
ZNTW	Zeitschrift für die neutestamentliche Wissenschaft
ZATW	Zeitschrift für die alttestamentliche Wissenschaft
ZPE	Zeitschrift für Papyrologie und Epigraphik

"Women are a nation unto themselves" (*bShabbat* 62a).

Introduction

In the Babylonian Talmud Ulla is reputed to have held the opinion that "women are a nation unto themselves (נשים עם לעצמן)" (*bShabbat* 62a). Because of the context in which it appears (Jewish Sabbath laws) it seems quite obvious that Ulla is in fact referring to *Jewish* women as being "a nation unto themselves." Nations have a history, a territory, a language, a culture, a religion (or religions), literature, enemies, allies and a great many other attributes which identify them and distinguish them from other nations. Did Jewish women have all these? Of course not. Did they have any of these? Perhaps, but not very likely. Ulla, in this statement, was not giving a positive, factual assessment of what women were, but typically, and candidly, stating what they were not. Jewish women are not full members of the Jewish nation. I say "typically," because when viewed from a feminist perspective, history (all history, including Jewish history) looks devoid of women. I say "candidly" because, unlike most, Ulla was willing to admit that in his opinion, there was a Jewish nation, with a history and all that went with it, and there were women—a nation unto themselves.

This book, however, puts into question Ulla's statement. If Jewish women were a separate nation, we would be able to write their history separately. This, however, we cannot do. For example, we have no separate literature to fall back on for information on Jewish women as opposed to Jewish men. While it is true that nations such as the Idumaeans also do not have a separate literature that has survived (for their history we rely on Jewish sources), it is important to note the fact that the Idumaeans as a nation are now extinct. Jewish women, on the other hand, are not. Furthermore, if they have no literature, the Idumaeans have at least an archaeology.[1] Even if some may argue that Jewish women have a literature of sorts,[2] all would agree they have no archaeology.[3]

---

[1] For example I. Efal and J. Naveh, *Aramaic Ostraca of the Fourth Century BC from Idumaea* (Jerusalem 1996).

[2] Ross Kraemer, "Women's Authorship of Jewish and Christian Literature in the Greco-Roman Period," in Amy-Jill Levine (ed.), *'Women Like This': New Perspectives on Jewish Women in the Greco-Roman World* (Atlanta 1991) 221-42.

[3] Carol Meyers, *Discovering Eve: Ancient Israelite Women in Context* (Oxford 1988) particularly 18-9.

Do Jewish women have a separate language, or a separate territory? No. They speak the same language as Jewish men and not only do they not live in a separate country, they are not even a minority living in another nation's country. For they have no cities or neighborhoods—they live with Jewish men in the same houses and even share the same beds. If their enemies are Jewish men, they are indeed "sleeping with the enemy."

Do Jewish women perhaps have a separate religion? This is where our answers become more involved. They were certainly excluded to a great extent from the religion of Jewish men. Every morning a Jewish man is instructed to utter a blessing extolling the fact that he was not made a woman (*tBerakhot* 7:18), much in the same manner that he congratulated himself for not being a gentile, that is a member of another nation. The rational behind this blessing is that women (like gentiles) were excluded from participating in the most important commandments of Judaism. The special commandments imposed on women, however, were not viewed as a blessing, but as a curse (*yShabbat* 2:4, 5b). These two sources indicate that Jewish men's religion was different from that of Jewish women.

Who was it, however, that formulated this women's religion? Surely its initiates rather than its detractors define a religion. We have no evidence that Jewish women defined their own religion. If ever they were asked what religion they belonged to, they would certainly have defined themselves as Jewish. In fact, we may safely assume that had they been allowed to participate in the religious life of the Jews, they would have done so willingly. Ulla's statement turns out to be more wishful thinking than description of a historical fact. Jewish women are not a nation unto themselves.

Because Jewish women are part of the entire nation of Jews, there is no way we can write a separate history for them. Their history is inexorably bound up with that of Jewish men. The sources we use to learn about men are the sources we will use to learn about women. The political events that shaped Jewish men's lives likewise shaped Jewish women's lives. The features that are typical of a given period affect women lives just as they affect men's. Therefore, the search for women's history should not be conducted in regions other than those where men's history is found. Some events certainly evoked different reactions from men and women, or influenced them in different ways, but this does not mean that men and women were not there together. Women's history should not be confined to the home, the family or the bed, just as men's history should not be confined to the battlefield. This book is an attempt to move Jewish women's history out of its prescribed territories and place it in the public, political, literary, economic and social centres where the nation's consciousness and identity are shaped. It sets out to integrate Jewish women into Jewish history.

The task is not an easy one. All the sources militate against such an approach. Most of them, when dealing with politics, with war, with religion, totally ignore women. When dealing with women, they confine them to the domestic sphere and identify them with the house, with the family, with child raising. The sources were, after all, written by men and for men. It is, therefore, no coincidence that most studies devoted to Jewish women also confine them quite naturally to the domestic sphere.[4] Scholars are slaves to their sources. They may suspect them, doubt them, denigrate them, but ultimately they are guided by them.

This book too is guided by the sources themselves. However, in addition, it is guided by the most vital tool of feminist inquiry—that of placing women at the center of the events. The basic assumption in this book is that the women mentioned in the sources are not a means by which to explain the events but an end in themselves. When we discover them, we do not inquire how they explain the source or the event related in the source, but rather how the source explains their presence. By this process, sources in which women appear as remote or obscure, or which appear at first sight to be discussing something completely different, turn out to yield much material on women. With the help of such texts, we can find them involved in political activity, or at the centre of a literary or theological debate.

This book is, therefore, all about gender and Jewish history in the Second Temple and Talmudic period. The history of this period is characterized by sectarianism and theological debate. It is characterized by Jewish independence and by subjugation to foreign rule. Thus it is also characterized by the elation of the fight for freedom and the degradation of the refugee. It is characterized by the emergence of two separate corpora of Jewish literature— first the books known as the Apocrypha and Pseudepigrapha, and then, with the emergence of rabbinic Judaism, the rejection and partial loss of these and the development of rabbinic literature. Furthermore, it is characterized by a daily life and a unique material culture, which are features of all periods, but differ in manifestation from time to time.

In all of these women were undoubtedly present. This books aims to seek them out in these territories and to expose their role. This, of course, is not always possible, and often, even when achieved, produces meager evidence, which could be brushed away as non-representative and misleading. In ancient history, however, one cannot often hope for more even in fields which are infinitely better documented. In some cases, however, I have been fortunate in that I was able to discover the presence of women where a less

---

[4] Léonie Archer, *Her Price is Beyond Rubies: The Jewish Woman in Graeco-Roman Palestine* (*JSOT Supplement Series* 60; Sheffield 1990); D. Boyarin, *Carnal Israel: Reading Sex in Talmudic Culture* (Berkeley 1993); T. Ilan, *Jewish Women in Greco-Roman Palestine: An Inquiry into Image and Status* (*Texte und Studien zum antiken Judentum* 44; Tübingen 1995); M. Satlow, *Tasting the Dish: Rabbinic Rhetoric of Sexuality* (*Brown Judaic Studies* 303; Atlanta 1995); Judith Hauptman, *Rereading the Rabbis: A Woman's Voice* (Boulder CO, 1997).

zealous observer would have missed them altogether. These discoveries, then, form the foundation on which this book is constructed.

I have divided the book into three parts. Part one deals with sectarianism. As mentioned above, Jewish history of the Second Temple Period was characteristically sectarian. Women's roles in this phenomenon, aside from the cases where the sources mention them explicitly,[5] has seldom been discussed. Yet, in a wider sociological context, one can observe that women have often been active in sectarian movements, especially when these were in opposition. Women's secondary status in ancient patriarchal societies, which renders them unfit for most offices society has to offer, makes non-establishment, radical groups an ideal field for women to make their presence felt.

Chapter 1 deals with women in association with the Pharisee movement of the Second Temple period. The enormous amount of secondary literature dealing with the Pharisees indicates just how important this group is for the study of Second Temple times. Whether this importance was real, or whether it is merely perceived because of the importance acquired by the heirs of the Pharisees after the destruction of the Temple, is largely irrelevant. Despite the fact that the allegiance of women to the Pharisees is mentioned more than once in the sources, the issue has never before been explored by scholars. Nevertheless, it appears that women followers were an accepted phenomenon on the Pharisee scene before the destruction of the Temple. I propose a sociological model which explains this within the framework of the attraction of women to marginal opposition groups. This model allows further discussion of women followers of two other Second Temple Jewish sects— Early Christianity and the Dead Sea Sect. With the model in mind, some interesting phenomena associated with these groups can easily be explained.

Once Pharisaism became the defining factor in Judaism, women were pushed aside. Their support was, apparently, no longer required. In Chapter 1, some indication of this trend is revealed. Chapter 2 also deals with a body of evidence which points in this direction. It discusses the famous schism within Pharisaism—the rift between Beit Shammai and Beit Hillel. Pinpointing the rulings of the two schools on women reveals the striking fact that, in general, Beit Shammai promoted a more positive (or at least more egalitarian) approach to women's personhood and sexuality than Beit Hillel. Consequently, the rejection of the rulings of Beit Shammai was on the whole detrimental to women in the debate over their social and legal status in Judaism.

The historical identity of Beit Shammai is enigmatic. Scholars throughout the ages have identified them either with later-day Sadducees or with the

---

[5] E.g. the Therapeutai, see Ross S. Kraemer, "Monastic Jewish Women in Greco-Roman Egypt: Philo on the Therapeutrides," *Signs: Journal of Women in Culture and Society* 14 (1989) 342-70.

freedom movements of Josephus' Fourth Philosophy (the Zealots?). The discussion of women and Beit Shammai affords us a brief exploration of the relationship between women and these two Second Temple movements, for which an initial survey of the sources reveals very little information. A second look, however, suggests that the field is not altogether barren. A discussion of women in the Fourth Philosophy also requires delving into the question of women and war, and women and martyrdom—two phenomena which are of paramount importance in Second Temple history.

Part two is devoted to the way women are presented by the sources. The object of this exercise, however, is not to paint a picture of woman's image in the literature, and with this image to extol or denigrate the authors of the sources (as in previous scholarship[6]) but rather, to understand how the image and stereotype of women distorts the actual role they may have played in the historical, political, social events of their day. Sometimes this role is, alas, lost forever, and a discovery of the distortion remains just that, but sometimes when the distortion is removed, a glimpse of the true events may be revealed.

Chapter 3 discusses Josephus' attitude to women. Naturally, because of the character of Josephus' writing, this discussion concentrates primarily on royal women of the Hasmonean and Herodian courts. The use of women as a "category of analysis" applied to the books of Josephus uncovers clues for the understanding of these writings and provides answers for questions which have long mystified scholars. My analysis reveals that there is a clear distinction between the attitude to women in material composed by Josephus himself and the attitude in other parts of his work where he borrowed from other historians, primarily Nicolaus of Damascus. This, for example, helps identify the point at which Josephus begins to utilise Nicolaus rather than other sources. Paying attention to the treatment of women thus generates several useful by-products.

All in all, having identified the bias of the author and discarded it as a-historical, some glimpses of the historical reality in which royal women operated come to light. Thus we learn, despite the confusion caused by the sources, that Mariamme, Herod's wife, was probably executed for political reasons, since she was rightly perceived by her husband as a threat to his royal power. Similarly, despite Josephus' protestations, Queen Shelamzion Alexandra ruled successfully and was admired by many of her subjects. The relevance of the queen's rise to power and her subsequent reign to the debate over women's suitability for such offices is the topic of Chapter 4.

In many respects Chapter 4 is the most speculative piece in the entire collection. It suggests a theory according to which the three dominant

---

[6] Extolling: Boyarin, *Carnal Israel*, 240-5; Hauptman, *Rereading the Rabbis*, 244-9; denigrating: Ross S. Kraemer, *Her Share of the Blessings: Women's Religions among Pagans, Jews and Christians in the Greco-Roman World* (Oxford 1992) 93-105; Satlow, *Tasting the Dish*, 332-3.

compositions on women which have come down to us from the Second Temple Period—Esther, *Judith* and *Susanna*—were in fact composed for the purpose of promoting the queenship of Hasmonean women, primarily Queen Shelamzion Alexandra. Unlike other claims of this sort made by previous scholars, this essay begins with a firm date which has been noted in the past but whose significance has been ignored—the date of the translation of Esther into Greek, just one year before the ascent to the throne of the aforementioned queen. The desired connection between this literary composition and Queen Shelamzion is thus concretized. The other connections suggested in this chapter are far more circumstantial, but the discussion of these three compositions against the background of Hellenistic views on women and power places the entire corpus in context.

Chapter 5 also deals with the image of women—this time women in general with reference to another composition, in which women feature prominently—*Ben Sira*. The question of *Ben Sira*'s misogyny has been the subject of some scholarly debate, and is, in any case, more a literary than a historical problem. In this chapter I explore the historical repercussions of *Ben Sira*'s attitude to women, by testing the extent to which his opinions on the subject were treasured and cited. For this purpose I explore the citations of *Ben Sira* in the Babylonian Talmud. As is well known, the book of *Ben Sira* enjoyed a special status with the rabbis, for although it was not canonized, it was often cited approvingly. It has, however, not been previously noted that the bulk of *Ben Sira* quotations cherished by the Babylonian rabbis were about women and displayed a marked misogynistic tone. This suggests two interesting conclusions. The first is that *Ben Sira*'s attitude to women was not "a voice in the wilderness," but rather a chorus of disapproval, and the other is that his book was appreciated in Babylonian circles less for its infinite wisdom and more for its blatant misogyny.

As opposed to Chapter 5, which inquires about the reflection of ancient women's images in rabbinic literature, Chapter 6 deals with the image of one woman—Beruriah—within the rabbinic corpus. The quest for the "historical Beruriah" allows the use of by now well tried literary tools of criticism of the rabbinic corpus. The tannaitic corpus is discussed separately from the amoraic one, and tannaitic compositions are discussed individually, allowing for differences in outlooks and purposes of the various editors. The historical Beruriah in this chapter turns out to be quite different from the literary Beruriah identified by previous (feminist) scholars. Her importance for feminist studies is, however, in no way diminished thereby.

Finally, Chapter 6 deals with a different kind of source altogether. The data it investigates is skeletal remains of Jews buried in Palestine during the Second Temple period. The assumption of this chapter is that the bones are not completely silent and when asked the right questions, may tell us much about the realities of Jewish women's lives in the period under discussion.

The questions I ask concern sex ratio, child mortality, age at death and violence in the family. The answers the bones give are not always straightforward, but the large data base I have collected allows for a fairly balanced assessment of the data.

Archaeological remains are also the topic of the last part of this book. The importance of the Judaean Desert documents for the study of Jewish women's history is so significant, that it merits special notice. These documents include two complete women's archives, as well as other personal documents owned by women, which contain a rich repository of information. However, because this information is in general confined to questions of marriage, divorce and women's ownership or lack of property under male tutelage, most of the discussions that these documents generate belong to the traditional realm of family and marriage. For this reason, the first two chapters in this section propose a special methodology with which these sources should be approached. The methodology is basically very simple. It suggests that the documents be read not only in order to establish generalizations about women's legal position within this particular Jewish society, but should likewise be mined for the unique, the unexpected, the sensational. For this reason chapters 8 and 9 each discuss only one detail mentioned in one document. Chapter 8 discusses the unique and unexpected; chapter 9 discusses the sensational.

Chapter 8 discusses a woman, Julia Crispina, who is mentioned in the Babatha archive as an *episcopos* (overseer), but whose presence and role there have eluded previous scholars. In this chapter it is suggested that her name and exalted position single her out as a member of the Herodian family. This allows one to incorporate her into Jewish women's history and to solve a few historical, social and legal mysteries associated with the Babatha archive.

Chapter 9 discusses a clause in the marriage document of Salome Komaise (the other owner of an archive), which suggests that the aforementioned Salome had been living together with her husband prior to their marriage. This clause is discussed in conjunction with information derived from rabbinic literature and places the social reality it reveals in a historical (even chronological) context.

Chapter 10, although equally engaged in discussing the sensational, is both a discussion of a complete document and deals specifically with the institution of marriage, with which women are traditionally associated, and which I have therefore, in general, avoided in this book. I have included this piece, however, because the document it discusses is a bill of divorce which a Jewish wife sent her Jewish husband under the auspices of a Jewish court in an independent Jewish state. The idea that such a document could exist, that such an action by a woman could ever have been possible is so foreign to any conventional scholar of Judaism that this straightforward document has universally been misunderstood in previous scholarship. Furthermore, it so radically alters our conception of the position of women in pre-rabbinic Judaism as to constitute a fitting finale for a book which proposes to revise, alter and fill in some gaps in our knowledge and understanding of women's role in Second Temple and Rabbinic Jewish history.

Part 1

Women and Sects

Chapter One

"Fear not the Pharisees" (*bSotah* 22b)
The Attraction of Aristocratic Women to
Pharisaism*

Unlike Christianity, which treats the words "Pharisee" as synonymous with "hypocrite,"[1] "legalist,"[2] "petty-bourgeois,"[3] Jews have always understood Pharisaism as the correct and trustworthy side of Judaism.[4] Since the eighteenth century all disputants who participated in the great controversies and schisms within Judaism have claimed to represent the true heirs of the Pharisees. For example, adherents of the strong anti-Hasidic movement initiated by R. Eliyahu of Vilna (usually called the "Ga'on of Vilna - הגר"א) in the second half of the eighteenth century, who are usually referred to in literature by the negative appellation "antagonists" (מתנגדים),[5] referred to themselves by the positive title "פרושים (Pharisees)."[6] When the Reform movement was founded in Germany in the first half of the nineteenth century, with the goal of reforming the Jewish religion to make it more "modern" and acceptable to its neighbors, they perceived themselves as the true heirs of the

---

* This chapter was read prior to its publication by my teacher D. R. Schwartz. I am grateful to him for many useful comments. I alone, of course, am responsible for the final product.

[1] Adolf von Harnack, *What is Christianity?* (New York 1957) 48. This book was first published in German in 1900.

[2] E.g. E. Schürer, G. Vermes, F. Millar and M. Black, *The History of the Jewish People in the Age of Jesus Christ (175 BC-AD 135)* 2 (Edinburgh 1979) 388.

[3] M. Weber, *Ancient Judaism* (Glencoe IL 1952) 388 (translation of a 1917 article).

[4] On disputes between Jews and Christians on the essence of Pharisaism, see: D. R. Schwartz, *Studies in the Jewish Background of Christianity* (*Wissenschaftliche Untersuchungen zum Neuen Testament* 60; Tübingen 1992) 66-70.

[5] See "Mitnaggedim," *Encyclopedia Judaica* 12 (Jerusalem 1971) 161.

[6] Y. Hisdai, "The Origins of the Conflict Between Hasidim and Mitnagdim," in B. Safran (ed.), *Hasidism: Continuity or Innovation?* (*Harvard Judaic Texts and Monographs* 5; Cambridge MA 1988) 27-45. See particularly pp. 39-44.

Pharisees.[7] In his important study of the Pharisees and Sadducees, Abraham Geiger, one of the founders of *"Wissenschaft des Judentums"*, and an important spokesman for the radical wing of the Reform movement,[8] fostered the view of the flexible open-minded Pharisees, who reformed Judaism to the point of contradicting the laws set out in the Pentateuch, in order to accommodate them to their changing needs.[9] Geiger's opponents easily produced evidence that negated his findings and proved beyond doubt that they, in their conservative strain, were the real heirs of Pharisaism. To his opponents Geiger was a representative of the detestable Sadducees, or their later counterparts, the Karaites.[10]

Despite their academic tone, more recent scholarly debates about the Pharisee can also be perceived as a dispute over who are the Pharisees' rightful heirs. Gedalyahu Alon, an Israeli scholar who harbored strong nationalistic feelings during the formative years of the state of Israel, argued in a highly polemical article that the Pharisees did not resign their political power with Herod's rise to power, but were politically active in opposition to his rule. Like Alon himself, the Pharisees must have opposed the Jews' subjugation to a foreign ruler or to Jewish collaborators and upheld a policy of resistance in a struggle for national independence.[11] Jacob Neusner, a Jewish scholar living in the Diaspora, argued that the ideological bent of these claims distorted Alon's methodology. He convincingly showed that where Alon found opposition to Herod there is no mention of Pharisees, and where Pharisees appear, opposition does not. Neusner maintained, therefore, that after the Hasmonean period the Pharisees withdrew from politics and became a religious sect.[12] Neusner strongly critiqued Alon's method as untenable; it is, however, interesting that Neusner's historical conclusions fit ideologically with his own agenda—the Pharisees, like present day Jews living in the

---

[7] D. Philipson, *The Reform Movement in Judaism* (Cincinnati 1907) 5: "In a word, Reform Judaism ... considers itself too a link in the chain of Jewish tradition, the product of this modern age, as Talmudism was of its age."

[8] On Geiger see: M. Wiener, *Abraham Geiger and Liberal Judaism: The Challenge of the Nineteenth Century* (Translation E. J. Schlochauer, Philadelphia 1962).

[9] A. Geiger, *Urschrift und Übersetzung der Bibel in ihrer Abhängigkeit von der inneren Entwicklung des Judenthums* (Breslau 1857) particularly pp. 101-58. For further bibliography on the identification of the reformers with the Pharisees, see D. R. Schwartz, *Jewish Background*, pp. 74-9.

[10] Solomon Eiger's letter, in S. A. Tiktin, *Darstellung des Sachverhältnisses in seiner hiesigen Rabbinatsangelegenheit* (Breslau 1842) 25.

[11] G. Alon, *Jews, Judaism and the Classical World* (Translation I. Abrahams; Jerusalem 1977) 18-47.

[12] A recent edition of Neusner's old theory is his "Josphus' Pharisees: A Complete Repetoire," in L. H. Feldman and G. Hata (eds.), *Josephus, Judaism and Christianity* (Detroit 1987) 274-92.

Diaspora, were content with religious freedom, and left politics to the foreign ruling power. Neusner has recently been criticized for his conclusions. It is striking that Daniel Schwartz, an Israeli scholar, concedes all of Neusner's criticism of Alon but opposes his ideological conclusions, arguing for an active political role for the Pharisees during the entire Second Temple period, even down to the war against Rome in 66-70 CE.[13]

Closer to the issue of the Pharisees is the identification of the tannaitic rabbis as the heirs of the Pharisees. The assertion that the Pharisees were not merely one of many sects, but encompassed the vast majority of the Jews comes from the circles of orthodox and traditional Jewish scholarship.[14] The rabbis, the true heirs of the Pharisees, effectively overcame all opposition to their political and religious system after the destruction of the Temple in 70 CE. Scholars describe this process as a move from pluralistic to monolithic Judaism.[15] These scholars maintain that even at the present time Jewish orthodoxy, the only true heir to the Pharisees, should assert itself over its insignificant and hardly Jewish opponents. This description has been opposed recently by the more liberal Shaye Cohen, another Jewish scholar living in the Diaspora; he maintains that rabbinic Judaism after 70, whose representatives were indeed former Pharisees, did not become monolithic but resigned its claim to exclusivity in the interest of a religious and social tolerance, which is the most common feature of rabbinic Judaism.[16] In Cohen's opinion, therefore, today's true heirs of the Pharisees should support a multifaceted interpretation of Judaism, including Conservative and Reform Judaism.

A variation on this attitude has prevailed in recent years, probably due to the greater interaction between Jewish and Christian scholarship. Current scholars commonly assert that Second-Temple Judaism could hardly be

---

[13] D. R. Schwartz, "Josephus and Nicolaus on the Pharisees," *JSJ* 14 (1983) 157-71.

[14] See e.g. E. Rivkin, *A Hidden Revolution: The Pharisees' Search for the Kingdom Within* (Nashville 1978).

[15] This idea certainly is found in early Christian works, see: Schürer, *History of the Jewish People,* 402-3; R. H. Pfeifer, *History of New Testament Times with an Introduction to the Apocrypha* (New York 1949) 44; G. F. Moore, *Judaism in the First Centuries of the Christian Era* 1 (Cambridge 1964) 83-7. The idea is also voiced by many Jewish historians, e.g. C. Roth, *A Short History of the Jewish People* (London 1969) 112; J. Neusner, *From Politics to Piety: The Emergence of Pharisaic Judaism* (Engelwood Cliffs NJ 1973) 143-54; S. Safrai, "The Era of the Mishnah and Talmud (70-640)," in H. H. Ben-Sasson (ed.), *A History of the Jewish People* (Cambridge MA 1976) 325-6; S. Zeitlin, *The Rise and Fall of the Judaean State* 3 (Philadelphia 1978) 155-8; M. D. Herr, *A History of Eretz Israel: The Roman Period* (Jerusalem 1984) 290 [Hebrew].

[16] S. J. D. Cohen, "The Significance of Yavneh: Pharisees, Rabbis, and the End of Jewish Sectarianism," *HUCA* 55 (1984) 27-53.

described as predominantly Pharisaic; they now talk of "many Judaisms."[17] The Pharisees, therefore, who previously had been viewed as normative in Second Temple times, and their heirs—the rabbis—who were similarly perceived in the following period, are relegated to equal footing with their one time inferiors, the other groups previously viewed as dissident or schismatic.[18] Scholars also apply this idea to the period after the destruction of the Temple, claiming that even in Palestine rabbinic Judaism was only one small group within the Jewish people at the time.[19] Interestingly this view is also propagated by Reform, Conservative and secular Jews, all of whom claim a share in modern-day Judaism.

The Jewish feminist movement, a product of the 1970s, can also be located on this "we-the-Pharisees" map. Judith Hauptman, a Conservative Jew, had written in 1972 (much like Reform Jews more than a hundred years earlier) that since the rabbis of the Talmud, the historical heirs of the Pharisees, had demonstrably improved the condition of womenfolk in their day, Judaism today should do likewise.[20] Hauptman adopted the attitude that the true heirs of the Pharisees can be feminists, much as the Pharisees themselves had probably been. Since 1972, however, much has been written to demonstrate that the Pharisees and their heirs were scarcely feminists—or even well-disposed toward women.[21] It is here that the proponents of the "many-Judaisms" approach enter the debate. The chief representative of this attitude is undoubtedly Ross Kraemer. Kraemer is convinced that rabbinic texts are misogynistic, and, what is more, fictional, representing attitudes of a small minority of Jews and certainly not describing the reality of the majority of Jewish women.[22] Kraemer, herself a Jew living in the Diaspora, devotes her studies to women in the Hellenistic-Roman Diaspora;[23] she maintains that

---

[17] See for example the two following titles: A. F. Segal, *The Other Judaisms of Late Antiquity* (*Brown Judaic Studies* 127; Atlanta 1987); G. D. Cohen, *Studies in the Variety of Rabbinic Cultures* (Philadelphia 1991).

[18] See recently, A. J. Saldarini, *Pharisees, Scribes and Sadducees* (Edinburgh 1989).

[19] E.g. I. L. Levine, *The Rabbinic Class of Roman Palestine in Late Antiquity* (Jerusalem 1985).

[20] Judith Hauptman, "Women's Liberation in the Talmudic Period: An Assessment," *Conservative Judaism* 26/4 (1972) 24-8. And see more recently, and in a more sophisticated style, but by no means with a new message, D. Boyarin, *Carnal Israel: Reading Sex in Talmudic Culture* (Berkeley 1993) 227-45.

[21] E.g. Judith Romeny Wegner, *Chattel or Person: The Status of Women in the Mishnah* (Oxford 1988); M. L. Satlow, "'Texts of Terror': Rabbinic Texts, Speech Acts and the Control of Mores," *AJS Review* 21 (1996) 273-97.

[22] Ross S. Kraemer, *Her Share of the Blessings: Women's Religions among Pagans, Jews and Christians in the Greco-Roman World* (Oxford 1992) 93-105.

[23] *Eadem*, "A New Inscription from Malta and the Question of Women Elders in Diaspora Jewish Communities," *HTR* 78 (1985) 431-8; "Hellenistic Jewish Women: The Epigraphic

while Pharisaic and rabbinic Judaism had little to offer women, Diaspora Judaism held them in great esteem and was, therefore, very attractive, even to non-Jewish women. This view obviously supports the legitimacy of present-day non-religious, assimilated Diaspora Judaism.

The present chapter obviously and consciously adds another brick to the Pharisaic edifice. It is written with the traditional historical methodology of presenting and evaluating the evidence and drawing historical conclusions. I certainly do not view feminism as the true heir of Pharisaism, although I hope to demonstrate that Pharisaism held great attraction for women. This claim greatly modifies the argument that the Pharisaic tradition was historically irrelevant to most Jewish women, as the "many-Judaisms" party claims. I am, nevertheless, certain that I can also be placed on the Pharisee research chart by someone standing at a distance from the present discussion and in command of a better view of the discipline.[24]

1. The Evidence

Two highly controversial and unrelated sources make the claim that Jewish women are ruled by the Pharisees, or at any rate follow their dicta. One source is Josephus, the other is rabbinic literature.

a. Josephus

In Josephus' description of the plot hatched against Herod by his son Antipater in alliance with Herod's brother Pheroras and the women of these two men's households, Josephus makes the following claim:

> There was also a group of Jews priding itself on its adherence to ancestral custom and claiming to observe the laws of which the Deity approves, and by these men, called Pharisees, the women were ruled. These men were able to help the king greatly because of their foresight, and yet they were obviously intent upon combating and injuring him. At least when the whole Jewish people affirmed by an oath that it would be loyal to Caesar and to the king's government, these men, over six thousand in number, refused to take this oath, and when the king punished them with a fine, Pheroras' wife paid the fine for them. In return for her friendliness they foretold—for they were believed to have foreknowledge of things through God's appearances to them—that by God's decree Herod's throne would be taken from him, both from himself and his descendants, and the royal power would fall to her and to Pheroras and to any children they might have (*Ant.* 17.41-3)

Evidence," *SBL Seminary Papers* 24 (1986) 183-200; "Non Literary Evidence for Jewish Women in Rome and Egypt," *Helios* 13 (1987) 85-101; "Monastic Jewish Women in Greco-Roman Egypt: Philo on the Therpeutrides," *Signs: Journal of Women in Culture and Society* 14 (1989) 342-70; "Jewish Women in the Diaspora World of Late Antiquity," in Judith R. Baskin (ed.), *Jewish Women in Historical Perspective* (Detroit 1991) 43-67.

[24] I have tried to place myself on this chart in my "Women Studies and Jewish Studies: When and Where do they Meet?" *JSQ* 3 (1996) 172-3.

This text is one of many highly-involved descriptions of the Herodian court found in Josephus' writings, and usually assigned to Herod's court historian, Nicolaus of Damascus. Elsewhere I show[25] that Nicolaus was much more interested than Josephus in the role women played in politics, and was usually quick to blame their sex for most calamities, political or otherwise, that befell Herod's court. Women's association with the Pharisees is, moreover, not intended as a compliment. The question we are addressing, however, is not whether Nicolaus liked the association women had with the Pharisees, but whether he is telling the truth.

In this text, one general claim and one particular claim are made about women and the Pharisees. In general the Pharisees have a special appeal for women—they "govern" them. The particular claim is contained in a case that proves this claim. When Herod fined the Pharisees, the fine was paid by a woman, in this case the wealthy wife of the king's brother. I will discuss the implication of the support rendered to the Pharisees by Pheroras' wife later. Here I am interested in the general claim voiced by Josephus, that women were governed by the Pharisees. I begin by inquiring whether this charge is fabricated.

Obviously the claim that the Pharisees ruled women is not intended as a compliment. Real rulers govern both men and women; rule over women alone is meant as a sign of weakness and softness. Furthermore, it is the husband's prerogative to rule over his wife (and Pheroras is here reprimanded for not ruling over his own wife) and the intrusion of the Pharisees is obviously intended to imply an encroachment on the natural rights of husbands. All this taken together raises doubts concerning the historical significance of this passage. Elsewhere, however, Nicolaus claims that the Pharisees had the support of the masses (*Ant.* 13.288; 13.401-2; and 18.15 apparently not based on Nicolaus). It has been shown that this claim likewise is not intended as a positive epithet.[26] Both Nicolaus and Josephus see the masses as an unruly, disruptive element in society, which should be contained rather than allowed to acquire power by rendering political support. Nevertheless, the question of the historical truth behind the assertion that the Pharisees enjoyed popular support and were actually in a position to influence the political, and particularly the religious, practices of their day is hotly debated. Sanders believes that there is no truth to this claim—that it is mere propaganda.[27] Schwartz sees it as a Nicolean slur.[28] Although Mason maintains that Josephus does not consider the Pharisees' popular following a compliment to

---

[25] On Nicolaus' treatment of royal women see chapter 3 below.

[26] Both by D. R. Schwartz, "Josephus and Nicolaus," 158-62, and S. Mason, *Flavius Josephus on the Pharisees: A Composition-Critical Study* (Leiden 1991) 222-9; 250-1; 300-6.

[27] E. P. Sanders, *Judaism: Practice and Belief 63 BCE-66 CE* (London 1992) 458-90.

[28] "Josephus and Nicolaus," 158-9; Schwartz does not refer specifically to the women.

them, he believes that historically they did exert significant power.[29] I think it is methodologically incorrect to dismiss the claim that the Pharisees held sway over women, while maintaining the view that they indeed exerted influence on the masses. If the one is correct, the other is probably also true and *vice versa*.

Assuming, therefore, that the statement is derogatory but true, I would inquire whether scholars have understood it correctly. Is this passage telling us that Pheroras' wife was a follower of the Pharisees like most Jewish women at the time but one of few supporters in Herod's court? If so, it is possible that Pheroras' wife's background made her susceptible to subversive Pharisee ideas. Nicolaus never names the woman, but she is often described in great detail and is even labeled a slave (*Ant.* 16.194). Whether she had been a slave, or whether the designation is a derogatory epithet for a woman of humbler origin is unclear from the text, but perhaps her attraction to Pharisaism stemmed from this background. In Ralph Marcus' translation of Josephus, however, the words "of the court" are inserted in parenthesis after the words "the women." This suggests that Marcus did not understand this statement to refer to a general following of the Pharisees by women but to a specific following by women within the court of Herod. Marcus' interpretation is obviously based on the fact that the words "the women" (which appear elsewhere in Josephus' description of the events leading to Antipater's plot against Herod and to the close death of the two) refer to a group of women at court. These women included Pheroras' wife, her mother and sister, and Antipater's mother, Doris. If Marcus' interpretation is correct, Josephus, *Ant.* 17.41-3 can serve as evidence that women were attracted to Pharisaism only in the royal court. While limiting the scope of Nicolaus' assertion about women and the Pharisees, Marcus' interpretation suggests a more interesting, and as we shall see, highly plausible pattern.

b. Rabbinic Literature

Rabbinic literature cannot be considered a sectarian writing of the Pharisees (equivalent, for example, to the Dead Sea Scrolls), particularly because of its late date. To a great extent, however, the rabbis were the heirs of the Pharisees and retained traditions originally held by the Pharisees.[30] As Neusner has aptly demonstrated, it is difficult to differentiate between the original Pharisaic stratum within rabbinic literature and the many embellishments added to it in the generations between its formulation and final redaction.[31]

Like Josephus, rabbinic literature also claims that the Pharisees exerted influence on the Temple functionaries, who despite Sadducean leanings,

---

[29] Mason, *Flavius Josephus*, 375.

[30] Even Cohen, "Significance of Yavneh," 50, concedes this.

[31] J. Neusner, *Rabbinic Traditions about the Pharisees Before 70* 1 (Leiden 1971) 6-7.

performed the cultic rituals according to Pharisaic dicta because the Pharisees had a large public following. For example, on the Day of Atonement the high priest followed Pharisaic rulings when he entered the Holy of Holies (*tKippurim* 5:8). Rabban Yohanan ben Zakkai reportedly supervised the immersion of the high priest before burning the red heifer (*tParah* 3:8) and ended the ordeal of the bitter water (*mSotah* 9:9). Whether any of this is historically true is a controversial question.[32] It is striking, however, that the claim of Pharisaic influence on the Temple corresponds, in theme if not in detail, to Josephus' description of Pharisaic influence, particularly over the Sadducees (*Ant.* 18.17). If Josephus in his *Antiquities* was the mouthpiece of the group that composed tannaitic literature in Yavneh, as suggested by Smith,[33] this correspondence would make sense. If, however, as Schwartz had argued, most of these claims go back to Nicolaus,[34] the similarities become more significant.

It is therefore striking that rabbinic literature retains a tradition, like Nicolaus, that women of the Sadducee sect followed the Pharisaic laws. Rabbinic tradition refers specifically to the laws of menstruation, devoting much space to them. Specialists within the rabbinic class could tell unclean menstrual blood from clean blood stemming from another source. The rabbis claimed that any woman who did not consult these specialists was theoretically unclean all the time. Samaritan women fell into this category. Sadducean women, however, were a different matter:

> Said Rabbi Yose: We (i.e. the rabbis, or the sages) are more knowledgeable about Sadducean women than about any other, since they are all examined by sages except for one who was among them and died (*tNiddah* 5:2).

Rabbinic literature tends to identify the Sadducees as the opponents of the Sages (as it terms the Pharisees). An anecdote appended to this text tells of a high priest's wife who confessed to her husband that she followed the rabbis dicta with regard to the laws of menstruation:

> There was a case of a Sadducean woman (צדוקה) who was conversing with a high priest and some spittle fell from her mouth on the clothes of the high priest, and the face of the high priest turned green. And they went and asked his wife and she said: My husband is a priest. Although we are Sadducean women, we are all examined by a [Pharisee] sage (*ibid.* 5:3).[35]

---

[32] See Sanders, *Judaism*, 399-402.

[33] M. Smith, "Palestinian Judaism in the First Century," in M. Davis (ed.), *Israel: Its Role in Civilization* (New York 1956) 71-8.

[34] "Josephus and Nicolaus," 158-62.

[35] It has been suggested by Cohen, "Significance of Yavneh," 32-3, that this second excerpt refers to Temple times, demonstrating the unique case of the specific woman, while

This story refers specifically to the time of the Second Temple, when a high priest had to be pure at all times in order to perform his priestly functions. A Sadducean woman was always perceived as a likely source of contamination. This text reassures the priest and its readers that this is not the case.

It seems, therefore, that rabbinic literature is making virtually the same claim as Josephus although in a more positive vein: the rabbis or sages (i.e. the Pharisees) had the support of the masses, and through them exerted influence on the political and religious institutions of their day. Texts making this claim are numerous and discussed elsewhere.[36] Furthermore, the Pharisees also exercised great influence on women not of their own sect, as is claimed in the text under discussion here. While the historical reliability of this claim may be highly suspect both as to the general claim and as to the specific claim about women's support, the fact that it is repeated independently by two sources does somewhat enhance its credibility.

In light of these conclusions, another source that has been virtually ignored or discarded may also be rehabilitated in the reconstruction of women's attraction to Pharisaism. At one point, the Mishnah puts forth a very negative view of a *perushah* woman (אשה פרושה). The text is very complex, and requires discussion of its context. In the third chapter of the mishnaic tractate Sotah we find a discussion of the desirability of teaching one's daughter Torah.

> Rabbi Eliezer says: "Whoever teaches his daughter Torah, it is as though he taught her תפלות" (*mSotah* 3:4).[37]

It is not clear what the last word means, but on the basis of the next sentence, it has usually been interpreted as sexual licentiousness:

> Rabbi Joshua says: A woman prefers one portion [of wealth] with sex (תפלות) rather than nine portions [of wealth] with abstinence (פרישות) (*ibid.*).

The word we are interested in here is פרישות. In this context it means sexual abstinence, but its root, פרש, is also the root of the word פרושי, meaning Pharisee. In this text, Rabbi Joshua asserts that women's sexual drives are

---

the former refers to Sadducean women of the time of the tannaitic sages. Jacob Neusner has demonstrated (*Reading and Believing: Ancient Judaism and Contemporary Gullibility* [Brown Judaic Studies 113; Atlanta 1986] 83-5), however, that it is not methodologically sound to accept this evidence at face value or to identify chronological strata on the basis of such source material.

[36] Sanders, *Judaism*, 399-402.

[37] On this text and its translations see my *Jewish Women in Greco-Roman Palestine: An Inquiry into Image and Status* (Texte und Studien zum antiken Judentum 44; Tübingen 1995) 139, and especially n. 13; and see also my *Mine and Yours are Hers: Retrieving Women's History from Rabbinic Literature* (Leiden 1997) 166.

paramount in their lives; the text's position in the Mishnah suggests that in order to avoid sexual misconduct, women should be married and ruled by their husbands. The text then proceeds as follows:

> Rabbi Joshua would say: A foolish *Hasid*, a sly villain (רשע ערום), a פרושה woman and the harms (מכות) done by the פרושים, these wear out the world (*mSotah* 3:4).

In using the word *perushah*, is Rabbi Joshua still referring to an abstinent woman? This is not clear, since he mentions also the harms of the פרושים, which probably refers to the Pharisees, after mentioning the woman. His reference to a פרושה woman may be a play on the two aspects of the word פרוש. A woman who follows the Pharisees disobeys her husband and therefore practices sexual abstinence. Correct sexual conduct can only be maintained if women are not פרושות in either meaning of the word. In other words, they must be ruled by their husbands rather than by פרישות (which can mean either Pharisaism or sexual abstinence). The sage thus acknowledges the phenomenon of "Pharisee" women, i.e. women who are not married to Pharisees, but adhere to the Pharisee ways. Had these women been merely the wives of Pharisees, there would have been no point in mentioning them. It is logical to assume that women married to non-Pharisee men, or not currently married, had followed the Pharisees; it is this that is so strongly criticized.

R. Joshua's statement is negative in its assessment of both the *perushah* woman and the harm done by the *perushim*. If the second use of the term should be identified with the Pharisees, so should the first. Scholars seem to have difficulty interpreting this text as referring to the Pharisees because of its provenance within the rabbinic corpus, which is assumed to be of Pharisaic origin.[38] Why would the Pharisees denigrate themselves in such a way? This particular negative statement, however, is presented as the opinion of a sage after the Temple's destruction; it may be a personal reflection of certain social phenomena associated with Pharisaism, of which the sage disapproved, without actually discrediting Pharisaism *per se*.[39] Perhaps when Pharisaism gained universal recognition after the destruction of the Temple, its members scoffed at some of the behavior of their forebears and at the following they had relied upon before attaining prominence. Once the constituency of women was no longer needed to bolster up the lines of the Pharisees, the women's

---

[38] See for example E. Rivkin, "Defining the Pharisees: The Tannaitic Sources," *HUCA* 40-41 (1970) 240-1. For an ingenious interpretation, intended to surmount the difficulty of the Pharisee woman, see A. Geiger, "On the Pharisee Woman in *mSotah* 3:4," *Otzar Nehmad* 2 (1857) 99-101 [Hebrew], who suggests that one should read, with Maimonides, אשה פרוצה (whore woman) instead. This suggestion clearly ignores the *lectio difficilior* principle.

[39] On the disparity between pre-70 Pharisees and post-70 sages, see P. Schäfer, "Der vorrabbinische Pharisäismus," in M. Hengel and U. Heckel (eds.), *Paulus und das antike Judentum: Tübingen-Durham-Symposium in Gedenken an den 50. Todestag Adolf Schlatters (Mai 1938)* (Tübingen 1988) 125-75.

loyalty was viewed as a burden rather than an asset. Regardless, this statement is further evidence for the existence of a body of women who followed Pharisaic ways.

The evidence amassed thus far may not amount to much but it certainly indicates that both within Pharisee circles and outside them the phenomenon of women who supported the movement separately from men was noticed and commented upon, mostly in a negative way. In order to investigate the historical truth behind these statements we must approach the issue from the perspective of individual women and their political leanings.

2. The Women

a. Queen Shelamzion Alexandra

It is a well-known historical fact that only during the nine short years of Queen Shelamzion's rule did the Pharisees gain the upper hand in Palestinian politics and were in a position to dictate their ideas of how to govern the Jewish people. Obviously based on Nicolaus of Damascus, Josephus explicitly states that they came to power because of the new regime headed by Queen Shelamzion Alexandra, the widow of King Alexander Yannai. Shelamzion's nine-year reign is the only period in Second Temple history when the land was ruled by the Pharisees, and it is also the only period in which the land was ruled by a woman. While these facts are universally recognized in Second Temple scholarship, no one has ever suggested that the Pharisees were favored for any reason other than Shelamzion's personal leanings. One should consider seriously, however, the possibility that these leanings were influenced strongly by the queen's gender. The appeal of Pharisaism for women seems to have paid off in the case of Shelamzion.

According to Josephus' *Jewish War*, Queen Shelamzion was responsible for investing supreme power in the Pharisees because "being herself intensely religious she listened [to them] with too great deference" (*War* 1.111). The queen followed the Pharisees for religious reasons, and in opposition to her husband's political leanings. The actions of Shelamzion are thus not governed by familial considerations; on the contrary, her choice was made over and against her family. While the text, undoubtedly based on Nicolaus, views Pharisaic influence on the woman negatively, there is little doubt that the good relations between the Pharisees and the queen in the text reflect historical reality.

In the version of the story in *Antiquities*, however, the wife follows her husband's advice in installing the Pharisees; this modifies the blatant claim that the queen made an independent choice. On his deathbed Yannai is said to have recommended that "on her return to Jerusalem ... she should yield a certain amount of power to the Pharisees, for if they praised her in return for this sign of regard, they would dispose the nation favorably toward her" (*Ant.* 13.401).[40] In my opinion this source is of a secondary nature, and should not be considered reliable. It is one of the texts found in *Antiquities* and absent in the *Jewish War*, that have parallels in the Babylonian Talmud, possibly suggesting that Josephus used a written Jewish source for this information. This now lost source was also available, in some form or another, to the redactors of the Babylonian Talmud.

The Hebrew version of this story is instructive; it indicates that a scene (legendary or historical) between the king and future queen was recorded in the lost source, and included reference to the Pharisees. The nature of the advice, however, is very different in the rabbinic text. The Talmud's discussion of the *mishnah*, which denigrates the "harms [done by] the פרושים" mentioned above, relates the following anecdote:

> King Yannai said to his wife: Fear not the פרושין nor those who are not פרושין, but fear rather the hypocrites (צבועין) who are like the פרושין, whose deeds are like the deeds of Zimri and who seek reward like Phineas (cf. Numbers 25) (*bSotah* 22b).

Although scholars have been uncertain whether the פרושים mentioned in *mSotah* 3:4 should be identified as Pharisees, no one has ever doubted that *bSotah* 22b refers to the Pharisees, because of its parallel in Josephus. The differences between this episode and the description found in Josephus, however, are numerous. The episode in the Babylonian Talmud is not a deathbed scene regulating the succession; the king does not recommend yielding power to the Pharisee, but suggests that the queen need not fear them. Others (who are called hypocrites, but unlike in the New Testament, not identified with the Pharisees) are the real source of a ruler's concern. Although the Babylonian text is evidently much later than the Josephus, and was probably transmitted orally over many generations, at least two considerations suggest that it preserves a better version. One consideration is the nature of oral traditions. When a story is transmitted orally much can be altered in the process, but concise sayings have a tendency to be transmitted precisely. Yannai's advice "Fear not ... nor ... but fear rather ..." is at the heart of the story in the form of an easily memorized epigram. The other consideration is the nature of Josephus' ordering of his source material. Josephus already knew a story of the reign of Shelamzion—the one he had

---

[40] The text goes on to state: "These men, he assured her, had so much influence with their fellow Jews that they could injure those whom they hated and help those to whom they were friendly; for they had the complete confidence of the masses when they spoke harshly of any person, even when they did so out of envy." Schwartz claimed ("Josephus and Nicolaus," 159) that this is one of the most obvious Nicolean texts on the Pharisees. If that were true, then my claim that the advice Yannai gave his wife comes from another source would be less likely. Josephus himself, however, could have inserted a statement he found in Nicolaus as part of Yannai's advice.

used in the *Jewish War*—which told of her alliance with the Pharisees.[41] Josephus then inserted another source that told of Yannai's advice to his wife—advice that mentioned the Pharisees. Josephus combined the two in a way that made the queens' choice of the Pharisees as co-rulers look like resignation to her husband's sound advice. Considering the relationship between Yannai and his opponents (most likely Pharisees—*Ant* 13.372-83),[42] however, it is doubtful whether even on his deathbed, this king would have been prepared for a reconciliation with his worst enemies.

I conclude, therefore, that the only support for the Pharisees that translated into political action during the Second Temple period, was given by a woman. Queen Shelamzion chose to invest the Pharisees with governing powers in an independent move, evidently in opposition to the policies followed by her late husband. Was her gender a coincidence, or did it play an important role in her decision? This question can only be answered with any degree of certainty if we can identify further women who supported the Pharisees.

b. Pheroras' Wife

As mentioned above, Josephus mentions another woman who rendered political and financial support to the Pharisees—the wife of Pheroras. Pheroras was Herod's younger brother, described in Josephus as an ungrateful weakling, who refused to support the king. He plotted against Herod and his sons (*Ant.* 16.68; 207), although Herod had shown him infinite kindness and compassion (*Ant.* 15.362). The worst influence on Pheroras' life appears to have been his wife. Although she is described by Nicolaus as a "slave," Pheroras chose to marry her instead of aligning himself with the king by marrying one of the king's daughters (*Ant.* 16.195-9). The entire description of this woman is influenced strongly by Nicolaus' biases. What stands out and

---

[41] Probably based on Nicolaus of Damascus, see Schwartz, "Josephus and Nicolaus," 159.

[42] Curiously, Josephus never identifies Yannai's opponents by name. The identification of these opponents with the Pharisees is usually argued along the following lines: The insurrection against Yannai was initiated on the feast of *Sukkot*, when the entire people pelted the King with their citrons, because he failed to perform the sacrifice in a satisfactory manner (*Ant.* 13.372). This same incident is recorded in rabbinic literature; the High Priest who is pelted by the mob is not identified by name but only by denomination as a Sadducee (*bSukkah* 48b). This text is another episode found both in rabbinic literature and Josephus' *Antiquities* but not in the *Jewish War*. The opponents of the Sadducean approach are identified in this text as העם, a designation the rabbis usually reserved for the allies of the Pharisees (see Cohen, "Significance of Yavneh," 41). Further, Yannai's opponents can be identified as Pharisees from the Qumranic *Pesher Nahum* (4QpNah), the only Qumranic document whose historical allusions are not contested. The Raging Lion in this text (=Yannai) is said to have crucified his opponents, the דורשי החלקות, usually identified as Pharisees. See: D. Flusser, "Pharisees, Sadducees and Essenes in Pesher Nahum," in M. Dorman, S. Safrai and M. Stern (eds.), *In Memory of Gedaliahu Alon: Essays in Jewish History and Philology* (Tel Aviv 1970) 133-68 [Hebrew].

rings true is the mention of the woman's support of the Pharisees, as I will now try to demonstrate.

One of the more debated issues in Herodian chronology is whether the two accounts of the oath of allegiance to the king that the Pharisees refused to take (*Ant.* 15.369-70 and 17.42) describe two events or only one.[43] If they describe two events, when did the second one—in which the Pharisees were fined for their refusal and the fine was paid by Pheroras' wife—take place? There are two possible approaches to this problem. First, the two-source theory suggests that these are two descriptions of the same event, which Josephus drew from two sources; perhaps he failed to realize that they were describing the same thing. Second, the harmonizing approach suggests that when Josephus tells two similar stories, he is describing two distinct events which took place at different occasions. If these were two events, one occurred in 20 BC, as its chronological ordering indicates. The other, which involves Pheroras' wife, occurred sometime close to Herod's death and Antipater's failed plot against Herod in 4 BCE, as suggested by its present position in the text.

I am convinced that the two-source theory, which claims that these are just two descriptions of the same event, is correct.[44] Josephus inserts the story of Pheroras' wife's alleged support of the Pharisees when describing a plot against Herod in which Pheroras was implicated. The outcome of this plot was that Pheroras himself died in mysterious circumstances and Herod suspected Pheroras' wife of poisoning her husband. The oath of allegiance story is presented in this context as an afterthought, or flashback, revealing that the woman's disloyal behavior toward Herod was deep-rooted and had been forgiven in the past. Precisely because this episode describes an event in the distant past, it sounds more authentic than other allegations Nicolaus hurled against Pheroras' wife. When describing the plot, Nicolaus wanted to blacken the woman's name, and conjured up the story of the oath because it was well known that the woman had supported the Pharisees against the king.

This story is a second clear case of a woman's support of the Pharisees in opposition to the expressed political leanings of her family. Pheroras' wife, therefore, is another woman who took an independent religious-political position by adopting Pharisaism.

The two examples discussed thus far presented women who are definitely identified by the sources as supporters of the Pharisees. As we move from the evidence of Josephus to that of rabbinic literature, we are left on less firm ground. Besides all the other complications of using rabbinic sources for the study of history, particularly the history of Judaism before the destruction of

---

[43] See D. R. Schwartz's summation of the topic with bibliography in "Josephus and Nicolaus," 160, n. 12.

[44] See Schwartz, *ibid.*

the Temple, the special problem of the words "Pharisee" and "Pharisees" in this literature must be addressed.

Although it is universally accepted that the Rabbis were the heirs of the Pharisees, rabbinic literature itself is hesitant in its use of the title Pharisee. This may be because the rabbis never used "Pharisee" as a name for themselves.[45] Since no rabbi is ever designated "the Pharisee," we can hardly expect to discover women thus designated.[46] The issues that interested the Pharisees, however, and that were eventually preserved in rabbinic literature, included stories about people who were either their close supporters or their enemies. The former, the rabbis, remembered favorably; the latter, they remembered in derogatory terms. Queen Shelamzion, therefore, is remembered in most favorable terms in rabbinic literature, and her name is connected with the chief Pharisee of her time, Shimeon ben Shatah (*Sifra Behuqotai* 1:1; *Sifre Deuteronomy* 42). The Babylonian Talmud even makes them brother and sister (*bBerakhot* 48a). By contrast, her husband, King Yannai, the Pharisees' great enemy, is featured only in unfavorable episodes.[47] Let us proceed to survey the evidence of other women mentioned in rabbinic literature in light of the rabbis' favorable assessment of supporters and derogatory treatment of enemies.

c. Queen Helene of Adiabene

Josephus describes in great detail the conversion of the royal house of Adiabene (the mother Helene and her two sons Izates and Monobazus) to Judaism (*Ant.* 20.17-96). Nowhere does he state that the queen or her sons adopted Pharisaic Judaism,[48] but references to the queen in rabbinic literature requires us to consider such an assumption.

Rabbinic literature suggests that Queen Helene immigrated to Palestine from abroad (*mNazir* 3:6), exhibited great piety, raised her sons as disciples of

---

[45] Other possible reasons for this have been discussed elsewhere, see: Rivkin, "Defining the Pharisees"; Cohen, "Significance of Yavneh," 36-42.

[46] On an abstinent woman in rabbinic literature and the hypocrisy assigned to her see S. Lieberman, "Sin and its Punishment: A Study in Jewish and Christian Visions of Hell," in S. Lieberman, S. Zeitlin, S. Spiegel and A. Marx (eds.), *Louis Ginzberg Jubilee Volume* (Philadelphia 1945) 254 [Hebrew].

[47] See: D. R. Schwartz, "Κατὰ τοῦτον τὸν καιρὸν: Josephus' Source on Agrippa II," *JQR* 72 (1981-2) 266-7. Schwartz refers to the work of J. Efron, *Studies on the Hasmonean Period* (Leiden 1987) 153-61, but Efron makes a distinction between the Yannai of the Babylonian Talmud and the Yannai of other rabbinic compilations. I find this distinction untenable.

[48] L. H. Schiffman discusses ("The Conversion of the Royal House of Adiabene in Josephus and Rabbinic Sources," in L. H. Feldman and G. Hata [eds.], *Josephus, Judaism and Christianity* [Detroit 1987] 293-312), Helene's conversion in light of rabbinic traditions. The Pharisaic aspect of the conversion process described in rabbinic literature, however, is not suggested.

the rabbis (*tSukkah* 1:1) and made substantial contributions to the Temple (*mYoma* 3:10), but she is nowhere portrayed as a convert. This does not imply that the rabbis did not know of her conversion, but rather that this was irrelevant for the sources that recorded Helene's actions.[49] Why would the rabbis have bothered to preserve the memory of this woman (when they failed to preserve the memory of so many others) unless she had had a special interest in their predecessors, or they an interest in her? Although it cannot be proven, it seems plausible that Queen Helene of Adiabene, a gentile proselyte, chose to convert to the Pharisaic form of Judaism.

Josephus' description of the conversion of the Adiabene royal household lays great stress on Izates, Helene's son.[50] Izates is not mentioned even once in rabbinic literature. Rabbinic sources do mention Monobazus, Izates' brother (*mYoma* 3:10; *tPeah* 4:18), but ultimately they seem more interested in Helene. This is a prime example of the rabbis' showing greater interest in a woman whose male relatives are known to us from Josephus. The next two examples present similar cases of women who were related to important politicians of the first century discussed by Josephus. In neither case does Josephus mention the women; rabbinic literature, by contrast, seems more interested in the women than in their male relatives.

d. Martha bat Boethus

The rabbinic corpus mentions Martha bat Boethus several times, although portraying her less favorably than Queen Helene. While Helene is mentioned only in early, tannaitic works, or in *baraitot* (tannaitic sources incorporated into the Talmudim), Martha bat Boethus appears in two separate strata of stories, the tannaitic stratum and the amoraic one. The tannaitic stratum, composed not much later than 200 CE, better reflects Pharisaic recollections of this woman than the Babylonian or even the (earlier) Palestinian Talmud. It is therefore noteworthy that a negative bias toward Martha only develops in the later strata.

Who was Martha bat Boethus? Scholars agree that the name Boethus places Martha within the family of high priests that first rose to prominence at the time of Herod (*Ant.* 15.320-2), and thereafter enjoyed a position of power until the destruction of the Temple.[51] The Mishnah states that she was the wife of the high priest Joshua ben Gamla:

---

[49] On the conversion source in *Genesis Rabbah* 46.19, which mentions an unnamed queen, obviously Helene in the original, see Schiffman (*ibid.,* 301-2), who rightly claims that the author of this tradition shows no indication that he knew the true identity of this woman.

[50] Schiffman, *ibid.,* 297-8, claims that the entire source in Josephus is in fact a *bios* composition whose subject is Izates.

[51] See M. Stern, "Aspects of Jewish Society: The Priesthood and Other Classes," in S. Safrai and M. Stern (eds.), *The Jewish People in the First Century* 2 (*Compendia Rerum Iudaicarum ad Novum Testamentum* Section One; Philadelphia 1976) 604-6.

A high priest shall not marry a widow ... but if he betrothed a widow and was nominated high priest—he may take her. There was the case of Joshua ben Gamla who had betrothed Martha bat Boethus and the king nominated him high priest and he took her to wife (*mYevamot* 6:4).

This mishnah indicates that the case of Martha was sufficiently important to create a precedent in the legal conception of the rabbis. Since the Mishnah is a halakhic construction of the rabbis alone, the halakhic rulings incorporated therein were probably never applied, unless also endorsed by the Sadducees and other ruling classes. In this case, it appears that the rabbis modified their previous rulings in light of an actual precedent involving Martha b. Boethus, thereby perhaps indicating her importance for them.

Josephus mentions Joshua ben Gamla in numerous instances (*War* 4.160; 238-70; 316; *Vita* 193; 204), but never refers to his wife. Rabbinic literature, on the other hand, seems far more interested in Martha than in her husband. The Babylonian Talmud identifies Joshua ben Gamla (*bBava Batra* 21a) as the founder of an egalitarian education system, but this may be an error, since a conflicting Palestinian tradition assigns this innovation to Shimeon ben Shatah (*yKetubbot* 8:11, 32c).[52] A Ben Gamla is mentioned as contributing toward the Temple (*mYoma* 3:9) but he is not necessarily to be identified with the high priest Joshua ben Gamla.

Martha, on the other hand, is mentioned much more frequently—four times in tannaitic collections (*ibid.*, and *tKippurim* 1:14; *Sifra Emor* 2:6; *Sifre Deuteronomy* 281), once in the Palestinian Talmud (*yKetubbot* 5:13, 30b), once or twice in *Lamentations Rabbah* (1:47; 49?) and five times in the Babylonian Talmud (*bYoma* 18a; *bSukkah* 52b; *bYevamot* 61a; *bKetubbot* 104a; *bGittin* 56a). In the tannaitic collection the attitude toward Martha is neutral, but her portrayal in the amoraic stratum is usually negative. The story of Joshua ben Gamla's appointment to the high priesthood following his betrothal to Martha, for example, told in the Mishnah in neutral terms, becomes in the Babylonian Talmud the result of a bribe his wife gave the king (*bYevamot* 61a).

The Babylonian Talmud records a unique legend of particular interest; it tells of Martha's misfortune and death during the siege of Jerusalem. Although it has no tannaitic parallel, this tradition is incorporated into a collection of stories that describe the horrors of the Roman siege of Jerusalem, Betar and other similar events, many of which are clearly tannaitic traditions.

And there was famine. Martha bat Boethus was of the wealthy of Jerusalem. She sent her messenger. She said to him: Go bring me fine flour. By the time he came, it was sold out. He went and said to her: There is no fine flour, there is [only] white flour. She said to him:

---

[52] On these traditions and their historical worth, see D. Goodblatt, "The Talmudic Sources on the Origins of Organized Jewish Education," *Studies in the History of the Jewish People and the Land of Israel* 5 (1980) 89-102 [Hebrew].

Go bring me white flour. By the time he came, it was sold out. He went and said to her:
There is no white flour, there is [only] plain flour. She said to him: Go bring me plain
flour. By the time he came, it was sold out. He went and said to her: There is no plain
flour, there is [only] barley flour. She said to him: Go bring me barley flour. By the time
he came, it was sold out. She removed her shoes. She said: I shall go and see if there is
anything left to eat. A piece of dung stuck to her heel and she died. Rabban Yohanan ben
Zakkai read this verse concerning her: "The most tender and delicately bred woman
among you, who would not venture to set the sole of her foot upon the ground"
(Deuteronomy 28:56). There are those who say she ate a fig [sucked by] Rabbi Zadoq, she
was disgusted and died ... when she was dying she produced all her gold and silver and
scattered the coins in the market, saying: what good are these to me? fulfilling the verse:
"They cast their silver into the streets [and their gold is like an unclean thing. Their silver
and gold are not able to deliver them in the day of the wrath of the Lord]" (Ezekiel 7:19)
(*bGittin* 56a).[53]

This story of Martha bat Boethus is one of two about the fate of wealthy
Jerusalemite women who lost all in the siege. The present redaction of
Martha's tale does not seem particularly sympathetic toward the heroine, but
the negative bias may be a Babylonian addition, similar to the bribe recorded
by the Talmud in the previous example.

Josephus, on the other hand, is not at all interested in the fate of Martha bat
Boethus, but does tell in great detail the fate of her husband, Joshua, who fell
prey to the purge instigated by the Idumaeans in the winter of 67-8 CE.
Josephus describes how he was killed together with another high priest,
Annanus, and how both were denied burial rites (*War* 4.316-25). What were
the political leanings of Joshua ben Gamla? Josephus is not really interested
in the old allegiances when describing the war against the Romans, because
throughout the war new parties and alliances were created.[54] He does stress,
however, that Joshua ben Gamla was Annanus' ally throughout the war;
elsewhere he states explicitly that Annanus was a Sadducee (*Ant.* 20.199).
From this, together with the fact that he was high priest, we may infer that
Joshua too was a Sadducee; this explains why rabbinic sources are not very
interested in him. Their interest in his wife, however, may suggest that she
had entirely different political leanings from those of her husband. Was she a
supporter of the Pharisees? Though this is mere conjecture, it is certainly a
plausible explanation for her prominence in rabbinic literature. If, Martha was
a Pharisee, we have here another example of a wealthy aristocratic woman
who was attracted to the Pharisees.[55]

[53] This tradition has been discussed in detail by Naomi G. Cohen, "The Theological
Stratum in the Martha b. Boethus Tradition: An Explication of the Text in *Gittin* 56a," *HTR*
69 (1976) 187-96.

[54] On the alliances of the war and their social implications see M. Goodman, *The Ruling
Class of Judaea* (Cambridge 1987).

[55] For a detailed analysis of the Martha bat Boethus traditions within their tannaitic and
amoraic contexts, see my *Mine and Yours*, 88-97.

e. The Daughter of Naqadimon ben Gurion

The next example is the least persuasive because it deals with an unnamed woman who appears in rabbinic literature in a highly literary context. The only reason I decided to include her here is because in several respects her appearance in rabbinic literature resembles that of Martha bat Boethus. She is the daughter of the famous millionaire of rabbinic literature—Naqadimon ben Gurion.[56] Naqadimon ben Gurion is a far more prominent and popular figure with the rabbis than Joshua ben Gamla; however, while his daughter appears in tannaitic sources (*tKetubbot* 5:9-10; *Sifre Deuteronomy* 305), Naqadimon ben Gurion himself is mentioned only in amoraic traditions (*yTaanit* 4:2, 68a; *bGittin* 56a; *Genesis Rabbah* 41:1; 98.8; *Lamentations Rabbah* 1:31; *Ecclesiastes Rabbah* 7:11; *ARNA* 6; *ARNB* 13). The Tosefta portrays the daughter negatively, as a spoiled "princess," who is taught a lesson by the war. Nevertheless the sages portray her fate as a tragedy:

> There was the case of the daughter of Naqadimon ben Gurion to whom the rabbis allotted five hundred golden denarii for perfumes every day, and she was only awaiting a levir (i.e. her husband had died childless and she was to marry his brother). She cursed them: May you allot thus and thus to your daughters. Said Rabbi Eliezer bar Zadoq: May I [not] see consolation if I did not see her collecting barley from beneath the hooves of horses in Akko (*tKetubbot* 5:9-10).

It is interesting to note that a woman is here associated with a rabbinic court of law. Whether rabbinic courts actually functioned during the Second Temple period in this capacity is unclear and beyond the scope of this paper. What is important is that the rabbis themselves associated women with their own system of jurisdiction.

Unlike the Tosefta, *Sifre Deuteronomy* portrays the daughter of Naqadimon ben Gurion as an innocent victim of the war. It also describes her as an associate of the ultimate Pharisee and survivor of the destruction of the Temple, Rabban Yohanan ben Zakkai.

> Once Rabban Yohanan ben Zakkai was riding a donkey and his disciples were walking after him He saw a young woman (ריבה) gathering barley from beneath the feet of the beasts of Arabs. When she saw Rabban Yohanan ben Zakkai she covered herself with her hair and stood before him and said: Rabbi, support me. He said to her: My daughter, whose daughter are you? She said to him: Naqadimon ben Gurion's daughter. She said to him: Rabbi, do you remember signing my *ketubbah* (i.e. marriage contract)? Rabban Yohanan ben Zakkai said to his disciples: I signed her *ketubbah* and it had one million golden denarii written in it. And members of her in-laws' house and members of her house would not enter the Temple Mount to pray unless carpets were spread beneath their feet ... (*Sifre Deuteronomy* 305).

---

[56] On this story see B. Visotzky, "Most Tender and Fairest of Women: A Study in the Transmission of Aggadah," *HTR* 76 (1983) 403-18; Ofra Meir, "The Story as a Hermeneutic Device," *AJS Review* 7-8 (1981-2) 231-62.

It seems, therefore, that at an early stage the rabbis entertained two contradictory traditions about the character of this woman. The importance of the two traditions lies in the fact that tannaitic rabbis were more interested in the fate of Naqadimon ben Gurion's daughter than in the fortunes and fate of her father.

Naqadimon ben Gurion is (probably) also mentioned in the *Jewish War*, where Josephus records a person by the name of Gorion the son of Nicomedes in a list of Jewish officials who negotiated with the besieged Roman garrison stationed in the Antonia (*War* 2.451). Despite the terms of surrender agreed upon by the besieged and this delegation, the Roman garisson was massacred upon laying down their weapons.

Gorion son of Nicomedes' political allegiance is rather obscure. His participation in these events, however, places him in one of two camps: either he was a revolutionary and dealt treacherously with the Romans in order to obtain a surrender, knowing all the time that his people had no intention of keeping their word; or he was part of a delegation from a more moderate party that genuinely intended to come to some agreement with the Romans but were then tricked by the extremists. The name of one other member of the delegation suggests that the second explanation is the correct one; he is called Ananias Sadouki (Σαδούκι). This is most simply understood as Ananias the Sadducee. Perhaps the delegation was a Sadducee idea, and Gorion son of Nicomedes (identified here as Naqadimon ben Gurion) was likewise of Sadducee leanings.

Another passage in Josephus may possibly refer to this man. In the *Jewish War,* when describing the wave of purges, of 67-8 CE, Josephus tells of the Zealots' murder of a certain Gurion "... a person of exalted rank and birth, and yet a democrat and filled with liberal principles, if ever a Jew was ...." (*War* 4.358). Traditionally, this Gurion has been identified with one Gorion ben Joseph, or Joseph ben Gorion,[57] but it is equally plausible to identify him with Gorion ben Nicomedes, also known as Naqadimon ben Gurion. If so, here Josephus once more describes the fate of a prominent Jerusalemite man whose political leanings are not Pharisaic, while the tannaitic stratum of rabbinic literature records a story about the fate of his daughter. Does this perhaps indicate that she had Pharisaic leanings?

The three examples cited here from rabbinic literature are extremely speculative, the last one being most tentative of all; in light of the character of rabbinic literature, we could hardly have expected anything more. Each of these examples in itself, and even all three taken together, do not amount to hard evidence. However, my reconstruction is strengthened and rendered more plausible by the repetitive theme of the rabbis showing an interest in

---

[57] See e.g. my article with Jonathan Price, "Seven Problems in Josephus' *Bellum Judiacum*," *JQR* 84 (1993-4) 200-3.

wealthy pre-destruction Jerusalemite women,[58] whose male relatives had been the object of Josephus' attention. This indicates a shift in emphasis. The only reason I can imagine for the rabbis' compassion for the fate of these women, rather than that of their more important male relatives, is a feeling of solidarity with them. The authors of these rabbinic tales may have felt an affinity with the women because of their interest in the cause of the Pharisees—the rabbis' own predecessors.

I have here discussed five women, either very wealthy or actually royal, who in varying degrees may have been attracted to Pharisaism. These examples, together with the general indications in the sources that the Pharisees had a large following among women, including particularly Sadducean women, suggests that the attraction of women to Pharisaism is indeed a topic worthy of pursuit. It is true that the evidence is scanty, but it is scarcely thinner than that adduced in support of claims made in Second Temple historiography, which have gained universal acceptance.[59] I surmise that Pharisaism may have been far more relevant for women than is assumed by scholars of Judaism in the Roman period.

3. Social Implications

If my assertion is correct, it is then pertinent to ask what made Pharisaism attractive to women, particularly wealthy women? The answer to this question is far from straightforward. Pharisaism, particularly the kind reflected in

---

[58] This preoccupation has been noted in the past, see e.g. Herr (*Eretz Israel*, 291), but the relationship to the information in Josephus has been ignored.

[59] For example, the identification of the Sadducees as a high-priestly party is one of the pillars of Second Temple historiography. The evidence for this identification is no less tentative. The two priests Josephus identifies as Sadducees are John Hyrcanus (*Ant.* 13.296), who had previously supported the Pharisees (and who, according to rabbinic literature, turned Sadducee at the end of his days *bBerakhot* 29a), and Ananus (*Ant.* 20.199). Josephus also mentions a certain Jonathan (*Ant.* 13.293) as a Sadducee, but we have no way of knowing whether he was a priest. Josephus does claim that the wealthy supported the Sadducees (*Ant.* 13.298; 18.17), but he does not necessarily identify them with priests. In fact we seem to know of more priests who are Pharisees than Sadducees, e.g. Josephus himself (*Vita* 12). Beside John Hyrcanus, rabbinic literature mentions only a few anonymous Sadducee priests: a priest whom the people pelted with citrons on *Sukkot* (see above, n. 42); and a priest who burned incense on the Day of Atonement in accordance with Sadducean ruling, and died (*bYoma* 19b). The rabbis, however, all agree that the Pharisees ran the Temple (and see above). In Acts the Sadducees are twice mentioned in conjunction with the priests (4:1; 5:17), but that is as close as the identification gets. The identification is based on this meager information, in addition to the name of the group—Sadducees, perhaps derived from the name of the high-priestly family, Zadoq. In light of this data, the rulings of the Sadducees are interpreted as priestly, see e.g. D. R. Schwartz, "Law and Truth: On Qumran-Sadducean and Rabbinic Views of Law," in Devorah Dimant and U. Rappaport (eds.), *The Dead Sea Scrolls: Forty Years of Research* (Leiden 1992) 229-40.

rabbinic literature, seems extremely hostile toward women, and women's status in society. This overtly hostile attitude produced the claim that Pharisaism in general was irrelevant to women. For example, with regard to the daughter's inheritance, which is debated between Pharisees and Sadducees in rabbinic literature, the Pharisees hold the stricter opinion (*tYadaim* 2:20; *yBava Batra* 8:1, 16a; cf. *bBava Batra* 115b).[60] The right of the daughter to inherit together with her brothers is, and always has been, a problem in Jewish law. The position taken by the Pharisees in their argument with the Sadducees is that, since biblical law explicitly bars the daughter from the inheritance, this ruling must be accepted. Such a decision certainly does not improve the position of women in Judaism. This is the only extant example, datable to the Second Temple period of the Pharisees' involvement in a specific issue pertaining to women, and it certainly does not explain why women found Pharisaism attractive.

It is methodologically unsound to treat rabbinic literature, even its tannaitic strata, or the more ancient layers of rabbinic literature as reflecting the legal opinions of the rabbis' forebears, the Pharisees. I suspect, however, that this is not the only reason why women's support of the Pharisees should not be sought in legal literature but rather in a sociological model. In order to discover such a model I shall refer to another Jewish movement, contemporary with the Pharisees, which enjoyed a large following of women.

Christian feminists have long noted that the Jesus movement, and later Paul's following, were bolstered by the support of women.[61] It has been noted that women not only populate the parables told by Jesus and the stories told of him, but that some women named in the Gospels, such as Mary Magdalene, the sisters Mary and Martha, and perhaps also Susanna and Joanna wife of Chuza, were real people who played an active role in the foundation of the Christian movement after Jesus' death.[62] It has also been noted that, although some of Paul's injunctions are less than favorable toward women, many of the notables he greets in his epistles are women. Some of the women in Jesus' Palestinian movement were not necessarily of the destitute classes whom Jesus addressed—the poor, the hungry, the sinners. On the contrary, Joanna, described as the wife of Chuza, Herod Antipas' treasurer (Luke 8:3), is clearly an aristocrat; Mary the mother of John Mark is described as the owner of a large house in which many believers resided (Acts 12:12) etc. What can

---

[60] For a detailed discussion of this text, see chapter 2, below.

[61] The literature is enormous. The foremost publication on the topic, which is still superior to all that was published subsequently is Elisabeth Schüssler-Fiorenza, *In Memory of Her: A Feminist Theological Reconstruction of Christian Beginnings* (New York 1982). On the Jesus movement see pp. 105-59; for Paul's movement see pp. 160-204.

[62] For my thesis on Jewish women in the Jesus movement, see my "In the Footsteps of Jesus: Jewish Women in a Jewish Movement," in Ingrid R. Kitzberger (ed.), *Transformative Encounters: Jesus and Women Re-viewed* (Leiden in press).

explain wealthy women's attraction to Christianity? Many have attempted to answer this question, but the answer of Christian feminism usually took the form of an apology for Christianity, and often turned into a denigration of the Judaism over and against which the Jesus movement developed. Naturally, Jewish feminists found themselves on the defensive. Rather than acknowledge the outstanding role of women in ancient Christianity, therefore, they found themselves defending a Judaism that probably did not exist at the time of Jesus.[63]

In the final analysis, however, Christian women did not find themselves historically in a more exalted position than their Jewish sisters. How can one explain the apparent discrepancy between women's role in the formative stages of Christianity and their subsequent subordinate position? Many theories have been raised to explain this, but I think a comparison with the position of women within Pharisaism can be instructive in answering this question. The agenda of the Pharisees was very different from that of the Jesus movement, but they did share one feature—both were opposition movements within Judaism during the first century. Soon their ways parted dramatically. Pharisaism survived the war against Rome and rose to a position of leadership within Judaism; from an opposition party it slowly developed into the only legitimate manifestation of Judaism. The Jesus movement evolved into Christianity, ceased to be a Palestinian or Jewish movement and became a subversive cosmopolitan religious movement within the Roman Empire. Eventually, in the fourth century, it became the official religion of the Roman Empire, superseding all other religions within it. Both movements, therefore, evolved from opposition party to a position of power.

Perhaps the initial similarity between the two movements explains the attraction of both for well-to-do women. The ruling parties were dominated by a male aristocracy, which by virtue of its political power found no need to seek support from larger segments of the population. Opposition movements, on the other hand, rallied support where they could, and thus had to adopt a more democratic attitude. Wealthy women could support opposition movements over and against their husbands' political leanings, demonstrating their financial independence by supporting charities of their choice. Through their financial contributions, such women may have influenced decision and policy making in the opposition parties they chose to support. Such a reconstruction is highly probable for early Christianity, and is just as plausible for the Pharisee movement.

These movements' attitudes toward women do not drastically alter the claim of this model. Women who supported them obviously expected to be treated with respect and to have their voices heard, not because they were women but because they were wealthy. Prior to the emergence of feminism

---

[63] For a survey of this relationship, see my introduction in *Jewish Women*, 3-14.

toward the end of the nineteenth century, stereotypical generalizations made about women were internalized by the subjects of these generalizations, as they still are in many traditional and less traditional societies the world over. Women probably agreed that they were, among other things, frivolous, jealous, talkative, gossip mongers; they certainly agreed, at least in theory, that the woman's place was in the home raising children, cooking, spinning and weaving. Women's support of opposition movements should not be expected to reflect positive legislation on the question of women. Elisabeth Schüssler-Fiorenza has shown, for example, that Jesus' pronouncements in favor of the poor do not specifically mention women as their object (although she believes that they were their chief beneficiaries).[64] Luise Schottroff has claimed that gender was no issue at all in the Jesus movement.[65] On the other hand, scholars who have tried to interpret Jesus' rulings about divorce as favoring women[66] have been rightly criticized for their naiveté.[67] The best way to describe the issue in Christianity is to say that women were not attracted to the Jesus movement because of its feminist legislation, yet, at the same time, the Jesus movement did not produce abusive anti-feminist legislation that alienated women supporters.[68]

---

[64] *In Memory of Her*, 122-30.

[65] "*Die unterschiedliche Situation von Frauen und Männern ist also kein Thema der Jesusbewegung in Palästina ...*" Luise Schottroff, "Frauen in der Nachfolge Jesu in neutestamentlicher Zeit," in W. Schottroff and W. Stegemann (eds.), *Traditionen der Befreiung 2: Frauen in der Bibel* (München 1980) 106.

[66] L. J. Swidler, *Biblical Affirmations of Women* (Philadelphia 1979) 173-6.

[67] Bernadette J. Brooten, "Early Christian Women and their Cultural Context: Issues of Method in Historical Reconstruction," in Adele Yarbro-Collins (ed.), *Feminist Perspectives on Biblical Scholarship* (Chico CA 1985) 74.

[68] Other oppositional and marginal cults and associations attracted women in the ancient world, and if pursued further, would probably conform to this model. For example, the Egyptian cult of Isis was a subversive, oppositional religious movement in Rome, which the authorities fought with legislation, and which attracted many women, although men also participated in it; see: Sharon K. Heyob, *The Cult of Isis among Women in the Graeco-Roman World* (Leiden 1975). Heyob contends that women were not the majority of Isis initiates but were more numerous in Rome than elsewhere. At the same time they served only as secondary priests in the cult. An investigation of the movement in light of my model would probably test positively. Many women took part in Montanism, an opposition movement within Christianity, see F. C. Klawiter, "The Role of Martyrdom and Persecution in Developing the Priestly Authority of Women in Early Christianity: The Case of Montanism," *Church History* 49 (1980) 251-61. His explanations are different from mine, but he shows that in the past Montanism had not been considered attractive to women because of the misogynistic writings of one of its members, Tertullian (p. 251). This certainly fits the Pharisee model. Similarly, the subversive Gnostic movements counted many women among their adherents; see Karen King, (ed.), *Images of the Feminine in Gnosticism* (Philadelphia 1988). In this volume J. E. Goehring makes a sociological claim similar to mine ("Libertine or Liberated: Women in So-called Libertine Gnostic Communities," 329-344), and see on p. 329: "It has been recognized that women found opportunities in Gnostic communities that

Exactly what attracted women to Pharisaism is equally unclear. Perhaps they were drawn to the Pharisees' belief in a life after death or the Pharisees' middle ground on the question of pre-destination (*Ant.* 13.171-3), or simply the Pharisee life-style (*War* 2.166). Women probably did not become Pharisee supporters in response to the group's legislation on the question of women. But did the Pharisees initiate strong anti-feminist legislation while they were seeking women's support? Or perhaps, as in early Christianity, this issue was not foremost in their minds. I suspect the latter is the correct answer. It is true that the Mishnah's Division of Women,[69] and much material in other mishnaic tractates which relates to women, is coercive and was composed in order to regulate and control women's behavior in every aspect of their life.[70] It is pertinent to ask, however, what material in the Division of Women was composed during the Pharisaic period.

Judith Hauptman's recent research into the relationship between the Mishnah and the Tosefta with regard to women may be instructive in this context. Hauptman has shown that the Mishnah was edited in such a way as to curtail, diminish and censor women's rights and participation in Jewish life both in general and in detail.[71] When Pharisaic Judaism finally gained the upper hand and composed its manifesto, the Mishnah, it chose to emphasize its control of women and reshape its attitude toward them from neutral to restrictive and patronizing. This is not to say that the attitude to women in the Tosefta is egalitarian or feminist; but it is certainly less vicious than the Mishnah. Irrespective of the time when the halakhot in the Tosefta were collected, therefore, the editing of the Mishnah marks a time period when controlling women and putting them in their place was of primary importance for the rabbis.

The *baraitot* found in the Tosefta and in some of the other tannaitic collections may reflect the Pharisaic period. For example, the Tosefta rules that women are not obligated to reside in a *sukkah* but recalls that Queen Helene had done so (*tSukkah* 1:1). This probably indicates that the halakhah

---

were closed to them in the 'orthodox' church." Goehring gives examples of medieval Christian movements that could also fit into this model (pp. 331-2). Modern religious and political movements could probably also fit the bill. This model may even explain the attraction of gentile women to Judaism in the Diaspora (see e.g. *War* 2.560, where Josephus claims that all the women in Damascus were attracted to Judaism).

[69] See J. Neusner, *A History of the Mishnaic Law of Women* 5 (Leiden 1988).

[70] See Wegner, *Chattel or Person.*

[71] Judith Hauptman, "Mishnah *Gittin* as a Pietist Document," *Proceedings of the Tenth World Congress of Jewish Studies* C/1 (Jerusalem 1990) 23-30 [Hebrew]; *eadem*, "Maternal Dissent: Women and Procreation in the Mishnah," *Tikkun* 6/6 (1991) 80-1; 94-5; *eadem*, "Pesach: A Liberating Experience for Women," *Masoret* (Winter 1993) 8-9; *eadem*, "Women's Voluntary Performance of Commandments from which They are Exempt," *Proceedings of the Eleventh World Congress of Jewish Studies* C/1 (Jerusalem 1994) 161-8 [Hebrew].

was formulated some time after the days of the queen, who, as demonstrated above, was probably a Pharisee supporter and is hardly likely to have disobeyed their rulings. This incident is not mentioned in the Mishnah (*mSukkah* 1:1). In another example, the *Mekhilta de Rabbi Ishmael* rules that women are exempt from wearing phylacteries; the text, however, refers to a woman by the name of Mikhal bat Kushi as having donned them (*Bo* 17). The Mishnah also exempts women from this commandment, but does not mention that women had not always followed this ruling. This probably indicates that the halakhah was formulated after the time of Helene and Mikhal. I think it is highly likely that the rabbis speak of these women because they were Pharisees. These two examples do not indicate what legislation concerning women the Pharisees enacted, but rather what areas of Jewish women's lives the Pharisees left untouched. Steering clear of these areas allowed women more freedom, and also enabled them to join and support the Pharisees. These examples demonstrate that, like early Christianity, Pharisaism avoided legislation concerning women, presumably in order to retain women's support of the movement.[72]

These two examples are passive, that is, they show what was not enacted by the rabbis. Interestingly, the Tosefta also records one law concerning women that supposedly was enacted by the foremost Pharisee, Shimeon ben Shatah. He enacted the clause in the *ketubbah* that makes all the husband's possessions surety for the *ketubbah* payment (*tKetubbot* 12:1).[73] Shimeon ben Shatah's enactment is also mentioned in the Palestinian Talmud (*yKetubbot* 8:11, 32b) and the Babylonian Talmud (*bKetubbot* 82b), but it is significantly absent from the Mishnah. This law is important because rabbinic sources dated it to the only time in Jewish history when a queen ruled, and as mentioned above, this was also the only time during the Second Temple period that the Pharisees were in power. It would be instructive to discover the precise significance of this period for women's social and legal standing in Judaism.

Few scholars have taken seriously the historical question of the sources assigning halakhah to early Pharisaic rabbis. The foremost study of the topic to date is Neusner's *Rabbinic Traditions about the Pharisees Before 70.*

---

[72] Perhaps the Pauline and deutero-Pauline legislation about women in Christianity follows the same pattern. Antoinette C. Wire suggests (*The Corinthian Women Prophets: A Reconstruction through Paul's Rhetoric* [Minneapolis 1990]) that Paul's legislation on women in his First Epistle to the Corinthians came to check the strong position that women attained in Corinth. If she is correct, this may also explain some of the anti-feminist backlash evident in the move from Tosefta to Mishnah. I am not certain, however, that the comparison is relevant in this case.

[73] That this was indeed the nature of Shimeon ben Shatah's enactment, see M. Satlow, "Reconsidering the Rabbinic *ketubbah* Payment," in S. J. D. Cohen (ed.), *The Jewish Family* (Atlanta 1993) 149-50.

Neusner surveyed all traditions about Pharisaic rabbis before the destruction of the Temple and concluded that none of the traditions can be verified, and they should, therefore, not be held historically reliable. On the attribution of the *ketubbah* clause to Shimeon ben Shetah, Neusner stated that "the pericope contains no evidence permitting the suggestion of a date. Attributing to Simeon such an ordinance may have been a way of saying: 'In very olden times'."[74] Whether one accepts or discards Neusner's opinion depends on the nihilist stance of the scholar, since there is equally no good reason to doubt this rabbinic statement. Some scholars have moved from believing everything stated in rabbinic literature, unless it contradicts nature, logic or other historical information, to disbelieving everything in it, unless manifestly proven correct. Both extreme attitudes should be modified, but even if the enactment of the *ketubbah* could be dated to the queen's reign, it would be difficult to decide whether she had any say in its enactment. Whether it was enacted for the improvement of women's position, or was indicative of the Pharisees' legal position on "the woman question" in the earlier stages of Pharisaic history, is the question at hand.

4. Conclusion

In this essay I have suggested a reconstruction of the continuous relationship between women and the Pharisees from the first century BCE to the redaction of the Mishnah at the end of the second century CE. The reconstruction can be outlined as follows: since both rabbinic literature and Josephus independently mention the influence of the Pharisees on women of a non-Pharisee background, and since both sources name some such women who were wealthy and influential, I assume that there is some evidence for a relationship between aristocratic women and the Pharisees. The Pharisees were an opposition party during most of the Second Temple period; this may be the reason why women supported them. A women was certainly instrumental in their rise to power between the years 76-67 BCE (the years of queen Shelamzion's reign). The Pharisees did not attract women's support by proposing egalitarian halakhah for women, but rather because they accepted their support and refrained from enacting detrimental rules against women. When the Pharisees came to power some time after the destruction of the Temple they turned their back on their previous following; the misogynistic Mishnah is proof of this development.

---

[74] Neusner, *Rabbinic Traditions*, 1. 94.

Appendix: The Case of the Dead Sea Sect

A claim that opposition groups in Second Temple Palestinian Judaism were more congenial to women and more readily accepted their support fails to account for the Essenes, the most typical opposition group of all. Of course none of what has been written up to now has any relevance to the Essenes, since they are described by Josephus and Philo as a celibate monastic group, that shunned the company of women (because of "women's wantonness"— *War* 2.120-1; cf. Philo, *Hypothetica* 11.14). Nothing beyond this can be said about the Essenes, since most of what we know about them comes from Josephus' and Philo's descriptions, both probably based on a common source.[75] For the purpose of this study it is useful, however, to note that the Essenes' Diaspora counterpart—the sect of the Therapeutics in upper Egypt— although celibate, admitted women (*De Vita Contemplativa*).[76]

The case of the Dead Sea Sect, however, is another matter. Since the discovery of the Dead Sea scrolls in 1947, scholars have debated whether the authors of these writings were or were not Josephus' Essenes.[77] On the whole, the scales have tipped toward a positive answer to this question. However, a principle reason for the reservations voiced by some scholars against this identification is the contradictory evidence concerning women which has come to light in association with the Dead Sea Sect.[78] While the Essenes were supposedly celibate, some of the scrolls (notably the *Damascus Document* and *1Qsa*) take into account the married status of members of the Qumran sect. Furthermore, the cemetery at Qumran yielded both male and female skeletons.[79] This data is not new and many scholars have grappled with it. Skeptics have rejected the identification of the two groups on the basis of this data. Others explained the problem away in some other fashion. In this appendix I shall not pronounce judgment on this problem. I shall merely show that the information pertinent to women that can be gleaned from the scrolls fits well into the sociological model I have set up above to explain the

---

[75] For the similarities in their description, see: F. H. Colson, *Philo: With an English Translation* (Cambridge MA 1941) 9. 514-5. For the assumption that both Philo and Josephus used Nicolaus of Damascus for their description of the Essenes, see: B.-Z. Wacholder, *Nicolaus of Damascus* (University of California Publications in History; Berkeley 1962) 70-2.

[76] On the female members of the Therapeutic sect, see Kraemer, "Monastic Jewish Women."

[77] For a fairly recent summary see: T. S. Beall, *Josephus' Description of the Essenes Illustrated by the Dead Sea Scrolls* (Cambridge 1988) 1-6 and footnotes; see also J. A. Sanders, "The Dead Sea Scrolls: A Quarter Century of Study," *BA* 36 (1973) 120-5.

[78] See e.g. Sanders, *ibid.*, 118-9; 125.

[79] On this see further in chapter 7, below.

similarity in the pattern of support that women rendered to the Jesus movement on the one hand, and to Pharisaism on the other.[80]

That the Dead Sea sect was an opposition party needs no demonstration in this context. Neither the sparsity of references to women in the Qumranic documents, nor the predominantly male language of the texts indicate that they were not addressed to women. Women are mentioned incidentally in the legislation but none of the legislation sets out to regulate women's life apart from that of men, or beyond what is found in the Hebrew Bible.[81] This fits the pattern we have seen above. Women, if drawn to the group, were drawn for reasons other than the promise of a more positive legal status. On the other hand, the absence of specific regulations over women's lives may suggest that women's support was welcome and not intentionally discouraged. It is true that the sect ruled against uncle-niece marriages as well as against divorce, or alternatively, against polygamy,[82] but like Jesus' injunction against divorce, these laws are no more relevant to women than to men. Thus the female skeletons at Qumran were probably skeletons of members of the sect, not merely of those wives of marrying Essenes, which seems to be the main thesis for explaining the presence of female skeletons.[83] This claim that the female skeletons were women sect members can be supported from a new angle. A recently published fragment from Cave 4 mentions a female scribe.[84] This could hardly be referring to women who are not members of the sect, since

---

[80] On women in the Dead Sea sect see Eileen M. Schuller, "Women in the Dead Sea Scrolls," in M. O. Wise, N. Golb, J. J. Collins and D. G. Pardee (eds.), *Methods of Investigation of the Dead Sea Scrolls and the Khirbet of Qumran Site: Present Realities and Future Prospects* (Annals of the New York Academy of Science 722; New York, 1993) 115-31; cf. Lena Cansdale, "Women Members in the *Yahad* According to the Qumran Scrolls," *Proceedings of the Eleventh World Congress of Jewish Studies* A (Jerusalem 1994) 215-22.

[81] On the latter see L. H. Schiffman, "Laws Pertaining to Women in the Temple Scroll," in Devorah Dimant and U. Rappaport (eds.), *The Dead Sea Scrolls: Forty Years of Research* (Leiden 1992) 210-28. Schiffman concludes: "The views of the Temple Scroll [*11QT*] on matters relating to women are extremely conservative. The text does not advocate a revision of previous norms ... (but rather) calls for the continued observance of ancient laws" (228). In other words, the text lets the Bible speak and is not interested in legislating on this topic.

[82] For a summary of the discussion see G. Vermes, "Sectarian Matrimonial Halakhah in the Damascus Rule," *JJS* 25 (1974) 197-202.

[83] See e.g. R. de Vaux, *Archaeology and the Dead Sea Scrolls* (Oxford 1973) 128-9; and see also: H. Stegemann, "The Qumran Essenes: Local Members of the Main Jewish Union in Late Second Temple Times," in J. T. Barrera and L. V. Montaner (eds.), *The Madrid Qumran Congress* (Leiden 1992) 126-34; J. M. Baumgarten, "The Qumran-Essene Restraints on Marriage," in L. H. Schiffman (ed.), *Archaeology and History in the Dead Sea Scrolls: The New York University Conference in Memory of Yigael Yadin* (JSP Supplement Series 8; Sheffield: 1990) 13-24; and see also chapter 7, below.

[84] R. H. Eisenman and M. Wise, *The Dead Sea Scrolls Uncovered* (Shaftsbury 1992) 207 (=4Q274 fragment 1,column 1:7).

the chances of meeting female scribes in the larger Jewish society were not high. A very fragmentary text from the same cave mentions זקנים וזקנות. Usually the term would mean "elders" but since women are also mentioned in it, Baumgarten suggested that it refers to aged members of the sect.[85] Eileen Schuller has noted correctly, that if for men זקנים refers to elders, that is leaders of the community, the same should be assumed for the female term זקנות.[86]

In view of this reconstruction, I suggest a new reading for a complicated paragraph from 1QSa. This document sets out to regulate the life of the sect in the messianic future, but describes a situation acutely similar to that of the sect in the present. In a discussion of the stages of a man's life in the sect, twenty is the age set for marriage. The text then moves on from masculine to feminine language and states that:

> At the age of twenty he [shall be] included in the lot of his family in the Yahad, the holy congregation. And he shall not approach a woman to lie with her before he is twenty years old when he can distinguish between good and evil. And she shall be received to testify to the laws of the Torah which concern him and appear at the hearing of judgment (וכן תקבל להעיד עליו משפטות התורה ולהתיצב במשמע משפטים) (*1QSa* 1:9-11).

Neil Richardson, the first scholar who discussed this text,[87] took this verse literally, and suggested that the wives of sect members were encouraged to testify against their husbands in cases where they transgressed the law. All subsequent scholars, beginning with Baumgarten,[88] have concluded that the text is faulty and should be emended. It is not the wife who is the subject but the sect-member himself.[89] When he takes a wife he has attained the right age to participate actively in the sect's legal and legislative activities. The arguments for emendation are: first, that the context of the pericope is a discussion of a man's position in the sect; second, that it is highly unlikely

---

[85] J. M. Baumgarten, "4Q502, Marriage or Golden Age Ritual?" *JJS* 34 (1983) 125-35.

[86] Schuller, "Women," 122-3.

[87] N. H. Richardson "Some Notes on *1QSa*," *JBL* 76 (1957) 108-22; He was preceded by D. Barthelemy, *Discoveries in the Judaean Desert* 1 (Oxford: Oxford University Press, 1955) 113, but his note is only an interpretation of the text, without a historical assessment.

[88] J. M. Baumgarten, "On the Testimony of Women in *1QSa*," *JBL* 76 (1957) 266-9; but see recently, P. R. Davies and Joan E. Taylor, "On the Testimony of Women in 1Qsa," *Dead Sea Discoveries* 3 (1996) 223-35 with an alternative interpretation.

[89] An emended text is found for example in J. Licht (ed.), *The Rule Scroll* (Jerusalem 1965) 257 [Hebrew]. The original reading is mentioned only in the footnotes. The new English translation of the scroll by G. Vermes (*The Dead Sea Scrolls in English* [London 1987] 101) does not even hint that the subject of the original sentence was feminine. Thus Cansdale ("Women Members," 218), who used Vermes' translation rather than the original, was ignorant of the fact that *1QSa* 11 refers to women's testimony and used the text only as a measure for the age of marriage in the sect.

that a woman's capacity to give evidence would be tied to her husband's age (what if she were a minor?); and third, that it is doubtful whether a sect such as the Dead Sea sect, which is probably a wing of the Essenes, would give women such an important role in its judicial system. I think the first two arguments can be easily dismissed as mere rhetoric: first, the context of the pericope is marriage, and once marriage takes place, women are integrated into the context; secondly, the woman's capacity to give evidence is not tied to the man's age, it is a function of her marriage to him. Perhaps the age of marriage for man was also the age of marriage for women in Qumran and the text does not state so explicitly because general male language included both? It may alternatively be that the definition of majority for Qumran women was the age of marriage. There is no explicit flaw, therefore, in the logic of the text.

The third argument, namely that it is unlikely that women would be given such an important role in the sect's legal system, is the most formidable, not because it is more convincing, but because it is so typical of the scholarly approach to unusual and unconventional texts dealing with women preserved from antiquity. Bernadette Brooten discusses this issue in her important book, *Women Leaders in the Ancient Synagogue.*[90] Brooten shows that a stereotyped view of women's role in society had created gross misjudgments on the part of scholars. I think that in the case of the Qumran evidence too, Brooten is right. Because the scrolls leave more mysteries unsolved than provide solutions to one's questions, one searches for evidence about the sect in external sources. An identification of the sect (say, with the Essenes) immediately burdens the scrolls with all other information available about the other sect. But if the Dead Sea Sect is not identified with some other sect, there is no need to look for traces of evidence about that sect in the Qumran scrolls. Indeed, if the sect is not identified with the Essenes, there is no reason to postulate a strong anti-feminist agenda for it.[91] Thus the text in *1QSa* can be taken at face value, as indicating that women were members of the sect, and legislation discovered concerning their function in it should not surprise, or be dismissed.

In the final analysis, this text, taken at face value, tells more about the sect than about its attitude to women. The text suggests that the wife turn informer on her husband's degree of compliance with the sect's laws. The Qumran sect thus favors loyalty to the sect over loyalty to one's spouse. It displays a

---

[90] Bernadette J. Brooten, *Women Leaders in the Ancient Synagogue* (*Brown Judaic Studies* 36; Atlanta 1982) 30-2.

[91] The discovery of *The Wiles of the Wicked Woman* in the sect's library (*4Q*184, see J. Allegro, "The Wiles of the Wicked Woman: A Sapiental Work from Qumran's Fourth Cave," *PEQ* 96 [1964] 53-5) is not strong evidence for misogyny since it was not composed by the sect, and was kept in their library together with other misogynist compositions like the Book of *Ben Sira*.

system which values regulating the lives of its members over respecting their privacy and conjugal intimacy.

Similarly, in the Damascus covenant (over and against biblical law, Numbers 30:14), a man is instructed to nullify his wife's vows only when she has vowed to transgress the laws of the sect. In cases where she has vowed to abide by the sect's dicta, the revocation is void:

> Concerning the oath of a wife/woman, which empowers her husband to annul it, he may not nullify an oath when he knows not if it was made to follow ... but if it were made to transgress the covenant, he may nullify it. And so too with respect to her father (*CD* 16:10-2).

This ruling shows that the sect valued loyalty to its institutions over all other loyalties. For that purpose it intruded on the privacy of the patriarchal home as portrayed in biblical and other Jewish law codes.[92]

Both of these laws suggest that woman's membership in the sect was accepted and acknowledged. Having reclaimed the first text for the study of women, and pointed out its connection to the second law, feminist scholars may be tempted to interpret them as revealing a Judaism of the Second Temple period more congenial to women and less patriarchal. Perhaps scholars will go to the extreme of naming the Dead Sea Sect the most "feminist" manifestation of Judaism: a woman can testify in court; her vows are her own, not controlled by her husband and so on. As a historian I feel compelled to object to such an interpretation. It is true that the subject of these two rulings are women, independent of men in the sect. This indicates that they were members of the sect, not just members' wives. It is important to note, however, that, in both cases, women are not the object of the rulings. The object of the rulings (both linguistically and literally) is the regulation of the sect's way of life. In order to achieve greater control of its members, it was occasionally profitable to pit the wife against the husband. This was done not for the good of women, but for the good of the sect.

However, my initial model is still valid. Not because of its pro-feminist legislation, but perhaps because of its marginal, oppositionary stance, the sect was supported by women and it accepted them as members. The female skeletons at Qumran attest unequivocally to that. The sources do not reveal, however, whether these women were wealthy or influential, as in the case of the women supporters of Pharisaism and Christianity.

---

[92] I wish to thank my colleague, Esther Chazon, for drawing my attention to this relevant text.

Chapter Two

"The Daughters of Israel are not Licentious" (*mYevamot* 13:1) Beit Shammai on the Legal Position of Women[1]

All the information we have concerning Beit Shammai and Beit Hillel is derived from rabbinic literature. Neither Hillel nor Shammai nor their disciples and the schools named after them are ever mentioned in any contemporary source, Jewish or otherwise, outside of rabbinic circles. Because of the nature of rabbinic literature and its total disinterest in history, its own as well as others', our knowledge of these groups (schools? sects? parties?) is fragmentary and enigmatic. Nevertheless the following details sum up what seems to be an agreed historical sketch of Beit Shammai and Beit Hillel and the relationship between them:

The two groups are named after their founders. Hillel and Shammai are mentioned last in a list of ancient pairs who, according to the testimony of rabbinic literature, led the Jewish people in Palestine during the Second Temple period (*mAvot* 1:1-12; *mHagigah* 2:2). Chronological considerations, which nobody contests, place the two founding fathers at the time of Herod. Some sources imply that Hillel emigrated to Palestine from Babylonia (*tNegaim* 1:16; *Sifra Tazria* pereq 9:16; cf. *yPesahim* 6:1, 33a). Of Shammai's background we know nothing at all. Since rabbinic literature is considered to

---

[1] In 1982 I attended Prof. Shmuel Safrai's M.A. seminar at the Hebrew University, Jerusalem. In one of its sessions Safrai made the comment that on the question of women's social status Beit Shammai was more congenial than Beit Hillel. That comment forms the basis of this paper. Although Safrai has written both on Beit Shammai ("The Decisions According to Beit Hillel in Yavneh," in his *In Times of Temple and Mishnah: Studies in Jewish History* 2 [Jerusalem 1994] 382-44 [Hebrew]) and on women ("Was There a Women's Gallery in the Synagogue of Antiquity?" *Tarbiz* 32 [1963] 329-38 [Hebrew]; "Torah Learned Women in the Mishnaic and Talmudic Period," *Mahanaim* 98 [1965] 58-9 [Hebrew]; and recently, with more feminist terminology and in English "The Role of Women in the Temple," *The Jerusalem Perspective* [July/August 1989] 5-6; "The Place of Women in First Century Synagogues," *The Jerusalem Perspective* [September/October 1993] 3-6; 14), his thesis on this issue has not been committed to writing. I thus take it upon myself to fill the void; I am grateful, however, to Safrai for setting me on this path.

be the product of the heirs of the Pharisees, the information it contains on Second Temple times emanates from Pharisaic chronicles, and it is, therefore, safe to assume that Hillel and Shammai were Pharisees, as were their schools.[2] Beit Shammai and Beit Hillel disagreed on an enormous corpus of legal points, encompassing questions of purity and impurity, religious practices, civil and criminal law. Their legal disputes form the basis of rabbinic halakhah (*tEduyot* 1:1). Somewhere along the way, the disagreements between Beit Shammai and Beit Hillel led to bloodshed (*yShabbat* 1:7, 3c; cf. *mShabbat* 1:4). Our sources suggest that this was a one-time event that was never repeated. Some time after the destruction of the Temple the rabbis rejected the halakhah of Beit Shammai en bloc (*tEduyot* 2:3; *yBerakhot* 1.7, 3b; *bEruvin* 13b), with a few exceptions, collected in one chapter of Mishnah *Eduyot* (1:12-14). Rabbinic Judaism thus evolved into the Judaism of Beit Hillel. Rabbinic literature explains that the views of Beit Hillel were adopted because they were more lenient in their approach than were their opponents, as well as being more humble and courteous to others (*bEruvin* 13b). Whether this statement is altogether true is, however, difficult to determine for several reasons. (1) A chapter in Mishnah *Eduyot* enumerates topics on which Beit Hillel was stricter than Beit Shammai (4:1-5:5), but on which the views of Beit Hillel were nevertheless adopted; (2) The statement obviously came from members of Beit Hillel, and is thus a self-portrait in which Beit Hillel may be complimenting themselves where others would not; (3) The question of what is strict and what is lenient generates different answers in different circles.[3] Certainly on issues where one group controls another, what seems lenient to the controlling group may seem very strict to those being controlled. This is true in general, but it is especially true for women, whom most ancient (and modern) legal systems set out to control, and who constitute a topic of debate or dispute between Beit Shammai and Beit Hillel.[4]

The subject of this article is Beit Shammai's view of the legal position of women. Although the legal disputes of Hillelites and Shammaites have been extensively mined and their conceptual differences discussed,[5] no scholar has

---

[2] J. Neusner, *The Rabbinic Traditions about the Pharisees before 70* 1 (Leiden 1971) 1-23; and against P. Schäfer, "Der vorrabbinische Pharisäismus," in M. Hengel and U. Heckel (eds.), *Paulus und das antike Judentum: Tübingen-Durham-Symposium in Gedenken an den 50. Todestag Adolf Schlatters (Mai 1938)* (Tübingen 1988) 125-70.

[3] For a discussion of this aspect see: A. Schwartz, *Die Erleichterungen der Schammaiten und die Erschwerungen der Hilleliten: Ein Beitrag zur Entwicklungsgeschichte der Halachah* (Wien 1893).

[4] For a similar observation by the rabbis themselves see *yKetubbot* 8:1, 32a.

[5] S. Zeitlin, "Studies in Tannaitic Jurisprudence: Intention as a Legal Principle," *Journal for Jewish Lore and Philosophy* 1 (1919) 297-311; I. Sonne, "The Schools of Shammai and

actually singled out this topic for academic discussion. Several comments, however, have been made on it in passing. I. Sonne[6] wrote: "...the attitude of the two schools toward the family ... has been the weakest point in the modern ... construction which takes for granted that the Shammaites represent the primitive, backward, unsympathetic attitude toward women, and the Hillelites, a more progressive, liberal one ... Modern scholars have tried to persuade us that even in this case the position of the Hillelites marks a considerable progress in comparison with that of the Shammaites; their arguments, however, have met with little success among sensible, unprejudiced scholars."

Recently, in his comprehensive book on Beit Shammai, Israel Ben-Shalom discussed under the rubric of "Marriage Laws" many of the laws pertaining to women, which were disputed by Hillelites and Shammaites.[7] Some of his conclusions were as follows: "... a formalistic attitude is evident in the case of Beit Hillel, which enfolds a certain insensitivity and lack of consideration for the other's sufferings. On the other hand, Beit Shammai demonstrates a straightforward approach which displays sensitivity to human suffering and injustice ... ;[8] ... Beit Shammai's attitude is clearly in favor of the woman, with the purpose of securing her future and safety ... ;[9] Beit Shammai's attitude reflects not only an ideal point of view of the institution of marriage, but also the protection of the social position and personal security of the married woman."[10] Ben Shalom attempts to incorporate the attitude of Beit Shammai on marriage into his overall view of the difference between the Houses, but he makes an important contribution to the issue of the Shammaites' position on women.

Both of these scholars raised an issue well worth pursuing. In contrast with their approach, however, I believe it is important to distinguish between the topics "marriage" and "women." Although the two are often conflated, they are clearly separate issues. While it is clear that women, in and of themselves, did not interest the rabbis,[11] marriage certainly did, and served as the mechanism through which women's position in society was manipulated. However, a closer look at the discussion of marriage between Beit Hillel and Beit Shammai reveals that while the former were indeed bothered by the

---

Hillel Seen from Within," in S. Lieberman, S. Zeitlin, S. Spiegel and A. Marx (eds.), *Louis Ginzberg Jubilee Volume* (English volume; New York 1945) 275-91.

[6] *Ibid.*, 287-8.

[7] I. Ben-Shalom, *The School of Shammai and the Zealots' Struggle against Rome* (Jerusalem 1993) 210-21 [Hebrew].

[8] *Ibid.*, 213; cf. p. 215-6.

[9] *Ibid.*, 214

[10] *Ibid.*, 217. The translations are my own.

[11] See J. Neusner, *A History of the Mishnaic Law of Women* 5 (Leiden 1985) 13-6.

marriage institution itself, the latter actually had the position of women in mind. This will become apparent in the first part of my discussion of the sources. The second part of my discussion turns to the other feminine topic on which Beit Shammai and Beit Hillel disagreed—menstruation and other bodily sources of cultic pollution. Next, I will discuss the unique relationship of Queen Helene of Adiabene to Beit Shammai. Finally I will attempt to locate Beit Shammai's attitude to women on the political map of the Second Temple period. I end this article with some observations on women's position and the implications of the decision taken in rabbinic circles to follow Beit Hillel's ruling on that issue.

1. Marriage Laws

a. Betrothal

According to Jewish law, betrothal is an indefinite period lasting from the point at which a man has betrothed (קידש) his wife to the actual consummation of the marriage.[12] Beit Shammai and Beit Hillel dispute three issues pertaining to the period of betrothal.

i. Tractate *Eduyot* contains a number of laws pertaining to marriage which were characterized by the Hillelites themselves as lenient rulings of Beit Shammai. The first rule concerns the price of betrothal:

> A wife may be acquired ... Beit Shammai holds: By a *denar* or a *denar*'s worth, whereas Beit Hillel holds: By a *perutah* or a *perutah*'s worth ... (*mEduyot* 4:7 cf. *mQiddushin* 1:1).[13]

The argument between the two houses in this source focuses on the sum of money a man is required to invest in securing a wife for himself—an initial sum he pays the prospective bride, "setting her apart" (מקדש) her for his exclusive use. It is assumed that in the distant past this action was one of acquisition,[14] but it has long been reduced to a symbolic act, or else it may be understood as the first installment in a long series of payments. Whichever is the correct legal or philosophical principle here, the houses of Hillel and Shammai dispute the amount of the consideration. Both suggest a symbolic

---

[12] See chapter 9, below.

[13] For some of the *mishnayot* in this chapter and elsewhere, I employ Judith Romney Wegner's translations from *Chattel or Person: The Status of Women in the Mishnah* (Oxford 1988).

[14] For the development of this institution in Israel see: Z. Falk, *Introduction to Jewish Law of the Second Commonwealth* 2 (Leiden 1978) 276-90; and see also my: *Jewish Women in Greco-Roman Palestine: An Inquiry into Image and Status (Texte und Studien zum Antiken Judentum* 44; Tübingen 1995) 88-9.

figure, certainly not representing the true value of a purchase, but while Beit Shammai maintains that this sum should be meaningful—a *denar*, Beit Hillel suggests a trifling sum of one *perutah* (192nd part of a *denar*[15]). Since neither house suggests that this transaction is a real acquisition, the difference between them seems to be in their attitude toward the sincerity of the man who performs the act. The Shammaites maintain that betrothal should be a serious decision, on which the prospective bridegroom should meditate and for which he should prepare himself. He must, therefore, carry with him the equivalent of a *denar* when setting out to negotiate the transaction. The Hillelites, on the other hand, assume that, since the sum involved in the action is purely symbolic, it may as well be minuscule. Almost any man could perform a betrothal ceremony on the spur of the moment. How the attitude of Beit Shammai can be interpreted as more lenient is not clear to me.[16] What is clear, however, is that the Shammaites have the other party to the betrothal in mind—namely the woman. They make betrothal more difficult, not so as to exclude anybody from it; only to force the man to reflect seriously on it. This ruling, therefore, defines one of Beit Shammai's principles in their attitude toward women—marriage is a serious life-long commitment, which should not be undertaken lightly by any man. At the same time, they also give the woman who receives the betrothal gift a feeling of greater self-esteem because of the size of the gift.

ii. Elsewhere in the Mishnah the betrothed woman is again discussed by the Shammaites and Hillelites, this time in connection with the most crucial issue of a woman's property:

> [Concerning] a woman to whom property fell before she became betrothed, Beit Shammai and Beit Hillel concur she may sell [it] or give [it] away and [her disposition] stands. [But if the property] fell to her after she became betrothed, Beit Shammai rules [that] she may sell it but Beit Hillel rules [that] she should not sell [it]. Both concur that if she has [in fact] sold [it] or given [it] away, [her disposition] stands (*mKetubbot* 8:1).

This ruling addresses the legal powers of the betrothed woman with respect to the ownership and disposal of private property. The ownership of property by women is, in general, a complicated issue in rabbinic literature. Although the rabbis acknowledge the power of women to own property, ideally they would have preferred all transactions to be handled by either her father or her

---

[15] See D. Sperber, *Roman Palestine 200-400: Money and Prices* (Ramat Gan 1991) 28-9 (especially Table B).

[16] Judith Romney Wegner suggested to me that "the Hillelites are stricter, or more rigorous because they will *insist* on the validity of the אירוסין even if he paid only a *perutah* (whereas Shammai will let him off the hook unless he paid an amount large enough to show he really meant business)" (personal communication, August 1998). I suppose this explanation makes sense but it once again shows an entirely male perspective, taking no notice of the woman involved.

husband acting as her trustee.[17] A documented disagreement between Beit Hillel and Beit Shammai on this issue is found only in connection with the legal powers of a betrothed woman who is not yet actually married. Essentially, there seems to be no disagreement between the Houses. Both concede that such a woman's legal transactions of acquisition and sale are valid in principle. However, they disagree as to the desirability of this situation. Beit Shammai fully endorses the principle, maintaining that since a betrothed woman is not yet married, she may continue to do as she pleases with her property. Beit Hillel, on the other hand, approaches this issue from the perspective of the woman's future station—the property she owns as a betrothed women is intended to become the responsibility of and inure to the benefit of her husband, and her independent transactions during the betrothal may diminish his potential gain. In light of this, the woman is warned against selling any property acquired after her betrothal. It is clear from this disagreement that while Beit Shammai have the woman's interest, independence and full mental capacity in mind, the Hillelites ride rough-shod over the woman, protecting the interests of her future husband instead. This ruling illustrates a second principle evident in Beit Shammai's attitude to women, namely that they are empowered, like men, to own property, and this power should not be curtailed because of gender considerations.

iii. Finally, the Mishnah records another disagreement between the Hillelites ·and the Shammaites on the position of a minor whose betrothal was arranged by her mother or brothers:

> Beit Shammai says: One allows only betrothed [minor orphans] to refuse [to marry husbands chosen to them by their mothers and brothers]. Beit Hillel says: Both betrothed and already married ones. Beit Shammai says: [They may refuse] a husband but not a levir; Beit Hillel says: Both a husband and a levir. Beit Shammai says: [Only] in his presence (literally: To his face). Beit Hillel says: Both in his presence and in his absence. Beit Shammai says: [Only] in a court of law; Beit Hillel says: Both in and out of a court of law. Said Beit Hillel to Beit Shammai: A minor may refuse even four or five times. Said Beit Shammai to Beit Hillel: The daughters of Israel are not licentious (הפקר). She refuses and then she waits until she comes of age and may refuse [again] and then marry [another] (*mYevamot* 13:1).

This is another halakhah pertaining to betrothal. It discusses the validity of a marriage contracted on behalf of a young girl by her mother or brothers in a case where her father had died.[18] The position espoused here by the Hillelites is that such a marriage is invalid and can only be validated by the daughter's consent. This means that, on coming of age, she may dissolve the marriage even after consummation—even after producing offspring. Beit Shammai,

---

[17] Ilan, *Jewish Women,* 167.

[18] See *ibid.,* 84.

however, maintains that although such a marriage is invalid to begin with, it may be dissolved by the girl only before consummation; not afterwards. In other words, the consummation of a marriage (obviously through sexual intercourse) cannot be lightly dismissed. The Houses further discuss the position of a minor who was married in this way to her levir (a biblical injunction—Deuteronomy 25:5-6) and even in this case Beit Hillel finds that she is at liberty to reject the marriage, while the Shammaites maintain that she may not. When one poses the question, which school has the woman's interest at heart here, a modern scholar would naturally suggest that the Hillelites do. The marriage was not contracted by the girl herself and allowing her the liberty of dissolving it in all circumstances places her in a position to make her own choice. However, we should view this issue in its larger historical context. Beit Hillel does not condemn arranged marriages altogether; it only denies the validity of such a marriage when arranged by insufficiently qualified members of the family (first and foremost the mother). It is, therefore, not the girl's interest that it upholds, but rather that of the traditional patriarchal household. This position undermines the mother's authority *vis à vis* her children in comparison with the father. Beit Shammai, in its dispute with Beit Hillel, upholds a very different principle. In arguing against giving the daughter the power to dissolve all such matches, the Shammaites maintain "the daughters of Israel are not licentious (הפקר)." In other words, the Shammaites have the good name of the girl in mind, and as mentioned above, they take a serious view of marriage. The consummation of marriage is, in their mind, of major importance, as is the maintenance of sexual purity. Sexual activity outside of marriage, they maintain, is a grave offense; they are not prepared to view sexual intercourse performed under a pretense of marriage as insignificant. This reflects a third principle, which Beit Shammai consistently espouses with regard to women, namely its belief in the supreme importance of the sexual act. Furthermore, as will be shown presently, Beit Shammai often treats a man's sexual misconduct almost as strictly as the woman's, and regards more actions taken by men in the sexual realm than those taken by women as halakhic offenses.

A *baraita* in the Babylonian Talmud, which is appended to this ruling (perhaps indicating that it reflects the original formulation of the law, which the editors of the Mishnah decided to remove), clearly demonstrates Beit Shammai's position toward women in this case too:

> Said Beit Hillel to them: The wife of Pishon the camel-driver exercised her right of refusal in his absence. Said Beit Shammai to them: Since Pishon the camel-driver dealt with her illegally (literally: Weighed for her with a fake weight), they dealt with him illegally (= weighed for him with a fake weight) (*bYevamot* 107b).

The incident of Pishon the camel-driver seems to have been a famous legal case on which the Shammaites and Hillelites both concurred. On the face of it, it seems to confirm the view of Beit Hillel—during the husband's absence a wife refused the match arranged for her by her mother or brother(s), and the court endorsed her action. Any number of scenarios could explain this, including the possibility that the man was violent and dangerous to his wife (so that she would have feared to exercise her right in his presence). Beit Hillel deduced from this case that the law allows all wives in a similar status to exercise the right of refusal in their husbands' absence. Beit Shammai, however, maintains that this case is not a precedent for all cases, but was limited to cases where the wife was abused. This suggests that while Beit Shammai held a stricter view of marriage, it was willing to consider individually and sympathetically cases where the husband was ill-treating the wife. Beit Hillel, on the other hand, was willing to accommodate the wife's plea only if it coincided with the letter of the law.

As we continue our survey of the sources we will see that this Shammaites view of sex, even where it appears to restrict women's actions, is in fact intended for their protection against accusations of unchastity, rather then the protection of the men who come in contact with them.

b. Divorce

i. Perhaps the most famous controversy between Beit Shammai and Beit Hillel involves the grounds on which divorce is permissible.

> Beit Shammai holds that a man may not divorce his wife unless he has found in her a matter of sexual impropriety, as stated in Scripture "since he finds something *improper* in her" (Deuteronomy 24:1). Beit Hillel holds [that he may divorce her] even if she [merely] burned his dinner, as it is stated "since he finds *something* improper in her" (Deuteronomy 24:1) (*mGittin* 9:10).

Both Beit Shammai and Beit Hillel would agree that the ultimate ground for divorce is sexual misconduct.[19] While for the Shammaites this remains, however, the sole ground for divorce, Beit Hillel takes a much broader view of the issue. This ruling makes it clear that Beit Shammai considered divorce, just like marriage, a weighty matter not to be lightly performed. Since it agreed with the Hillelites that divorce is a unilateral transaction, which can only be executed by the husband, it suggested limiting his prerogative to matters that bear directly on the marriage itself. A woman is taken in marriage for the purpose of sexual intercourse and reproduction; it is, therefore, only with relation to misconduct in this context that she may be put away. Modern feminists may rightly wonder if it is in any woman's best interest to remain married to a man who has lost interest in her, and may, in light of this approach, suggest that the Hillelite view greatly supports women. In answer to this, it may be pointed out that the Hillelite view does not give the woman the

---

[19] *Ibid.*, 141-3.

right to dissolve an unsuccessful marriage. It simply allows a man to reduce his wife to a piece of property that can be disposed at whim; with the almost certain result that the woman would be plunged into economic hardship as has historically been the lot of single women in ancient patriarchal societies (and is true even today, the world over).[20] The question which interests us here is not the social effect of the ruling, but rather the intention of the legislator. For Beit Shammai the object(ive) of this ruling is clearly (and even grammatically) the woman—her sexual conduct—whereas for the Beit Hillel the man's interest becomes the object(ive)—his satisfaction—to which woman is subject(ed). Beit Shammai also bears in mind the woman's correct sexual conduct, viewing divorce as a punishment for impropriety alone. Two of the above mentioned Shammaitic principles appear here—the demand that the husband make a serious commitment to marriage, and a stringent attitude toward sexual behavior.

ii. That Beit Shammai considered divorce a serious matter is further demonstrated by another halakhah on which the two Houses disagreed:

> If a man wrote a divorce bill for his wife and then changed his mind, Beit Shammai says: He has disqualified her from [marrying into] the priesthood; Beit Hillel says: Even if he gave it to her on a condition which was not fulfilled, he has not disqualified her from [marrying into] the priesthood (*mGittin* 8:8).[21]

Marriage into the priestly caste, although it appears central to the formulation of this halakhah, is not in fact the issue here. Because priests may not marry divorcées,[22] marriage into the priesthood is taken as the code word for the validity or otherwise of a divorce. Beit Shammai contends that once a bill of divorce has been sent to the wife it is always valid, even if the writer's intention is not reflected in it. Beit Hillel maintains that if a man who sent the divorce bill changes his mind before it reaches his wife, the divorce is revoked. Thus, we see again that for Beit Shammai the decision to divorce is a serious matter, which may not be easily revoked. The Shammaites maintain that a man should not act in haste when executing a bill of divorce.

iii. Another divorce issue debated by Beit Shammai and Beit Hillel touches on the extent to which a man and a woman may fraternize after the divorce has been formalized.

> Beit Shammai says: A man may divorce his wife with an outdated bill of divorce (*get*), but Beit Hillel forbids it. What is an old bill of divorce? Any case where [the husband] was alone with [his wife] after he wrote it (cf. *mGittin* 8:4).

---

[20] *Ibid.*, 147-8.

[21] Cf. also *tGittin* 8:8.

[22] Ilan, *Ibid.*, 71-2.

If a man has divorced his wife and [then] she sleeps with him in an inn, Beit Shammai says: She does not need another bill of divorce, while Beit Hillel says: She does need another bill of divorce from him ... (*mEduyot* 4:7; *mGittin* 8:9 Cf. also *tGittin* 8:8 for additional information).

The meaning of this law, according to Beit Hillel, is that if a man gave his wife a bill of divorce and subsequently sequestered himself with her, this raises a presumption that they were sexually intimate, with the effect (according to Jewish law) that they have remarried, and thus require a fresh divorce. Beit Shammai, however, trusts the divorced couple not to indulge in sexual intercourse as soon as they find themselves alone together. This suggests that the Shammaites took a much more positive view of gender mingling, entertaining the possibility that such associations do not inevitably lead to sexual activity.

Since the bill of divorce is issued by the man to the woman, it may be assumed to represent the man's intention rather than the woman's. Thus, when formulating its opinion, Beit Hillel suspects the woman of an intention to seduce her husband once they are alone together, in the hope of making him change his mind. The Hillelite position therefore reflects badly on the woman (as also on the man, who is easily seduced). Beit Shammai on the other hand, assumes that both man and woman may be trusted after the divorce to avoid sexual misconduct. Thus, despite the fact that Beit Shammai is more interested in sexual misconduct pertaining to marriage, and takes a stricter view of it (as we have seen, and as we shall see), it nevertheless takes a more positive view of human capacity for self-restraint, in the case of men and women alike, than Beit Hillel does. This approach allows Beit Shammai a more positive view of marriage, in that although its primary purpose is sexual consummation, it may in practice encompass also a closer, non-sexual relationship between spouses.

These two rulings, incidentally, appear in a chapter in *mEduyot* that contrasts the stringent rulings of Beit Hillel with the lenient rulings of Beit Shammai.[23]

c. Widowhood

In Jewish law a woman's widowhood entails two problems—verification of the husband's death (in order to free his wife to remarry) and settlement of his property (to allow his wife to collect her marriage settlement). Since a widow is in no way responsible for her misfortune, and since no sexual misconduct is involved, on both of these issues Beit Shammai seems to favor the position of the woman more than Beit Hillel does.

---

[23] And for a possible further halakhah on divorce see *tArakhin* 4:5.

i. The best example of the relative leniency with which Beit Shammai permitted the establishment of a husband's death is their position that a woman may testify to the death of her own husband:

> These are issues on which Beit Hillel revised [their view] to teach according to the opinion of Beit Shammai: A woman who came back [alone] from overseas and said "My husband is dead," she may marry; or "My husband died [childless]," she may enter levirate union. Beit Hillel says: We have heard [such a ruling] only of a woman who came back from the reaping. Beit Shammai said to them: It is all one, whether she came from the reaping or from the olive-picking or whether she came from overseas; the sages mentioned the reaping only as a commonplace event. Thus Beit Hillel revised [their view] to teach according to the opinion of Beit Shammai (*mEduyot* 1:12; cf. *mYevamot* 15:2).

Establishment of the husband's death is essential for allowing a Jewish widow to remarry. Death may be established through the evidence of witnesses, but women, as a rule, are incompetent as witnesses according to Jewish law (*Ant.* 4.219; *Sifre Deuteronomy* 190; cf. *mShevuot* 4:1). Social reality has proven, however, that the plight of a woman whose husband has died an unwitnessed death is extremely severe. For this reason, rabbinic literature goes a long way to simplify the legal procedure of establishing the man's death[24]—one witness (as opposed to the usual two) suffices; a woman or even a gentile may serve as witness in this case (*mKetubbot* 16:5-7); etc. The question here is whether the widow herself, testifying in her own self-interest, is reliable. Beit Shammai answers this question in the affirmative. Whether this is an appropriate legal procedure is debatable, but Beit Shammai preferred to ignore it here. What clearly emerges is that they sought to alleviate the woman's hardships by dispensing with formal court requirements. Furthermore, they even succeeded in persuading the Hillelites to adopt their view. The Hillelites knew of a precedent which followed the procedure favored by Beit Shammai, but sought to limit its application to specific cases, where a woman's husband died during the harvest and she came home and related his death. In general, they preferred the more rigid rules of evidence. Beit Shammai, on the other hand, clearly supported the woman's interest, and incidentally enhanced her legal capacity.

The source goes on as follows:

> Beit Shammai says: She may remarry and receive her marriage settlement (*ketubbah*). Beit Hillel says: She may remarry but may not receive her marriage settlement. Said Beit Shammai to them: You have dispensed with the stringent sexual [prohibition], will you not dispense with the lenient monetary [prohibition]? Said Beit Hillel to them: We have learnt that the brothers [of the deceased husband] do not inherit his property on her testimony [since they need two Jewish male witnesses for this purpose]. Said Beit Shammai to them: From her very marriage contract we learn that he wrote for her benefit:

---

[24] Ilan, *Jewish Women*, 148-9.

If you marry another, you may take what is assigned to you. Beit Hillel revised [their view] to teach according to the opinion of Beit Shammai (*ibid.*, cf. *mYevamot* 15:3).

This text goes on to discuss the legal situation that ensues as a result of the decision arrived at in the previous halakhah. The death of the husband having been established, the woman may remarry. What sort of bride will she be? Poor and helpless or prosperous and desirable? The very institution of the marriage settlement (*ketubbah*) was developed in the hope of producing the second result.[25] In the situation prevailing in this case, however, Beit Hillel deprives the newly-declared widow of her marriage settlement, on the basis of a formality that would stand up in any court of law. The marriage settlement, after all, is part of the entire inheritance arrangement, and legally no one can inherit the dead man's property until two reliable witnesses have come forward and testified to his death. As stated above, the Hillelites agreed with the Shammaites that for the purposes of matrimonial status, one witness, even though it be the woman herself, suffices to establish the husband's death. They would both probably agree that her testimony is not sufficient to allow the heirs to inherit their father's property. The argument of Beit Hillel, therefore, has its legal merits. Beit Shammai, in both of its refutations of the Hillelites' position, ignores this legal point altogether. First, with its usual value judgment, it holds that sexual misconduct is a far worse problem than monetary disorder. If Beit Hillel is willing to adopt Beit Shammai's lenient approach on this issue, the danger of an invalid remarriage and the production of bastard offspring notwithstanding, surely it will overlook the minor problem, that the return of the woman's *ketubbah*-money may have been procured under false pretenses. The second argument involves the text of the *ketubbah* itself.[26] That document expressly states that a widow who remarries is entitled to keep her marriage settlement from her previous marriage. Common to both arguments is a genuine interest in the widow's plight. If she loses her marriage settlement, rightfully or wrongfully, she will surely fail to

---

[25] On the date of the Jewish marriage settlement and its various developments see: L. M. Epstein, *The Jewish Marriage Contract: A Study in the Status of Women in Jewish Law* (New York 1927). There seems little doubt that by the time of Shammai and Hillel some form of the *ketubbah* already existed. A most important amendment of it is assigned to Shimeon ben Shetah, two generations before Hillel and Shammai (*tKetubbot* 12:1; *yKetubbot* 8:11, 32b-c; *bKetubbot* 82b; and see above, chapter 1). See also Hillel's treatment of a *ketubbah* clause in Alexandria (*tKetubbot* 4:9). On the form of *ketubbot* and other Jewish marriage contracts see: Hannah M. Cotton, "A Canceled Marriage Contract from the Judaean Desert (*XHev/Se GR.* 2)," *JRS* 84 (1994) 64-86; M. Satlow, "Reconsidering the Rabbinic *ketubbah* Payment," in S. J. D. Cohen (ed.), *The Jewish Family* (*Brown Judaic Studies* 289; Atlanta 1993) 133-51.

[26] This may have been a soft spot with the Hillelites, in light of the tradition that Hillel himself had expounded the text of the *ketubbah* in order to reach unusual halakhic conclusions. See previous note.

contract a second marriage and remain a pauper.[27] This ruling is also in line with Beit Shammai's interest in women's economic independence.

ii. Widowhood is again disputed by the Shammaites and the Hillelites, this time in relation to another issue—the *sotah* (wayward wife):

> If her husband died before she had drunk [the bitter water] Beit Shammai says: She may receive her marriage settlement (*ketubbah*) and does not drink. Beit Hillel says: Either she drinks or she receives no marriage settlement (mss. version) (*mSotah* 4:2).

The Hebrew Bible (Numbers 5:11-31) prescribes an ordeal which a wife suspected by her husband of infidelity must undergo, in order to "prove" her innocence.[28] This ordeal includes drinking a certain potion which is designated "bitter water." The halakhah under discussion here involves a case where the husband has voiced his suspicion of his wife, decided to submit her to the ordeal, and then died without carrying out his plan. Beit Shammai maintains that since the wife's unfaithfulness is a matter of mere suspicion, which can now no longer be tested, the woman should receive the benefit of the doubt and be treated like any other widow. Beit Hillel, to the contrary, upholds the husband's suspicion as of primary importance and maintains that the widow should be treated as an unfaithful wife, who would forfeit her marriage settlement upon divorce. The formulation of the printed editions reads: "she need not drink, but she does not receive her marriage settlement." This version says what I have maintained above, but it is, in fact an interpretation of the manuscript texts, which read: "Either she drinks or she receives no marriage settlement." In other words, payment of the marriage settlement to a suspected adulteress depends on the results of the bitter water test. Nevertheless, the interpretation of the printed editions is valid because,

---

[27] In this context a *baraita* from the Babylonian Talmud (*bYevamot* 122a) seems to qualify the compassionate attitude displayed by Beit Shammai toward the widow under similar circumstances: "Said Rabba bar Samuel: It has been taught [by the early rabbis, i.e. it is a *baraita*] Beit Shammai says: One may not marry [a widow] on the evidence of rumor (בת קול) and Beit Hillel says: One may marry [a widow] on the evidence of rumor." Rabba bar Samuel recites this *baraita* with relation to *mYevamot* 16:6: "One may marry [a widow] on the evidence of rumor." The meaning of this mishnah is that if rumor has it that the woman's husband has died, this evidence should be accepted and the woman may remarry. According to *bYevamot* 122a this considerate approach was upheld by Beit Hillel and rejected by Beit Shammai. However, a closer examination reveals that this *baraita* is in fact a composite tradition, based on the mishnah cited above, and on another *baraita* found in the Tosefta (*tNezirut* 1:1) "Beit Shammai says: One may not accept the evidence of rumor (בת קול), and Beit Hillel says: One may accept the evidence of rumor." This says nothing about Beit Shammai's attitude to rumor in the specific case of a widow. It appears that Rabba bar Samuel harmonized the mishnah with the *baraita* in putting an inconsiderate ruling on the specific topic of the widow's remarriage into the mouth of Beit Shammai. That this was indeed their opinion seems unlikely.

[28] Ilan, *Jewish Women*, 136-41.

with the husband gone, no-one can bring the suspected adulteress to the Temple to undergo the *sotah* ordeal, and so in practice Beit Hillel's position terminates her chances of receiving her marriage settlement. Here, as in the previous cases, it is clear that Beit Shammai sees no reason to mix the issue of property ownership with the issue of marital status and firmly supports the woman's right to her own property.

iii. A special case of widowhood is the case of the levirate widow, whose husband has died childless, and who is, thus, required to remarry his brother. This issue seems to have been a subject of frequent debate between Shammaites and Hillelites, and appears among the lenient rulings of Beit Shammai and the stringent rulings of Beit Hillel:

> Beit Shammai permits the co-wives [of women who cannot marry their dead husband's brother because of consanguinity] to [marry] the [surviving] brothers but Beit Hillel forbids [this]. If [such co-wives] have performed *halitzah* [as required by the Shammaites], Beit Shammai declares them ineligible for [marriage into] the priesthood [because they are classified as divorcées], but Beth Hillel [for whom the release ceremony was unnecessary, hence lacks legal significance] declares them eligible. If they performed levirate marriage, Beit Shammai permits [their offspring to be considered unblemished Jews], but Beit Hillel does not. Despite the fact that the former permit it and the latter forbid it, Beit Shammai did not hesitate to marry women of Beit Hillel nor Beit Hillel to marry women of Beit Shammai ... (*mEduyot* 4:8; cf. *mYevamot* 1:4).

According to biblical law (Deuteronomy 25:5-10), when a man dies childless his widow is required to marry the deceased husband's brother, in order to produce offspring for the dead man. This is called levirate marriage, or *yibbum,* and is considered commendable. If, however, the dead brother had produced offspring, the consanguinity laws forbid the widow to marry her brother-in-law. If the brother declines to perform levirate marriage he may choose the humiliating alternative of *halitzah*—release. During the Second Temple period levirate marriage was still very much in vogue, although it seems to have lost its appeal soon afterwards.[29]

The argument between Beit Shammai and Beit Hillel involves a very specific case of levirate marriage, in which a man is married to two women, one of them his brother's daughter.[30] On the death of the husband, what should the brother do? Certainly he cannot marry his own daughter, and in her case he is exempt from both levirate marriage and *halitzah.* How, then, should he act toward the co-wife? Beit Shammai says he should act normally—either take her in levirate marriage or free her by *halitzah.* Beit Hillel claims the ineligible widow releases the co-wife from these obligations. On the face of it this looks like a simple debate about mere formalities. Its implications,

---

[29] *Ibid.,* 152-5.

[30] A very favorable match according to rabbinic law. See *ibid.,* 76-7.

however, are far-reaching. According to Beit Hillel, if the first co-wife is exempt from the levirate union, any co-wife who marries the husband's brother will be committing incest. In other words, according to Beit Hillel, an act permitted by Beit Shammai would result in a blemished marriage and the production of bastard offspring. But if the brother chose to follow Beit Shammai and release his brother's widow by *halitzah,* Beit Hillel considers the action superfluous but harmless. The woman is, after all, a widow and thus free to remarry. Beit Shammai, however, considers the *halitzah* release valid, and the woman is thus a form of divorcée. As such she is ineligible to marry a priest, and if she did so, the Shammaites would consider her children blemished priests. This would suggest that persons who followed Beit Hillel would not be able to marry people who followed the ruling of Beit Shammai because they may be suspected bastards. Followers of Beit Shammai, on the other hand, would have difficulty accepting some members of the priesthood acceptable to Beit Hillel. The source states explicitly that Hillelites continued to marry Shammaites, but from the gravity of the situation, this sounds like part of Beit Hillel's after-the-fact "love" rhetoric.

Even though this controversy seems to broach a rather hypothetical topic, it is one of the most famous controversies between the two Houses, frequently discussed in the literature, both rabbinic and modern.[31] The reason for this is, on the one hand, the grave social implications that could result from an application of this law one way or the other. It would create not merely two schools of thought but also two castes who do not intermarry, clearly making the Hillelites a sect in the narrow sense of the word.[32] On the other hand, rabbinic literature contains several examples of cases in which this problem came to a head during Temple times and after, and in all cases the parties involved followed Beit Shammai, indicating that at some past time Shammaite rulings had been followed.[33] It has, therefore, been an intriguing topic for historians.

In what way does this ruling illustrate Beit Shammai's social attitude to women? Its assumption is that if biblical law recommends levirate marriage, it must be a good thing. Its application should, therefore, be extended to as many cases as possible. Certainly a man cannot marry his daughter, but there is nothing to stop him from marrying her co-wife. Levirate marriage, although it may sometimes be objectionable to the woman, did at least offer her

---

[31] See A. Büchler, "The Practice of Halakhah According to Beit Shammai During the Second Temple Period and After the Destruction," *Emlékkönyn Bloch Mózes Tiszteletére (Moses Bloch Festschrift)* (Budapest 1905) 22-4 [Hebrew]; Safrai, "Decision According to Beit Hillel," 24-5; Ben Shalom, *The School of Shammai,* 232-3.

[32] For a definition of Jewish sectarianism at this period, including just this parameter, see S. J. D. Cohen, *From the Maccabees to the Mishnah* (Philadelphia 1987) 124-73, and see particularly pp. 128-31.

[33] See Büchler, *ibid.,* Safrai, "Decisions According to Beit Hillel," *ibid.*

economic security. Beit Shammai is also less stringent about the status of the offspring of such a marriage. Beit Hillel's attitude, on the other hand, represents a departure from the biblical law, which, when the halakhic rulings of Beit Hillel were eventually adopted, culminated in a saying found in the Babylonian Talmud: "If a man marries his deceased brother's wife on account of her beauty, or in order to gratify his sexual desires, or with any other ulterior motive, it is as if he has infringed the laws of incest and ... the child [of such a union] is a bastard" (*bYevamot* 39b). This pro-and-anti-biblical-law dichotomy pervades the disputes of Beit Shammai and Beit Hillel, but seldom bears directly on women's issues.[34]

iv. The next example, which also pertains to levirate marriage, further demonstrates the Houses' attitude toward the topic, revealing a less formalistic approach to marriage on the part of Beit Shammai:

> [There was a case of] three brothers; two married to two sisters and one a bachelor. One of the husbands [of the sisters] died, and the bachelor came unto [his wife], and then his other brother died. The House of Shammai says: His wife is with him, and the [second sister] must be released because she is his wife's sister. Beth Hillel says: He must divorce his wife both by a bill of divorce and by *halitzah* and his brother's wife by *halitzah*. On this it was said: Woe to him on account of his wife, Woe to him on account of his brother's wife (*mEduyot* 4:9; cf. *mYevamot* 3:4; cf. also *mEduyot* 5:5).

The situation here is similar to the one discussed above, although somewhat more acute. This is a case where a levirate marriage has actually taken place, and is valid according to both Houses. When a second brother dies, who was married to the sister of the levir's newly acquired wife, however, Beit Hillel compels the levir to divorce his levirate wife. How it arrives at this conclusion is not clear. Beit Shammai, on the other hand, upholds the validity of his first marriage. Its consideration of the humane rather than formal aspect of marriage is clearly visible. That the Hillelite position is considered tough is evident from the lament appended to it: "Woe to him on account of his wife, Woe to him on account of his brother's wife." This lament however focuses only on the man's plight in this situation. No less pitiful is the women's situation in this case. The approach of Beit Shammai, by contrast, clearly champions marriage against legal formalities.

v. Another ruling with a similar moral is this:

> If two of four brothers were married to two sisters, and if the married brothers died, their wives are subjected to *halitzah* and not to levirate marriage. If, however, they have married them, they must divorce them. Rabbi Eliezer says in the name of Beit Shammai:

---

[34] On this see now D. R. Schwartz, "Hillel and Scripture: From Authority to Exegesis," in J. H. Charlesworth and L. L. Johns (eds.), *Hillel and Jesus* (Minneapolis 1997) 335-62. See also below in a dispute between Pharisees and Sadducees.

They may keep them. But Beit Hillel says: They must divorce them (*mEduyot* 5:5; cf. *mYevamot* 3:1).

There is no need to expand on this ruling. It mirrors the tradition of the two previous ones, clearly conveying the sense that Beit Hillel favors *halitzah* over and against levirate marriage, and it disregards the human suffering that may result from dissolving a forbidden marriage. Beit Shammai initially agrees with Beit Hillel's rulings, but is willing to make an exception in order to save a marriage performed in error, but which is not really incestuous. The two last rulings, even more than the first one concerning levirate marriage discussed above, address hypothetical situations, rather than any actual case. Nevertheless, it is worth noting that the Shammaites continue to champion the human aspect of marriage, over and against its precise legal formalities.

d. Other Topics Pertaining to Marriage

Jewish marriage is clearly much more than the rules of betrothal, divorce and widowhood. It is the institution through which the important commandment to be fruitful and multiply is realized, and is the only framework within which sex is viewed as licit. It is also the institution in which children are raised as a joint project of husband and wife. A small number of Beit Shammai and Beit Hillel disputes pertain to these issues, and I have collected them here:

i. An interesting topic is the difference in the views of Beit Shammai and Beit Hillel on the question of sexual continence. Rabbinic Judaism as a whole displays a positive, almost compulsive affirmation of sex.[35] As is evident from dissident readings, however,[36] some rabbinic Jews expressed other views, some of them decidedly ascetic. Although we have but one dispute between Beit Hillel and Beit Shammai on this topic, it may suggest to us that Beit Shammai, by inclination, belonged to this latter trend:

[As for] one who forswears sexual intercourse with his wife, Beit Shammai rules [that he may keep his vow] For two weeks (literally: two Shabbatot), Beit Hillel rules one week [only] (*mEduyot* 4:10; cf. *mKetubbot* 5:6).

This text suggests that a man may occasionally wish to abstain from having sex with his wife, usually by making a binding vow. Since rabbinic literature tends to view sex as an essential component of marriage, it maintains that a prolonged period of abstinence necessitates divorce. The issue under

---

[35] See D. Boyarin, *Carnal Israel: Reading Sex in Talmudic Culture* (Berkeley 1993) particularly pp. 61-76.

[36] D. Biale, *Eros and the Jews: From Biblical Israel to Contemporary America* (New York 1992) 33-59; H. Eilberg-Schwartz, *God's Phallus (and Other Problems for Men and Monotheism)* (Boston 1994) 211-22; S. Fraade, "Ascetical Aspects of Ancient Judaism," in A. Green (ed.), *Jewish Spirituality* 1 (New York 1986) 274-5.

discussion between the Hillelites and the Shammaites is the maximum duration of this abstinence period. Beit Shammai is the more flexible, suggesting that a two-week abstinence period is not too much. Beit Hillel, however, permits only one week. Who benefits from this period of abstinence? Obviously, although the man is the one whom this law contemplates, sex is an issue that intimately affects women. Thus, some feminists would maintain that if a man decides, of his own accord, to abstain, it may be in the woman's interest to compel him to resume his sexual activity as soon as possible.[37] Indeed, the Mishnah views this law as a lenient ruling of the Shammaites, and as we have seen, these lenient rulings usually benefit the man. It is, therefore, assumed that compelling the husband to resume his sexual activity is hard on him, but probably beneficial to the wife. This is, however, the Hillelite view of the issue, which totally ignores the Shammaite *raison d'être*. According to the latter, forcing the husband to resume sexual activity even after two weeks is probably in itself a concession. This may have to do with Beit Shammai's general attitude to sex—since it is such a serious issue, occasional abstention may relax the tension of following the rigid sexual code precisely. Thus, if, according to the Shammaites, sexual continence is legitimate, the purpose of marriage is not limited to procreation alone, and a situation in which a man and a woman live together without being sexually active is not considered obscene. This suggests once again that Beit Shammai, who adhered to a stricter sexual code, nevertheless did not consider marriage as an exclusively sexual relationship, imagining other possible common interests of husband and wife.

ii. The Hillelites and Shammaites also discussed what constitutes a man's required offspring:

> No man is exempt from the duty to be fruitful and multiply unless he [already] has sons. Beit Shammai says: [This means] two sons. Beit Hillel says: [This means] a son and a daughter (*mYevamot* 6:6).

This ruling is clearly associated with the previous one, because it contemplates a man who wishes to desist from sexual activity, legally requiring him to fulfill the duty of procreation before he abstains. According to the Mishnah, Beit Shammai and Beit Hillel dispute the nature of this obligation. They agree that it entails producing two offspring, but while Beit Shammai requires two sons, Beit Hillel maintains they should be a son and a daughter. This ruling, suggests that Beit Hillel has a higher opinion of daughters. Since procreation is the oldest commandment, issued to Adam and Eve, Beit Hillel sees women are part of the order of creation, while Beit Shammai does not. Indeed, the Palestinian Talmud lists this halakhah among

---

[37] See the nuanced discussion of this topic in Boyarin, *Carnal Israel*, 142-6.

the lenient rulings of Beit Shammai (*yYevamot* 6:6, 7c). It is useful, however, to compare this text with a similar tradition in the Tosefta:

> Rabbi Nathan says: Beit Shammai says: [This, i.e. the commandment to be fruitful and multiply, means] two sons. Beit Hillel says: [This means] a son and a daughter. Rabbi Jonathan says: Beit Shammai says: [This means] a male and a female; Beit Hillel says: [This means] either a male or a female (*tYevamot* 8:4).

Clearly the mishnaic version represents Judah the Patriarch's choice of one version of the tradition (Rabbi Nathan's, namely that of the school of Rabbi Aqiva), over against another (that of Rabbi Jonathan's, namely of the school of Rabbi Ishmael). We may never know what exactly Beit Shammai maintained, but the Tosefta version of Rabbi Jonathan suggests that Beit Shammai did not necessarily display a preference for sons.

iii. The two rulings that follow revolve around the woman as a mother:

> A nursing woman whose husband has died may not become betrothed and may not marry ... Beit Shammai says: For twenty four months. Beit Hillel says: For eighteen months (*tNiddah* 2:2).

The issue here is the well-being of a fatherless infant, who is dependent on his mother for sustenance. The question is, must the mother nurse him for two years or does a year and a half suffice? In the eyes of Beit Hillel remarriage is so desirable that a minimum period of eighteen months for the infants nourishment suffices. Beit Shammai, however, with the infant's well-being in mind, decrees a longer period of nursing, namely 24 months. Clearly its opinion suggests once again that it considers marriage an obligation into which one should not rush. If the intended husband is a serious man, he will probably wait for his intended wife another six months, and in this way make the marriage more sound.

This attitude seems to contradict their approach to the issue of nursing, under different circumstances:

> If she vowed not to nurse her son, Beit Shammai says: She may remove the nipple from his mouth; Beit Hillel says: [Her husband] can compel her, and she must nurse [her son]. But if she is divorced he cannot compel her (*bNiddah* 59a).

Here, although the issue is again a nursing baby, Beit Shammai maintains that a woman's vow is sacred and takes precedence over her obligation to nurse her son, while Beit Hillel upholds the authority of the husband over his wife. Since neither seems concerned about the baby, the argument digresses to the question of a woman's autonomy, which Beit Shammai upholds, while Beit Hillel denies. We may surmise, therefore, that, in conjunction with the previous ruling, according to Beit Shammai's scale of values, a woman's autonomy took precedence over her child's welfare, but the child's welfare took precedence over new matrimonial plans of the mother. According to Beit Hillel, on the other hand, the father/husband's authority is paramount; then comes the requirement to marry off an unattached woman, thus ensuring her control by a man. The welfare of the child is no consideration at all.

iv. Finally, another discussion between the two schools touches on the mother-son relationship:

> If a woman fondled her minor son and he ejaculated on (or penetrated) her, Beth Shammai disqualifies her [from marrying into the priesthood] but Beth Hillel permits her [to marry into the priesthood] (*tSotah* 5:7).

This ruling discusses the consequences of a woman's (involuntary) sexual involvement with her (apparently adolescent) son. Beit Hillel views such conduct as insignificant, and therefore inconsequential for the woman's marital status. For Beit Shammai, that always upholds more stringent sexual norms, this amounts to a sexual act, which should be considered as nothing less than incest, which naturally makes the woman ineligible for marriage with a priest.

In this context the Palestinian Talmud cites another *baraita* not found in the Tosefta:

> As for two women who fondle (מסללדת) one another, Beit Shammai disqualifies [them from marrying into the priesthood] and Beit Hillel permits [them to marry into the priesthood] (*yGittin* 8:10, 48c).

This text is extremely interesting, because it is one of the few sources in rabbinic literature which discusses a lesbian relationship, while indicating the Houses' attitude toward it.[38] As in the case of the mother and son, Beit Hillel considers such a relationship as insignificant, and women who engage in homoerotic activity are not perceived as performing a sexual act. Beit Shammai, on the contrary, considers female homoeroticism a sexual activity, and the women who engage in it as sexually perverted. Obviously they cannot enter a marriage with a priest. Once again we see Beit Shammai's more stringent attitude to sex. Feminists may surmise that Beit Hillel's attitude, which tends to dismiss lesbianism as not amounting to a sexual offense, is more beneficial to lesbian women. However, it is interesting to note that the Shammaites, by according greater significance to women's sexual activity among themselves, even while expressing a negative attitude toward lesbianism, at the same time uphold the personhood and importance of women, by maintaining that actions women perform among themselves also

---

[38] On this text, see Bernadette J. Brooten, *Love Between Women: Early Christian Responses to Homoeroticism* (Chicago 1996) 66-70; M. Satlow, "'They Abused Him Like a Woman': Homoeroticism, Gender Blurring, and the Rabbis in Late Antiquity," *Journal of the History of Sexuality* 5 (1994) 15-7.

count in the halakhic context. Sex does not necessarily require a male or an act of penetration[39] to be meaningful.

In sum, the attitude of Beit Shammai to marriage and women's place in it is very different from that of Beit Hillel. In the first instance, Beit Shammai supported women's property rights. It held that, whenever in doubt about her marital position, the woman should enjoy the economic benefits available.[40] Such an approach afforded greater personhood to women.

Secondly, Beit Shammai viewed marriage as a serious matter, rather than a whim; a man must bear the consequences of his decisions regarding marriage. Beit Shammai also believed that marriage should not be easily dissolved. Therefore it should also not be entered lightly. This approach is even evident in a *baraita* in the Babylonian Talmud, in which the Hillelites and Shammaites argue about the correct procedure of dancing before the bride at her wedding:

> How does one dance before the bride? Beit Shammai says: "Bride, Bride," as she is. Beit Hillel says: "Beautiful bride, Gracious bride." Said Beit Shammai to them: And if she were lame or blind, does one say to her: A beautiful and gracious bride? And it is written in the Torah "You shall not utter a false report" (Exodus 23:1). Said Beit Hillel to them: In your opinion, if a person makes a bad bargain in the market place, what will [the merchant] do, praise or denigrate it? Surely praise it! (*bKetubbot* 16b-17a).

In matters of marriage Beit Shammai believes in being truthful, even when the truth is unpleasant (to husband and wife). Beit Hillel believes the merriment of the wedding, and the happiness of the groom (nothing about the feelings of the bride appears in their argument) justify even a deviation from the absolute truth.

Finally, Beit Shammai took a stricter view than Beit Hillel on the question of sexual conduct. It believed that sexual licentiousness is a grave offense, and should therefore be strictly avoided. Its rulings, however, hint that this strict approach pertains to the male partner in marriage no less than to the female one, somewhat minimizing the double standard which other Jewish groups employed in their ordering of the lives of men and women.

---

[39] On this definition see: M. L. Satlow, *Tasting the Dish: Rabbinic Rhetorics of Sexuality* (*Brown Judaic Studies* 303; Atlanta 1995) 316-7. His discussion of the text presented here is on pp. 189-90.

[40] Another economic dispute between the houses (*bYevamot* 89b) focuses on the husband's right to inherit from his wife, who is a minor on which "Beit Shammai says: [From the time] when she attains womanhood (עמדה בקומתה). Beit Hillel says: [From the time] when she enters the bridal canopy." However, this dispute involves the husband's, not the wife's economic rights and is therefore not relevant here.

2. Purity Laws

A cursory view of the debates between Shammaites and Hillelites on the question of menstruation laws and other issues pertinent to women's purity reveals a far stricter approach on the part of the Shammaites. For example, "Beit Shammai says: All dead women are [in the category of] menstruants. Beit Hillel says: Only women who die menstruating are menstruants" (*mNiddah* 10:4). This is hardly a considerate view of women, although another halakhah seems to imply that the opinion of Beit Shammai eventually prevailed (*tNiddah* 9:16).

Beit Shammai adopts a broader approach to what kinds of bleeding should be considered menstruation: "Five kinds of women's bloods cause impurity: the red, the black, the crocus color, the color of earth water and the color of mixed drink [of wine and water]. Beit Shammai says: also like water with trefoil leaves and as the water of roast meat. Beit Hillel, however, declares these pure" (*mNiddah* 2:6). Thus Beit Shammai would in general more readily consider women in a state of ritual impurity than Beit Hillel.

An interesting debate exists between Beit Shammai and Beit Hillel over the state of ritual impurity of a woman who has just given birth. The biblical law (Leviticus 12) provides for her to be impure for seven days on the birth of a male and for fourteen days on the birth of a female. Thereafter a purification period extends to forty days in the case of a male child and eighty days for a female. During this period the woman is still impure, but not to the same extent, and may, for example, engage in sexual intercourse. Beit Shammai and Beit Hillel discuss various cultic options available to women over this extended period. It is interesting to note that Beit Shammai always upholds the more stringent view:

> At first they said: A parturient who is bleeding pure blood [after a week for a male and two weeks for a female] would pour water on the Pesah [sacrifice]. They enacted, however, that contact with her be considered unclean as with one who has had contact with a corpse, according to Beit Hillel. Beit Shammai says: Even as a corpse itself.

> But they concede that she may eat tithes, puts aside *hallah* offering ... and if her saliva or blood fell on a loaf of *terumah* offering it is clean.[41] Beit Shammai says: She is required to immerse [in water] at the end [of the forty or eighty days] and Beit Hillel says: She is not required to immerse at the end [of the period] (*mNiddah* 10:6-7).

Interestingly, these laws, which obviously place the Shammaite attitude at the more stringent end of the scale, deal with the question of women's participation in the cult. The first law deals with her participation in the ritual

---

[41] One of two rulings described in the Mishnah as leniencies of Beit Shammai does in fact suggest that Beit Shammai viewed these women as less polluting than Beit Hillel, see: *mEduyot* 5:4; cf. *mNiddah* 4:3 and see also *mEduyot* 5:1.

of the *Pesah* sacrifice, a commandment from which women were later exempt, according to rabbinic dicta (*mQiddushin* 1:7). Another cultic activity in which Beit Shammai holds a stricter view appears in the Tosefta:

> The meat of the first-born, Beit Shammai says: It is forbidden to a menstruating woman and Beit Hillel permits it to a menstruating woman (*tBekhorot* 3:16).

Beit Shammai further maintains that purity regulations are so important that they override any other considerations:

> All women are considered pure for their husbands when they come home from a journey .... Beit Shammai says: She needs two tests for every intercourse, or intercourse should be performed by the light of a candle. Beit Hillel says: Two tests are sufficient for the entire night (*mNiddah* 2:4).[42]

This text begins with a positive statement, suggesting that when a man comes home to his wife from a long journey he expects to have sex with her and should be gratified. *A priori* all women are clean. This attitude seems to be that of the redactor of the Mishnah. Nevertheless, the text immediately limits this sweeping generalization by juxtaposing it with the view of Beit Shammai which maintains that, on the contrary, a man should always suspect his wife of being unclean. She should check herself for a flow of blood twice before she can actually have sex with her husband, and then repeat the test before every intercourse. Beit Hillel holds an intermediate position, not as lenient as the Mishnah, not as stringent as Beit Shammai.

These and several other examples all point in the same direction: Beit Shammai was stricter than Beit Hillel on issues of women's ritual purity. This is consistent with Beit Shammai's attitude to sexual impropriety. Its sober attitude to sex in marriage spills over to the realm of ritual purity in this way. Not surprisingly, Beit Shammai was also stricter than Beit Hillel with regard to the ritual purity of men. For example we read in *mZavim*:

> Concerning a man who observes a [gonorrheal] discharge, Beit Shammai says: He is like a [menstruating] woman [checking herself] from day to day. Beit Hillel says: He is like [a man] who had a seminal emission ... As to one who had a seminal emission on the third day [of checking himself for ritual impurity], Beit Shammai says: He has [retrospectively] defiled the two previous [clean] days; Beit Hillel says: He has defiled only that day (*mZavim* 1:1-2).

These two examples indicate, that Shammaite strictness in the realm of ritual purity was not confined to the affairs of women alone. Beit Shammai demanded strict sexual control and ritual purity from men and women alike.

Nevertheless, when discussing the question of control over women's discharges and the responsibility for reporting the pollution thereof,

---

[42] Cf. *bNiddah* 16b.

Shammaites are again found on the side that accords women greater autonomy. In a law, dated by the mishnaic redactors to the founders of the houses, we read:

> Shammai says: All women [are polluting] only from the time [at which they saw menstruation blood]. Hillel says: From when they last examined themselves and even [if this means] many days (*mNiddah* 1:1).

This law deals with the question, when does a woman begin polluting everything she touches because she is menstruating? Shammai says this happens from the point when she observes herself bleeding. Hillel maintains, however, that she may have been polluting before she actually observed her blood, and so it is necessary to retroactively declare unclean all that she touched since her previous examination. Obviously the latter rule is the harsher and less accommodating to women, because it objectifies them, making their capacity to pollute uncontrollable. Since we have observed that in general Beit Shammai considered menstruation more polluting than did Beit Hillel, a legitimate question is, why is Shammai's ruling on the beginning of menstruation more lenient? Was he not afraid that such leniency would bring about greater pollution? The answer to this question is not straightforward, but it is instructive to see one opinion cited in the Babylonian Talmud to explain Shammai's view—a woman only pollutes from the moment she observes bleeding "since a woman feels [when she begins to bleed], but according to Hillel, she feels it only as she feels urine" (*bNiddah* 3a).[43] The rabbis themselves, therefore, assign to Shammai an attitude which presupposes a woman's personhood and responsibility—women themselves can know and will tell when they begin to pollute. If this explanation is correct, this ruling shows that even though Beit Shammai accorded greater significance to menstrual uncleanness, this did not reflect negatively on its attitude to women.

Could women find the Shammaite views appealing? We have very little to go on, in answering this question, but perhaps the case of Queen Helene of Adiabene can shed some light on it.

3. Queen Helene of Adiabene

Although Josephus claims that Queen Helene of Adiabene became a convert to Judaism around the middle of the first century CE (20.17-96), our

---

[43] I learnt this explanation from Charlotte Fonrobert in a lecture entitled "Whose House is This Body? Conflicting Conceptions of the Woman's Body in Talmudic Literature," given at the AJS Conference in Boston on December 18, 1995.

information about her from rabbinic literature suggests no such detail.[44] Nevertheless, we may assume that she did convert, and it is therefore pertinent to ask, what form of Judaism did she adopt? In the previous chapter I argued that the Judaism she adopted was of the Pharisee variety.[45] Here I would like to explore the possibility that the Pharisaism she adhered to was that of Beit Shammai.

Queen Helene is mentioned in rabbinic literature in three separate traditions, all of them tannaitic. One of them is directly associated with a controversy between Beit Hillel and Beit Shammai:

> Concerning one who vowed an extended *nazirite* vow and fulfilled her/his vow and then came to the Land [of Israel]. Beit Shammai says: S/he shall be a *nazir* for thirty days, but Beit Hillel says: S/he shall be a *nazir* from the beginning [of her/his vow period]. There was the case of Queen Helene, whose son went to war, and she said: If my son comes home safely I shall be a *nazirite* for seven years. Her son came back from the war and she became a *nazirite* for seven years. At the end of seven years she migrated to the Land [of Israel] and Beit Hillel instructed her to remain a *nazirite* for another seven years. At the end of seven years she became unclean and she was thus a *nazirite* for twenty one years. Rabbi Judah said: She was only a *nazirite* for fourteen years (*mNazir* 3:6).

This tradition is obviously legendary, as the thrice repeated number seven indicates. Yet, it does have a historical background, since Helene's sons did go off to war (e.g. *Ant.* 20.75-80), and Helene did come to Jerusalem (*Ant.* 20.49-53), if not actually to reside there, at least for a visit, and then again, to be buried there (*Ant.* 20.95). It is interesting to note, therefore, that according to this tradition, Beit Hillel instructed Helene as to the proper conduct required of a *nazirite*. I am interested, however, in the dissenting tradition preserved by Rabbi Judah. He maintains that Helene was a *nazirite* for only two spans of time (fourteen years) and not three. His commentary can be interpreted in one of two ways: either Helene was not contaminated after fourteen years, or she did not follow Beit Hillel's ruling after the first seven. The suggestion that the second of these interpretations represents Rabbi Judah's rule can be underscored by the fact that Rabbi Judah is often reported as transmitting traditions in the name of Beit Shammai.[46] If this is the correct reading of the tradition, it suggests that, in Rabbi Judah's view, Queen Helene was not instructed by Beit Hillel but by Beit Shammai. Obviously, Rabbi Judah's opinion is transmitted as a minority opinion in this debate, but

---

[44] See L. H. Schiffman, "The Conversion of the Royal House of Adiabene in Josephus and Rabbinic Sources," in L. H. Feldman and G. Hata (eds.), *Josephus, Judaism and Christianity* (Detroit 1987) 293-312. A discussion of this problem is found on p. 301.

[45] See chapter 1.

[46] On Rabbi Judah's relationship to Beit Shammai and its traditions, see J. N. Epstein, "On the Mishnah of Rabbi Judah," *Tarbiz* 15 (1944) 1-13 [Hebrew].

perhaps the rest of the information on Queen Helene embedded in tannaitic traditions supports this opinion as more genuine.

Another tradition about Queen Helene is recorded in the Tosefta as reported by the same Rabbi Judah:

> A *sukkah* higher than twenty cubits is invalid. Rabbi Judah said: It is valid. He said to them: It is told of Queen Helene's *sukkah* that it was twenty cubits high and the sages went in and out of it, and none of them said anything. They said to him: That is because she is a woman, and women are exempt from the commandment of *sukkah*. He said to them: Did she not have seven sons who were all disciples of the sages, and all dwelt in that *sukkah*? (*tSukkah* 1:1).

This tradition does not address primarily the question whether women are exempt from residing in the *sukkah*, although it is raised as a side issue, when Rabbi Judah insists that a royal precedent, Queen Helene's *sukkah*, fits his paradigm of the legal requirements for such a structure. I suspect, however, that Rabbi Judah's information was originally associated with the question of women's participation in the commandment of *sukkah*.[47] Relics of a debate on this issue between Beit Shammai and Beit Hillel are preserved in the Mishnah:

> Women, slaves and minors are exempt from [residing in the] *sukkah*. A minor who does not need his mother is obligated [to reside in the] *sukkah*. Once Shammai the Elder's daughter-in-law gave birth, and he removed the ceiling [over her] and covered it with branches for the sake of the minor (*mSukkah* 2:8).

This mishnah spells out two laws and then appends an episode involving Shammai the Elder, which is intended to dispute one of these rulings. The way it appears now implies that Shammai the Elder's action was intended to refute the claim that only a minor who no longer needs to remain with his mother is obligated to reside in the *sukkah*, since his action implies that even a newborn is so obligated. However, scholars have rightly noted that the last words in this example (בשביל קטן) are a later gloss,[48] added so as to conform to a version of this tradition suggested by the Babylonian Talmud.[49] Originally Shammai's actions were reported to refute the first ruling, namely that women are exempt from residing in the *sukkah*, by allowing the parturient mother to participate in the commandment. If Beit Shammai followed Shammai in requiring women to participate in *sukkah*, and Helene built a *sukkah* and dwelt in it (as reported by Rabbi Judah), she was obviously following the ruling of that school. That Rabbi Judah, who often transmits

---

[47] And further on this, see my *Mine and Yours are Hers: Retrieving Women's History from Rabbinic Literature* (Leiden 1997) 189.

[48] Sonne, "The Schools," 280-1, n. 13.

[49] See *bSukkah* 28b.

Shammaite traditions, relates this one, makes such a reconstruction not altogether improbable.

Finally, Helene is mentioned in one more tannaitic tradition. The Mishnah relates that

> King Monbaz made all the handles of the vessels of the Day of Atonement of gold. Helene, his mother, made a golden chandelier to hang over the entrance to the sanctuary. She also made a golden plaque with the *sotah* episode inscribed on it (*mYoma* 3:10).

Wealthy women are known to have contributed to the Temple, and an action of this sort on the part of Helene could therefore be viewed as historically correct, though insignificant, were it not that Helene chose to inscribe on the golden plaque which she donated to the Temple a biblical text which was somewhat controversial at the time. Some sources seem to suggest that toward the end of the Second Temple, the ordeal of the suspected wife came under attack from several quarters. The reasons for this attack will be suggested presently. For now it is interesting to note that, concerning Helene's younger contemporary, Rabban Yohanan ben Zakkai, the Mishnah relates:

> When adulterers became many [the rite of] the bitter water ceased; and Rabban Yohanan ben Zakkai brought it to an end (*mSotah* 9:9).

As mentioned above,[50] rabbinic literature has a tendency to describe the Temple as being under the control of ancient Pharisee leaders, and therefore reports the cessation of the bitter water ordeal as a historical fact. Many scholars today would doubt this statement, claiming that it is a retrojection of Rabban Yohanan ben Zakkai's post-70 authority onto the Temple cult and rituals.[51] I choose not to side with anyone on this issue. But if Rabban Yohanan did not oversee the cessation of the bitter water ritual, he obviously took the view that the ritual was redundant, even while the Temple was still standing. Helene's plaque, which reflects a more stringent adherence to the biblical injunction of the bitter water, represents, therefore, a statement in an ongoing debate within Pharisaic circles. Was this a Beit-Shammai vs. Beit-Hillel debate? Unfortunately, we have no way of knowing. The only Beit-Shammai—Beit-Hillel debate preserved on the *sotah* issue is the one quoted above (*mSotah* 4:2), which does not touch directly on the question implied by the Helene and Rabban Yohanan ben Zakkai traditions, namely whether the *sotah* ritual is still valid. Other information, however, may be relevant here. First of all, note that Helene is upholding strict observance of a biblical law against an approach that devalues it. This, as shown above, would

---

[50] Chapter 1.

[51] See Adriana Destro, *The Law of Jealousy: Anthropology of Sotah* (*Brown Judaic Studies* 181; Atlanta 1989) 6-13; in more general terms, see E. P. Sanders, *Judaism: Practice and Belief 63 BCE-66 CE* (Philadelphia 1992) 458-90.

be typical of the Shammaites in their disputes with Beit Hillel. Secondly, in a *baraita*, Rabban Yohanan ben Zakkai is described as the youngest of Hillel's disciples (*bSukkah* 28a). This statement places Yohanan squarely within the chain of tradition of the Hillelites. If his opinion on the *sotah* ordeal represents the entire House of Hillel, Helene's statement obviously represents Beit Shammai.

The evidence I have adduced here for a Shammaite conversion of Helene is sparse and circumstantial, and could probably be interpreted in other ways by other scholars. My reconstruction could also be attacked as naive, ignoring as it goes the a-historical character of rabbinic literature. The sources about Helene (such an approach would claim) cannot be treated as historical. How can we believe that the rabbis report accurately that Queen Helene, who flourished some 150 years before their traditions were collected, built a *sukkah* or took a *nazirite* vow, or even donated a golden plaque to the Temple? We cannot, of course, but in this case, each objection could be answered from a historical perspective. The fact that the rabbis recollected a historical figure is not disputed. There is, therefore, no reason to doubt that Helene could, like another wealthy queen of her time (Berenice—*War* 2.313), make a *nazirite* vow. She could also, like other women,[52] have dedicated money or furnishings to religious institutions. Since there is no external parallel to a woman building a *sukkah*, if she had not in fact built such an outrageously enormous one, who would have bothered to invent it? I believe the credibility of rabbinic recollections may be stretched just a little beyond what is usually acceptable among scholars today.[53]

What is the significance of retrieving for history a real woman who identified with Beit Shammai? If true, it suggests that women felt comfortable with Beit Shammai's attitude toward them and their place within the family. Beit Shammai offered women economic independence and greater social standing, together with tighter control of all that was associated with the sexual aspects of marriage. In other words, if a woman behaved chastely in marriage she could lead an independent life in other respects. So it is not surprising to find a woman—Helene—supporting the side that recommended continuation of the ordeal of the suspected adulteress, while a man—Rabban Yohanan ben Zakkai—supports the opposite side.[54] If Helene abided by Beit Shammai's strict approach to sexual misconduct she could hardly adopt

---

[52] See Bernadette J. Brooten, *Women Leaders in the Ancient Synagogue: Inscriptional Evidence and Background Issues* (*Brown Judaic Studies* 36; Chico CA. 1982) 157-65.

[53] In this last sentence I have employed text critical methods which I recommend in my book, *Mine and Yours*, 237-77.

[54] This has been understood by Miriam Peskowitz ("Spinning Tales: On Reading Gender and Otherness in Tannaitic Texts," in J. L. Silberstein and R. L. Cohn [eds.], *The Other in Jewish Thought and History: Construction of Jewish Culture and Identity* [New York 1994] 119-20, n. 46) as a "mechanism assigning to women the power to police" other women.

another opinion. One of the reasons the *sotah* ordeal was coming under attack from Rabban Yohanan's circles is the feeling voiced by the sages that it was not working. In the Tosefta Rabban Yohanan ben Zakkai is reputed to have said: "When adulterers became many the (bitter) water ceased" (*tSotah* 14:2). Another new idea, developed in rabbinic circles, suggested that meritorious women could pass the bitter water test even when guilty (*mSotah* 3:4).[55] In other words, Rabban Yohanan ben Zakkai and his party had ceased to rely on the test of the bitter water. In their opinion, even women who were vindicated by the ordeal remained suspect. A counter opinion, which demanded a stricter adherence to the ordeal would perhaps support the opposite point of view: Women who are suspect should be given a chance to prove their innocence by submitting to the ordeal, and if they survived it they should be allowed to go on with their lives. A lingering suspicion, this view would maintain, is unhealthy and does no good for any marriage. Helene's actions are, therefore, not altogether incomprehensible. She could live with Beit Shammai's strict sexual demands, given the freedom they allowed women in other spheres of life.

4. Historical Discussion

Most scholarship on Beit Shammai and Beit Hillel has tended to concentrate on legal issues.[56] In light of rabbinic sources, this is not surprising. However, historians who discussed Beit Shammai and Beit Hillel have puzzled over the interpretation which should be placed on this phenomenon. The historical approach has been to find evidence for the existence of schools outside of rabbinic literature, primarily in the writings of the chief historian for this period, Josephus. As a result one can detect two competing views concerning Beit Shammai and Beit Hillel. Both approaches are very old. One was sponsored by Abraham Geiger, a founder of the Reform movement within Judaism in the nineteenth century, who suggested that Beit Hillel should be identified with the Pharisees and Beit Shammai with the Sadducees.[57] The other approach was suggested by Heinrich Graetz, the father of modern

---

[55] For a date to this idea see Ilan, *Jewish Women*, 138-40.

[56] A. Goldberg, "The Eighteen Measures of Bet-Shammai and Bet-Hillel," in A. M. Rabello (ed.), *Studies in Judaism: Jubilee Volume Presented to David Kotlar by his Students, Colleagues and Friends* (Tel Aviv 1975) 216-25 [Hebrew]; M. Weiss, "The Authenticity of the Explicit Discussions in Bet Shammai-Bet Hillel Discussion," *Sidra: A Journal for the Study of Rabbinic Literature* 4 (1988) 53-66 [Hebrew] and others.

[57] A. Geiger, "About the Controversies between the Sadducees and their Followers and the Pharisees and the Difference between the Old and the New Halakhah," *HeHalutz* 6 (1862) 13-30 [Hebrew]. And see also: L. Finkelstein, *The Pharisees: The Sociological Background of their Faith* 1 (Philadelphia 1966) 3; 2: 637-753.

Jewish historiography. Graetz believed that the Hillelites were indeed the Pharisees, but identified Beit Shammai with the "fourth Philosophy" of Josephus, i.e. the zealots.[58]

a. Beit Shammai and the Sadducees

Geiger assumed that Beit Shammai should be identified with (or viewed as the successors of) the Sadducees because in his opinion both groups upheld and supported an archaic, rigid legal system, refusing to part with it in favor of a more modern, humane, and viable halakhah. After the Sadducees were defeated by the more liberal, open-minded Pharisees, their heirs joined the latter but continued to fight against reform from within. This caused a rift within Pharisaism itself—that between Beit Shammai and Beit Hillel.

Geiger's view is no longer in vogue today, but since I do not wish to pass judgment on its plausibility, and am only interested in the question of women's status, I feel justified in inquiring whether the portrait of the Sadducees in the sources and the position they hold concerning women in any way supports such an identification.

The Sadducees are, without doubt, the least documented sect of the Second Temple period, although they are mentioned in Josephus, the New Testament, Rabbinic Literature, and possibly also Qumran. Only once are they portrayed as engaging in a dispute over a topic relevant to the issue of women's legal status;[59] interestingly the issue they discuss is women's rights of inheritance, a question that would certainly have been of interest to the Shammaites:

> The Sadducees argue as follows: The daughter of the son and the daughter should be equivalent to one another. For they interpret the passage as follows: Now if the daughter of the son, who inherits by virtue of my son, can inherit indirectly from me, my daughter, who inherits by virtue of direct relationship to me—is it not a matter of logic that she should inherit from me? They said to them: No. If you claim that the daughter of the son inherits, who does so only through a stronger claim than the brothers of [her] father, will you say so in the case of the daughter, who inherits solely through her direct relationship to the deceased (i.e. her father) (*yBava Batra* 8:1, 16a[60]).

The issue of the daughter's inheritance in Judaism is long and complex, having its roots in the biblical text itself. The injustice of the biblical law, which permitted only the sons to inherit, was already recognized by the

---

[58] H. Graetz, *Geschichte der Judäer* 3/2 (Leipzig 1906[5]) 797-9 (n. 24); 813-5 (n. 27).

[59] In the New Testament, when discussing the issue of life after death, the Sadducees bring levirate marriage as an example (Mark 12:18-24; Matthew 22:23-30; Luke 20:27-36). This could hardly be considered a discussion of women's status. But note that, like the Shammaites, the Sadducees take levirate marriage for granted.

[60] The text is found also in the *tYadaim* 2:20, where the Pharisees' opponents are the Boethusians. And cf. also *bBava Batra* 115b. For a discussion of this ruling within another context see chapter 1, above.

authors, or compilers of the biblical text itself. This is evident from the story found in the Book of Numbers (27:1-11) about the daughters of Zelophehad, who complain to Moses on the injustice of this law, and whose logic and eloquence result in an amendment, whereby daughters who have no brothers may inherit from their father. To a certain extent this biblical ruling, undoubtedly intended to improve the position of women, had the opposite effect on the development of women's inheritance in Jewish history, because it made a specific statement about where sons inherit and where daughters do, so that biblical law could not be loosely interpreted. In the rabbinic text at hand, the Sadducees try to circumvent the biblical injunction by using a logical principle—inference (הקש). If a man had a son, who died and left an only daughter, this daughter would inherit along with her uncles. The man's own daughter, however, would not. The Sadducees argue by inference that this cannot be the intention of the biblical law and therefore uphold the right of the daughter to inherit. The Pharisees, however, turn out to be strict constructionists, following the word of the biblical law closely: The biblical law says that daughters do not normally inherit, and the biblical law, so they maintain, should be followed.

By all criteria according to which the Pharisees and Sadducees are normally measured, the two parties have here changed positions. Generally, Sadducees are said to follow the biblical law to the letter (*Ant.* 13.297; 18.16; *Scholion to Megillat Taanit* Tamuz 4) while the Pharisees are said to hold to traditions not emanating from the biblical text (*Ant.* 13.297). Yet here the Pharisees rigidly uphold the biblical text. The Pharisees are further portrayed as great exponents of the law (*War* 2.162), who are willing to read new meanings into the text (*Scholion ibid.*). But here it is the Sadducees who engage in such activity, while the Pharisees resist it. Interestingly, the idea of applying logical principles to the biblical text in order to deduce new rulings is traditionally assigned to Hillel, the founder of Beit Hillel (*tPesahim* 4:13; *bPesahim* 66a; *yPesahim* 6:1, 33a). Should one then conclude, contrary to Geiger's thesis, that it is Beit Hillel who was the follower of the Sadducees rather than Beit Shammai? I think not. I do think, however, that if Geiger is right, and if Beit Shammai is the historical heir of the Sadducees, then the topic of this tradition, rather than its external exegetical modes, demonstrates this.

The Sadducees here uphold a daughter's inheritance rights, thereby affirming her legal right to own property. In this they are certainly the forerunners of Beit Shammai, which maintains that a woman who acquires property prior to her marriage is entitled to dispose of it at her own discretion; and that on the death of the husband the woman is always entitled to manage her settlement property. The Pharisees, on the other hand, who deny the daughter's inheritance rights, are clearly the forerunners of Beit Hillel, who believe a woman should have less control of her property.

b. Beit Shammai and the Zealots

By contrast with Geiger's unpopular thesis, Graetz's theory that Beit Shammai should be identified as members of the zealot movement of the first century, which initiated the great revolt against Rome in 66-73 CE, is still quite popular.[61] Graetz maintained that Beit Shammai should be identified with the zealots for several reasons, among them the fact that the Shammaites kept strict Sabbath laws, yet Shammai supports fighting on the Sabbath (*tEruvin* 3:7), much like Josephus' description of Jewish freedom fighters in the first revolt against Rome (*War* 2.517). Furthermore, Graetz identified Eleazar ben Hananiah, who, according to Josephus, initiated the revolt with the cessation of the sacrifice for the Emperor's well-being (*War* 2.409), with Eleazar ben Hananiah ben Hezekiah the Shammaite (*mShabbat* 1:4). He also identified Zadok the Pharisee, co-founder of the Fourth Philosophy according to Josephus (*Ant.* 18.4), with Rabbi Zadok of rabbinic literature, who may, according to one source, be considered a Shammaite (*bYevamot* 15b). Most of Graetz's evidence, however, pertains to events during and even before Herod's reign. Today most scholars agree that the revolutionary movement which led the rebellion against Rome cannot be dated to any time earlier than 6 CE, the date Josephus gives for the foundation of the Fourth Philosophy.

Although after the works of Zeitlin[62] and Morton Smith[63] no sound scholarship can encompass the entire revolutionary movement of the first revolt against Rome under the heading "Zealots," scholars have, nonetheless, continued to support the thesis that Beit Shammai should be identified with some form of radical thinking on the issue of freedom and the relationship between the people of Israel and foreign hegemony. This view was furthered by the growing interest in the revolutionaries of the Second Temple in the wake of the emergence of the State of Israel.[64] One scholar found new evidence for the connection between Beit Shammai and a very specific group of freedom fighters from a Geniza fragment of a lost *midrash*, in which the students of Beit Shammai were identified as אדומים (Idumaeans—*Sifre Zuta, Para*). Josephus expressly mentions a group of "Idumaeans" who took part in the fighting and civil war inside Jerusalem during 67-8 CE (*War* 4.224-333; 7.267 and elsewhere).[65] The ultimate study of the entire topic, which

---

[61] See particularly Ben Shalom, *Beit Shammai*.

[62] S. Zeitlin, "Zealots and Sicarii," *JBL* 81 (1962) 395-8.

[63] M. Smith, "Zealots and Sicarii: Their Origins and Relations," *HTR* 64 (1971) 1-19.

[64] See D. R. Schwartz, *Studies in the Jewish Background of Christianity* (*Wissenschaftliche Untersuchungen zum Neuen Testament* 60; Tübingen 1992) 128-46.

[65] J. N. Epstein, "Sifre Zuta: Parah," *Tarbiz* 1 (1940) 52-3 [Hebrew].

integrates all existing evidence, is that of Ben Shalom.[66] As a whole, the prevailing theory can be summed up as follows:

In *War* Josephus usually describes the Jewish freedom movement as a *creatio ex nihilo* (*War* 2.118). When he finally tells the truth about its foundation in 6 CE in his later work, the *Antiquities,* he describes the new group (which he calls "philosophy") as being founded by a Pharisee, and as being in all aspects similar to Pharisaism, except for its founders' great love of freedom (*Ant.* 18.4, 23). This is, in effect, a description of a schism within Pharisaism. Rabbinic literature, although not using the word Philosophy, also knows of a division within the Pharisee movement, which culminated in the creation of two "philosophies (תורות)"—the division between Beit Shammai and Beit Hillel (*tHagigah* 2:9; *tSanhedrin* 7:1). Unless we assume that the two literatures are speaking of two completely unrelated events within the same movement, i.e. that there was a schism between Pharisaism and the fourth Philosophy (not mentioned in rabbinic literature) and, at the same time, a separate a schism between Beit Hillel and Beit Shammai (not mentioned by Josephus), we should assume that the two are recording the same event. If so, than it is more logical to identify Beit Shammai with the new freedom party of 6 CE, if for no other reason than that they both ceased to exist after the destruction of the Temple. But positive reasons for this association also exist, the most compelling of which is the contents of eighteen decrees which Beit Shammai forced on Beit Hillel under duress.[67] According to the most reliable tradition, these decrees were designed to separate Jews from gentiles on all social levels (*yShabbat* 1:4, 3c). For present purposes the most important of these decrees is the one requiring Jewish men to separate themselves from the daughters of gentiles (בנותיהם). Obviously this group believed it was entitled to regulate men's sex life. Interestingly, the only passage in the Mishnah which mentions zealots (קנאין) directly, refers to them in this context: "... [a man] who has intercourse with (literally penetrates) an Aramean woman, is attacked by zealots" (*mSanhedrin* 9:6). The Aramean symbolizes all gentile women. The zealots here are portrayed as a vigilance committee, which takes it upon itself to impose Beit Shammai's decree.

Beit Shammai should, therefore, not be identified with any specific faction which took part in the struggle against Rome, but rather as the study-house in which the freedom ideology was formulated, and in which the leaders of all the parties were educated: Menahem the Sicarius as well as Eleazar son of Simon the Zealot, Simon Bar Giora as well as John of Gischala. Beit Shammai is Josephus' "Fourth Philosophy." It is an ideology, rather than a political party, guerrilla group, or military formation. And their ideology

---

[66] *Beit Shammai.*

[67] On this in detail see *ibid.*, 252-76.

should be defined as zealotry. It is in this sense that I use the word "zealot" in what follows.

If Graetz's theory with all its later embellishments still holds, it is appropriate to inquire whether the attitude of Beit Shammai toward women is in any way significant for the historical reconstruction of the zealot movement between 6 and 73 CE. The questions we should be asking are whether Beit Shammai's accommodating attitude toward women was, in any way, designed to attract women to support their philosophy, and, if so, whether they met with success in this venture. Since the first question is difficult to answer from the sources, we should, perhaps, begin from the opposite direction, inspecting the evidence for women's support of revolutionary movements during the first Jewish revolt against Rome.

Two of the most important ideological aspects of the revolutionary movement of the first century CE were zealotry and martyrdom. These were relatively new ideas, developed and perfected during the Second Temple period.[68] Although the ideal role models of zealotry were biblical (Phineas—Numbers 25:7-13; and Elijah—1 Kings 18:20-40, 19:10, 14), it was Mattathias the Hasmonean who perfected this trait by applying it to the political scene of Second Temple Palestinian Judaism. Mattathias had killed with his own hands, using a common dagger, both the Greek official (the representative of foreign hegemony) who came to impose religious persecutions on the people of his village, and the Jewish collaborator, who cooperated with that rule (*1 Maccabees* 2:23-6). His actions triggered the outbreak of the Hasmonean revolt. Mattathias probably served as role model for many of the Jewish freedom fighters in the war against Rome,[69] not least among them the dagger carrying Sicarii, who not only fought the Romans but also carried out reprisals against their own people. Similarly, the martyrdom ideal, which demanded from the believer a willingness to sacrifice his life in face of religious persecution, had its root in the Hasmonean revolt. *2 Maccabees* tells of Eleazar the Elder, and of seven brothers who died under the worst possible forms of torture rather than renounce their Jewish religion (*2 Maccabees* 6-7). Acts of great self-sacrifice in face of danger, with suicide as their ultimate expression, are recorded often throughout Josephus' description of the Jewish war against Rome (*War* 4.28; 79; 7.389-401 and elsewhere). The Maccabean martyrs, therefore, no less than the Maccabean zealots, served as role models for the Jewish revolutionary movement of the first revolt against Rome.

---

[68] On martyrdom, see G. W. Nickelsburg, *Resurrection, Immortality and Eternal Life in Intertestamental Judaism* (Cambridge MA 1972) 11-111; on zealotry see M. Hengel, *The Zealots* (Edinburgh 1989) 150-1.

[69] Hengel, *ibid.*, 151-3.

It is interesting to note that, parallel to the great male heroes of the Maccabean era, women who wished to join in the revolutionary movement found equally compelling role models. Just like Mattathias of *1 Maccabees*, Judith, the heroine of the book that bears her name, saved the Jewish people by a personal act of zealotry. With her own hands she killed Holofernes, the commander of the Assyrian forces who had subdued the country and oppressed her people (*Judith* 13:1-10). Judith served as proof that a woman, no less than a man, could save the Jewish people.[70] For this, no special education or social position were required; personal zealotry was all that was needed. Exactly when Judith was written, and for what purpose, is a debated issue.[71] Whether the book provided a role model for women in the Maccabean revolt cannot be proven; that it could have served as such in the revolt against Rome seems beyond dispute.

Martyrdom too had a female role model for women to emulate. That women actually died a martyr's death in the Hasmonean revolt seems beyond doubt (*1 Maccabees* 1:60-1; *2 Maccabees* 6:10). The story of the seven brothers who chose to die rather than desecrate the Jewish commandments is crowned by the actions of their own mother, who not only encouraged her sons to choose death rather than idolatry, but herself died along with them at the end of the ordeal (*2 Maccabees* 7:41). "[I]n each audience there were quite likely women for whom the mother, in her virtuous conduct and sacrifice, was meant to be a model to emulate."[72] Interestingly, while *2 Maccabees* mentions the mother's death as an afterthought, following the detailed description of the death of all her sons, in *4 Maccabees* (a later, elaborated reworking of the story) the mother commits suicide, in order to avoid defilement by the enemy (*4 Maccabees* 17:1). This suggests that a new rhetoric had became fashionable. Indeed, during the revolt against Rome, revolutionary groups recommended to their members suicide rather than surrender. The mother in *4*

---

[70] For a compelling interpretation of *Judith* along these lines, see Elisabeth Schüssler-Fiorenza, *In Memory of Her: A Feminist Theological Reconstruction of Christian Origins* (New York 1983) 115-8.

[71] See C. A. Moore, *Judith: A New Translation with Introduction and Commentary* (The Anchor Bible; New York 1985) 67-71; and see chapter 4 in this volume.

[72] Quoted from: Robin D. Young, " 'The Woman with the Soul of Abraham': Traditions about the Mother of the Maccabean Martyrs," in Amy-Jill Levine (ed.), *'Women Like This': New Perspectives on Jewish Women in the Greco-Roman World* (Atlanta 1991) 68. The entire article is on pages 67-81. For further reading see I. Levi, "Le martyre de sept Macchabees dans la Pesikta Rabbati," *REJ* 54 (1907) 138-41; J. Guttman, "The Mother and her Seven Sons in Legend and in Books II and IV Maccabees," in M. Schwabe and J. Guttman (eds.), *Johanan Levi Memorial Volume* (Jerusalem 1949) 25-37 [Hebrew]. This article only discusses the sons' martyrdom and totally ignores the mother; R. Duran, "The Martyr: A Synoptic View of the Mother and her Seven Sons," in J. J. Collins and G. W. E. Nickelsburg (eds.), *Ideal Figures in Ancient Judaism: Profiles and Paradigms* (Chico CA 1980) 189-221; G. Cohen, *Studies in the Variety of Rabbinic Culture* (New York 1991) 39-60.

Maccabees probably served as a legitimate role-model for the novel form of martyrdom practiced in the war of 66-73 CE—suicide in the face of defeat. Women, like men, could show the highest degree of this form of self-sacrifice, for which none of the typical male attributes was essential.

All this may suggest that women were actually incited by the revolutionary movements' propaganda to join the fighting against Rome. Did they heed the call? Did they join? Much speculation and creative rewriting of events would be needed in order to make a convincing argument to that effect. A careful historian can only collect relevant data, leaving lacunae unfilled. It should be remembered, however, that for Josephus, our main source for the events under discussion, as for most ancient historians, the role of women in the rhetoric of war was that of innocent victims. Josephus periodically refers to women in their victim role—they are butchered (*War* 3.336; 4.81), raped (*War* 4.560), sold into slavery (*War* 6.384). Occasionally, however, one can get a broader glimpse of what is going on even through this rhetoric.

To begin with it is worth noting that the one non-Jewish historian who wrote a detailed account (most of it, alas, lost) of the war between Rome and the Jews, Tacitus, mentions the striking fact that in Jerusalem women as much as men hampered the advance of the Roman army (*Histories* 5.13.3). This could be merely a rhetorical device, designed to demonstrate to the reader just how total was the opposition the Romans encountered. On the other hand, rhetoric or not, it may be a true statement. Although Josephus does not mention women fighters in Jerusalem, he does point out the women of Japhia in Galilee as having fought the Romans alongside their husbands (*War* 3.303). Beside the fate of the men (they were all killed), Josephus relates also the fate of the women of Japhia (they were all sold into slavery—*War* 3.304). This should be compared with the fate of Gabara for example (*War* 3.133), where Josephus also mentions the slaughter of all the men but says nothing there about the fate of the women. These two pieces of evidence placed side by side suggest perhaps that the phenomenon was, possibly, more widespread than reported. Also in the two cases of mass suicide described by Josephus—in Gamla and in Masada—women are counted among the dead (*War* 4.79; 7.393); although Josephus suggests that their death was the result of the decisions of their husbands, this may be no more than his own reconstruction of events which he witnessed only second-hand. The wives and daughters (and other women?) who were party to these events were, at the very least, compliant. Otherwise it is doubtful whether their husbands could have succeeded in carrying out their plans. Therefore, when two women with their children in Masada (*War* 7.399) and two other women in Gamla (*War* 4.81) decided not to participate in the suicide pact, they succeeded in escaping.

Factional strife between the various groups also provides some relevant information. Two episodes associated with Simon Bar Giora refer to women—one general and one more specific. In general, it is surprising to discover that at one point Josephus describes Simon Bar Giora's followers as a band of women (*War* 4.505). Describing Simon's activities before his final arrival in Jerusalem, Josephus relates how this leader attempted to rally the support of the Sicarii on Masada to his cause. The latter, however, viewed him with suspicion and would not allow him to ascend to the top, leaving him and his entourage of "women" half way up the mountain. This mention of women is indeed puzzling. It could be merely a derogatory reference to Simon's army, but the fact that Josephus mentions the women in passing suggests that this may be partly true.

The second reference is to Simon Bar Giora's wife. During the struggle between John of Gischala and Simon Bar Giora's factions the former is reported to have kidnapped the wife of the latter. This was obviously done in order to blackmail Simon into accepting John's terms, but Simon must have called his opponent's bluff, for he did not capitulate and John's faction finally released the woman unharmed. This entire action could be seen as an exploitation of the woman as a pawn in men's warfare, but Josephus' description of the events suggests otherwise. The wife was captured in an ambush, which was obviously laid for Simon himself, because she was captured "with a large number of his attendants." Simon's wife, therefore, was found in the entourage of her warring husband, but not actually with him at all times. Simon had taken her with him either because he was a jealous patriarchal husband who never let his wife out of his sight, or because she was an important partner in his exploits. At least it partly confirms the former statement found in Josephus, about Simon Bar Giora's female entourage. In support of the interpretation that his wife was his helpmate one could quote Josephus' statement, that when bringing her prisoner to Jerusalem her captors celebrated "as if their prisoner had been Simon himself" (*War* 4.538); the wife, no less then the husband, shared in the life of brigandage led by Simon Bar Giora's group.

This evidence may not amount to much, but given Josephus' attitude to women, it is surprising that these slips of the pen have been preserved at all.[73] It certainly suggests that women may have been active participants in the war against Rome. If Beit Shammai supplied the ideology behind the freedom movement of the first century CE, as Graetz's school asserts, women's participation in the latter could be a result of their identification with the former.

---

[73] And see further on this in chapter 3, below.

5. Postscript:
The Decision According to Beit Hillel and Women's Position in Judaism

As mentioned in Chapter 1, during Second Temple times Pharisaism was an opposition movement within a multi-faceted Judaism, defined by a plethora of sectarian ideologies. It produced one variety of Judaism and participated in the ongoing legal and ideological debate of the day. Since sectarianism defined the very essence of Judaism, Pharisaism itself at one time witnessed an internal sectarian split between Beit Shammai and Beit Hillel.

After 70 CE a slow process of evolution began within the Pharisee movement, transforming it from a sect to a religion, and from an opposition force to a position of leadership.[74] This process probably began with the founding of the study center of Yavneh by Rabban Yohanan ben Zakkai in 68-9 CE, and came to full fruition with the official recognition by the Roman authorities of the leadership of a Jewish patriarch genealogically descended from Hillel with legal authority over the entire Jewish people sometime during the third or early fourth century.[75] Cohen has demonstrated that this shift was characterized, to begin with, by a refusal to tolerate sectarian dissent. Instead, disputes within the Pharisaic academy itself were encouraged, creating a unique, non-dogmatic literature, which records conflicting opinions without making judgments about the correctness of the one and fallacy of the other.[76] However that may be, at a second stage, and also in a unique style which emphasized the dispute, the new Pharisaism, which came to be known as rabbinic, or tannaitic Judaism, began making judgments, discarding some tradition and adopting others. One such decision is that which favored the entire corpus of Hillelite rulings over that of Beit Shammai,[77] without erasing it from the corpus; merely declaring its opinions redundant. Another such choice of some rulings over others occurred in the compilation of the Mishnah. This process of choice and rejection of traditions canonized part of the tannaitic corpus of disputes. But the rest were not censored or forgotten. On the contrary, they continued to be studied and were even collected in various corpora such as the Tosefta and the halakhic *midrashim*. Nevertheless, their exclusion from the Mishnah reduced their

---

[74] See S. J. D. Cohen, "The Significance of Yavne: Pharisees, Rabbis, and the End of Jewish Sectarianism," *HUCA* 55 (1984) 27-53.

[75] See L. I. Levine, "The Jewish Patriarch (Nasi) in the Third Century," in W. Haase (ed.), *Aufstieg und Niedergang der römischen Welt* 2.19.2 (Berlin 1979) 649-88. On Roman recognition in the fourth century, see 650-1. Now see M. Jacobs, *Die Institution des jüdischen Patriarchen* (*Texte und Studien zum antiken Judentum* 52; Tübingen 1995).

[76] Cohen, *ibid.*, 47-50.

[77] On the date of this decision see Safrai, "Decision According to Beit Hillel," 34.

status from law to a stage in the development of Jewish law. They were no longer authoritative rulings. Furthermore, even within the Mishnah itself a complex system of choice and rejection made anonymous opinions represent the halakhic ruling, while dissident views were transmitted in the name of the sage who held this minority opinion. This intricate and subtle process was definitive in shaping what eventually came to be considered normative Jewish practice and was codified during the middle ages by various legal scholars such as Maimonides and Karo.

Since the issue of this chapter is the position of women, it is important to inquire how this process of determining Jewish law influenced women's status. In the previous chapter I argued that Pharisaism held a special attraction for women, while it was still an opposition movement, because of its very nature as such. What happened to the special relationship between women and Pharisaism when the latter became first a majority group and ultimately the supreme force in Judaism? It appears from the choices made by rabbinic Judaism, that the heirs of the Pharisees were no longer interested in rallying women's support. The wholesale rejection of Beit Shammai's ideology, together with its decidedly favorable attitude toward women's economic independence and personhood, is an indication of this.[78] As mentioned above, another rejection of rulings favoring women has been pointed out by Judith Hauptman, in her detailed comparative study of laws governing women in the Mishnah and the Tosefta.[79] She has shown that almost on every score, when the Mishnah is compared to the Tosefta on parallel issues, the Tosefta's ruling gave greater freedom, more opportunities and more options to women. The Mishnah, on the other hand, either altered the rulings so as to diminish women's roles, or actually omitted the tradition altogether. A topic for another study is whether minority opinions within the Mishnah were more beneficial to women than the anonymous views adopted by the editor of the text. At this point, however, I make no such claim.

In sum, it appears that the selection process which rabbinic literature underwent on the way to becoming canonical, led to choices that downgraded the position of women. The preference for the rulings of Beit Hillel over Beit Shammai was only one stage in this process.

---

[78] It is also true that a rejection of Beit Shammai's more ascetic approach to sex could be a reaction to the manifest monastic tendencies of emerging Christianity, see: Biale, *Eros and the Jews*, 48-50; P. Brown, *The Body and Society: Men, Women and Sexual Renunciation in Early Christianity* (New York 1988) 61-4.

[79] In chapter 1, and see especially n. 71, there.

Part 2

Women and Sources

Chapter Three

"Things Unbecoming a Woman" (*Ant.* 13.431)
Josephus and Nicolaus on Women[1]

Despite much recent research into the question of Jewish women in Greco-Roman time and sources, the writings of Josephus, the most important historian for this period, have been almost entirely ignored. A case in point would be a collection of articles edited by Amy-Jill Levine and published in 1991[2] that discuss the position of women in practically all Jewish documents preserved in Greek from the Greco-Roman world (*Ben Sira*; Philo; *Maccabees*; *Pseudo-Philo*; *Tobit*; *Testament of Job*; *Joseph and Aseneth*; *Judith*; *Susanna*; even the New Testament). Josephus is conspicuously missing from the list. The little research carried out on Josephus' women has tended to concentrate on his portrayal of biblical women in the *Antiquities*,[3] with the aim of demonstrating Josephus' attitude to women by comparing his work with the original descriptions of these women in the Hebrew Bible. Louis Feldman stated explicitly that this was his aim: "...we may expect that Josephus' portraits of women may reflect his own personal life."[4] It appears, however, that Feldman held some preconceived notions of Josephus' attitude to women, based on data not derived from biblical women: (1) The sparse information Josephus volunteers about his female relatives. Here Feldman

---

[1] In 1983 my teacher D. R. Schwartz published an article entitled "Josephus and Nicolaus on the Pharisees" (*JSJ* 14, 157-71). His assumption had been that much of the information found in Josephus on the Pharisees should be ascribed to his main source for the Herodian period—Nicolaus of Damascus. In a similar vein I wish to suggest that much of the material found in Josephus on women is taken from the same source.

[2] *"Women Like This": New Perspectives on Jewish Women in the Greco-Roman World* (Atlanta).

[3] L. H. Feldman, "Josephus' Portrait of Deborah," in A. Caquot, M. Hadas-Lebel and J. Riand (eds.), *Hellenica et Judaica: Hommage à Valentin Nikiprowetzky* (Leuvan 1986) 115-28; J. L. Bailey, "Josephus' Portrayal of the Matriarchs," in L. H. Feldman and G. Hata (eds.), *Josephus, Judaism and Christianity* (Detroit 1987) 154-79; Betsy H. Amaru, "Portraits of Biblical Women in Josephus' Antiquities," *JJS* 39 (1988) 143-70; Cheryl-Ann Brown, *No Longer be Silent: First-Century Portraits of Biblical Women* (Louisville KY 1992); Eileen Schuller, "Women of the Exodus in Biblical Retellings of the Second Temple Period," in Peggy L. Day (ed.), *Gender and Difference in Ancient Israel* (Minneapolis 1989) 178-94; for Josephus see pp. 186-9.

[4] Feldman, *ibid.*, 115.

makes comments such as "...one guesses that Josephus must have been difficult to live with, to judge from the fact that he was, it appears, married three times,"[5] a statement that can hardly be corroborated from the little information at our disposal, and, even if true, is certainly not an indication of Josephus' intellectual attitude to women. (2) General negative statements he makes about women as a group: "... in his summary of the commandments, he adds the detail (*Ant.* 4.219) not found in the Bible, that the testimony of women is inadmissible in Jewish law because of their levity (κουφότητα) and because of the boldness (θράσος) of their sex."[6] While it is undeniable that Josephus does make this statement and half a dozen others (all of which, according to my inventory, are cited either by Feldman or by Bailey), these proclamations are few and far between, occasionally contradicted by Josephus himself, and can hardly be counted as a major issue which preoccupied Josephus.[7] (3) Feldman stands amazed by Josephus' negative description of the reign of the Jewish Hasmonean queen Shelamzion Alexandra (76-67 BCE), of whom he claims, "[t]he Talmudic rabbis poured lavish praise upon her piety ... [while] Josephus disparages her for listening to the Pharisees with too great deference." "This criticism [of Josephus'']," Feldman goes on to claim, "is particularly striking in view of the fact that Josephus identifies himself with these selfsame Pharisees."[8]

This last observation by Feldman is the topic of this chapter. Josephus' portrayal of the Hasmonean queen is only the most blatant part of a larger and very detrimental picture emerging from his description of the royal women in the Hasmonean and Herodian courts. The vehemently negative portrayal of royal women (the queen, her granddaughter Alexandra, Mariamme Herod's wife, Salome Herod's sister, Pheroras' wife), which has no precedent in Josephus' earlier writings, and is unsurpassed in his description of later events, leaves the reader with an uneasy impression that the author of these texts believed that behind every calamity lurks a woman, or as the French would have it—*cherchez la femme*. Small wonder that Feldman felt inclined

---

[5] *Ibid.*, 116 = *Vita* 414; 415; 426-7. Actually, Josephus was probably married four times. Feldman has missed the wife Josephus left in Jerusalem, whom he mentions in his speech to the besieged in the city, *War* 5.419.

[6] *Ibid.*, 117.

[7] Unlike his counterparts, Ben Sira and Philo, who are often grouped together with Josephus as the prime examples of Jewish misogyny of the Greco-Roman period. For Ben Sira and women see: C. W. Trenchard, *Ben Sira's View of Women: A Literary Analysis* (*Brown Judaic Studies* 38; Chico CA 1983); Claudia V. Camp, "Understanding a Patriarchy: Women in Second Century Jerusalem Through the Eyes of Ben Sira," in Amy-Jill Levine (ed.), *Women Like This*, 1-39, and see below, chapter 5. On Philo and women see recently: Dorothy Sly, *Philo's Perceptions of Women* (*Brown Judaic Studies* 209; Atlanta 1990); Sharon L. Mattila, "Wisdom, Sense Perception, Nature and Philo's Gender Gradient," *HTR* 89 (1996) 103-29.

[8] Feldman, "Deborah," 118-9.

to brand Josephus a misogynist. In his article about the Pharisees in Josephus, however, D. R. Schwartz had argued convincingly that Josephus did not originate the description of the Pharisees during Shelamzion's reign.[9] It stems from the writings of a non-Jew and sworn enemy of the Pharisees, whose writings Josephus dutifully followed, often contradicting his own statements elsewhere. The most likely candidate for this role, in Schwartz's mind, was Herod's court historian, Nicolaus of Damascus. Endorsing Schwartz's assertion, I would like to test the case that not just Shelamzion's Pharisees, but Shelamzion herself, and all the other royal Hasmonean and Herodian women, as portrayed in Josephus, are creatures of Nicolaus' imagination. The purpose of this claim is not to acquit Josephus and lay the charge of misogynism at someone else's doorstep, but rather, as will become clear, to demonstrate that this assertion has far-reaching consequences for the issue of Josephus as a historian of women, for the history of royal Judaean women during the Second Temple period and for the personal involvement of Nicolaus, as a court-historian, with the heroines/villainesses of his history.

Josephus himself freely admits that he read the *Histories* of Nicolaus (*Ant.* 1.94; 108; 159; 7.101; 13.250-1; 347; 14.9; 68; 104; 16.183-6 *CA* 2.84). That he is far more indebted to them than he concedes is a common assertion. Scholarly debate revolves around the ways in which he borrowed from Nicolaus. Some scholars claim he copied directly from Nicolaus, seldom checking for internal inconsistencies that resulted.[10] Others would have him mold the material he found in his source to fit his own agenda.[11] Some scholars, with no clear methodology, mention Nicolaus occasionally but totally ignore him elsewhere.[12] Still others disregard Nicolaus altogether.[13] Many scholars claim that while in *War* Josephus used Nicolaus slavishly, in *Antiquities* he had meanwhile come across other sources and rewrote his material independent of Nicolaus.[14] Yet others claim that in *Antiquities* he is not less but more dependent on Nicolaus because he wrote in greater detail.[15]

---

[9] "Josephus and Nicolaus," 159; 162.

[10] O. Michel and O. Bauernfeind, *De Bello Judaico* (München 1959) XXV-XXVI.

[11] S. J. D. Cohen, *Josephus in Galilee and Rome* (Leiden 1979) 232-3.

[12] See e.g. A. Schalit, *König Herodes: Der Mann und sein Werk* (Berlin 1969) who mentions Nicolaus, Herod's advisor, often, but only very rarely as Josephus' source, primarily in the story of Mariamme's execution, 566-71.

[13] E.g. S. Zeitlin, "Herod: A Malevolent Maniac," *JQR* 54 (1963-4) 1-27. On p. 1 Zeitlin mention Nicolaus as source but never refers to him again. And see also his "Queen Salome and King Jannaeus Alexander: A Chapter in the History of the Second Jewish Commonwealth," *JQR* 51 (1960-1) 1-33.

[14] G. Hölscher, *Die Quellen des Josephus für die Zeit vom Exil bis zum jüdischen Krieg* (Leipzig 1904); R. Laquer, *Der jüdische Historiker Flavius Josephus* (Gießen 1920) 128-221.

[15] H. St. J. Thackery, *Josephus: The Man and the Historian* (New York 1929) 66; B.-Z. Wacholder, *Nicolaus of Damascus* (Berkeley 1962) 60-1, 63; Cohen, *Josephus,* 57-8; M. Stern *Greek and Latin Authors on Jews and Judaism* 1 (Jerusalem 1976) 229.

In what follows I will make the case that the *cherchez-la-femme* syndrome
found in Josephus' descriptions of the Hasmoneans and Herodians is typically
Nicolean, and Josephus does not resort to it before, or after he exhausts
Nicolaus as a source.

1. Josephus on Women

Josephus' attitude to women probably could be inferred from his rewriting of
biblical women's roles. The way he reworked their roles, when systematic,
could teach us, for example, something about how he reworked the roles of
women he found in his lost source—Nicolaus' *Histories*. The results of such
an investigation, however, are not straightforward, and interpreting them
requires *finesse*. Unfortunately, no work done up to now has discovered
significant trends and attitudes, primarily because the question scholars have
posed, namely, "Is Josephus more positive or more negative to women than
his source?" is not very sophisticated, and most data adduced could be interpreted either way. Thus, Feldman claimed that Josephus denigrated and be-
littled Deborah's role,[16] but Bailey, to his own astonishment, found Josephus'
description of the matriarchs exceptionally accommodating, and in fact an
improvement on the Bible.[17] These contradictory finds show that the criteria
"positive" and "negative" are not useful in determining Josephus' attitude to
women. In a footnote, however, Feldman points out a useful indicator as to
the way Josephus reworked his material on women: "[he] often heightens the
romantic element in his retelling of the Biblical narrative."[18] This observation
is very interesting, but the two best examples Feldman brings to demonstrate
this trait—Josephus' retelling of the story of Joseph and Potiphar's wife (*Ant.*
2.41-58), and his story of Moses' marriage to the Ethiopian princess
(2.243-53)—are notorious as narratives Josephus borrowed from other
sources.[19] So while it is true that the romantic element in some of Josephus'
retellings of the Bible is greater than the original, we should legitimately ask,

---

[16] Feldman, "Deborah."

[17] Bailey, "Josephus' Matriarchs," 168-76.

[18] Feldman, "Deborah," 127, n. 28.

[19] For Potiphar's wife see M. Braun, *Griechischer Roman und hellenistische
Geschichtsschreibung* (Frankfurt 1934) 17ff.; *idem, History and Romance in Graeco-Oriental
Literature* (Oxford 1938) 92; Maren Niehoff, *The Figure of Joseph in Post-Biblical Jewish
Literature* (Leiden 1992) 105-6. For the Ethiopian princess, see Braun, *Romance,* 98-102;
Tessa Rajak, "Moses in Ethiopia: Legend and Literature," *JJS* 29 (1978) 120-1; A. Shinan,
"Moses and the Ethiopian Woman: Sources of a Story in the Chronicles of Moses," in J.
Heinemann and S. Werses (eds.), *Studies in Hebrew Narrative Art* (*Scripta Hierosolymitana*
27; Jerusalem 1978) 69-72; Donna Runnalls, "Moses' Ethiopian Campaign," *JSJ* 14 (1983)
135-56. Wacholder, *Nicolaus,* 57-8 suggests that for these two accounts Josephus' source is
also Nicolaus.

is this a trait of Josephus' own writing, or does it stem from his sources? If the latter is correct, we need to test Josephus' attitude to women in another way.

I propose examining Josephus' texts on women in places where no historiographic or aggadic sources were available to him, and where he can be described, so to speak, as his own source, namely, the latter parts of *War*, beginning in the middle of the second book, and his *Vita*. In composing them he may have used his own notes, or notes taken by military and imperial clerks during Vespasian's campaign to Judaea in 67-70 CE, but these can hardly be considered historiographic sources.

The most striking feature of these texts is the almost complete absence of women in them. Only two women (Queen Berenice, and Mary daughter of Eleazar of the Peraea—*War* 6.201) are mentioned by name, and those only briefly. All other women mentioned on these pages are nameless, characterless and float out of the text almost as soon as they appear. One may, justifiably, claim that Josephus ignores women because he is describing a war, and, as is natural, women are the victims rather than the perpetrators of wars. Josephus acknowledges their victimization by mentioning numerous cases of women who suffered and died of hunger during siege (*War* 5.430; 433; 513); were captured (4.115), raped (4.560), slaughtered (3.336; 4.81) and sold into slavery (6.384). These stereotypical descriptions, however, cannot tell the whole story, for women's roles in the war must have been more varied, as Josephus himself occasionally admits. Minor notices indicate that some women took a greater active interest in the war than Josephus cared to explore.[20] Apart from ignoring the general contribution of women to the war, however, some specific women were too important for the narrative to be completely omitted, and the way they are introduced may help discover the nature of Josephus' interest in them.

a. The Sister of Justus of Tiberias.

One of Josephus' most worthy literary opponents, and perhaps the man whose attack on Josephus' historical integrity spurred the composition of the *Vita*, was a certain Justus of Tiberias. Justus' career was in some ways similar to that of Josephus. They both toyed with the idea of fighting against Rome, but they both, finally ended up on the Roman side, Josephus as a direct client of the emperor Vespasian and Justus as a loyal servant of the client king Agrippa II. Josephus, thus, moved in higher circles, and his history of the war received royal sanction. Justus too eventually published his version of the war in which he portrayed Josephus in a less than favorable light. Because of the antagonism between Josephus and Justus, the former, in his *Vita*, volunteers new information not found in *War* about Justus' activities during the Galilee campaign.

---

[20] And see more on this in chapter 2, above.

In *Vita* 186 Josephus relates certain events that took place in Gamla, in which Philip son of Jacimus, another of Agrippa's men, was involved. Josephus recounts a purge carried out by the inhabitants of Gamla on Philip's and Justus' relatives, when these two and their forces were out of town. According to Josephus, the inhabitants of Gamla executed a certain Chares, Jesus his kinsman, and the sister of Justus. This last victim of the purge is curiously absent from most modern editions of Josephus. For example, in his translation, Thackery writes "the brother(!) of Justus." A glance at the Greek text is just as misleading for it reads ἀδελφόν, and the only indication that another reading is available is found in a footnote, which states: "Most mss. read ἀδελφήν (i.e. sister)." If this is indeed true, why did the editor choose the version "brother"? Surely not because of the principle of *lectio difficilior*. While that principle warns against reliance on the quantity of the readings, a reading should not be dismissed *because* it is represented in the majority of manuscripts. The question should rather be: In what direction would we expect a scribe to "correct" his misunderstood, or bizarre manuscript? In the case before us I think the *lectio difficilior* is "sister" for three reasons. First of all, the involvement of women in the business of war is unexpected. It is true that the woman here seems to have been a pawn in some political maneuver, but even so, this is the only political assassination of a woman described by Josephus in the entire war. For this reason alone a scribal correction of the text from female to male is more logical than a move in the other direction. Secondly, I believe we can detect a general tendency in the transmission process of ancient texts, whereby women are gradually eliminated.[21] Thirdly, and most importantly, the copyist who altered "sister" into "brother" did so, in this case, not as a result of a whim, but presumably under the influence of an earlier passage in *Vita*. For this reason too, modern editors and translators have chosen the version "brother." Let us now turn to that other text.

In *Vita* 177 Josephus tells of the same incident in quite a different context. Sitting at table with Justus, after having tricked him, taken him prisoner and then cordially released him, Josephus urges Justus to realize that he is his natural ally, while the Galileans and inhabitant of Gamla are not. He reminds him that the Galileans had cut off his brother's hands, and that at Gamla (obviously referring to the same incident of *Vita* 186), associates of Justus had been murdered: Chares and Jesus the husband of Justus' sister.[22] The

---

[21] On this see *Mine and Yours are Hers: Retrieving Women's History from Rabbinic Literature* (Leiden 1997) 51-84.

[22] In the literature about Justus of Tiberias mention of the sister is also missing. For example, Tessa Rajak, "Josephus and Justus of Tiberias," in L. H. Feldman and G. Hata (eds.), *Josephus, Judaism and Christianity* (Detroit 1987) 89, mentions only *Vita* 177, where a brother is mentioned, and totally ignores *Vita* 186. Y. Dan, "Josephus Flavius and Justus of Tiberias," in U. Rappaport (ed.), *Josephus Flavius: Historian of Eretz Israel in the Hellenistic-Roman Period* (Jerusalem 1982) 71-2, uses *Vita* 177 as evidence that Justus was a

discrepancies between the two lists of victims are probably irreconcilable.[23] The inhabitants of Gamla killed either Justus' sister, in which case *Vita* 186 is correct, or his brother-in-law, in which case *Vita* 177 is correct, or both, in which cases both lists are correct, or neither, in which case neither list is correct. It remains unclear whether the inhabitants of Gamla killed Justus' sister. The correction "brother," however, is obviously based on *Vita* 177, where Justus' brother is mentioned, but in another context and with another fate.

On the basis of *lectio difficilior,* I suspect the version "sister" in *Vita* 186 is, if not the only, at least one of the correct readings. The confusion results, in my opinion, from Josephus' utter lack of interest in the role women *qua* women played in politics. For Josephus politics is a dangerous game in which people can get killed and the gender of the victims is unimportant. Furthermore, by not mentioning the sister in his conversation with Justus, Josephus fails to capitalize on the emotional consequences of the woman's death. He makes it clear to Justus that her death, like the death of his other associates, spelt danger, but does not suggest that it may have been emotionally more traumatic for him.

b. Eleazar ben Yair's Wise Relative

Although some scholars doubt Josephus' description of the dramatic and tragic fate of the defenders of Masada,[24] the story in itself seems credible,[25] and sufficiently supported by the archaeological data.[26] Its one flaw is the disturbing fact that in cases of mass suicide there are usually no survivors to tell the tale. So who told Josephus about the fate of the Sicarii on Masada? Josephus seems to be quite clear about that. In the wake of the events "... an old woman and another [female] relative of Eleazar, superior in sagacity and training to most of her sex, with five children ..." (*War* 7.399) had hidden themselves in the subterranean water system of Masada. If, as I maintain, Josephus recorded the true fate of Masada, his source for the events leading

---

relative of Philip b. Jacimus, and also ignores 186; Cohen, *Josephus*, 167, does state that *Vita* 186 mentions a sister, but further down he states: "Josephus even suggests that Justus' brother was harmed before the war, but here *Vita* 177 is refuted by *Vita* 186." In other words, Cohen discards the reading "sister" in 186.

[23] For an attempt at reconciliation, see: J. J. Price, "The Enigma of Philip ben Jakimos," *Historia* 40 (1991) 90-2, although Price ignored the reading "sister" altogether.

[24] See primarily Trude Weiss-Rosemarine, "Josephus' 'Eleazar Speech' and Historical Credibility," *Proceedings of the Sixth World Congress of Jewish Studies* 1 (Jerusalem 1973) 417-27.

[25] M. Stern, "Sicarii and Zealots," in M. Avi-Yonah and Z. Baras (eds.), *The World History of the Jewish People: Society and Religion in the Second Temple Period* (Jerusalem 1977) 278-81.

[26] See Y. Yadin, *Masada: Herod's Fortress and the Zealots' Last Stand* (London 1966) 193-201.

up to the mass suicide, for the life of the defenders during the years between the fall of Jerusalem and the fall of Masada, and perhaps even for his surprisingly accurate description of the fortress[27] was the evidence of the younger woman, the relative of Eleazar, for unless she were his source, Josephus would not have praised her superior wisdom, which, because of his apparent prejudice against women, seems to him greater than he usually expected to find in members of the second sex.[28]

Nevertheless, Josephus' description displays no characteristics even remotely related to a woman's perspective on the events. We do not know whether the wives of the defenders supported the decision to commit suicide. They are found in their traditional role as victims of men's wars, and the only emotions described are those of the men: "Like men possessed they went their way ... so ardent the passion that had seized them to slaughter their wives and little ones and themselves ... For while they caressed and embraced their wives and their children in their arms, clinging in tears to those parting kisses, at that instant, as though served by hands other than their own, they accomplished their purpose ... Wretched victims of necessity, to whom to slay with their own hands their own wives and children seemed the lightest of evils!" (*War* 7.389-94) Furthermore, Josephus nowhere explains the motives behind the actions of Eleazar's relative—when, why and how did she defect? For him she was a source of information, but not a protagonist in the events.

c. Queen Berenice

The historical importance of the two women discussed thus far may be inferred only by conjecture. Josephus leaves them as hazy as possible. A completely different case is that of Queen Berenice, Agrippa II's sister, an important historical figure of Josephus' times, who genuinely influenced events in the highest political circles. A biographical sketch of Queen Berenice runs as follows: Daughter of King Agrippa I, as a teenager she was married to Marcus, the nephew of the philosopher Philo, and almost immediately widowed by his death. She earned the title "queen" through her second marriage, to her uncle Herod, King of Chalcis (*Ant.* 19.277). Widowed a second time, she married and divorced yet another king—Polemo of Cilicia—and then lived alone for many years next to her brother, king

---

[27] It is not clear whether Josephus ever visited Masada. Yadin asserts that his description of the walls is of an external observer, *ibid.*, 141: S. J. D. Cohen, "Masada: Literary Tradition, Archaeological Remains and the Literary Credibility of Josephus," *JJS* 33 (1982) 398, n. 41, claims that Josephus described the fortress from the notes of Romans who surveyed the site after its capture.

[28] That the woman was Josephus' source is the opinion of L. H. Feldman, *Josephus and Modern Scholarship (1937-80)* (Berlin 1984) 776. Tessa Rajak, *Josephus: The Historian and his Society* (London 1983) 219 maintains that the woman gave this information to the Romans, and not directly to Josephus.

Agrippa II, causing gossips to brand their relationship incestuous (20.145-6). During the war of 66-70 CE, Berenice met the general Titus, son of the emperor Vespasian, and became his lover (Tacitus, *Histories* 2.2.1). She must have harbored hopes of yet another, and still greater, royal marriage, but if so, her hopes were dashed (Suetonius, *Titus* 7.1; Cassius Dio, *Roman History* 66.15.3-4). Nothing more is known of her.[29]

Although Josephus' writings are the most important and extensive source of our knowledge for the Herodian dynasty, most of this information is absent from *War*, and his later *Antiquities* is only slightly more informative. Details about the most important aspect of Berenice's career, her relationship with the soon-to-be emperor Titus, are available only in the writings of contemporary and later Roman historians. It is not as though Josephus did not know of her. On the contrary, he probably knew her personally.[30] The best explanation for Josephus' total silence on the question of her relationship with Titus is, probably, his own special relationship with the general. Josephus was a *protégé* and friend of the emperor-designate; and his history of the war, beyond being the official Flavian version thereof, was the chronicle of Titus' campaign and victory.[31] It has often been claimed that Josephus deliberately concealed damning information about Titus' conduct. For example, he acquits Titus of the charge of burning the Temple, although most historians doubt the historical accuracy of this claim.[32] If the romantic attachment of Titus to the Jewish queen was viewed in Rome as a drawback rather than an asset, it should come as no surprise that the details are totally absent from Josephus' account.

Josephus, however, does not totally ignore the existence of Berenice, and her appearance on and disappearance from the scene in *War* is reminiscent of

---

[29] For the historical sources, see: Stern, *Greek and Latin Authors, index* s.v. Berenice. For epigraphic data see: W. Dittenberger, *Orientis Graeci Inscriptiones Selectae* 1 (Lipsiae 1903) 638-9; *L'Année épigraphique* (1928) 23, no. 82. On Berenice see also: Grace H. Macurdy, *Vassal Queens and Some Contemporary Women in the Roman Empire* (Baltimore 1937) 84-90; J. A. Crook, "Titus and Berenice," *American Journal of Philology* 72 (1951) 162-75; E. Mireaux, *La Riene Bérénice* (Paris 1951); Ruth Jordan, *Berenice* (London 1974); P. M. Rogers, "Titus, Berenice and Mucianus," *Historia* 29 (1980) 86-95; D. C. Braud, "Berenice in Rome," *Historia* 33 (1984) 12-3. An important contribution to the study of Berenice is S. Schwartz, *Josephus and Judaean Politics* (Leiden 1990) 110-69. Schwartz did to Josephus' works what I am trying to do here to Nicolaus', namely search in his writings for a personal motivation. His work, however, has no particular bearing on women.

[30] Rajak, *Josephus*, 75; Schwartz, *ibid.*, 156. Schwartz comments and speculates on the absence of Agrippa from Josephus' description of the siege of Jerusalem, but the absence of Berenice, which I find more intriguing, he totally ignores (pp. 132-3).

[31] On the publication of *War* during Titus' reign see: M. Stern, "The Date of the Composition of *BJ*," in *Studies in Jewish History: The Second Temple Period* (Jerusalem 1991) 402-7 [Hebrew].

[32] E.g. G. Alon, *Jews, Judaism and the Classical World* (Translation I. Abrahams; Jerusalem 1977) 252-68.

the way other women enter and exit Josephus' account of the war. Berenice is mentioned as present in Jerusalem when hostilities erupted between the Roman governor Gasius Florus and the Jerusalem Jews.[33] Josephus incidentally discloses the fact that she was present in Jerusalem in a private, religious, rather than public, political context. She had apparently made a *nazirite* vow, and now came to fulfill it. This gives us a glimpse of her physical appearance at the time, for Josephus says: "it is customary for those ... [who take this vow] to shave their heads ... and she would come barefoot before the tribunal" (*War* 2.313). Berenice intervened, so we understand, to try and stop the massacre and plunder carried out by the procurator's troops in Jerusalem, but ultimately failed (*War* 2.310-4). She is then mentioned, in the same context, as, on the one hand, writing to the Roman governor of Syria, to report the outrages of the procurator (*War* 2.333) and, on the other hand, attempting, along with her brother, who had now also arrived in Jerusalem, to restrain the Jewish insurgents' eagerness to fight Rome (*War* 2.333; 402-5). Then she abruptly disappears from the scene. Even in the story of Agrippa's escape from Jerusalem, which must have included Berenice as well, she is not mentioned (*War* 2.407).[34] Berenice's importance and influence are never followed up in *War*, although Tacitus names her as an ally in her own right of the general Vespasian (Tacitus, *Histories* 2.81.2), probably indicating that she played a prominent role in the later events of the war, beyond being Titus' mistress. Had we known nothing more of Berenice than Josephus tells us in *War*, therefore, her role in the events would be only slightly less obscure than that of Justus' sister or the wise woman from Masada.

Josephus, however, wrote other books after *War*, and his personal situation was sufficiently altered by that time (by several events, not the least among them the death of his one-time patron, Titus) to merit a different evaluation of Berenice and her role in history.[35] The detailed information concerning her marriages comes mainly from *Antiquities*. Her marriage to Marcus, Philo's

---

[33] Berenice is mentioned earlier three times, all in genealogical contexts. In *War* 2.217 as the wife of Herod of Chalcis; in *War* 2.220, as the daughter of king Agrippa I; and in *War* 2.221 as the widow of Herod of Chalcis and mother of his two sons. All these descriptions come from genealogical lists Josephus used in his description of Agrippa's reign, not from a literary account.

[34] Berenice is further mentioned by name together with Agrippa II as the joint owner of a palace in Jerusalem burnt down by the rebels (*War* 2.426) and as the joint employer of a certain Ptolemy, who is robbed by some Jewish rebels (*War* 2.595), but these could hardly be counted as events in which she took part. After book 2 of *War* Berenice is never mentioned again.

[35] It is also S. Schwartz's assertion (*Josephus*, 151-2), that Josephus' portrayal of the Herodians in *Ant.* is a result of a change in personal interests, but, in his analysis, he does not single out Berenice.

nephew, is mentioned only in *Antiquities* (19.276-7).[36] Then, on the death of Agrippa I, Josephus describes the outrageous treatment of the statues of Agrippa's daughters by the Caesarean mob (*Ant.* 19.357).[37] *Antiquities* further records Berenice's marriage to her uncle, King Herod of Chalcis (*Ant.* 19.277; 354; 20.104—where Berenice's children are mentioned by name[38]). These rather dry, factual details add little to the description of Berenice's role in Jewish politics, except to indicate that her father used her as a pawn in his political power games, marrying her off to desirable allies and close relatives.[39]

Berenice's last two appearances on the pages of *Antiquities,* however, have a completely different function. *Antiquities* 20.143 informs us that Berenice's jealousy of her sister Drusilla made the latter's life unbearable, so that, violating the ancestral laws of the Jews, she married the Roman procurator, Felix—a strange charge indeed, which cannot be corroborated, sounds very unconvincing, and is, without doubt, intended to damn Berenice. It contains one of the two stock charges against bad women—jealousy. Finally, Berenice's marriage to king Polemo of Cilicia is described in *Antiquities* 20.145-6 with no less malice:

> After the death of Herod, who had been her uncle and husband, Berenice lived for a long time as a widow. But when a report gained currency that she had a liaison with her brother, she induced Polemo king of Cilicia to be circumcised and to take her in marriage; for she thought that she would demonstrate in this way that the reports were false. Polemo was prevailed upon chiefly on account of her wealth. The marriage did not, however, last long, for Berenice, out of licentiousness, according to report, deserted Polemo. And he was relieved simultaneously of his marriage and of further adherence to the Jewish way of life (*Ant.* 20.145).

The licentious sexual behavior mentioned here is the second stock charge against bad women. Berenice is accused both of incest with her brother and of deserting her husband "out of licentiousness." While the charge of incest may

---

[36] Berenice is mentioned earlier, in *Ant.* 18, on two occasions: Once in a genealogical list of Agrippa I's children (132), probably the same source Josephus had used in less detail in *War* 2.220; another time as co-heir with her brother Agrippa II to the services of a certain Thaumastus. Neither references can be considered an account of Berenice's role in Jewish history.

[37] Jordan (*Berenice*, 89-90) suggested that Josephus, for reasons of modesty, is here refraining from relating a shocking tale of how the kings daughters themselves were violated. On this episode, see below, chapter 6.

[38] And further on Berenice's children, see chapter 7, below.

[39] In *Vita* also Berenice is mentioned only as a co-ruler with Agrippa II. Twice Josephus tells of a letter Their Majesties received from Philip son of Jacimus (*Vita* 48; 180), and twice Josephus reminds Justus of Tiberias that king Agrippa had planned to put him to death, and it was only at the interception of the queen that this punishment was averted (*Vita* 343; 355). Berenice is further mentioned incidentally as the owner of lands in the vicinity of Besara (=Beit She'arim—*Vita* 119).

have been a current rumor (see Juvenal, *Saturae* 6.155-8), a negative view of Berenice's marriage to Polemo need not have been.

These last two comments on Berenice belie Josephus' restrained attitude toward the woman in all his previous discussions of her. It both puts Berenice in a position to influence negatively the flow of events, and makes her capacity to cause shame through sexual misconduct a liability for her relatives. The report is so damning for both Berenice and her family, that some scholars surmise that Josephus must have written it after the death of Agrippa II, who according to Josephus' own account, was also his patron (*Vita* 362-4).[40] This suggestion, however, contradicts the dates both of the publication of *Antiquities* (93/4 CE), and of Agrippa II's death (100 CE).[41] Therefore, Schwartz has come up with what he terms "a partial solution" to the problem, by suggesting, based on a whole body of evidence, that here too Josephus is not espousing the "*cherchez la femme*" approach, but simply following his source—a priest whose concern seems to have been the preservation of the ancestral Jewish laws,[42] as appears from the two incidents involving Berenice. If Schwartz is correct in his assumption (and I for one, am convinced he is), then here too it is not Josephus but his source who puts a woman at the center of events.

Thus, to sum up Josephus' account of queen Berenice, the historian was convinced that her attempt to influence Florus in the summer of 66 CE could, if successful, have had major historical repercussions. However, it failed. No other action taken by Berenice seemed to him worth mentioning. His apparent lack of interest in her romantic entanglement with Titus may be explained by his need for discretion when discussing Titus, but that he was not tempted to return to the topic after his patron's death suggests that Josephus did not view the episode as sufficiently important in the historical scheme of things. Thus, in the words of Grace Macurdy: "Josephus is no Plutarch, and we do not get from him an impression of Berenice's character and charm to equal that of which Plutarch gives of Cleopatra ..."[43]

In these examples of Josephus' treatment of women's viewpoint, fate and involvement in Jewish history, the meager and fragmented data demonstrate

---

[40] On this problem see: D. R. Schwartz, "Κατὰ τοῦτον τὸν καιρὸν: Josephus' Source on Agrippa II," *JQR* 72 (1981-2) 241-3. S. Schwartz, on the other hand (*Josephus*, 150-7) suggests it was probably oral and perhaps came from a competing line of Herodians—the descendants of Herod of Chalcis. Such a claim ignores the fact that Berenice had at one time been married to Herod of Chalcis and two of his descendants were her sons.

[41] On the date of Agrippa II's death see now: D. R. Schwartz, *Studies in the Jewish Background of Christianity* (*Wissenschaftliche Untersuchungen zum Neuen Testament* 60; Tübingen 1992) 243-75.

[42] D. R. Schwartz, "Agrippa II," 241-68. On the nature of this source, see particularly pp. 258-9.

[43] *Vassal Queens*, 90-1.

quite convincingly that Josephus, as historian, found women a topic of little interest. He neither found it necessary to blame them for negatively affecting the course or events, nor did he see sexual misconduct lurking behind every catastrophe. This conclusion, of course, tells us nothing about Josephus' personal attitude toward women; and even if he can be branded a misogynist, he certainly did not allow such sentiments to affect his analysis of the cause and effect in political and social life. I am tempted to conclude that Josephus is an even poorer source for women's history than has previously been suggested.

Josephus' writings, however, are replete with passages that place women precisely in a position to negatively influence political events through their intrigue, cunning, jealousy and capacity to bring shame through sexual misconduct. These texts are curiously concentrated in books 1 and 2 of *War* and between books 13 and 17 in *Antiquities*—the very same texts that describe the Hasmonean and Herodian Kingdoms, a period for which Josephus is principally dependent on Nicolaus of Damascus.

2. Nicolaus on Women

A short biographical note on Nicolaus is in order here. A native of the city of Damascus, Nicolaus received a formal Greek education and emerged as an important rhetor, dramatist and historian. Anthony and Cleopatra hired his services as tutor to their children. After the battle of Actium, in which his patrons were defeated and subsequently committed suicide, Nicolaus found himself unemployed, and was duly grateful for king Herod's generosity in taking him into his service. Nicolaus served as companion, mentor, court historian and political advisor to the king, until the latter's death, when he retired, apparently to Rome, to finish writing his World History.[44]

Nicolaus belonged to the peripatetic school of thought, whose philosophical theory maintained that written history should be dramatic, emotional and entertaining, much like a good play. It is the historian's imperative to add to dry historical data psychological effects and dramatic moments, as well as to share with the reader the emotions of the heroes. In such matters the historian need not furnish actual historical proof. In this vein did Nicolaus write his *Histories*.[45] In Wacholder's words: "... faced with the conflict between telling a good story and telling the truth[, t]here is no doubt that Nicolaus preferred a

---

[44] On Nicolaus see: Wacholder, *Nicolaus*; Stern, *Greek and Latin Authors* 1, 227-32.

[45] For a discussion of Nicolaus as a peripatetic, and a demonstration of his techniques in the description of events which have no bearing on Herod, see: Schalit, *Herodes*, 583-4, nn. 38-9; G. Giangrande, "On an Alleged Fragment of Ctesias," *Quadesni Urbinati di cultura classica* 23 (1976) 38; Deborah Gera, *Warrior Women: The Anonymous Tractatus de Mulieribus* (Leiden 1997) 91-2; 96.

good story."[46] The historian Polybius, who counted himself among the disciples of Thucydides, attacked the peripatetic school for its deceitfulness. It is, therefore, not surprising that Josephus, who had read Thucydides (*CA* 1.18; 66), though not mentioning him by name, also considered himself a member of Thucydides' historical school (*War* 1.3; 14), and therefore wrote very differently.

Furthermore, Nicolaus seems also to have had a personal preference for describing the domestic, rather than the political, and for concentrating on peace rather than war.[47] That perspective naturally accords women a greater role in the events, whether real or imagined. It is, thus, not surprising that of the thirty nine women mentioned by name in the entire corpus of Josephus' writings on the Second Temple period (*Ant.* 11-20; *War*; *Vita*), no fewer than twenty appear in those sections dependent on Nicolaus; and of these women only one (Acme—*War* 1.641; *Ant.* 17.134) is not of royal blood. The women are mentioned numerous times, and play a decisive role in the events described by Nicolaus, which include much plotting and court intrigue. The difference between Josephus' and Nicolaus' attitude to women, therefore, can be a useful marker for scholars of Josephus, in seeking to differentiate the writings of one from the other.

For example, a much debated question is how far does Josephus rely on Nicolaus for his description of the Hasmoneans? M. Stern claimed that Josephus relies quite heavily on him, and "[t]his explains the rather strange fact that Josephus, notwithstanding his patriotism and the pride he took in his kinship with the Hasmoneans, presents us with a rather cold picture of the three main figures of the Hasmonean monarchy, namely Aristobulus I, Alexander Jannaeus and Salome-Alexandra."[48] Stern says nothing about Josephus' portrayal of John Hyrcanus, however, presumably because the latter is portrayed far more favorably than the former mentioned three monarchs; and Stern may have suspected that for the description of his reign Josephus had used as a primary source some author more accommodating than Nicolaus (see *1 Maccabees* 16.23-4). I think, however, that we are now in a position to ascribe to Nicolaus the primary description of the reign of John Hyrcanus too.

In his description of the Hasmonean revolt and its aftermath in *Antiquities*, Josephus depends on *1 Maccabees* as his primary source. *1 Maccabees*' lack of interest in women surpasses the apathy of Josephus himself. Women are mentioned only in a casual way, as victims of Antiochus' persecutions (*1 Maccabees* 1.60-1; 2.37), or the hardships of war (*1 Maccabees* 5.13). No female relative of the Hasmonean brothers is ever mentioned by name; we

---

[46] Wacholder, *Nicolaus*, 67. Thackery, *Josephus,* 66 also stresses Nicolaus the dramatist.

[47] For a discussion and an example unrelated to Herodian history, see: Wacholder, *ibid.,* 57; 80.

[48] *Greek and Latin Authors* I, 230.

learn of their mother only when Simon is described as building a monumental tomb for his father, *mother* and brothers (*1 Maccabees* 13.28), of Jonathan's and Simon's wives (by implication), because they had sons (*1 Maccabees* 13.16-20; 16.16) and of Simon's daughter (again by implication), only because he had a son-in-law (*1 Maccabees* 16.11). It would be instructive had Josephus found it necessary to mention more women in his narrative than does *1 Maccabees*, but he did not—not even his own ancestor, the daughter of Jonathan the Hasmonean (*Vita* 4). Thus, we see that Josephus was absolutely loyal to his source.[49]

1 Maccabees ends with the death of Simon the Hasmonean. Simon, we are told, was tricked by his son-in-law, who invited him to a banquet, took advantage of his drunken stupor and murdered him along with his two sons.[50] No woman is mentioned and the last words of the book reassure the reader that one of Simon's sons, John, succeeded in escaping and took power after his father. In Josephus' account, however, both in *War* and in *Antiquities* the same story ends with an extensive epilogue on the behavior and fate of the wife of Simon the Hasmonean, who is mentioned there for the first time:

> Attacking the fort, (Hyrcanus) proved superior in other ways, but was overcome by his righteous feelings. For Ptolemy, as often as he was hard pressed, brought forward his mother and brothers upon the ramparts and tortured them within full view of Hyrcanus, threatening to hurl them over the battlements, if he did not instantly retire. At this spectacle indignation in the breast of Hyrcanus gave way to pity and terror. His mother, unshaken by her torments or the menace of death, with outstretched hands implored her son not to be moved by her outrageous treatment to spare the monster; to her death at Ptolemy's hands would be better than immortality, if he paid the penalty for the wrongs

---

[49] Although there is scholarly consensus that Josephus is *not* dependent on *1 Maccabees* for his account of the first generation Hasmoneans in *War* 1 (31-54), women are not featured in that narrative either. The assumption is that in *War* Josephus was dependent on Nicolaus' description of the Hasmonean revolt (e.g. Hölscher, *Quellen*, 17-8; Thackery, *Josephus*, 40-1). Thus, it *is* surprising that *War* does not mention women either. A partial solution to the problem would be an investigation into Nicolaus' sources for the revolt. I would submit that Nicolaus himself used *1 Maccabees* for his narrative. Josephus account in *War* is thus a shorthand version of Nicolaus, which, in itself, must have been an epitome of his source (*1 Maccabees?*), leaving little room for elaboration. But note that Josephus' (Nicolaus'?) description of Eleazar's death under the elephant in *War* (1.42-4) is slightly more dramatic than in *1 Maccabees* (6.43-7); while the episode is completely absent from *2 Maccabees* 13. In L. H. Feldman, "Flavius Josephus Revisited," in W. Haase (ed.) *Aufstieg und Niedergang der römischen Welt* 22.2 (Berlin 1984) 808 this episode is discussed but the differences between *Antiquities* and *War* are shrouded because of a comparison between *War* and *1 Maccabees*. Further on this topic see now my "King David, King Herod and Nicolaus of Damascus," *JSQ* 5 (1998) 222-4.

[50] It is not important for the present study, that for most of Simon's reign Josephus did not use *1 Maccabees* (see: J. von Destinon, *Die Quellen des Flavius Josephus* [Kiel 1882] 80-6; N. Bentwich, *Josephus* [Philadelphia 1914] 181-2), because this does not add any women to the narrative and they appear in *Antiquities* (as well as in *War*) exactly were *1 Maccabees* ends.

which he had done to their house. John (Hyrcanus), as often as he took his mother's unflinching courage to heart and gave ear to her entreaties, was impelled to assault; but when he beheld her beaten and mangled, he was unmanned and quite overcome by emotion. The siege consequently dragged on .... Ptolemy, now relieved of the siege, put John's brethren and their mother to death (*War* 1.57-60; cf. *Ant.* 13.230-5).

This description surely comes from the pen of another author. Obviously the entire scene was composed for the purpose of drama and psychology. Since it ends with the death of the mother, her heroic actions add nothing to the course of events, and are, therefore, utterly superfluous. Precisely because of Nicolaus' known interest in just such elements, and their ever-increasing occurrence as we move from events described by Nicolaus second hand (the Hasmonean period) to events to which he was an eye-witness (the later years of Herod's reign), I would claim that this drama comes from the pen of Nicolaus. Nicolaus, then, is Josephus' major source for John Hyrcanus' reign, beginning with his rise to power.

The rest of this chapter will be devoted to Josephus' (i.e., Nicolaus') treatment of three prominent Hasmonean and Herodian women: Queen Shelamzion, Herod's wife, Mariamme the Hasmonean, and Herod's sister, Salome.

a. Queen Shelamzion

Joseph Sievers discussed the women of the Hasmonean court,[51] correctly noting that in the Hasmonean dynasty women played a surprisingly prominent role. All wives of Hasmonean rulers, beginning with John Hyrcanus, make a brief appearance on the pages of Josephus' two books, in almost identical form, and always in connection with the succession, i.e., on the death of one monarch and the ascent to the throne of his heir. (1) John Hyrcanus nominates his wife as successor, but his son, Judah Aristobulus, usurps the throne and starves the woman to death (*War* 1.71; *Ant.* 13.302); (2) Judah Aristobulus' wife plots against and murders his brother Antigonus (*War* 1.76; *Ant.* 13.308) and then (3) nominates his brother Alexander as successor (*War* 1.85; *Ant.* 13.320); (4) finally, the wife of Alexander Yannai assumes the royal power herself (*War* 1.107; *Ant.* 13.407). Most of this information, which Josephus obviously and studiously copied from Nicolaus, had been reworked by the latter from some unknown source on the Hasmoneans, since Nicolaus himself was not a contemporary of these kings, and thus could not write about them at first-hand. One indication of the existence of this source is the absence of names for the women. Nicolaus did not write of women in this fashion. When we arrive at the Herodian period, he names all the royal women.[52] The case of

---

[51] "The Role of Women in the Hasmonean Dynasty," in L. H. Feldman and G. Hata (eds.), *Josephus, Bible and History* (Detroit 1988) 132-46.

[52] Save one, Pheroras' wife. On this woman, see chapter 1, above.

the earlier period is different. Nicolaus' source seems to have had little interest in women—perhaps in the same tradition as *1 Maccabees*. But he had to mention them because they evidently played an important historical role. Why else would Hyrcanus nominate his wife to succeed him, than because she had proved a capable co-ruler, whom Hyrcanus trusted to manage the affairs of state better than his sons? Yet the source does not mention her even once during her husband's reign, indicating how little it was interested in her. Nicolaus, on the other hand, delighted in describing the murder of this woman at the hands of her son, as part of the gruesome scenario of Aristobulus' court.

In the same way, and as part of the same train of events, Aristobulus I's wife is likewise implicated in the plot to murder Antigonus (*War* 1.76; *Ant.* 13.308). How anybody could have known such a detail is not clear, as the plot was a secret, and Aristobulus himself was duped by it. Also, since it succeeded, who could know and publish the members of the court responsible for it? At best it could have been a malicious rumor, which a historian could have chosen to ignore. At worst it was not even a rumor, but a mere literary assumption on the part of the author. The historian, therefore, placed himself in the position of a novelist, who not only records the events, but also supplies the motivation for them himself. This, as I shall show presently, is precisely the sort of writing in which Nicolaus described the Herodian court. I would guess that in this case, Nicolaus found Aristobulus' widow in his source choosing her husband's successor, but I suspect it was Nicolaus himself who made her responsible for the murder of Antigonus. This would create a neat pattern. The original plan of succession, laid out by Aristobulus himself, was for his brother Antigonus to take his place. The inexplicable execution of Antigonus frustrated this plan, and a new heir had to be named. The queen chose the heir, so Nicolaus connected her action with Antigonus' murder.[53] What is the root of all evil? *Cherchez la femme!*

This brings us to the main female hero of the Hasmonean dynasty— Shelamzion Alexandra. Josephus' two descriptions of her reign, in *War* and *Antiquities*, differ greatly in emphasis, if not in detail. Both narratives include the following details: Shelamzion succeeded her husband, even though she had adult sons (*War* 1.107; *Ant.* 13.407). In her domestic policy, she installed the Pharisees in power (*War* 1.110-1; *Ant.* 13.409), and her eldest son, Hyrcanus, in the high priesthood (*War* 1.109; *Ant.* 13.408). The Pharisees carried out reprisals against their former (Sadducee?) enemies (*War* 1.113; *Ant.* 13.410). Shelamzion's foreign policy consisted of recruiting a large force

---

[53] But even Nicolaus did not marry them to each other, although this would have made the story more romantic. This was to become the prerogative of modern scholars, and see my "Queen Salamzion Alexandra and Judas Aristobulus' Widow: Did Jannaeus Alexander Contract a Levirate Marriage?" *JSJ* 24 (1993) 181-90, and see particularly pp. 189-90. I would guess that Nicolaus could not marry the dowager to the new king because the identity of Yannai's wife was too well known.

of mercenaries (*War* 1.112; *Ant.* 13.409), sending an abortive expedition to
Damascus (*War* 1.115; *Ant.* 13.418) and contracting a peace agreement with
Tigranes of Armenia (*War* 1.116; *Ant.* 13.419-21). When she lay sick on her
deathbed, her younger son, Aristobulus, attempted to take the reins of power
by force (*War* 1.117; *Ant.* 13.422-7). While all these details appear in both
accounts, their appraisal is, surprisingly, quite different. In *War*, Josephus
gives the following evaluation of the queen's reign:

> Alexander bequeathed the kingdom to his wife Alexandra, being convinced that the Jews
> would bow to her authority as they would to no other, because by her utter lack of his
> brutality and by her opposition to his crimes she had won the affections of the populace.
> Nor was he mistaken in these expectations; for this frail woman firmly held the reins of
> government, thanks to her reputation for piety. She was, indeed, the very strictest observer
> of the national traditions and would deprive of office any offenders against the sacred
> laws (*War* 1.107-8).

War further states that Alexandra's association with the Pharisees was
negative, while saying only positive things about the queen herself. She
listened to the Pharisees overmuch because she was "intensely religious,"
while they took advantage of her "sincerity (ἁπλότητα τῆς ἀνθρώπου)" (*War*
1.111). As opposed to the Pharisees, however, "[s]he proved ... to be a
wonderful administrator in larger affairs" (*War* 1.112).

Antiquities, on the other hand, while adding only one important detail, i.e.
that the queen appointed the Pharisees on her husband's advice (*Ant.*
13.399-404),[54] usually views the queen's reign very negatively.[55] In the first
place, her ascent to the throne is characterized as a mistake: "Now although
Alexander had left two sons, Hyrcanus and Aristobulus, he had bequeathed
the royal power to Alexandra" (*Ant.* 13.407). This statement has a negative
thrust, which is reinforced by the author's later portrayal of Aristobulus and
his (Sadducee?) followers in a far more favorable light than in *War*, making
their fate the topic of a melodramatic diatribe. It ends, however, with the
words: "But still they themselves were to blame for their misfortunes, in
allowing a woman to reign who madly desired it in her unreasonable love for
power, and when her sons were in the prime of life" (*Ant.* 13.417). The worst
publicity accorded to Shelamzion, however, occurs in the penultimate
statement of book 13:

> She was a woman who showed none of the weakness of her sex; for being one of those
> inordinately desirous of power to rule, she showed by her deeds the ability to carry out her
> plans, and at the same time she exposed the folly of those men who continually fail to
> maintain sovereign power. For she valued the present more than the future, and making

---

[54] This detail is not taken from Nicolaus, but is rather Josephus' own reworking of a
Jewish tradition, see: *bSotah* 22b. And see on this further in chapter 1, above.

[55] For a comparison of the two accounts, see S. Mason, *Flavius Josephus on the Pharisees*
(Leiden 1991) 248-59.

everything secondary to absolute rule, she had, on account of this, no consideration for either decency or justice. At least matters turned out so unfortunately for her house that the sovereign power which it had acquired in the face of greatest dangers and difficulties was not long afterward taken from it because of her desire of things unbecoming a woman and because she left the kingdom without anyone who had their interests at heart. And even after her death she caused the palace to be filled with misfortunes and disturbances which arose from the public measures taken during her lifetime (*Ant.* 13.430-2).

This text blames the queen for all the misfortunes of the Hasmonean household, including the Roman conquest of Palestine, for no specific reason except that she was a woman and women should not assume supreme power! Indeed, her very conduct is described as unfeminine. This is a typical trait of the *cherchez-la-femme* attitude, usually absent in Josephus' historical writings, and it is a very strong misogynistic statement. But who made it? The usual reconstruction of the relationship between the descriptions in *Antiquities* and *War* maintains that in *War* Josephus is slavishly loyal to his source (Nicolaus?) while in *Antiquities* he voices his own opinion.[56] This, however, is not the only possible reconstruction. For, as Stern had amply demonstrated: "In his *Antiquities* ... Josephus continues to draw upon the *Histories* of Nicolaus,"[57] and elsewhere Josephus makes it quite clear that, in his opinion, the blame for the fall of the Hasmoneans should be laid at someone else's door. In the fourteenth book of the *Antiquities*, after describing the dynastic squabble between Hyrcanus and Aristobulus, the sons of Shelamzion, and the conquest of Jerusalem by Pompey, Josephus makes the following statement:

> For this misfortune which befell Jerusalem Hyrcanus and Aristobulus were responsible, because of their dissension. For we lost our freedom and became subject to the Romans, and the territory which we had gained by our arms and taken from the Syrians we were compelled to give back to them ... and the royal power which had formerly been bestowed on those who were high priests by birth became the privilege of commoners (*Ant.* 14.78).

Josephus is clearly blaming the brothers for the fall of the Hasmonean dynasty. Blaming Shelamzion for the downfall of the Hasmonean state does not necessarily imply that Josephus could not also blame other accomplices for the crime; but the different styles of the two paragraphs leaves one in no doubt as to which one was authored by Josephus. That Josephus speaks in the

---

[56] For such an assumption see Laquer, *Flavius Josephus*, 128-34. See however, Sievers, "Hasmonean Women," 139, who, on our passage, while claiming this is not Nicolaus, cannot bring himself to convict Josephus of such bad language; Mason, *Pharisees,* 257-8, does charge Josephus with this judgment; see also S. Schwartz, "Review of S. Mason, *Flavius Josephus on the Pharisees: A Composition-Critical Study*," *AJS Review* 19 (1994) 86-7; but see D. R. Schwartz, "Josephus on Hyrcanus II," in F. Parente and J. Sievers (eds.), *Josephus and the History of the Greco-Roman Period* (Leiden 1994) 219-23, who thinks this part was written by Josephus and not copied. (The fact that this article is formulated much like mine is mere coincidence. I only saw it after most of this work was already completed).

[57] *Greek and Latin Authors* 1, 229.

second one is clear from his digression into first person plural ("we," the Jews of Palestine) and from the description of the Hasmoneans as respectable high priests, while branding the Herodians "commoners." Josephus here gives true voice to his opinion of the royal Hasmonean dynasty, the family of his ancestors.[58] By contrast, the earlier paragraph describes the Hasmonean fate in a distant, third person, and while the blame is placed squarely on the queen, the consequences of the Hasmoneans' demise (Roman and Herodian rule) are not spelled out. If indeed Nicolaus is its author, this should come as no surprise. As Herod's servant, Nicolaus took pleasure in gloating over the downfall of the Hasmoneans, while blaming them for what he saw as the greatest incompetence—leaving royal power in the hand of a woman—but he certainly had no motivation to denigrate the beneficiaries of the Hasmonean stupidity.

There is yet another reason why this summation of Shelamzion's rule should not be assigned to Josephus. In the last line of book 13 the following words are added to the derogatory description of queen's reign: "Nevertheless, in spite of reigning in this manner, she kept the nation in peace" (*Ant.* 13.432). This is indeed an unexpected assessment. At least two scholars have solved this contradiction in the same way. Sievers wrote: "This contradiction ... is hard to explain by any other means than by Josephus' careless juxtaposition of sources."[59] Klausner ventures a bolder suggestion: "This obvious contradiction can only be explained by presuming that the two conflicting statements have their origin in two different sources: a Jewish Pharisee source in defense of Salome (*sic!*) and a Greek source hostile to the Jews."[60] Neither author pursued the issue further. I myself believe that, having faithfully copied Nicolaus' summation of Shelamzion's rule, Josephus was suddenly taken aback. After all, as is shown in his description in *War*, he knew very well that queen Shelamzion had been exceptionally popular with the people—or at any rate with those associated, like himself, with the Pharisees.[61] So he modified the words of Nicolaus. In this last sentence, therefore, we hear the voice of Josephus himself.

Shelamzion is only the most prominent example of Nicolaus' treatment of his Hasmonean female subjects. These women (except, perhaps John Hyrcanus' mother) were not creatures of his imagination. They were mentioned in a source he used, of which we now know nothing. Nicolaus merely highlighted their role, and, when possible, blamed them for adverse consequences. One question, however, remains open. Given that *1 Maccabees* mentions no women, and Nicolaus was not the original source of the

---

[58] And see further on this: D. R. Schwartz, "Hyrcanus II," 217-20.

[59] "Hasmonean Women," 139.

[60] J. Klausner, "Queen Salome Alexandra," in A. Schalit (ed.), *The World History of the Jewish People: The Hellenistic Age* (London 1972) 243.

[61] For her popularity in rabbinic literature, see: Klausner, *ibid.*, 247-54.

subsequent Hasmonean history, but was using an earlier Hasmonean source similar in character to *1 Maccabees*, how did women come to be so prominent in the narrative? I think the answer is not far to seek. Later Hasmonean sources mentioned women because they became historically prominent in later Hasmonean history. John Hyrcanus really thought it would be best for his people if his wife were to succeed him. However, his plan failed. Alexander Yannai really thought Shelamzion would be the best queen for the Jewish commonwealth. And she did rule. Some sources concur that she did it rather well. For the Hasmoneans, therefore, it was clearly not anathema for a woman to rule.[62] As the next part of this discussion will show, this notion had far-reaching consequences in the continued history of Hasmonean women.

b. Mariamme the Hasmonean

Herod married Mariamme, the great-granddaughter of Shelamzion Alexandra (*War* 1.344; *Ant.* 14.465). He was married to her from 37 BCE to 27 BCE. They had five children: three boys and two girls (*War* 1.435). Then he put her to death (*War* 1.444; *Ant.* 15.231). These details seem beyond dispute. Yet in *War*, and to a far greater extent in *Antiquities*, Mariamme dominates large sections of the narrative. She is described as the subject of Herod's great passion and consuming love, yet portrayed as proud and arrogant:

> For the love which he felt for Mariamme was no less intense than those justly celebrated in story. As for her, she was in most respects prudent and faithful to him, but she had in her nature something that was at once womanly and cruel, and she took full advantage of his enslavement to passion. Since she did not take into account that she was subject to the king and that he was her master, as would have been proper under the circumstances, she frequently treated him with arrogance (*Ant.* 15.218-9).

Furthermore, Mariamme is repeatedly portrayed as the subject of Herod's uncontrolled jealousy. Her death, we learn, came about in a storm of terrible jealousy. Herod suspected her of committing adultery with his servant (*War* 1.443; *Ant.* 15.227-8). On this score, however, Josephus feels that he should set the record straight. In one of his rare attacks on Nicolaus' credibility, Josephus makes the following comment:

> ... since [Nicolaus] lived in Herod's realm and was one of his associates, he wrote to please him and to be of service to him, dwelling only on those things that redounded to his glory, and transforming his obviously unjust acts to the opposite or concealing them with the greatest care. For example, in his desire to give a color of respectability to the putting to death of Mariamme and her sons, which had been so cruelly ordered by the king, Nicolaus makes false charges of licentiousness against her and treachery against the youths ... We, however, being of a family closely related to the kings descended from

---

[62] For the Hellenistic milieu of this notion, see: Macurdy, *Vassal Queens*, 65-6; Ilan, "Salamzion Alexandra," 189-90, and below, Chapter 4.

Asmonaios ... have considered it unfitting to tell any falsehoods about them (*Ant.* 16.183-7).

Indeed, Josephus refrains from charging Mariamme's sons with plotting against their father, and from accusing Mariamme of infidelity. So, did Nicolaus accuse Mariamme of such a crime, or is Josephus using Nicolaus when he acquits her of the charge?[63] We have no direct way of knowing the answer, because Nicolaus' description of this event is, alas, lost. Fortunately we do have a text from the pen of Nicolaus, not mediated to us by Josephus, reporting his position on the accusations Herod leveled against his two sons by Mariamme—accusations that resulted in their execution. In an excerpt from his autobiography, preserved in the writings of the tenth-century Byzantine scholar-emperor Constantinus Porphyrogenitus, Nicolaus makes the following statement:

> At the same time the court of Herod was thrown into confusion since the eldest of his sons *falsely* accused the two next born of plotting against their father. These were indeed younger than he, but were his superiors in rank, because they were children of a queen, whereas his mother was a commoner. Before Nicolaus had returned from Rome, the young men were convicted by the council, and the father, having been much exasperated, was on the point of having them executed. After Nicolaus had sailed home, Herod informed him of what happened and asked his advice. Nicolaus suggested that they should be removed to one of the fortresses, in order to gain time for better consultation, and thus not appear to make a fatal decision concerning his nearest while actuated by anger. Antipater, perceiving this, looked on Nicolaus with suspicion, and, suborning various persons, frightened his father into the belief that he was in danger of being immediately killed by his sons, who had corrupted the whole army ... and that his only safety lay in their quick execution. And Herod, being afraid for his life, took a quick but not a good decision. No more did he communicate about the matter with Nicolaus, but at night he secretly sent the executioners. Thus the sons died ...[64]

Nicolaus is here clearly counseling Herod not to execute his sons, suspecting that they are not guilty of treachery, as charged. If the opinion voiced by Nicolaus in his *Vita* is the same as the one he gave in his *Histories*—and I see no reason for him to have changed his mind[65]—then Nicolaus' opinion on the execution of Mariamme's sons sounds suspiciously similar to the version presented by Josephus in his *Antiquities*. So whose story is it? And if Josephus misrepresented Nicolaus' opinion on the execution of Herod's sons, may he not be equally incorrect in his claim that Nicolaus accused Mariamme of adultery? I would, therefore, suggest that, notwithstanding Josephus' outburst of indignation in *Antiquities* 16, his description of Mariamme's

---

[63] Much of the reconstruction suggested in the following lines has been anticipated by Destinon, *Quellen*, 94-102; 108-20.

[64] Stern, *Greek and Latin Authors* 1, 253 (emphasis mine).

[65] For a different view see S. Schwartz, *Josephus*, 121-3.

relations with Herod, culminating in her trial and execution in *Antiquities* 15, all stem from Nicolaus.

A notoriously difficult problem in the writings of Josephus is the confusion over Herod's command concerning Mariamme in his absence. In *War* we are told that when in 35 or 34 BCE Herod was summoned by Mark Anthony, he entrusted Mariamme to the care of his brother-in-law Joseph, ordering him to kill the woman in the event that Anthony is displeased with him and has him executed. In his absence Joseph tells Mariamme of the order, in an effort to persuade her of Herod's love, and when Herod returns and discovers that Mariamme knows of the order, he is convinced that only sexual intimacy would have induced Joseph to reveal the secret, so he executes both partners for adultery (*War* 1.441-3). In *Antiquities*, the situation is far more complex. First we are told that in 35-34 BCE, when summoned by Anthony, Herod did in fact leave Mariamme in the charge of the same Joseph, who did indeed disclose the secret to the woman. Curiously, when Herod returns and discovers his servant's breach of faith, he does suspect the two of misconduct, but executes only Joseph (*Ant.* 15.65-70; 80-7), allowing Mariamme to live on until 30 BCE, when Herod was again summoned, this time by the victor of Actium, Octavian. Here Josephus tells a similar tale—Herod left Mariamme in the charge of his servant, Soemus, with a similar order to kill her if Herod failed to return. On his return, he discovers that Soemus had also disclosed the order to Mariamme, and immediately suspects the two of sexual misconduct. Soemus is executed at once and shortly afterwards Mariamme is brought to trial as well. This tribunal condemns and then executes her.

Which is the preferable version? The problem is extremely complex. If *Antiquities* is correct, we have an inexplicable literary doublet, which a historian should reject whenever possible. If *War* is correct, the entire chronology is in jeopardy, for a post-Actium date for Mariamme's execution seems imperative if she was to bear Herod five children, as well as for another reason I will suggest further on.[66] Furthermore, the account in *War* occurs in a summary description of the Hasmoneans' fate at the hands of Herod, and is deliberately concise. If this were Nicolaus' version of Mariamme's death, she was executed (whether in 34 BCE or in 27 BCE) on a charge of adultery, but Nicolaus thought the charge was false. I am not convinced, however, that this

---

[66] For a recognition of the difficulty and a bold attempt to solve it, see: W. Otto, "Herodes," in *Pauly-Wissowa Real-Encyclopädie der klassischen Altertumswissenschaft* Supplementband 2 (Stuttgart 1913) 8-9, n. Otto, however, was misguided because of his adoption of Hölscher's thesis on the anonymous Jewish author who reworked Nicolaus and which Josephus used, a theory that is greatly out of favor these days, see e.g. Stern, *Greek and Latin Authors* 1, 229-30; D. R. Schwartz, "Agrippa II," 244-5. Other scholars discussed the problem but offered no solution for it, see: Thackery, *Josephus*, 66-7; Zeitlin, "Herod," 9-16; M. Grant, *Herod the Great* (London 1971) 83.

was the entire story found in Nicolaus, or even that Nicolaus claimed adultery as the charge brought against Mariamme.

In order to disentangle the problem, several other factors must be brought into the debate. (1) In the summary description in *War* that records the death of Mariamme's brother Jonathan, that of her grandfather Hyrcanus, and her own execution, another Hasmonean execution is quite conspicuous by its absence—that of Alexandra, Mariamme's mother, who, according to *Antiquities* (15.247-51) was put to death shortly after her daughter. A closer look at the text in *War* reveals a strange fact not previously noted, namely that Alexandra is totally missing from the entire work.[67] This absence is truly curious. Is it possible that Nicolaus, Josephus' main source for *War*, knew nothing of Alexandra, who plays such a prominent part in *Antiquities*, and that all the information about her in the latter work derives from another source? Conversely, is it possible that Josephus, who so slavishly followed Nicolaus in *War*, effectively eliminated all traces of Alexandra? What possible motive could he have had for this? (2) *War*'s description of the deliberate drowning of Mariamme's brother's in Jericho at dead of night is very damning to Herod (*War* 1.437). It has been suggested that in this description Josephus cannot be relying on Nicolaus, because it is so negative to Herod.[68] The description in *Antiquities* also assumes that (Jonathan) Aristobulus was drowned intentionally, but the way the story is told, namely that the murder was made to look like an accident (*Ant.* 15.54-6), suggests that someone else may have recorded the story not as a murder but as an accident. Perhaps this was Nicolaus' apologetic version, which in *Antiquities* Josephus turned upside down. Since Herod obviously never admitted planning or implementing such an assassination, we today should be very cautious in our judgment. After all, accidents do happen. (3) In *Antiquities* (15.174), Josephus admits that he had used two sources in the description of Hyrcanus' attempted escape, trial and execution. One he describes as Herod's personal memoirs (ὑπομνήματα); but scholars have considerable doubts that Josephus had access to the king's personal archives.[69] Nicolaus, on the other hand, probably did, and it should come as no surprise that, for the period prior to his arrival at court, Nicolaus used Herod's personal notes. So Josephus is probably quoting Herod indirectly, through Nicolaus. Not surprisingly, in the account of Hyrcanus' defection, which Josephus claims is derived from Herod's memoirs, Alexandra, Hyrcanus' daughter plays a prominent role. This is in keeping

---

[67] Even S. Schwartz (*Josephus*, 119-28), who is on the lookout for differences in the description of the Hasmoneans in *War* and *Antiquities* missed this one.

[68] M. Stern, "Nicolaus of Damascus as a Source of Jewish History in the Time of Herod and the Hasmoneans," in *Studies in Jewish History: The Second Temple Period* (Jerusalem 1991) 453 [Hebrew].

[69] See e.g. R. Marcus' note in his translation to the passage, p. 83, n. c; Thackery, *Josephus*, 66.

with Nicolaus' style, where behind every evil deed lurks a woman. In the other description, Alexandra plays no part in the plot at all.

This information in my view dictates the following general conclusions: The source used by Josephus in *War* to describe Herod's relations with the Hasmoneans does not seem to have been Nicolaus, for two reasons. The first reason is literary-formal. Scholars who claimed that Josephus used Nicolaus for Herodian history puzzled over the question, why all the information in *War* about the elimination of the Hasmoneans by Herod is condensed together, rather than placed in correct chronological sequence. The solutions they have come up with vary,[70] but no one has proposed the most natural solution, namely that Josephus interrupted his main source, obviously Nicolaus, in order to insert information on two topics (Herod's building activities and his relations with the Hasmoneans 1.401-44) from other sources.[71] The second reason stems from content. This source was pro-Hasmonean and anti-Herodian, describing the death of the Hasmoneans as a serial killing. This could hardly be a Nicolean description. In answer to the claim that it may be Josephan, one may note that while in *Antiquities* Josephus is usually more negative toward Herod, precisely on this topic Josephus becomes more moderate toward him. What was the nature of this alien source? It seems to have been Jewish, for it uses the Hebrew name of Mariamme's brother—Jonathan; some information on the Hasmoneans is unique to *War*—for example, the story of Antigonus' sister, who held the fortress of Hyrcania, resisting Herod's assault for close to seven years (*War* 1.364); the story of Mariamme's portrait sent to Anthony differs from the one in *Antiquities* in not mentioning Mariamme's mother (*War* 1.439); as a matter of fact the source seems curiously unaware of the significance of Alexandra, the mother of Mariamme. This source may also have mentioned the marriage between Pheroras, Herod's brother, and another Hasmonean princess—a detail unknown to the source of *Antiquities* (*War* 1.483). Finally, this source related the story of Herod's journey, his command to Joseph, his return and the execution of Mariamme, as taking place under Anthony's reign, and made the chronological error of placing Mariamme's death in 34 BCE.

In *Antiquities* Josephus still used the *War* source, but supplemented it with information that he had now found in Nicolaus. Several factors support this conjecture. Mariamme's brother, who is described as dying in an accident rather than murdered, is called Aristobulus, rather than Jonathan; the defection of Hyrcanus is told from Herod's point of view; and Alexandra, Mariamme's mother, enters the scene. Nicolaus probably also correctly placed Herod's journey, and his instructions to kill his wife should he not return,

---

[70] On Josephus arrangement of the material concerning his domestic difficulties and building activity in *War*, see: Thackery, *Josephus*, 65; and especially Cohen, *Josephus,* 52-8.

[71] On Josephus' method of writing this way, see D. R. Schwartz, "Agrippa II," 248-54 and elsewhere.

after the battle of Actium and its aftermath. Josephus, however, faced with two versions of the story, one about Actium and one about Anthony, told them both. If my conclusions are correct, I suggest a very unconventional reconstruction of source relationships. For the description of the death of the first three Hasmoneans (Aristobulus III, Hyrcanus II and Mariamme) at the hands of Herod in *War,* Josephus was not dependent on Nicolaus, and only in *Antiquities* is the latter's influence evident. The only explanation I can suggest is that when Josephus was writing *War,* of the 144 books of Nicolaus' *Histories,* he did not have the relevant volumes on this topic, and he came by them only later and then used the information in them to supplement his material in *Antiquities.*

Returning to the question of Mariamme's execution, if in *War,* not based on Nicolaus, it is clear that she was charged with adultery, in *Antiquities* the picture is not so clear. For while we are told that Soemus was executed because the king suspected him of seducing his wife (*Ant.* 15.229), Mariamme seems to have been charged with a different offense. We read the following in Josephus:

> One noon the king lay down to rest and out of the great fondness which he always had for her called for Mariamme. And so she came but she did not lie down [with him] in spite of his urging. Instead she expressed contempt for him and bitterly reproached him for having killed both her [grand]father and her brother. And when he showed resentment of her arrogance and was about to do something rash, the king's sister Salome, who perceived how greatly he was disturbed, sent his butler, who had long before been prepared for this, and ordered him to say that Mariamme had tried to persuade him to help her prepare a love-potion for the king. And [she said] if Herod should be disturbed and ask what it was [he should reply that he did not know], for Mariamme had poured the drug while he had [merely] been requested to serve it ... Having given him these instructions in advance, she sent him to speak to Herod on that occasion. And so he went in obediently and with alacrity, saying that Mariamme had ... tried to persuade him to give the love-potion to the king. ... Herod showed great excitement[over this and asked what the love potion was[. T]he butler said that it was a drug given him by Mariamme ... On hearing these statements Herod, who was already in an ugly mood, was even more provoked ... (*Ant.* 15.222-6).

The story than goes on to tell of the torture of Mariamme's household slaves and, in the end, when Mariamme was brought to trial "[Herod] brought an elaborately framed accusation against her concerning the love potions and drugs which she was alleged to prepare" (*Ant.* 15.229). This description obviously shows that Mariamme was not charged with adultery at her trial, but with attempted poisoning of the king.[72] If I am right in my conjecture that this text comes from Nicolaus, the historian thought Mariamme was innocent, and was framed by another woman, who, as we shall presently see, Nicolaus considered the root of all evil—Salome, Herod's sister. Josephus had misread Nicolaus. Nicolaus claimed neither that Mariamme's sons were guilty of

---

[72] And see on this Otto, "Herodes," 51; Zeitlin, "Herod," 18-9.

treason nor that Mariamme was guilty of adultery—nor, for that matter, of attempted poisoning, for which charge she was brought to trial.[73] If Nicolaus believed Mariamme innocent, however, would that not make Herod all the more guilty for her death? Not from Nicolaus' perspective.

In describing Herod's domestic misfortunes, Nicolaus, who knew he could not acquit his master of doing away with numerous family members, decided to portray the entire affair as a "tragedy"—that is a tragedy in Greek philosophical terms. By definition Greek tragedy postulates that the chief characters suffer greatly but the cause of their suffering is beyond their control. This is how Nicolaus decided to portray Herod and Mariamme's relationship. The king had married her not for political advantage but out of a great and passionate love. This love is so powerfully described that historians, beginning with Josephus, have been totally misled. Schalit, for example, agreed with Nicolaus that Herod actually had little to gain from marrying the Hasmonean.[74] Most other scholars, even when conceding that Herod had much to gain from a Hasmonean match, nevertheless stress the love element in the relationship between the two.[75] Nicolaus further described Mariamme as an ideal tragic heroine. She was beautiful, good, tender, and above all innocent. Her only weakness was her arrogance (ὕβρις—*Ant.* 15.219), a fatal flaw of a tragic hero. This combination of passionate love and hybris was deadly. It made both heroes vulnerable, and wicked people soon took advantage of this vulnerability. Court intrigue and sheer wickedness teamed together to devise the downfall of these "star-crossed" lovers.[76] The malicious, scheming individuals, who brought about this tragedy were (as is usually the case in the writings of Nicolaus) two women—on Mariamme's side her mother, Alexandra, and on Herod's side his sister, Salome. A third woman, who seems no less guilty, but remains somewhat in the shadowy background, is none other than that *femme fatale*, Cleopatra.

The figure of Alexandra is, from the outset, that of a ruthless insurgent who will stop at nothing to obtain for her family their rightful patrimony. She first appears on the scene when Herod appoints a high priest other than her son (*Ant.* 15.23) whereupon she immediately enlists in her cause the aid of the most powerful (but evil) woman in the world—Cleopatra (24). Even after her

---

[73] And see already Destinon, *Quellen*, 110-3.

[74] *Herodes*, 61-6; elsewhere Schalit claims that, on the contrary, it was in the Hasmoneans' political interest to form a marriage alliance with the Herodians, 564; and see also S. Perowne, *The Life and Times of Herod the Great* (London 1960) 81.

[75] Otto, "Herodes," 21; 50; A. H. M. Jones, *The Herods of Judaea* (Oxford 1938) 37; 55; Zeitlin, "Herod," 15-6; 22; Grant, *Herod*, 57. Even Edith Mary Smallwood (*The Jews Under Roman Rule: From Pompey to Diocletian* [Leiden 1976] 49; 77) who stresses most the political motive, does not doubt the emotional element involved (pp. 71-2).

[76] Although I have used a phrase from Shakespeare's *Romeo and Juliet*, I think a better Shakespearean model for Herod and Mariamme's story is actually *Othello*, and see on this Perowne, *Herod*, 86.

scheme succeeds, and her son is appointed high priest (41), she does not rest but plots further with Cleopatra to escape the country with her son (probably in order to return at the head of an army, remove Herod and place her son on his rightful throne—44-6). The plot is discovered (47-9) and is immediately followed by the death of Aristobulus (53-6), which may have been an accident, but which Alexandra interpreted, once again to her friend Cleopatra, as murder (62-3). Cleopatra urges Anthony to summon Herod to a hearing, and Anthony, who is totally enslaved by this woman, complies (64-5). At this point in the narrative, Josephus inserts the story of Herod's order to his brother-in-law Joseph, but the Nicolean narrative is soon resumed, with the presentation of the scheming Alexandra, now enlisting her daughter's aid, and for the first time interfering in the relationship of the king and his wife. When a rumor spreads in town that Anthony has executed Herod, Alexandra persuades her guard to flee with her and her daughter to the Roman legions stationed outside the city, so that "they might recover the throne ... which it was proper for those of royal blood to have" (71-73). Herod's safe return, however, frustrates this new conspiracy. For this failed attempt Alexandra, no longer in favor of Herod, is put in chains (87). Next we hear of Alexandra plotting with her father his escape to the Arabs, who are, at the time, Herod's bitterest enemies (166-8); this plan also fails (169-73); her execution, which follows close on that of her daughter, is also for a failed conspiracy. When Herod falls into deep depression following his wife's death, and leaves town, Alexandra makes a final attempt to seize power (247-50), and when the king hears of it, he "without delay ... gave orders for her to be put to death" (251). Somewhat out of character is her behavior at the execution of her daughter:

> Alexandra considered the situation and having small hope of escaping similar treatment from Herod, changed her attitude in very unseemly fashion to one which was the opposite of her former boldness. For in her desire to make plain her ignorance of the things with which Mariamme was charged, she sprang up and in the hearing of all the people cried out and reproached her daughter with having been wicked and ungrateful to her husband, and said that she was suffering just punishment for her reckless behavior, for she had not properly requited the benefactor of them all. In so indecently acting a part and even daring to seize Mariamme by the hair she naturally incurred the strong disapproval of the others for her unseemly play-acting. Especially was this clear in the case of the condemned woman herself, for she spoke not a single word nor did she show confusion as she watched her mother's disgusting behavior, but in her greatness of spirit she did make it plain that she was indeed greatly distressed by her offense in behaving in this conspicuously disgraceful manner (*Ant.* 15.232-5).

This presentation of Alexandra, so out of character with the woman, is included in order to stress the wickedness of the one compared with the magnanimity of the other. Thus, on Mariamme's side, Alexandra, the ever-scheming Hasmonean, did all that was in her power to create tension and discord between the lovers, and justly deserved to die for her constant disloyalty. One may even commend Herod for his patience in keeping up with her constant disloyalty, and only executing her when all other measures proved ineffective.

Herod's sister, Salome, is cut from another cloth altogether, but is no less wicked than Alexandra. Since I intend to return to her latter, I will outline here only her participation in the death of Mariamme. She is portrayed as having a personal grudge against the queen, because she "had shown a proud spirit in their disputes and had reproached Salome's family with their low birth" (*Ant.* 15.81). Salome's malice was so effective, and her counsel so trustworthy in the king's eyes, however, that almost all her accusations ended in the death of her victim. When blaming Mariamme and her mother for attempting to escape to the Roman camp, she persuaded Herod of her husband Joseph's disloyalty, and he was put to death (81; 87). Further, Salome was also responsible for framing Mariamme for attempted murder (213; 223-4). Even after the condemnation of Mariamme, when Herod was seriously considering clemency, Salome pressed her brother to carry out the execution (231). Alexandra's treachery together with Salome's loyalty conspired to defeat the tragic and ill-fated love of Herod and Mariamme. Herod and his perfect wife, Mariamme, were the victims of two evil women. Mariamme died guiltless and Herod was destined to suffer the intolerable grief of the loss of his loved one (*Ant.* 15.240-6).

While we are on the subject of women, Nicolaus' treatment of Cleopatra is also interesting. It should be remembered that, like Herod, Nicolaus himself had been in the service of Anthony and Cleopatra prior to Actium, and if he is apologizing for Herod's conduct at the time, he is, at the same time, excusing himself. In a typical Nicolean trait, his line of defense is to lay the blame of all ills at a woman's door. In this case the woman was readily available. Cleopatra was an object of hatred and reproach of many Roman writers, and Nicolaus followed suit. Rather than blame his master, Nicolaus brought charges against his mistress. Cleopatra was, thus, held responsible not only for Hasmonean plotting against Herod, and for the occasional discord between him and Anthony, but also for trying to seduce the king (*Ant.* 15.97-9). Sexual danger lurks everywhere. Herod, on the other hand, is portrayed as contemplating the removal of Cleopatra (99-101), and, in his speech before Octavian following the battle of Actium, he claims he advised Anthony to rid himself of the woman.

Let us now return to Mariamme. The description of her execution, which is undoubtedly Nicolean, fits the reconstruction I have proposed:

> Mariamme herself, at least, went to her death with a wholly calm demeanor and without change of color, and so even in her last moments she made her nobility of descent clear to those who were looking on. Thus died Mariamme, a woman unexcelled in continence and in greatness of soul, though lacking in reasonableness and of too quarrelsome a nature. But in beauty of body and in dignity of bearing in the presence of others she surpassed her

contemporaries more greatly than one can say. And this was the chief source of her failure to please the king and to live with him agreeably. For being constantly courted by him because of his love, and expecting no harsh treatment from him, she maintained an excessive freedom of speech. And since she was also distressed by what had happened to her relatives, she saw fit to speak to Herod of all her feelings, and finally succeeded in incurring the enmity of the king's mother and sister and his own as well, though he was the one person from whom she had mistakenly expected not to suffer any harm (*Ant.* 15.236-9).

Here all the elements of the tragedy are brought together. The description begins with the disgraceful behavior of one villain—Mariamme's mother— and ends with the malicious actions of the other—Salome. Mariamme comes out unscathed. Rightly had she been loved by the king; she was indeed worthy of his love. The end of love is the tragedy composed by Nicolaus.

But is it true? Did Herod indeed love Mariamme? I think that as historians we are not in a position to answer this question, as even Nicolaus was not. The more important historical question, however, still remains, why did Herod execute Mariamme? For example, we may suspect that it was not Salome who sent the butler with the poison, but Mariamme, in which case the charge against her was justified. Or we may conjecture that Mariamme had indeed been unfaithful to Herod; after all, she would not be the first woman to deceive her husband. If we remain within the framework of the information Nicolaus and Josephus want us to contemplate, however, we will be missing the main point. As nicely put in *War*, Mariamme's death at the hands of Herod was preceded by those of her brother and grandfather, and followed by the execution of (her mother and) two sons. This pattern aroused attention in the past, beginning with Josephus himself in *War*,[77] but no one has drawn logical conclusions from it. I think, however, that the picture emerging here is quite clear. Herod's attitude to the Hasmoneans had always been one of possible gain and loss. From the very beginning he realized he had no chance of winning the favor of Aristobulus II's house, so he courted Hyrcanus II. When fighting against the Hasmonean pretender Antigonus, Herod felt that he stood a better chance of rising to the purple if he were to come in the name of another Hasmonean pretender, so he became engaged to Mariamme. Although both Anthony and Octavian appointed him king, the animosity that arose between them almost immediately made him proceed with his Hasmonean match in the hope that, if one triumvir rejected him, he could return to the throne through the person of his wife. This becomes clear when Nicolaus explains the motives for Soemus' revealing to Mariamme Herod's order: "the women (Mariamme and Alexandra) ... it was natural to suppose, would not lose their present rank, but would improve their position either by becoming sovereign themselves or by being close to the sovereign" (*Ant.* 15.206). Before his visit to Octavian after Actium, Herod eliminated the most serious

---

[77] E.g. Zeitlin, "Herod," 22; Smallwood, *Roman Rule*, 64.

Hasmonean contender to the throne, Hyrcanus II, thereby making himself the most eligible candidate, if not by virtue of his past services, than because he was married to a Hasmonean. All these measures, however, turned out unnecessary, and Herod returned to Judaea sole ruler, and married to a woman who was no longer an asset. On the contrary, she constituted a constant danger to the stability of his regime. So he executed first her and then her mother. For the time being, there were no more Hasmoneans left. It is impossible to know whether Mariamme was charged with adultery or attempted murder, but in either case the charges were trumped up.

But was she indeed innocent, as Nicolaus would have us believe? I think Nicolaus himself knew better. Herod executed the male Hasmoneans first because they posed a more imminent threat to him. In the Hasmonean dynasty, however there had been a precedent. A woman (Shelamzion) had ruled, and she had done so successfully. The people could hope for a repetition of such a reign. With no male candidates around, Mariamme and her mother Alexandra were themselves legitimate Hasmoneans, worthy of the throne, who could rally popular support. The repeated attempts of Alexandra to dominate centers of power, such as the army, were probably matched by Mariamme. I doubt very much that from Herod's standpoint Mariamme could ever be described as innocent.[78]

c. Herod's Sister Salome

Finally, I shall discuss Salome, the sister of Herod. An outline of her life runs as follows: Daughter of Antipater, Hyrcanus II's advisor, early in life she married a certain Joseph, who was, perhaps, her uncle (*War* 1.441; *Ant.* 15.65).[79] After his fall from favor and execution, Salome remarried, this time a certain Costobarus, an Idumaean noble. From these two marriages Salome had three (or four) children (*War* 1.446; 566; 2.26; *Ant.* 17.9), two of whom we know by name: a son, Antipater who may have been the son of Costobarus (*Ant.* 16.227), and a daughter, Berenice, whose father *was* Costobarus (*Ant.* 18.133). Costobarus was also executed, for the only Idumaean attempt during the Second Temple period to revolt against the Jewish establishment that had forcefully converted them (*Ant.* 15.253-66). Salome's precise role in his downfall is unknown, although Nicolaus made much of it, as we shall presently see. After Costobarus' death, Salome remained a widow for several years, arousing the interest of gossip-mongers, who claimed that she was infatuated with a certain Arab diplomat—Syllaeus (*Ant.* 16.220-6). Meanwhile her daughter, Berenice, who was by now a grown woman, married one of Herod's sons by Mariamme, Aristobulus. Toward the end of Herod's

---

[78]And see also Grant, *Herod*, 99.

[79] On the problem of his identity, see R. Marcus, note d in his translations to *Antiquities*, *ad loc.*

rule, the king matched Salome to one of his close friends, Alexas (*Ant.* 17.10; *War* 1.566). Apart from these biographical details of marriage and divorce, we may add that Salome was on good terms with the empress Livia, wife of Augustus (*ibid.*). In his will Herod left Salome the revenues of the cities: Jamnia (Yavneh), Azotus, and Phasaelis, as well as his residential palace at Ascalon (*War* 1.646; 2.98; *Ant.* 17.147; 189; 321), and these Salome in turn willed to the empress (*Ant.* 13.81). Salome's final appearance on the scene is in Rome, where she contests Herod's last will, claiming that Judaea should be handed to Herod Antipas rather than to Archelaus (*War* 2.15; 26; *Ant.* 17.220; 224; 230). Presumably she stayed in the capital with her family, because we next hear of her grandson, Agrippa I growing up there (*Ant.* 18.143).

Despite this rather unimpressive record, Salome dominates the pages of books 15, 16 and 17 of the *Antiquities* in an unprecedented sequence. We have already seen Nicolaus' judgment of her involvement in the downfall of her first husband, Joseph, whom she denounced for seducing Mariamme, and in the indictment of Mariamme herself. These are, however, hardly the only victims of her intrigue. Further down Nicolaus convicts her of denouncing her second husband, Costobarus, before Herod.[80] This, however, is not portrayed as an act of loyalty on her part. Herod appointed Costobarus governor of Idumaea (*Ant.* 15.254). When Costobarus conspired against Herod, approaching Cleopatra with an offer to defect to her side together with the territories under his charge (256-8), and the conspiracy was discovered, Salome, rather than side with her brother, chose to protected her husband (258). It was not loyalty to Herod, therefore, but a falling-out with her husband that eventually made her denounce him. Nicolaus reports that Salome sent Costobarus a bill of divorce (259), a statement which Josephus feels he needs to comment upon, saying that it "was not in accordance with Jewish law. For it is the man who is permitted by us to do this, and not even a divorced woman may marry again on her own initiative unless her former husband consents" (*Ant.* 15.259).[81] Whether Josephus' legal statement has any significance here is at this point unimportant. What is of significance is that Costobarus had been plotting against Herod throughout these years, and Salome had disloyally protected him, denouncing him only when she fell out with him on a personal matter. This indicates that Nicolaus is out to rob

---

[80] In support of my claim that for these years (35-25 BCE) Josephus did not have Nicolaus' account when writing *War*, is the fact that this entire episode, although not connected with the Hasmoneans, is missing in *War*, while Costabarus is mentioned in passing in the descriptions of the events of 10 BCE (*War* 1.486) as though he is familiar to the reader.

[81] Salome's action and Josephus' response have been the subject of much debate. See: e.g. E. Bammel, "Markus 10, 11f. und das jüdische Eherecht," *ZNTW* 61 (1970) 95-101; Bernadette J. Brooten, "Konnten Frauen im alten Judentum die Scheidung betreiben? Überlegung zu Mk 10, 11-12 und 1Kor 7, 10-11," *Evangelische Theologie* 42 (1982) 65-80; A. M. Rabello "Divorce of Jews in the Roman Empire," *The Jewish Law Annual* 4 (1981) 92-3; and see also chapter 10, below.

Salome of her one positive asset, her loyalty to her brother. The end of the story is already set out: Costobarus turns out to be hiding dangerous Jewish opposition leaders who had been on Herod's "wanted" list for a long time and Costobarus, together with several accomplices, is executed (260-6).

Salome is also portrayed unkindly in two other personal affairs. The first involves Syllaeus the Arab. Syllaeus, the Nabatean king's most trusted advisor, is portrayed throughout Josephus' writings as Herod's bitterest enemy (*Ant.* 16.275-85), and the only person who actually succeeds in bringing discord between Herod and Augustus (286-99). He is also accused of collaborating in a plot to assassinate Herod (*War* 1.574-7; *Ant.* 17.54-7), and then to poison him (*War* 1.583, cf. *Ant.* 17.63). His eventual downfall was facilitated through the mediation of Nicolaus of Damascus (*Ant.* 17.336-50). Nicolaus' personal involvement suggests that this absolutely negative portrait may require modification. As is often claimed of Josephus' description of the war against Rome, it is where he is personally involved with his characters, that his description is least trustworthy.[82] It is, therefore, interesting that in his first appearance on the pages of *Antiquities*,[83] the description of this man is not so negative, but it allows for a further denigration of Salome.

The king of Arabia, Obadas, was inactive and sluggish by nature; for the most part his realm was governed by Syllaeus, who was a clever man, still young in years and handsome. Having come to Herod on some business or other, as he was dining with him, he saw Salome and set his heart on having her. And as he knew that she was a widow, he spoke to her about his feeling. Salome ... regarded the young man with anything but indifference [and] was eager for marriage with him, and during the following days, when many people came together for dinner, there appeared numerous and unmistakable signs of an understanding between these two. These were reported to the king by other women, who derided their lack of discretion. Herod then inquired further about it of Pheroras and asked him to watch them during dinner to see how they felt about each other. Pheroras reported that they both made their passion clear by gestures and looks. Some time after this the Arab left under suspicion but after the lapse of two or three months he came again on the same matter and made proposals to Herod, asking that Salome be given him in marriage. This connection, he said, would not be unprofitable to Herod through his association with the government of Arabia, which was even now virtually in his hands and by rights should be more so. When Herod brought the proposal to his sister and inquired whether she was ready for this marriage, Salome quickly agreed. But when they asked Syllaeus to be initiated into the customs of the Jews before the wedding—otherwise, they said, marriage would be impossible—he would not submit to this but took his departure, saying that if he did submit, he would be stoned to death by the Arabs. Then Pheroras began to accuse Salome of lewd behavior, and even more did the women of the court, who said that she had been intimate with the Arab (*Ant.* 16.220-6).

---

[82] See e.g. Rajak, *Josephus*, 161.

[83] Again, this episode is missing from *War*, but is alluded to occasionally in flashback: 1.487; 534; 566. The date of the event has been suggested by Otto ("Herodes," 100) to be 25 BCE (and not 14-12 BCE, as would result from the present position of this passage in *Antiquities*). This date would help explain its absence in *War*. These are, apparently, still the dates in which Josephus did not use Nicolaus.

Without the hindsight of Nicolaus, who knows the trouble in which Syllaeus eventually landed Herod, this story sounds very simple. An important diplomat proposes to the king's sister but is not prepared to meet the conditions of the marriage. Nothing comes of the affair. Here, however, Nicolaus stresses the indecent behavior of the woman in question, who though not married to the suitor, is rumored to have yielded to his seduction, a common slander, designed to defile the name of any decent women. That it is mere rumor does not matter. Most of what Nicolaus writes of Salome is in the form of gossip or rumor. Ignoring the indignant tone of the storyteller from the episode, however, we discover a serious blunder on Herod's part. Had he given Salome in marriage to the Arab, he might have gained an important ally instead of a dangerous enemy.[84]

In connection with the previous event, Josephus records Salome's last marriage to Alexas:

> And though Salome was eager to be married to the Arab Syllaeus, for whom she felt an erotic desire, Herod forced her to become the wife of Alexas; in this situation Julia (i.e. the empress Livia) cooperated with him, persuading Salome not to refuse the marriage lest open enmity be declared between them, for Herod had sworn that he would not be on good terms with Salome if she did not accept marriage with Alexas. And she took Julia's advice, both because she was the wife of Caesar and because on other occasions she would give her very helpful counsel (*Ant.* 17.10; cf. *War* 1.566).

Instead of simply describing Salome's last marriage, Nicolaus again felt inclined to report Salome's continuing infatuation with Herod's deadly enemy. Yet it is evident from this text that Salome, whether against her will or not, dutifully complied with Herod's demands, and was again used as a pawn in Herod's political alliances.

According to Nicolaus, however, Salome's most wicked and most spectacular "success" was the removal of Mariamme's two sons, Alexander and Aristobulus, from the scene. Space does not permit detailed treatment of both *War* 1 and *Antiquities* 16's descriptions of Salome's constant hunting down of Mariamme's two sons: spying on them by getting her daughter to inform against her husband, Aristobulus (*Ant.* 16.201; cf. *War* 1.478), spreading rumor against them (*Ant.* 16.9-10; 69), denouncing them (*War* 1.479; cf. *Ant.* 16.205), accusing them (*War* 1.535; *Ant.* 16.73-4), and finally testifying against them in their trial (*War* 1.538). Here is a sample of some of these statements:

> Salome had taken over hatred for the youths as if it were a legacy, and was trying everything that had succeeded against their mother in a desperate and reckless way so as not to leave alive any of her offspring who would be able to avenge the death of the woman who had been destroyed by her .... Thus there was equal amount of hatred on both sides but the form of their hatred was not the same, for the youths were open in their

---

[84] And see also Smallwood, *Roman Rule*, 95-6.

abuse and rash in their reproaches, believing in their inexperience, that it was noble to let their anger be unstrained, while the other ... did not act in the same way but made use of slander in a calculatedly malicious way ... (*Ant.* 16.66; 69; cf. 8-10).

Nicolaus further feels he should demonstrate what a thoroughly wicked woman Salome was, charging her with both jealousy and sexual immorality. The object of her jealousy is her nephew, Alexander's wife:

Salome's hostility was aggravated by Glaphyra, Alexander's wife, who boasted of her noble ancestry ... On the other hand, she was constantly taunting with their low birth Herod's sister and his wives ... (*War* 1.476; cf. *Ant.* 16.193).

Sexually, Salome is accused of raping her nephew:

[Salome, Alexander] declared, had one night even forced her way into his chamber and, against his will, had immoral relations with him (*War* 1.498; cf. *Ant.* 16.256).

This story seems no more true than Nicolaus' account of Cleopatra's seduction of Herod, but certainly belongs to the same literary genre that assumes that an evil woman must of necessity be sexually immoral also.

The execution of Herod's sons undoubtedly has the makings of another tragedy. The innocent, young and inexperienced orphan princes are pitched against evil itself, personified in Salome. The woman hates the princes with a vengeance and would stop at nothing to bring them to their grave. The other tragic hero of these events is of course Herod himself, whose *naiveté*, blind trust in his sister and suspicious nature Salome exploits to the utmost. The bottom line is, again, the success of the plot. The sons are brought to trial, found guilty on the basis of false evidence, and executed. This took place, according to all indications, in the year 7 BCE.

Salome's ally in these feats is none other than Herod's eldest son, Antipater, who was soon to meet his own death at the hands of his father in 4 BCE. Salome features often in the events that led to the latter's execution: She informs about Antipater's plot against his father, as well as his alliance with Pheroras (*War* 1.269-71; *Ant.* 17.36-40); she reveals to Herod the Pharisees' alliance with Pheroras' family (*Ant.* 17.44) and is eventually herself the victim of a plot by Antipater (*War* 1.641-4; *Ant.* 17.137-41). At his trial, she serves as witness for the prosecution (*Ant.* 17.93). Surprisingly, even though these actions also lead to the death of a prince at the hands of his father, Salome here is not portrayed as negatively as in the preceding events. Probably this is due to the fact that at Antipater's trial, Nicolaus, as Herod's advisor, also played a very active role for the prosecution, serving as the accuser and denouncing the son in the presence of his father (*Ant.* 17.106-21). Nicolaus' participation in this trial, his access to the evidence and his patent dislike of Antipater, convinced him that the king's son had been the main force behind the execution of Mariamme's sons. Nicolaus says as much in his autobiography, as we saw above.

Why then, in his *Histories,* did Nicolaus implicate Salome along with Antipater? She was not branded guilty of the crime at the princes' trial, nor in Antipater's trial, nor any time later. Her guilt is mere conjecture. Furthermore, why is Salome so negatively portrayed in all of Nicolaus writings? One answer is that Nicolaus portrays Salome as an absolute monster because that is what she was. This is the unqualified opinion of many scholars who have studied the woman. Schalit wrote of her *"Alles, was uns über diese Frau berichtet wird, läßt mit Sicherheit darauf schließen, daß sie ein durch und durch verdorbenes Geschöpf war. Ihre hervorstechenden Charakterzüge sind die Fähigkeit zu abgrundtiefem Haß und das Fehlen aller moralischen Hemmungen bei der Verfolgung ihrer verbrecherischen Absichten."*[85] Jones describes her as follows: "... jealous and vindictive, she had pursued Mariamme ... with relentless hatred, and it was to her indefatigable intrigues that Mariamme owed her disgrace and death. She had few scruples and rarely allowed sentimental considerations to stand in her way. She callously sacrificed her first husband ... to her schemes against Mariamme. Her second husband Costobarus she also delivered to the executioner."[86] Somewhat less vehement, but still thoroughly negative is Perowne: "Capable she may have been, and faithful to Herod in her fashion. But as a character she was ... vile ..."[87] More accommodating, but still indebted to Josephus, is Grant: "Whatever her faults, and they were numerous—including an extremely ready ear for gossip—she was never lacking in what she regarded, often wrongly, as her duty to her royal brother."[88]

I suspect that this solution is rather naive. While it is true that the only record of Salome outside the writings of Josephus is a very brief note by Strabo on her *good* relations with Augustus,[89] it would be instructive to

---

[85] Schalit, *Herodes,* 571.

[86] Jones, *Herods,* 111.

[87] Perowne, *Herod,* 104.

[88] Grant, *Herod,* 84.

[89] *Geographica* 16.2.46. It has been claimed that Salome is mentioned in one of the papyri designated "Acts of the Alexandrian Martyrs" (see: V. A. Tcherikover and A. Fuks [eds.], *Corpus Papyrorum Judaicarum* 2 [Cambridge MA 1960] 80, no. 156d). In this document, in a derogatory diatribe against the emperor Claudius by a citizen of Alexandria, he is accused of being "the outcast son of the Jewess Salome." Scholars have assumed that this Salome is none other than Herod's sister (*ibid.,* 81; Smallwood, *Roman Rule,* 252, n. 123; Stern, *Greek and Latin Authors* 1, 310). In my opinion, however, there is nothing to warrant such an assumption. The woman in the document is identified as "Jewess," and as such could be any Jewish woman, because, in the eyes of the Alexandrians, being of Jewish blood is derogatory enough. And indeed, they could hardly have chosen a more typical name for a Jewish woman, since Salome was the name borne by practically a quarter of the Jewish women of Palestine at the time, see my "Notes on the Distribution of Women's Names in

inquire whether Josephus himself had acquired some information about her from a source other than Nicolaus. I think two such scraps can be culled from Josephus. A study of the attitude to Salome displayed by these texts would be very enlightening. The first derives from the fact that Salome outlived Nicolaus, or if not the man himself, at least his written source. There is scholarly consensus that Josephus ceases to use Nicolaus after his description of the outbursts of violence following Herod's death, which were crushed by Varus, the Roman legate of Syria (*War* 2.110; *Ant*. 17.339).[90] After the detailed description of these events Josephus' writings become brief and sketchy. Among the notes Josephus inserts after this date is a mention of Salome's death:

> His successor in office was Marcus Ambivulus, during whose administration Salome, the sister of king Herod died. To Julia she bequeathed Jamnia and its territory, together with Phasaelis, which lay on the plain, and Archelais, where palms are planted in great numbers and the dates are of the highest quality (*Ant* 18.31; cf. *War* 2.167).

This description is brief indeed. Unlike the end of Shelamzion's reign, or the execution of Mariamme, it is not followed by a summation of her activities. Nicolaus would not have ended Salome's story so abruptly. Josephus, however, did not feel compelled to conclude the life of this woman with a note, either based on the evidence he had previously adduced from Nicolaus, or from his own personal repository of historical data. He did feel, however, that she was important enough to merit a mention of her death. His source for this information is unclear, but it is obvious that wherever he found it, it did not include a long diatribe on the faulty character of the woman. Furthermore, this notice, together with some earlier information found in Nicolaus, on Herod's bequest to Salome of lands and money (*War* 1.646; 2.98; *Ant*. 17.147; 189; 321), show that the king too, at his death, did not consider Salome an evil woman. In this he differed from Nicolaus. This raises the question: How did the historian dare to go against his master in so serious a matter?

The second detail that is independent of Nicolaus is the description of Salome's action immediately on the death of Herod. We are told that before Herod died, he assembled all the elders of the Jews at the hippodrome in Jericho giving instructions to his sister to have them executed in the event that he die, so that the mourning of the elders be interpreted as a mourning of the king. When he died, however,

> Before the death of the king became known, Salome and Alexas dismissed those who had been summoned to the hippodrome and sent them to their own homes, telling them that

---

Palestine in the Second Temple and Mishnaic Period," *JJS* 40 (1989) 191-2. And see also Chapter 8, below.

[90] E.g. Stern, *Greek and Latin Authors* 1, 229.

the king ordered them to go off to their fields and look after own affairs. And this act of theirs came as the greatest benefaction to the nation (*Ant.* 17.193; cf. *War* 1.666).

The story, although told both in *Antiquities* and in *War*, is so anti-Herodian that it could hardly have come from the pen of Nicolaus.[91] This contention derives further support from the fact that the same story is found also in rabbinic literature, albeit told of King Alexander Yannai, and his wife Shelamzion:

They said: when King Yannai fell ill, he seized seventy of the elders of Israel. He put them in chains ordering the prison guard: When I die, kill the elders, so that even as Israel rejoice, they shall mourn their masters. It was said: He had a good wife named Shalminon and when he died, she removed his ring from his finger, presented it to the prison guard and said: Your master released them in a dream. He released them and they went home. Then she said king Yannai was dead (*Scholion to Megillat Taanit Shevat* 2).

Josephus, particularly in *Antiquities*, often quotes sources that are also narrated in some form in rabbinic literature. It is usually assumed that these traditions derive from a Jewish source or sources, rather than Hellenistic or Roman sources.[92] The mistaken identity of the participants in the rabbinic story is easy to explain. The original story had Salome and Herod, but since it is common in rabbinic literature to blame any evil doings of a wicked king on Yannai,[93] and since Yannai had a famous wife with a name quite similar to, or actually the same as Salome,[94] the mistake became almost inevitable.[95]

So what does this source tell us? It tells us that other circles, quite far removed from Nicolaus, and probably Jewish, portrayed Salome in a favorable light, as a sort of savior who could counter with wit and courage the evil plans of her brother. I return therefore to my initial claim—wicked Salome is the literary creation of Nicolaus.

Why did Nicolaus hate Salome so much? The answer to this question, I think, has to do with the personal relationship between the historian and the

---

[91] *Ibid.*, 230.

[92] E.g. Hölscher, *Quellen*, 81-5, who claims that these traditions were Pharisaic and oral; cf. B. Dinur, "Historiographical Fragments in Talmudic Literature and their Investigation," *Proceedings of the Fifth World Congress of Jewish Studies* 2 (Jerusalem 1969) 142-3 [Hebrew], who claims, on the contrary, that these are traces of written documents in rabbinic literature. And see also S. J. D. Cohen, "Parallel Historical Traditions in Josephus and Rabbinic Literature," *Proceedings of the Ninth World Congress of Jewish Studies* 2 (Jerusalem 1986) 7-14, especially pp. 12-3; but on p. 9, n. 3 Cohen states explicitly that his conclusions do not extend to the Scholion.

[93] J. Efron, *Studies on the Hasmonean Period* (Leiden 1987) 143-218.

[94] On the two names see my: "New Ossuary Inscriptions from Jerusalem," *Scripta Classica Israelica* 11 (1991-2) 156-7.

[95] On the curious fact that Herod comes out unscathed from rabbinic literature, see: D. R. Schwartz, "Herod in Jewish Sources," in M. Naor (ed.), *King Herod and his Age* (*Idan* 5; Jerusalem 1985) 38-42 [Hebrew].

king's sister. This becomes apparent when we survey the way Nicolaus portrays himself in the pages of his *magnum opus*. He participates in four major episodes in the life of Herod, in each case delivering a blazing speech and carrying the day. Stern, in his *Greek and Latin Authors on Jews and Judaism*, refrained from including these speeches in the Josephan excerpts of Nicolaus, on the assumption that, given Josephus' inclination to write speeches, he could easily have composed them himself.[96] However, while Stern may be right about the contents of the speeches, I suspect that the situation in which Nicolaus is addressing an audience, and probably also to a great extent the themes found therein, derive directly from Nicolaus. In Josephus' entire description of the Herodian period, one finds only twelve direct speeches, all of which, save for one short address by a certain Tiro in the trial of Alexander and Aristobulus (*Ant.* 16.346-50) are delivered by either Herod or his sons or Nicolaus. Moreover, he is the single person with the most numerous and longest speeches recorded in *Antiquities* 15-17. This aggrandizement of Nicolaus could hardly be the work of Josephus. It would, therefore, be instructive to follow Nicolaus through his speeches. The first speech, given before Marcus Vipsanius Agrippa in favor of the Jews of Asia Minor (*Ant.* 16.31-57), results in impressive legislation in their favor (59-60). His next two speeches, however, are made for the prosecution rather than for the defense. In the first of these he accuses the above mentioned Syllaeus before Augustus of treachery and treason (16.346-50). His accusations are so successful that not only is Herod reconciled with his patron Augustus, but Syllaeus is found guilty and executed (352). Nicolaus wants us to think his use of language is so efficient that it can be deadly. Whether this episode is also true is not absolutely clear, because some time later we meet Syllaeus still very much alive, and because elsewhere Herod's son, Antipater, claims for himself the success of removing Syllaeus (*Ant.* 17.54 cf. *War* 1.574; *Ant.* 17.81; cf. *War* 1.605; 633). In light of Nicolaus' hatred for Antipater, it should come as no surprise that he would credit himself with the positive deeds of his enemy. Nicolaus' third address is his famous prosecution speech in the trail of Antipater, Herod's son (*Ant.* 17.110-20; cf. *War* 1.637). Once again, Nicolaus' eloquence overrides Antipater's passionate appeal to his father (*War* 1.630-5; cf. *Ant.* 17.100-5), and even though Herod himself was fatally ill, and had already executed two of his sons, an action viewed negatively in the Roman empire,[97] Antipater was executed (17.187). Nicolaus, therefore, credits himself with the same characteristics he denigrates in Salome—the ability of his words to secure life or death.

---

[96] *Greek and Latin Authors* 1, 231-2.

[97] See Augustus' comment made on Herod, and recorded by Macrobius (*Saturnalia* 2.4.11), that it is safer to be Herod's pig than to be his son: Stern, *Greek and Latin Authors* 2, 665.

Finally, and this time in indirect speech, Nicolaus is portrayed as defending Archelaus' claim for Herod's throne in Judaea, in accordance with Herod's last will and testimony (*War* 2.34-6; *Ant.* 17.240-7; 315-6). In this episode, Archelaus was challenged by his brother, Herod Antipas, who claimed that in an earlier draft of Herod's will, when the king was still of sound mind, he had bequeathed Judaea to him (*War* 2.31; *Ant.* 17.238) and by a delegation of Jews who wished to rid themselves of Herodian rule altogether (*Ant.* 17.299-314). Just as Archelaus had Nicolaus as his counsel, Antipas too brought his legal aides and advisors with him. Standing up against Nicolaus at Augustus' court was Antipater, Salome's son (*War* 2.26; *Ant.* 17.230), but Nicolaus makes it quite clear that the real power behind the Antipas' appeal was Salome herself. Nicolaus describes Salome's actions as follows:

> With [Archelaus] also went Salome, the sister of Herod, who took her family ... [who] ostensibly meant to help Archelaus in his attempt to obtain the throne but in reality meant to work against him and in particularly to protest against the things he had done in the Temple (*Ant.* 17.220; cf. *War* 2.14).

Further down Nicolaus continues:

> At this time Herod's son Antipas also sailed to Rome to claim the throne, for he was encouraged by Salome's promises to believe and considered that he would be taking over the government with greater right ... (*Ant.* 17.224; cf. *War* 2.20).

We can, therefore, see that a real feud developed between Salome and Nicolaus, and Nicolaus in his greater eloquence won. Augustus ruled in favor of Archelaus who became the governor of Judaea, while Herod Antipas had to make do with Galilee and the Peraea (*War* 2.93-5; *Ant.* 17.317-20). Salome, apparently remained in Rome with her family, possibly under the protection of Livia. We do not hear of her again until her death. Nicolaus, conceivably, did the same, and settled down to complete his *magnum opus*, particularly his detailed description of the end of Herod's reign. His predilection for drama, his belief that behind every calamity lurks a bad woman, and his personal hatred of Salome made her the target of his deadly pen. His writings could be as venomous as his speech. Salome has come down to later generations as evil, ruthless, cunning, the ultimate *femme fatale* whose mere presence kills. Against such accusations she had no way to defend herself.

A final sober note, however, should be made on Salome's political choice of Antipas as Herod's successor. Because Nicolaus no longer supplied material for Josephus for events after 4 BCE, we cannot know why Archelaus was so unsuccessful as a ruler; but very soon we hear that in the year 6 CE Augustus found his services intolerable and had him removed and exiled (*War* 2.111; *Ant.* 17.344). Thus, perhaps Nicolaus had indeed defended the wrong candidate for Herod's succession. Antipas' reign, however is another matter altogether. He ruled Galilee for 42 years, and survived not only Augustus but also his successor, Tiberius. When he was finally removed in 38 CE, it was by the mad emperor Caligula, on a false charge brought as a childish prank or a mere whim (*War* 2.183; *Ant.* 18.250-3). Interestingly, whoever is our source for Antipas' downfall, blames this too on a woman (*War* 2.182; *Ant.* 18.240-6).[98] Thus, Salome again made a better political judgment. She recommended a person who truly had the administrative capability to rule. One wonders what history would have looked like had her recommendation been followed. This, however, is where the task of the historian ends.

3. Summary and Conclusions

In this article I have claimed that the powerful women of the Hasmonean and Herodian dynasties who dominate Josephus' writings are the literary creations of Nicolaus of Damascus, who wrote drama and firmly believed that women were the root of all evil. This belief led to women attaining prominent, often demonic roles on the pages of his writings; but whether his historical judgment can be believed is another matter altogether. We have seen that Nicolaus' personal resentment of his heroines in some of the cases, and dramatic requirements in others, can easily cloud our vision of these women's real roles. One wonders, therefore, whether the situation of a historian like Josephus, who totally ignored women *qua* women, and wrote about them only when they become absolutely essential to his narrative, is not preferable.

Nicolaus of Damascus was not alone in his belief that women, through cunning and craft, dominate everything. The idea is well developed in the Jewish apocryphal book *Esdras*, where Zerubabel proves to king Cyrus that women have more power than kings (4.14-32). Many ancient histories, beginning with Herodotus, accord royal women a major role in influencing events through their counsel, intrigue and sexual irresponsibility. In historiography of the Herodians too, Nicolaus was not alone. D. R. Schwartz had shown that one of the sources about Agrippa I's rule which Josephus used, described women as forceful actors on the historical stage.[99] A story on the evil character of Herodian women has even entered the New Testament (Matthew 14:3-12; Mark 6:17-28). One wonders whether the morbid impression we have of the Julio-Claudian dynasty and its family intrigues is not the result of the same historical genre. I hope that this study will generate similar criticism of other classical works where the negative portrayal of women has been uncritically accepted.[100]

---

[98] On the source see: D. R. Schwartz, *Agrippa I: The Last King of Judaea* (*Texte und Studien zum antiken Judentum* 23; Tübingen 1990) 48.

[99] *Ibid.*

[100] The best example of this sort of gullibility still remains: Grace H. Macurdy, *Hellenistic Queens* (Baltimore 1932).

Chapter Four

"And Who Knows Whether You have not Come to Dominion for a Time Like This?" (Esther 4:14) Esther, *Judith* and *Susanna* as Propaganda for Shelamzion's Queenship

In 76 BCE Shelamzion ascended the Hasmonean throne in Palestine. She was the only Jewish queen during Second Temple times, and despite her subsequent success (hailed in rabbinic literature, and grudgingly conceded by Josephus), her ascent to the throne must have been opposed in several quarters, not only because she was the former king's widow rather than his descendant, but even more so because of her gender. If we are to believe Josephus, we may assume that her willingness to accept the appointment must have required a brave decision, since twenty eight years earlier her father-in-law, John Hyrcanus, had also attempted to nominate his wife queen after him, but that experiment failed miserably and had cost the (nameless) pretender her life; she was starved to death by her son and successor Judah Aristobulus I (*War* 1.71; *Ant.* 13.302). One could interpret this failed reign as just another internal dynastic squabble, but the fact that even during Shelamzion's reign, this pattern of son overthrowing mother threatened to repeat itself, and Aristobulus II, her son, did all in his power to dethrone the queen (*War* 1.117; *Ant.* 13.411; 416; 422-8), suggests rather that sons viewed this form of succession as faulty (even though the repeated pattern may suggest that it was the norm in the Hasmonean commonwealth). That the issue was primarily a gender issue, however, comes out most succinctly in Josephus' long description of the queen's reign in *Antiquities*. First, when describing the plight of her husband's comrades-in-arms under the new Pharisee rule initiated by the queen, Josephus writes: "But still, they themselves were to blame for their misfortunes, in allowing a woman to reign, who madly desired it, in her unreasonable love for power" (*Ant.* 13.417). This is the first we hear that Shelamzion's love of power was unreasonable (ἐκλελυσσηκυία); but that it was unreasonable precisely because she was a woman becomes quite clear in Josephus' final words about the queen (*Ant.* 13.430-1). "She was a woman," he says, "who showed none of the weakness of her sex; for being one of those inordinately desirous of power to rule, she showed by her deeds the ability to carry out her plans ..." This statement could actually be viewed as a compliment—the queen relinquished her female traits; consequently, her reign was a success. This is, however, not the intention of Josephus, and gender is at the heart of the underlying assumption of this sentence—women, even if capable, should not assume male traits. Later, Josephus states this explicitly "... matters turned out so unfortunately for her house ... because of her desire for things unbecoming a woman ..." In other words, because she was a woman who desired to rule—a function ill-suited for women—she failed. Furthermore, it was not only she who failed, but the entire royal house, since her rule marked the end of its independence. Had the Hasmoneans not made the blunder of allowing a woman to rule, they would most likely still be in power.[1]

Josephus is not the only ancient thinker who commented on the question of women's ability to rule, and the desirability of their ruling. The issue was tackled by the leading thinkers of fourth century BCE Athens and by various authors of the Hellenistic period right down to the time of Queen Shelamzion herself and long afterward. Here I shall discuss some of the arguments put forward in this debate, in order to play out the background against which Shelamzion's rise to power should be viewed.

All ancient authors seem to agree that the women they know are unfit to rule. A philosophical dispute is evident, however, in the writings of the Greeks as to whether this is the result of nature or nurture, or, in other words, whether women were genetically incapable of ruling, because they were created subservient, or whether they were ill-fitted for it by the education they received. Plato, in his Republic, puts forward the argument that intelligent women, given the right education, may serve together with men as co-guardians in a utopian republic (*De Republica* 5.454E-457C; cf. *Laws* 7.804E-805A). Plato, thus, supports the view that women's subservience is the result of nurture.

Plato's views, however, were greatly overshadowed by the formative thinking of his pupil, Aristotle, who claimed that "the temperance of a woman and that of a man are not the same, nor their courage and justice ... but the one is the courage of command and the other that of subordination" (*Politics* 1.5.1260a). In light of this formulation, he believed that leaving power in the hands of women could lead to regression into tyranny (*Politics* 5.9.1313b). He, therefore, blames Sparta's downfall on the freedom they accorded their womenfolk: "...this characteristic (allowing women positions of power) existed among the Spartans and in the time of their empire many things were controlled by women ... (and) in war ... the Spartans' women were most harmful, and they showed this at the time of the ban invasion (369 BCE) for

---

[1] For a further discussion of this text, see chapter 3, above.

they rendered no useful service like the women of other states, while they caused more confusion than the enemy" (*Politics* 2.6.1269b).[2]

Aristotle's formulation, which maintained that women were by nature subservient, carried the day. More than three hundred years later, during the reign of Augustus, when Livy in Rome wrote two speeches, one for Lucius Valerus and one for Cato the Elder, for and against the repeal of the Oppian Laws, although the two were said to hold diametrically opposing views on the laws themselves (which directly affected women), their basic approach to the subservient nature of females is one and the same. Thus, while Cato maintains that if you "[g]ive loose reign to this untamed creature and ... it is complete liberty .... that they desire ... If you suffer them to ... wrench themselves free and finally to be placed on a parity with their husbands ... the moment they begin to be your equals they will be your superiors" (36.2), Lucius Valerius claims that: "... you should keep them in control, not in slavery" for "in reality their frail nature must endure whatever you decree. The greater the authority you exercise, the greater the self-restraint with which you should use your power" (*ibid.*, 7). Therefore, although they propose different strategies for dealing with women, both Cato and Lucius Valerus (and implicitly Livy) believed that women were by nature created subservient to men.

Greek mythology preserved the ancient tradition of the Amazons—a warlike nation of women against whom the bravest Greek heroes had made war. The image of the Amazons was so potent that legend had it that even Alexander the Great had met and cohabited with the Amazon queen of his day (e.g. Diodorus Sycalus 17.77.1-4; Strabo, *Geographia* 11.5.4; Quintius Curtius, *A History of Alexander* 6.6; cf. Arrianus 17.13.3).[3] These myths are alluded to in the most ancient literature, but the earliest extant sources that relate an Amazon anthropology, describing their whereabouts, exploits and fate date to no earlier than the second century BCE.[4] The most detailed

[2] Interestingly, Plato also criticizes the Spartans with regard to their womenfolk, but from the other direction, namely that they had given them some freedom but had not followed their logic to its conclusion (*Laws* 7.805E-806 C).

[3] This legend also found its way into the Babylonian Talmud, see *bTamid* 32a-b on Alexander the Macedonian visiting a country of women (in Africa).

[4] The presentation of the Amazons in the most ancient extant sources is rather superficial—in visual art amazonomachia was a favorite theme, see e.g. Eva C. Keuls, *The Reign of the Phallus: Sexual Politics in Classical Athens* (New York 1985) 3-4; 44-7. Keuls affirms that the Athenian evidence is mostly pictorial and usually describes the actual slaughter of Amazons. The oldest extant written sources mention them as a matter-of-fact, without detiled explanations or judgment (e.g. Homer, *Iliad* 3.189; 6.186; Aeschilus *Prometheus* 723; *Suppliant Maidens* 287; *Eumenides* 628; 685-90; Xenophon, *Anabasis* 4.4.16; Aristophanes, *Lysistrata* 676; Plato, *Menexenus* 9B; *Laws* 7.806B; Euripides, *Madness of Hercules* 408-17; *Ion* 1145). Even Herodotus (4.110-7) explains only the disappearance of the Amazons, and not their mode of life. It could be claimed that earlier sources did relate these extended versions of the myth, but they are now lost, since fragments, like e.g. those of Ephorus of Kyme in the middle of the fourth century BCE do mention the

account of the Amazons comes from the writings of Diodorus.[5] This first
century author describes two tribes of Amazons—one in Anatolia (2.44-6)
and the other in Libya (3.52-5). For this second group, Diodorus claims
Dionysius Skytobrachion as his source (3.52.3) but he too is famous as a
second century BCE Alexandrian writer. In his description Diodorus is the
first to maintain that the Amazons subjugated men and raised their daughters
as warriors, while maiming their sons. Another, apparently contemporary
source maintains that they actually killed their sons (Justinus, 2.4). These
women occupied themselves with war, physical exercise and hunting while
their men spun and wove performed other tasks reserved for women.
Diodorus' description is all-embracing, claiming that not only Amazons ruled
this way, but a sister nation of Gorgons likewise occupied territory in North
Africa and terrorized their male neighbors (3.52.4; 55.3). As far as I know,
Diodorus is the only ancient interpreter of mythology who identified the
Gorgons as such a nation. This description of a topsy-turvy world, in which
"the men of those time were women and women were men," (Strabo,
Geographia 11.5.3) does not constitute an attempt to describe the world as it
would look had it been ruled by women, but rather describes the rule of
women as a male nightmare, since in it women do to men what in the present
world men do to women. It is no wonder, therefore, that Strabo at the end of
the first century BCE makes the comment that

> a peculiar thing has happened in the case of the account of the Amazons; for our accounts
> of other peoples keep a distinction between the mythical and the historical elements; for
> the things that are ancient and false and monstrous are called myths, but history wishes for
> the truth, whether ancient or recent, and contains no monstrous elements, or else very
> rarely. But as regards the Amazons, the same stories are told now as in early times, though
> they are marvelous and beyond belief (*ibid.*).

Thus, Strabo confirms my suspicion that the second and first centuries BCE
saw a rising interest in the Amazon myth. He, however, had his doubts about

---

Amazons (Ephoros, frg. 103, in C. and T. Müller, *Fragmenta Historicorum Graecum* [Paris
1928] 262). However, from the fragments themselves it appears that they did not contain
further details. See e.g. the statement made by Josine H. Blok (*The Early Amazons: Modern
and Ancient Perspectives on a Persistent Myth* [Leiden 1995] 134) in the most definitive
study of the subject: " ... the Amazons are females who fight, and every imaginative fantasy
which is added to this is a commentary on this single, fixed datum." Some research has been
done into the Amazon myth in Athens. From these it now appears that the Athenians for
example were far less interested in an "anthropology" of the Amazons than writers of the
second and first century BCE. "The Athenians thought about the Amazons first as warriors
and then as women" wrote W. B. Tyrrel, *Amazons: A Study of Athenian Mythmaking*
(Baltimore 1984) 22. On the Amazons of the Athenians see also Page DuBois, *Centaurs and
Amazons: Women and the Pre-History of the Great Chain of Being* (Ann Arbor 1991).

[5] Tyrrel, *ibid.*, pp. 41; 45-9; 52-9, attempts to prove that this late description derives from
earlier traditions, but I suspect his explanations are intended to bolster up his body of
evidence more than to make a coherent argument.

the reliability of these legends, for in conformity with Aristotle's views he adds: " ... who could believe that an army of women, or a city or a tribe, could ever be organized without men." Much like him, when commenting on the fate of the Amazons, his early contemporary Diodorus writes: "And in the end (the Gorgons) and the race of Amazons were entirely destroyed by Hercules, when he visited the regions of the west and set up his pillars in Libya, since he felt that it would ill accord with his resolve to be the benefactor of the whole race of mankind if he should suffer any nation to be under the rule of women" (3.55.3). The nation of the Amazons, women who ruled over men, was in his opinion destroyed, because it was an unnatural, monstrous creation that distorted the natural order, and must therefore be removed.

Why this sudden interest in the Amazons? What happened in the Hellenistic world in the second and first centuries BCE to bring the topic of the Amazons and their like to the fore? The answer to this question may lie in the increasing power amassed by Hellenistic, particularly Ptolemaic, queens during the second half of the second century BCE. Despite the poor state of our sources for this period, it becomes obvious, particularly from the writings of Justinus, who abridged the history of the first-century-BCE Roman author Peompeus Trogus, that the Egyptian political scene was dominated during these years by two powerful queens by the name of Cleopatra (II and III), a mother and her daughter. The first was the wife and then the widow of her brother, Ptolemy Philometer, and after his death she was in position to recall her other brother, Ptolemy Physcon, marry him and nominate him his brother's successor (Justinus, 37.8). She, however, did not serve merely as a pawn in the power struggles over the Alexandrian throne, for when, some years later, her second husband proved cruel and overbearing, the Alexandrians chose Cleopatra as their champion over and against Ptolemy Physcon, from whom she became estranged (*ibid.* 132-27 BCE). This Cleopatra played her hand at court intrigue, using her daughters to cement political alliances (Justinus 38.7; 39.1), but the latter themselves proved capable political manipulators. One daughter, Cleopatra III, married her mother's brother and ex-husband Ptolemy Physcon in 142 BCE. When the latter died in 116 BCE, Cleopatra became his true heir and nominated to the throne each of her sons in turn, when the policies of the one suited her and those of the other did not. She too fought wars and engaged in political alliance marrying her daughters to potential allies. These intrigues proved the death of her (Justinus 39.4), but her daughters continued to exert influence on their royal husbands (*ibid.*, 3).

These series of charged political events in which women played active roles as political leaders could easily have brought to the fore the heated debate over the suitability of women as rulers, generating horrible descriptions of the rule of Amazons and heated arguments about women's inferior nature and subservient status. However, a positive impression of women's rule may also be discerned.[6] It was, therefore, probably under Ptolemaic influence that first John Hyrcanus the Hasmonean, and then his son Alexander Yannai, each nominated his wife as his successor. In Egypt too, it appears that the Jews were duly impressed. Thus Josephus tells us that both Cleopatra II and Cleopatra III were strongly supported by an Egyptian Jewish military contingent that showed loyalty to the women under great duress (*CA* 2.49-52; *Ant.* 13.284-7). These two responses may suggest that the Jewish political scene reacted more favorably to women as rulers. What was the reaction of their philosophers and thinkers on the issue, however?

A contemporary Jewish variation on the debate about women's nature and their place in society can be found in a statement, explicitly addressing the issue of women and power in a Jewish composition of the second century BCE. As part of the learned discourse between King Ptolemy and the elders of Jerusalem in the *Letter of Aristeas*,[7] one of the elders describes to the king how a man should conduct the affairs of his wife by "realizing that the female sex are rash and energetic in pursuing their desire,[8] and fickle through fallacious reasoning and of naturally weak constitution, [o]ne must deal with them sanely ... Life is steered straight when the pilot knows to what haven he must set his course" (*Aristeas* 250). Here men deal with women and steer their lives. In other words, they lord it over them. This Jewish author, most likely living in Egypt during the century dominated by Hellenistic queens striving for power, repeats many of Aristotle's arguments for viewing women as weak and confused, created to be ruled by men.[9]

In light of negative popular and philosophical thinking on women as potential rulers at the time, and after John Hyrcanus failed to bequeath the throne to his wife, in order for Shelamzion to succeed to the throne, some measures had to be taken, to prepare the ground for the woman's queenship. Are there any traces in the ancient sources that support my contention that some sort of propaganda on Shelamzion's behalf was attempted? The thesis of this paper is that three unusual and closely related compositions—Esther, *Judith* and

---

[6] For a possible literary example composed at this period in favor of women in power see now Deborah Gera, *The Anonymous Tractatus De Mulieribus* (Leiden 1997) especially pp. 59-61.

[7] For a dating of this book to second century BCE Jewish Egypt, see: M. Hadas, *Aristeas to Philocrates* (*Jewish Apocryphal Literature*; Philadelphia 1951) 9-54, particularly p. 54.

[8] Compare Josephus' description of Shelamzion's reign cited above.

[9] Much has been written on the negative portrayal of women in Jewish Apocryphal Literature, see e.g. Léonie Archer, "The 'Evil Women' in Apocryphal and Pseudepigraphical Writings," *Proceedings of the Ninth World Congress of Jewish Studies* A (Jerusalem 1986) 239-246; J. Prusak, "Women, Seductive Siren and the Source of Sin? Pseudepigraphical Myth and Christian Origin," in Rosemary R. Ruether (ed.), *Religion and Sexism: Images of Women in the Jewish Christian Traditions* (New York 1974) 89-116. These works, however, gloss over nuances and ignore contradictory evidence. This is partly due to the fact that they were composed during the early stages of feminist writing.

Susanna,[10] all three named after women—could be considered as such pamphlets.

In the following I will outline my argument in favor of this premise. I wish, however, to state from the outset that as Esther, *Judith* and *Susanna* yield little or no direct information about their authors' time or whereabouts, a wide variety of suggestions about the date, provenance, language or genre of these books has been put forward; and because of space limitations I shall not analyze the texts themselves to support my case, but will rather make use of the results of the studies of scholars whose conclusions fit my thesis, but who have reached them without the objective I have in mind, thereby enhancing the credibility of my argument.

1. The Date of Esther

I begin with a date, because a date places a given event firmly within a chronological/historical framework. The one absolute date underpinning my claim appears in the colophon to the Septuagint book of Esther. In that appendix to the Greek translation the following details are found:

> In the fourth year of Ptolemy and Cleopatra, Dositheos claiming to be a priest, and Levitas, and Ptolemy his son brought this Purim epistle and testified to its truth. It was translated by Lysimachus son of Ptolemy residing in Jerusalem.

This tells us when and by whom the Scroll of Esther was translated into Greek. Bickerman has shown, quite convincingly in my opinion, that this translation was made in 78-77 BCE,[11] just one year before the death of Alexander Yannai and the ascent of his wife, Shelamzion Alexandra, to the throne of Judaea. The translation was made in Jerusalem, capital of Judaea, and then officially dispatched to the Egyptian Jewish community by a delegation which included a member of the priestly aristocracy to recommend the Book of Esther to them. What was the purpose of this translation and distribution?

Many scholars use the date of 78-77 BCE as a *terminus-post-quem*, after which there can be little doubt that the Scroll of Esther was in circulation. Few however maintain that this was actually the date of composition, because the appending of a date to a translation militates against dating the composition itself to the same period. But this is where agreement between

---

[10] For the reader's convenience, all references to and translations from these books, unless otherwise stated, are from C. A. Moore, *Esther: Introduction, Translation and Notes* (*The Anchor Bible*; New York 1971); *Daniel, Esther and Jeremiah—The Additions: A New Translation with Introduction and Commentary* (*The Anchor Bible*; New York 1977); *Judith: A New Translation with Introduction and Commentary* (*The Anchor Bible*; New York 1985).

[11] E. J. Bickerman, "The Colophon of the Greek Book of Esther," *JBL* 63 (1944) 346-7.

scholars ends. The existence of two very different ancient translations of Esther into Greek, of a retelling of the scroll by Josephus, of two quite ancient translations into Aramaic and of apocryphal additions in both Greek versions to Esther, not found in the Hebrew Masoretic text but some obviously translated from a Semitic *Vorlage*, has led various scholars to make elaborate reconstructions of the relationships between these texts.[12] The two most extreme positions were voiced in the 1940s, when Torrey suggested that the Greek is a translation of a now lost Aramaic text,[13] and I. Levy maintained that the Hebrew text of Esther as it now stands is a translation from a Greek version.[14] In addition, disagreement as to the date of the original Semitic Esther Scroll (and whether that original is identical with our Masoretic Esther) is widespread. Broadly, there are two schools of thought—one that prefers to view Esther within a Hellenistic setting,[15] and another that prefers a Persian date for the book.[16] The arguments for the Persian date include the internal evidence of the scroll itself as well as the realistic descriptions of the Persian court, including the use of numerous Persian words (and the absence of any Greek words). The arguments for a Hellenistic date are more external. (1) Esther (and Mordechai) are not mentioned among the heroes of Israel diligently listed by *Ben Sira* (44-50). *Ben Sira* mentions Nehemiah, who is Esther's contemporary, and Simon the Just, who is his (Ben Sira's) contemporary (beginning of the second century BCE), but fails to mention Esther in between the two. (2) On the other hand, Purim, the event commemorated by the Esther Scroll, is listed among the Jewish festivals introduced into the Jewish calendar during the Second Temple period in *Megillat Taanit* (the "Fast" Scroll), a document, probably dating from the Great Revolt against Rome.[17] (3) The feast of Purim curiously falls on the

---

[12] For various suggestions see e.g.: C. A. Moore, "On the Origins of the LXX Additions to the Book of Esther," *JBL* 92 (1973) 382-93; E. Tov, "The Lucanic Text of the Canonical and Apocryphal Sections of Esther: A Rewritten Biblical Book," *Textus* 10 (1982) 1-25; D. J. A. Clines, *The Esther Scroll: The Story of the Story* (*JSOT Supplement Series* 30; Sheffield 1984).

[13] C. C. Torrey, "The Older Book of Esther," *HTR* 37 (1944) 1-40.

[14] I. Levy, "La Repudiation de Vashti," *Actes du XXIe Congres International des Orientalistes (1948)* (Paris 1949) 114f. I was not able to see this work. For details see L. H. Feldman, "Hellenization in Josephus' Version of Esther," *Transactions and Proceedings of the American Philological Association* 101 (1970) 143, n. 1.

[15] See e.g. L. B. Paton, *International Critical Commentary: Esther* (Edinburgh 1908) 60-2; Ruth Stiehl, "Das Buch Esther," *Wiener Zeitschrift für die Kunde des Morgenlandes* 53 (1956) 4-22; R. E. Herst, "The Purim Connection," *Union Seminary Review* 28 (1973) 139-45.

[16] E.g. S. Talmon "'Wisdom' in the Book of Esther," *VT* 13 (1963) 452-3; Moore, *Esther*, lvii-lx; Susan Niditch, "Esther: Folklore, Wisdom, Feminism and Authority," in Athalya Brenner (ed.), *A Feminist Companion to Esther, Judith and Susanna* (Sheffield 1995) 42-6.

[17] For a good summary of the details see N. N. Glazer, "Megillat Ta'anit," *Encyclopedia Judaica* 11 (Jerusalem 1971) 1230-1.

exact date of an important Second Temple celebration—the Day of Nicanor.[18] While *2 Maccabees*, which was probably written sometime during the first century BCE,[19] synchronizes the Day of Nicanor with an event it calls "The Day of Mordechai" (*2 Maccabees* 15.36),[20] the older *1 Maccabees* mentions no such festival, perhaps indicating that it was not yet in existence. Most of these claims are based on the unpopular "argument from silence," but such arguments may be the only ones available when something does not exist.

In light of the diverse opinions about Esther's date of composition, a proposition that it was not only translated in 78-7 BCE, but also composed only shortly before, is not altogether untenable. Support for this claim will be adduced below, in conjunction with the discussion of Judith and Susanna. For the present it suffices to clarify that even if 77 BCE, when the Book of Esther was introduced into Egypt, is only a translation date, this proves that official policy was seeking to promote the importance of this book about a Jewish heroine, a queen who saved her people. The fact that this policy was initiated in Jerusalem, that the old king in the Judaean capital was ailing and that a year later his widow was crowned queen in Jerusalem seems to me more than mere coincidence. The decision to promote the book of Esther could well be associated with the coronation of Shelamzion. The composition of Esther may thus have been part of a larger literary campaign designed to promote the leadership of women through dialogue with other contemporary points of view, which, as I have shown above, were hostile to the idea of women in power. The Book of Esther, like its close contemporaries, the books of Judith and Susanna, is highly aware of gender issues, stressing time and again the unusual, yet positive roles which women can play in society. I, therefore, conclude that Esther, Judith and Susanna form a literary group of some uniformity—in content as well as context—which could serve as propaganda literature for promoting the queenship of Shelamzion. If Esther was written, translated and distributed among Jewish communities toward the end of Alexander Yannai's reign, the same may be true of the other two. Before discussing the common features of the three, and their possible utility in the debate about women and power, I shall first comment on the composition dates of Susanna and Judith.

---

[18] Today the feast of Purim is celebrated on the 14th of Adar, i.e. one day after the day of Nicanor, while it is the Fast of Esther which is commemorated on the 13th, but the scroll itself refers to the events of Purim as taking place on the 13th (Esther 8:12; 9.1; 17), and see: B. Schneider, "Esther Revised According to the Maccabees," *Liber Annus* 13 (1962-3) 190-218.

[19] On this date see J. A. Goldstein, *II Maccabees* (*The Anchor Bible*; New York 1983) 71-83.

[20] Note that the day is designated "The Day of Mordechai," suggesting perhaps that it was, as yet, not Esther's day. On a possible ancient explanation of the Day of Mordechai, see J. C. H. Lebram, "Purimfest und Estherbuch," *VT* 22 (1972) 208-22. On the possibility that Esther was later superimposed onto the scroll bearing her name, see below.

2. The Dating of Judith and Susanna

Unlike Esther, which is already attested in 78-77 BCE in the colophon to the Greek translation, and again in Josephus' retelling of the story during the 90s of the first century CE, there is no evidence for *Judith* or *Susanna* predating the second century CE, when the former is mentioned by the apostolic father Clement in his first epistle to the Corinthians (LV),[21] and the latter by Irenaeus of Lyons in his *Contra Haeresis* (XXVI.3).[22] Another feature common to the two books is the absence of any mention of them in Josephus. Some scholars maintain that this indicates that the books were not yet in circulation in his time. Josephus' choice of biblical and post-biblical sources, however, is somewhat arbitrary. While he uses *1 Maccabees*, he appears to know nothing of *2 Maccabees*. While he quotes *Esdras*, *Aristeas* and *3 Maccabees* from the Apocrypha, he seems oblivious of *Tobit* and *Ben Sira*, although there is no doubt that both were already in extant in his time. While he knows Ruth and (apparently Greek) Esther, he seems to be unfamiliar with Job. Josephus' attitude to the Hagiographa and the Apocrypha is, therefore, evenhanded, indicating that the contents of both collections were still fluid in his day, and Josephus treated none of them as Scripture.[23] He may have overlooked *Susanna* because it is a less important document for political history, but I would guess that he rejected *Judith* because of its striking internal contradictions (on which see below) which prevented him from placing it within any historical setting of which he was aware.

In the final analysis, most scholars are agreed that both *Judith* and *Susanna* date from a period earlier than Josephus. They are, however, divided, as with Esther, between a Persian date[24] and a Hellenistic, or more specifically Hasmonean one.[25] Many identify Judith symbolically with Judah Maccabee, whether positively or in protest.[26] The display of Holophernes' head on the

---

[21] See in *The Anti-Nicene Fathers* 1 (Grand Rapids 1989) 20. Interestingly, Clement refers to Judith's exploits in conjunction with a reference to Esther and her accomplishments.

[22] *Ibid.*, 497.

[23] Josephus does mention that the Jewish Scriptures include 22 books, divided as the five books of Moses, the thirteen books of the prophets and four books of wisdom (*CA* 1.37-41) but since he does not name them, any reconstruction of their contents is plausible.

[24] For *Judith* see particularly: Y. M. Grintz, *Sefer Yehudit* (Jerusalem 1957) [Hebrew]; but see also J. C. Greenfield, "The Jewish Historical Novella of the Persian Period," in H. Tadmor and I. Efal (eds.), *The World History of the Jewish People: The Persian Period* (Jerusalem 1983) 208-9 [Hebrew]; for *Susanna*, see: Moor, *The Additions*, 13; 91-2.

[25] E.g. W. O. E. Oesterley, *An Introduction to the Books of the Apocrypha* (New York 1935) 178-80.

[26] For Judith as symbolizing Judah Maccabee, see e.g. S. Zeitlin, "The Books of Esther and *Judith*: A Parallel," in M. S. Enslin (ed.), *The Book of Judith* (*Jewish Apocryphal Literature* 7; Philadelphia 1972) 29-30; for Judith as an alternative and protest figure against the later misdeeds of the Hasmoneans, see: J. W. van Henten, "Judith as Alternative Leader: A Reading of *Judith* 7-13," in Brenner (ed.), *ibid.*, 244.

walls of Bethulia after Judith had decapitated him is compared to the display of Nicanor's hand and head on the walls of Jerusalem after Judah Maccabee's great victory over him. Even André LaCocque, whose introduction suggests that *Judith*, Esther and *Susanna* (and Ruth) are all treatises composed in protest of the attitude to women displayed by the returnees from the Babylonian exile at the time of Ezra and Nehemiah,[27] actually assigns *Judith* a Hasmonean date.[28] One interpreter even dates the composition of *Judith* to the actual reign of Queen Shelamzion.[29] As for *Susanna*, Nehemiah Brüll, who wrote one of the most influential articles on this book, interpreted the legal debate about the questioning of witnesses as referring to the Pharisee-Sadducee dispute on the issue in the days of Shimeon ben Shetah, Queen Shelamzion's contemporary.[30] Even if Brüll's theory is now outdated,[31] the attention it draws to the interest in precisely the same issues that loomed large during the days of the last Hasmoneans[32] indicates that the date he assigned it may still be relevant. Enough scholarly arguments have, therefore, been put forward to support the dating of *Judith* and *Susanna* to the Hellenistic, and specifically the Hasmonean period. My thesis is based on the conclusions of these scholars.

---

[27] A. LaCocque, *The Feminine Unconventional: Four Subversive Figures in Israel's Tradition* (Minneapolis 1990) 1-6.

[28] *Ibid.*, 39.

[29] Enslin, *Judith*, 180-1: "Since numerous other emphases in the book suggest a date well beyond the Maccabean days, it is to my mind far from improbable that this choice is deliberate as a reflection of Alexandra, idealized in the eyes of the Pharisees under the name of Salome, who ruled for nine years (78-69 *sic!*) as queen ... While no act of Alexandra is to be seen as prompting the story, it does seem to me not unlikely that the author casts his heroine, unlike the other famous heroines of Israel's history, out of compliment to this doughty queen." An unusual opinion about the date of *Judith* is found in E. Mireaux, *La reine Bérénice* (Paris 1951) 167-178. He suggests that *Judith* was written during the Roman siege of Jerusalem in 69-70 CE with the purpose of persuading the Jewish Queen Berenice to do to her lover, the general Titus, what Judith had done to Holophernes.

[30] N. Brüll, "Das apokryphische *Susanna*-Buch," *Jahrbuch für jüdische Geschichte und Literatur* 3 (1877) 1-69.

[31] Primarily because it is difficult to determine whether *Susanna* is promoting the Pharisee or Sadducee point of view, see Moore, *Additions* 88.

[32] Rabbinic literature seems particularly consistent about this, beginning with the description in the Mishnah of the Pharisee-Sadducee debate (from which it is not clear what exactly the position of each sect is, see *mMakkot* 1:6), continuing with the assignment of a saying to Shimeon Ben Shetah in the formative Tractate Avot about the importance of interrogating witnesses (*mAvot* 1:9), and with a story about how the same Shimeon conducted himself (correctly or incorrectly—the sources are divided about this) in one specific case (*tSanhedrin* 6:6; *Mekhilta de Rabbi Ishmael, Mishpatim* 20; cf. *tSanhedrin* 8:3), and culminating in a story in the Palestinian Talmud which tests the sage exactly on this issue (*ySanhedrin* 6:5, 23b).

3. Esther, Judith and Susanna—The Common Premise

The features common to Esther, *Judith* and *Susanna* have been shown by many and implied by many others. Thus in the 1970s and 1980s Carey A. Moore authored the Anchor Bible commentaries on Esther, *Judith*, the Greek additions to Esther, and the Greek additions to Daniel (which include *Susanna*).[33] This indicates that Moore's specialization made him the best interpreter of all these books.[34] In 1983 Michael P. Carroll published an article claiming that a structural analysis along the lines of Claude Levy-Strauss' theory of the development of myths, exposes the three stories as transformations of one and the same myth.[35] In 1990 André LaCocque published a monograph in which he analyzed the three books side by side (together with Ruth) as unusual examples of biblical books with feminine heroes.[36] In one of her feminist companions to the Old Testament, Athalya Brenner assembled articles on these three books, even though by this procedure *Judith* and *Susanna*, which were not canonized by the Hebrew Bible, became the first apocryphal books to be included in this series.[37] All three books are also discussed by Lawrence Wills in his newly published study of ancient Jewish novels.[38]

These details, however, say more about scholars than about the books themselves. As for the latter, the internal similarities between them are extensive, and I shall mention here only some general ones, which can hardly be disputed. First of all, the three books are named after women. They are, of course not the only biblical or apocryphal compositions named for women, but unlike most other apocryphal stories in which women attain a prominent role (such as *Joseph and Aseneth* or the *Testament of Job*[39]), none of the three is an extended *midrashic* composition on biblical verses.[40] In other words, they are independent literary works freely composed by their authors.[41] The Book of Ruth bears these same characteristics, but it does not conform to the next category.

---

[33] See above, n. 10.

[34] And interestingly, he did not author the commentary for Daniel itself.

[35] M. P. Carroll, "Myth, Methodology and Transformation in the Old Testament: The Stories of Esther, Judith and Susanna," *Studies in Religion* 12 (1983) 301-12.

[36] LaCocque, *Feminine Unconventional.*

[37] Athalya Brenner (ed.), *A Feminist Companion to Esther, Judith and Susanna* (Sheffield 1995).

[38] L. M. Wills, *The Jewish Novel in the Ancient World* (Ithaca 1995).

[39] For other possible and more feminine ancient names of these books, see: Elisabeth Schüssler-Fiorenza (ed.), *Searching the Scripture* 2 (New York 1994) 139; 859.

[40] It is true that *Susanna* was eventually associated with the biblical Daniel, but his name may be an addition to the original story, as suggested by Moore, *Additions*, 109.

[41] Obviously using popular literary motifs.

Esther, *Judith* and *Susanna* all claim a post-exilic setting (Esther: "Now there was in the acropolis of Susa a Jew ... he had been carried away from Jerusalem with the exiles who had been deported with Jeconiah King of Judah, whom Nebuchadnezzar king of Babylon had taken into exile" [2:5-6]; *Judith*: "For they had returned from the exile only a short time before" [4:3]; *Susanna*: "There once lived in Babylon a man named Joakim" [1]), indicating a post-exilic date of composition. How far into the post-exilic period they were composed remains unclear because of the strategy, common to these authors, of portraying an "imaginary history"[42] as their background. This approach is carried to extremes by the book of *Judith,* which identifies Nebuchadnezzar as king of Assyria(!) after the return of the Jews from exile, and in which the tribe of Simon, also recently returned from the Judaean(!) exile, is settled in the mountains of Samaria. But even the other two books display similar features. The historical difficulties with Esther are well known. Therefore, despite the Septuagint's identification of the Persian king with Artaxerxes, modern scholars maintain that, if anything, he should be identified with Xerxes. This identification gained prominence because the king Ahasuerus mentioned in Ezra 4:6 should probably be identified with Xerxes, but since it is already disputed by the Septuagint,[43] it is unclear why after making this identification, scholars bother to refute it with the help of conventional historical criteria.[44] Esther too is obviously an imaginary history. Somewhat less striking are the difficulties in *Susanna,* mainly because its author proceeds directly to tell his story, giving as little background detail as possible. Nevertheless his claim that the story takes place in the Diaspora[45] is immediately thrown into question by the fact that not a single gentile makes an appearance in the book, and that the Jewish community is autonomous, being free to practice its own laws and even to mete out capital punishment to offenders.

In all these aspects, the three books under discussion display similarities with another apocryphal book, *Tobit*—likewise a post-exilic ("This is the story of Tobit ... of the tribe of Naphtali. He, in the days of Shalmaneser, king

---

[42] For this definition regarding the book of *Judith* see: J. Licht, "The Book of *Judith* as a Work of Literature," in M. Z. Kaddari, A. Saltman and M. Schwarcz (eds.), *Baruch Kurzweil Memorial Volume* (Ramat Gan 1975) 173 [Hebrew]. On the "historical blunder" in all these and other biblical and apocryphal books, see now Wills, *Jewish Novels,* 217-24.

[43] Interestingly, Ezra 4.6 of the Septuagint does not mention the king at all, but rather queen Esther.

[44] E.g. M. V. Fox, *Character and Ideology in the Book of Esther* (Columbia SC 1991) 131-4.

[45] For an elaborate exegesis of the book, based primarily on its Diaspora setting, see: Amy-Jill Levine, "'Hemmed in on Every Side': Jews and Women in the Book of *Susanna,*" in Brenner (ed.), *ibid.,* 303-23.

of the Assyrians, was carried away captive ..." [1:1-2][46]), non-biblical story
with an imaginary history and geography. Another similarity is found between
Tobit, Judith and *Esther*. In the former, Tobit is related to the tribe of
Naphtali, obviously one of the lost tribes of Israel, rather than the extant tribe
of Judah which produced the book. So too, Judith is said to be of the tribe of
Simeon (9:2) and Esther of the tribe of Benjamin (2:5). The shorthand version
of *Susanna* does not include this sort of genealogical information about the
heroine. These details, together with the previous ones, add up to group these
books together into the category of "imaginary history."[47]

We have thus established a firm link between the books of Esther, *Judith*
and *Susanna* and the Book of *Tobit*. However, in contrast with *Tobit*, of which
several copies were found in Qumran,[48] the three books that concern us here
were not.[49] This discrepancy is usually explained as stemming from the
particular interests of the Dead Sea community. Thus, on the absence of the
book of Esther from Qumran, Moore writes: "Evidently Esther was not
regarded as canonical by the Essene community of Qumran ... Perhaps the
Essenes resented the absence of any explicit mention of God in the book; or
possibly they did not consider Esther a 'good' Jewess because she failed to
observe the laws of *kashrut* and was evidently at first not willing to help her
own people."[50] Canonicity is not the issue, though, since books like *Tobit* (and
Enoch, and *Jubilees* and the *Genesis Apocryphon*) *were* found in Qumran.
When discussing *Judith*, on the other hand, Moore does mention that it was
lacking in Qumran, but ventures no explanation for this.[51] Since the book
never made the Hebrew canon, the question seemed less interesting to him,
even though, unlike Esther, Judith does eat kosher and does all in her power
to save her people. As for *Susanna*, Moore does not even bother to mention its

---

[46] The translation is that of F. Zimmerman, *The Book of Tobit* (*Jewish Apocryphal Literature*; New York 1958).

[47] On the imaginary history and topography of *Tobit*, see: Amy-Jill Levine, "Diaspora as Metaphor: Bodies and Boundaries in the Book of *Tobit*," in J. A. Overman and R. S. MacLennan (eds.), *Diaspora Jews and Judaism: Essays in Honor of and in Dialogue with A. Thomas Kraabel* (Atlanta 1992) 106.

[48] J. T. Milik, "La Patrie de Tobie," *RB* 73 (1966) 522, n. 3; and see now: B.-Z. Wacholder and M. G. Abegg, *A Preliminary Edition of the Unpublished Dead Sea Scrolls* 3 (Washington DC 1995) 1-5.

[49] I totally disagree with J. T. Milik ("*Daniel et Susanne* à Qumrân?" in J. Dore, P. Gerlot, and M. Carrez [eds.], *De la Tôrah au Messie: Mélanges Henri Cazelles* [Paris 1981] 337-59) that the fragment he assigned to *Susanna* is part of this book. His suggestion is particularly contested by the name יהונתן בר ישוע בר ישמעאל which can be clearly read in the text but which cannot be identified with any of the figures featuring in *Susanna*.

[50] Moore, *Esther*, xxi-xxii. Also claiming that the Qumranites did not canonize Esther (but did know it) is S. Talmon, "Was the Book of Esther Known at Qumran?" *Dead Sea Discoveries* 2 (1995) 249-67.

[51] Moore, *Judith*, 86. In a footnote, Moore is willing to consider a late composition date for *Judith* as the reason, see *ibid.*, n. 86.

absence from Qumran.[52] Nevertheless, the absence of these three books suggests some common denominator among them. They (unlike the Book of *Tobit*) were not brought to Qumran by the settlers at the beginning of the second century BCE, most likely because they were not yet in existence; nor were they added to the sect's library later, presumably because they did not fit well with the sect's ideology.[53] If this is the scenario, then it is pertinent to ask in what way they offended the sect's point of view.

It cannot have been the imaginary history contained in these books that discredited them in the eyes of the Qumranites, since *Tobit*, with a similar "history," was adopted by them. Neither are their female heroes the reason, since the Scroll of Ruth, which also has a female hero whose name is, moreover, the name of the scroll, was found in their library.[54] Another feature common to the three books is the positive depiction of their heroines as exceedingly beautiful. But this is clearly not the reason for their exclusion from the Dead Sea library, since the Qumran *Genesis Apocryphon*, a pseudepigraphical composition hitherto unknown describes Sarah the matriarch as exceptionally beautiful.[55] We have also seen that the reasons suggested by Moore for the rejection of Esther do not hold for *Judith* etc. I therefore propose that the reason for the rejection of all three books at Qumran must be associated with the circle which produced them—the Hasmoneans. If Esther, *Judith* and *Susanna* were indeed composed as propaganda for Hasmonean queenship, their absence from Qumran matches the absence of the Books of *Maccabees* from that library.[56] Since the Qumranites were clearly hostile to the Hasmonean dynasty, any books promoted by that regime, or that promoted its interests, would have *ipso facto* been rejected by the Dead Sea Sect.[57] Thus although gender is the overriding

---

[52] Moore, *Daniel*, 29-30.

[53] This is not intended to deny, as suggested by J. Finkel ("The Author of the *Genesis Apocryphon* Knew the Book of Esther," in C. Rabin and Y. Yadin [eds.], *Essays on the Dead Sea Scrolls* [Jerusalem 1961] 163-82 [Hebrew]), and Talmon ("Esther at Qumran?"), that some compositions found in Qumran knew of the Book of Esther and used expressions found in it.

[54] On the Book of Ruth at Qumran see for now P. W. Skehan, "The Biblical Scrolls from Qumran and the Text of the Old Testament," *BA* 28 (1965) 88-9.

[55] *1QapGen* 20.2-6, see N. Avigad and Y. Yadin (eds.), *A Genesis Apocryphon: A Scroll from the Wilderness of Judaea* (Jerusalem 1956) 43.

[56] For a similar assessment of Esther, see Skehan, *ibid.*, 89: "... when one considers the late origin of the Purim festival with which Esther is connected, its partial identification with the victories of Judas the Maccabee (whose Hasmonean kindred were abhorred at Qumran) ... it seems more likely that the book was avoided than it was simply not known."

[57] The dislike of the Sect for the Hasmoneans is one of the famous historical assumptions, which has not been systematically described. One of its promoters recently is H. Eshel, and see his "The Historical Background of the Pesher Interpreting Joshua's Curse on the Rebuilder of Jericho," *RQ* 15 (1991-2) 409-20; with Esther Eshel and Ada Yardeni, "A

issue of Esther, *Judith* and *Susanna*, as we shall see presently, this does not seem to be the reason for their rejection at Qumran. That rejection, however, supplies another chronological clue for their dating, although admittedly this criterion too is based on an argument from silence.

The formal similarities between *Tobit* and the three books under discussion here are of some importance. Under what influence the author of *Tobit* wrote is difficult to assess, and is beyond the scope of this chapter. It appears to me, though, that it may have served as a literary model for the authors of Esther, *Judith* and *Susanna* in its non-biblical, imaginary background, as well as in its use of popular folklore motifs. It is not absolutely clear why this strategy was adopted, but it may be that the author(s) chose to avoid a head-on collision with misogynist philosophies of his day, writing fiction instead. This, s/he/they may have assumed, would make the books more entertaining, and thereby reach a broader audience. To this end, folklore motifs were applied. The imaginary history may have been employed to make the stories look historical; the author(s) wanted the audience to believe that they were describing events of the not-so-distant past, but sufficiently far back that no one could actually refute them. The authors therefore used sources that included some plausible facts and details, including Persian technical terms from earlier times.

Such a claim may be made in light of a Qumran text recently published by Milik.[58] He designated the text *Proto-Esther*, because it contains many elements in common with the Esther Scroll we know. For example, the events take place in the court of the son of the Persian king Darius (*4QprEsthera* 5-6); the text includes a royal edict of that king which is, unfortunately, very fragmentary (*ibid.*, 6-7). The text also seems to be reporting a rivalry between two of the king's advisors (*ibid.*, fragment *d*). Similarly to Esther, this text also lays great stress on royal robes (fragments *a*, *d*), assigns to its hero a genealogy from the tribe of Benjamin (fragment *d*), and (perhaps) refers to the king's restlessness which led to the reading of the royal chronicles to him (fragment *a*). However, the scroll differs from Esther in several important features. First of all it is written in Aramaic. Secondly, its hero is neither Esther[59] nor Mordechai, but rather a man by the name of Patriza (fragments *a*, *b*, *c*, *d*). The similarities of this text to Esther are striking, but in some features it resembles *Tobit*—it is in Aramaic, was found in Qumran, suggests an imaginary history with an imaginary genealogy, and its heroes are male. This is the kind of book the authors of Esther, *Judith* and *Susanna* used in order to get their historical details and *minutiae* straight. The fact that the historicity of

---

Qumran Composition Containing Part of Ps. 154 and a Prayer for the Welfare of King Jonathan and his Kingdom," *IEJ* 42 (1992) 216-9.

[58] J. T. Milik, "Les modèles Araméens du livre d'Esther dans la grotte 4 de Qumrân," *RQ* 15 (1991-2) 321-99.

[59] Despite Milik's attempt to read this name in fragment *d* col. IV, 4 (p. 337).

Esther and *Judith* was still being argued down into the twentieth century[60] clearly indicates that they succeeded in "fooling" their readers.

The most important difference between Esther, *Judith* and *Susanna* and their earlier models is, therefore, the reversal of gender. Onto a male setting, sometimes onto an all-male story, they imposed a female heroine. This was best shown for Esther by Lawrence Wills, in his careful literary analysis of the scroll. In previous studies, the artificial connection between a story featuring Esther and another featuring Mordechai was noted, and various reconstructions were suggested to deal with this problem—the most popular being the two-source hypothesis. According to this theory, the Mordechai source, describing a rivalry between two courtiers, and the Esther source, describing a harem intrigue, were combined together.[61] In discussing these theories, Wills wrote: "I do not believe that we need to posit an independent Esther narrative which circulated as a court intrigue story. It is difficult to isolate an entire, self contained Esther story from what we have at hand without bringing in the bulk of the Mordechai/Haman conflict."[62] On the other hand, he shows that if Esther is removed from the scroll the events run on just as smoothly. He, therefore, concludes that "it is ... clear that Esther has been introduced into the story as an emotional ally or foil for the audience's emotional response to the position of being in 'ethnic jeopardy.' The audience—male and female—identifies with her as the one in the throes of a crisis of moral decision, just as it does with several other important women characters of the same period: Susanna, Judith, Aseneth and the martyred mother of *2 Maccabees* 7."[63] Wills, therefore, sets Esther clearly within the same context as *Judith* and *Susanna*, although he does not prove for the latter that there too the women are secondary. Nevertheless, in *Susanna*, the story of Daniel's rise to fame by cross-examining false witnesses does not necessarily require a woman falsely accused of adultery. It could be told, for example, against a story similar to that of Naboth the Jezreelite in the biblical Book of Kings (1 Kings 21). Similarly, half of the Book of *Judith* is over before the heroine even appears on the scene! While it is true that Judith's presence in the final chapters gives the book its unique character, we can still conjecture,

---

[60] For a survey of the arguments in favor of *Judith*'s historicity, see: R. H. Pfeifer, *History of New Testament Times with an Introduction to the Apocrypha* (New York 1949) 291; for Esther, see Fox, *Esther*, 134-6.

[61] For the most prominent see: E. J. Bickerman, *Four Strange Books of the Bible* (New York 1967) 172-88; H. Cazalles, "Notes sur la composition de roleau d'Esther," in H. Gross and F. Mussner (eds.), *Lex tua veritas: Festschrift für Hubert Junker* (Trier 1961) 18-29; Lebram, "Purimfest und Estherbuch."

[62] L. M. Wills, *The Jews in the Courts of Foreign Kings* (*Harvard Dissertations in Religion* 26; Minneapolis 1990) 180. Wills further backs these claims in his more recent *Jewish Novel*, and suggest a Hasmonean date for Esther, see pp. 109-11.

[63] *Ibid.*, 188.

that some source, which told a very different story, forms the basis of the book.[64]

Assuming that the special feature of the books of Esther, *Judith* and *Susanna* is their female hero, it is important to inquire how these books operated as propaganda for the queenship of a Jewish women. To answer this question some discussion of the books' contents is necessary, as well as of some useful insights provided by recent feminist analyses of the texts.

4. Gender and Leadership in Israel: The Ideological Message of Esther, Judith and Susanna

Esther, *Judith* and *Susanna* all tell good stories. They were composed by talented author(s) who knew how to captivate her/his/their audiences. As such they could be powerful tools. Not one of them, however, involves a woman who usurps man's position in social hierarchy or threatens the "natural order" described by the philosophers cited above and also implied in the biblical Genesis narrative (3:16) according to which the man shall rule over the woman. In what way do these books serve as propaganda for the rule of a queen?

In the first place it is instructive to note that all three books are highly aware of gender issues, and of some of the suppositions of the philosophical treatises quoted above about the "natural hierarchy" between men and women. Thus for example, in the book of Esther, Vashti's refusal to appear before King Ahasuerus is immediately interpreted as a scandal threatening men's natural rule over women:

> It is not only the king whom Queen Vashti has wronged but also all the officials and people in the provinces of King Ahasuerus.[65] When all women hear the rumor about the queen, they will look down on their husbands ... and there will be contempt and anger to spare" (Esther 1:16-8).

To counter this "doomsday" forecast, the advisors of the king suggest that he issue a decree according to which "all women, regardless of their status, shall show proper respect to their husbands" (1:20). The writer's awareness of gender and hierarchy questions is beyond doubt. Yet the extent to which s/he justifies the King's drastic action is not altogether clear. Esther is a very ironic

---

[64] See e.g. J. C. Greenfield "Nebuchadnezzar's Campaign in the Book of *Judith*," *Bulletin of the Israel Exploration Society* 28 (1964) 204-8 [Hebrew].

[65] Moore uses the name Xerxes, but since I dispute the identification, I prefer the name found in the Hebrew Bible.

book, and its portrait of the King is rather grotesque.[66] The author seems to suggest to the reader that the king overreacts to the crisis of Vashti. This interpretation can be reinforced by a resort to a recent feminist reading of Esther, which compares Ahasuerus' reaction to Vashti's behavior with his reaction to Mordechai's behavior. The former refuses to obey her husband, and consequently all women should be punished; the latter refuses to obey the king's order to prostrate himself before the king's chief advisor and consequently all his nation should suffer. Or in the words of Bea Wyler:

> Those who have smiled about the funny, even farcical, setting and the totally exaggerated reaction of male chauvinism in ch. 1 are given a shock in ch. 3. The exercise of power in ch. 1 can still be accepted as fairly normal, particularly by an audience not sensitive to gender issues. This does not apply to the execution of power as presented in ch. 3, where 'execution' is to be taken in its most literal sense. Chapter 1 needs ch. 3 in order to uncover the pattern of power abuse, whereas ch. 3 can do without ch. 1, since the abuse is so obvious.[67]

A comparison of the seemingly unimportant question of gender hierarchy with the threat to the very existence of the Jewish people, which is the central theme of Esther, alerts us to the importance of the former theme. As we shall see presently, the author of Esther is not propagating a feminist revolution to overthrow the present patriarchal order, but it does challenge some of the more blatant assumptions of its promoters about the thoroughly negative and subordinate nature of women.

The Book of *Judith* is no less alert to the question of gender. When praying to God that she may succeed in her quest and overcome, single-handed, the might of Assyria, Judith says:

> By the guile of my lips strike down the slave with the ruler and the ruler with his servant. Break their pride by the hand of a female. For your strength does not depend upon numbers, nor your might upon powerful men. Rather, you are God of the humble; you are the ally of the insignificant, the champion of the weak, the protector of the despairing, the savior of those without hope (*Judith* 9:10-11).

Judith is here describing the irony of the downfall of a great general at the hands of a woman—the weakest will overcome the strongest. In her prayer the single hand is contrasted with the "number" of the enemy; but the woman is clearly contrasted with "powerful men." When Judith describes God as the champion of the humble, the insignificant, the despairing, she is traditionally assumed to refer to the Jewish nation. Yet within the present context she may

---

[66] See Y. T. Radday, "Esther with Humour," in Y. T. Radday and Athalya Brenner (eds.), *On Humour and the Comic in the Hebrew Bible* (*JTOS Supplement Series* 23; Sheffield 1990) 295-313.

[67] See Bea Wyler, "Esther: The Incomplete Emancipation of a Queen," in Brenner (ed.), *ibid.*, 122-3.

just as well be referring to the plight of women. Just as the *real* situation of Israel as humble and despairing is descriptive rather than prescriptive, so too the weakness of a woman and her subordinate position with regard to men, implied in these verses, may be interpreted as descriptive rather than prescriptive. In other words, just as Israel is now weak and subdued, but this is by no means the natural order of things, so too women are weak and subdued, but this is not, by definition, the ideal of a perfectly ordered world.

Somewhat subtler, but still undeniable, is *Susanna's* reference to gender hierarchies. When condemning the first of the elders for perjury, Daniel says to him:

> [Y]ou descendant of Canaan, not Judah ... This is how you have been treating the daughters of Israel, and being afraid of you, they had relations with you two. But this daughter of Judah would not submit to your villainy (56-7).

Daniel is making it clear that the dividing line between righteous and wicked does not run along the gender divide. It is not women who are wicked and men who are righteous (even when they are elders) but rather it runs along the divide between Jews and non-Jews. The wicked elders are not true Jews (despite their impeccable ancestry) for their behavior is that of Canaanites.[68] Women who are threatened the way these elders threatened Susanna, and who submit out of fear, are not as utterly wicked—they are designated "daughters of Israel." In order to attain the name "Judaean," however, one has to risk one's life for the sake of righteousness. Susanna—a woman—is the true Judaean, despite her sex. This statement constitutes in fact a powerful critique of the gender assumptions of the day. It suggests that women are not necessarily more prone to sexual license than men, and are, therefore, also not morally inferior.

These passages indicate that the authors of Esther, *Judith* and *Susanna* not only promoted female heroes in their books, but subtly questioned gender relationships expressly promoted in their day. The portrayal of heroines in these books, however, does more than undermine traditional feminine models; it also presents a positive model for women to follow.

Both Esther and Susanna have been compared by scholars with the righteous biblical Joseph. Susanna, like Joseph, was falsely accused by her assailants because she refused to submit to their sexual propositions. Amy-Jill Levine writes:

> Both Susanna and Joseph are chaste, beautiful, naked individuals displaced from their homeland. Both are propositioned by people in positions of authority, and both fail to

---

[68] For the association of Canaanites with sexual license, see e.g. Ezekiel 16:4.

confront their accusers. Both stories depict impotent husbands and leaders, and both required supernaturally inspired knowledge for redemption.[69]

Esther too has been compared to Joseph. Like him, she is a foreigner in a king's court, who must rely on her wits to survive. She is in a precarious position, but ultimately she prevails. Susan Niditch calls Esther and Joseph "wisdom heroes" and characterizes them as using

> the stealthy, home-based power of the woman; the emphasis on clever, behind-the-scenes manipulation of those of higher status to secure oneself benefits ... The wisdom heroes and heroines seek to become part of the system that threatens them and, like Esther and Joseph, enjoy being part of the establishment, deriving much benefit from it.[70]

These two parallels cover two different phases in Joseph's life—his misfortunes in Egypt and his later rise to prominence. But no-one has noted that the Joseph story is also an intertext for the book of *Judith*.[71] Nevertheless, it is interesting to note that a site often mentioned in the book is Dothan: Judith's patrimony lies in Dothan (8:3). The Assyrian army is stationed there (7:3). Consequently, Judith's great act of faith takes place on that plain. Now, it is in Dothan that the first drama in Joseph's life took place—having grown up as the pampered child of his father, he was sold to slavery by his brothers on the plain of Dothan (Genesis 37:17). Judith in no way reenacts Joseph's life; but the choice of location for the drama of *Judith* (for once, not an imaginary location) strongly suggests that her exploits are in some sense designed to set straight the record of Joseph's misfortunes.

Judith, *Susanna* and Esther, taken together, in their overt and covert reference to the Joseph story, cover the entire scope of his biblical life— Judith attains glory at the site of Joseph's disgrace, Susanna undergoes Joseph's ultimate test of chastity and prevails, and Esther reenacts his wisdom and rise to power in a foreign court. Why is Joseph so important for the authors of these books? The answer to this question is not immediately

---

[69] Levine, "Hemmed in," 316. This comparison was, apparently already drawn in antiquity, by the fourth century Bishop of Antioch, John Chrysostom, see, B. M. Metzger, *An Introduction to the Apocrypha* (New York 1957) 112; due to the incomplete reference I was not able to check Chrysostom's work itself.

[70] Niditch, "Esther," 41; on other similarities between the two, see e.g. L. A. Rosenthal, "Die Josephgeschichte mit dem Büchern Esther und Daniel verglichen," *ZATW* 15 (1895) 278-84.

[71] On a very long list of biblical heroes against which Judith is modeled, but which does not include Joseph, see Linda Bennet-Elder, *Transformations in the Judith Mythos: A Feminist Critical Analysis* (Unpublished Ph.D. Dissertation; Florida State University 1991) 259ff. For an implied reference to Joseph, see Amy-Jill Levine, "Sacrifice and Salvation: Otherness and Domestication in the Book of *Judith*," in Brenner (ed.), *ibid.*, 214-5: "... as the connection to Israel (that is Jacob) signals Judith's talents for deception and crossing boundaries, so names like Gideon, Elijah ... *Joseph* and Merari (in Judith's genealogy) portend her ability to function in such roles as judge, prophet, *ambassador* and priest."

obvious. First, it is important to note, with James Kugel, that in post-biblical literature, "among all of Israel's illustrious ancestors, Abraham, Isaac, Jacob and the rest, it was Joseph who had received the lion's share of attention."[72] Kugel goes on to state that "Joseph, like so many biblical figures, developed a particular title or appellation that was paired with his name ... comparable to 'Abraham our Father,' 'Moses our Teacher' .... in this case it was 'Joseph the Righteous' ... *Yosef ha-saddiq*."[73] The importance of Joseph as a point of reference for the educated reader of the first century BCE seems, therefore, beyond doubt. Furthermore Kugel emphasizes that Joseph acquired this title because "for ancient readers of the Joseph story, the adulterous proposal of Potiphar's wife, and Joseph's virtuous refusal to cooperate, came to loom larger and larger in the imagination."[74] To educated readers, therefore, Joseph acquired God's favor and rose to splendor through his refusal to benefit from sexual politics. "That a slave, even one of his relatively lofty position should permit himself to refuse such a request from his master's wife, that he should refuse what amounted to repeated requests ('day after day') bespeaks both high moral standards and no small amount of courage."[75] As a result of his refusal to submit to his subservient position, he was slandered and cast into prison, but from the depth of the pit he was saved by God. This story is a repetition of Judith's assertion in her prayer cited above, that God is "God of the humble; ... the ally of the insignificant, the champion of the weak, the protector of the despairing, the savior of those without hope" (*Judith* 9:10-11). The story of Joseph proves this. And yet, God's intervention is subtle—no miracles occur. Joseph rises to greatness, because of his own resources and trust in God. In their stories, the women—Esther, Judith and Susanna—do the same. When heroines transcend their subordinate position and refuse to submit to their role in sexual politics, they imitate Joseph the Righteous. God's intervention in their behalf is subtle (sometimes, like in Esther, extremely subtle[76]), but it ensures their success and they rise to prominence, much as Joseph did.

Finally, it is pertinent to ask whether each of the books discussed here presents a justification for women's transcendence of their traditional role in order to rise into a position of prominence. If the answer to this question is positive, we should proceed to ask how they do it, and in what way they serve, each separately and all together, as propaganda for Jewish queenship.

---

[72] J. L. Kugel, *In Potiphar's House: The Interpretive Life of Biblical Texts* (Cambridge MA 1990) 18.

[73] *Ibid.*, 25.

[74] *Ibid.*, 22.

[75] *Ibid.*, 126.

[76] For a sympathetic, feminist approach to God in Esther, see e.g. Sidnie-Ann White, "Esther: A Feminine Model for Jewish Diaspora," in Peggy L. Day (ed.), *Gender and Difference in Ancient Israel* (Minneapolis 1989) 162.

a. Susanna

The book of *Susanna* does not discuss women's leadership. Susanna, although giving the book its title, is its object rather than its subject.[77] Ultimately, she does not actively help herself. Her only self-assertive act is actually a refusal to take action—she is propositioned by the two elders of the community but refuses to yield to their sexual overtures. Other than that she trusts in God. In this she is critiqued from a feminist perspective by Jennifer Glancy:

> Readers can recognize Susanna's courage and still reject the moral code which implies that the preservation of women as intact property is more important than the preservation of women's lives.[78]

From a feminist point of view, therefore, the text of *Susanna* is rather disappointing. It has much to say about the conventional androcentric approach to seduction and rape, but nothing to say about the leadership of women. On the other hand, however, it is a blatant critique of traditional male leadership. The community leaders, its elders, prove to be incompetent and outright criminal. They take advantage of their exalted position first by their intrusion into Susanna's garden, then by threatening Susanna and finally by testifying against her, in the knowledge that their prominence in the community will render their testimony credible.

The description of corrupt politicians must have sounded convincing to most audiences and their downfall must have rendered the book popular. Corrupt politicians, however, may be apprehended for taking bribes, embezzlement, extortion, even murder by proxy. This story chose to concentrate on the advantage such men can take of women. Instead of concentrating on the negative aspects of women's sexuality and temptation for men,[79] it chose to highlight the danger of men's sexuality for women. When the elders implicate Susanna in a sexual liaison, they know they will succeed, not only because they are elders, but also because in the society in which they live (which generates the view that women are sexually loose) such allegations are believable. The first part of *Susanna* ends predictably— Susanna is found guilty and condemned to death. The justification for the book is found in the second part, where Daniel intervenes on Susanna's behalf and turns the expected result on its head—the elders are wicked, Susanna is righteous. If this book is not a direct piece of propaganda for women's leadership, it certainly undermines the assumption underlying the opposite point of view, namely that men are made to rule over women. It does so by pointing out the wickedness and high-handed behavior of some male rulers on

---

[77] Jennifer A. Glancy, "The Accused: Susanna and her Readers," in Brenner (ed.), *ibid.*, 290-1.

[78] *Ibid.*, 295.

[79] On this sort of attitude to women in most post-biblical Jewish literature, see above n. 9.

the one hand, and the righteousness and sexual innocence of some women on the other. The stage is set for a possible role reversal.

b. Judith

One place in which such a role-reversal takes place is the book of *Judith*. The leaders of Bethulia, Judith's home town, are not criminal as their counterparts in the Book of *Susanna*. They are just downright incompetent. Role reversal is evident in that the leaders are inactive, while Judith takes action. The author of *Judith* also takes account of men's traditional view of women's weakness and rampant sexuality. As described by Elisabeth Schüssler-Fiorenza,

> ... Judith is a woman who fights with a woman's weapons, yet far from being defined by her 'femininity,' she uses it to her own ends. Far from accepting such circumscription by feminine beauty and behavior, she uses it against those male enemies who reduce her to mere feminine beauty and in so doing seriously misjudge her real power. Intelligent wisdom, observant piety, shrewd observation and faithful dedication to the liberation of her people are Judith's true definition and personal assets ... The male enemies walk into her trap because they are beguiled by her attractiveness and femininity, but they have not the faintest idea of her religious and national identity and strength. In taking her just as 'woman'—and no more—they walk into the trap and their own destruction ...[80]

Nevertheless, the Book of *Judith* does not propose to upset the patriarchal order of society. As formulated by Amy-Jill Levine

> ... inversion of male-female leadership patterns are permitted if not necessitated by the extraordinary circumstances of Judith's deed and Israel's rescue. They cannot, however, be allowed to continue unchecked ... 'Judith went to Bethulia and remained on her estate' (16:21) ... The inversion of gender roles is ended and the *status quo* is reinforced ... Judith's only remaining public appearance is her burial; not surprisingly, 16:23 explicitly notes that 'they buried her in the cave of her husband Manasseh.' In death, she is made to conform to her traditional role as wife.[81]

The Book of *Judith* is, therefore, a story of a woman who comes forward as a savior of her people in an *ad hoc* capacity. In a time of crisis traditional roles are abandoned and anyone who is resourceful, even a woman, can save the day. Judith, therefore, in her emergence, her one-time action and her return to her solitude, resembles the ancient biblical judge (Judges 2:11-9). And the judge, as is well formulated in biblical tradition, is the antithesis of the king (1 Samuel 8:10-8). Therefore, if the story of *Judith* is propaganda for women's leadership, it recommends this only under extreme conditions, in times of national crisis and the failure of leadership. The author of *Judith* set out to promote Shelamzion's queenship as an emergency measure prompted by a

---

[80] Elisabeth Schüssler-Fiorenza, *In Memory of Her: A Feminist Theological Reconstruction of Christian Origins* (New York 1983) 117.

[81] Levine, "Sacrifice and Salvation," 218-22.

terrible crisis and leadership failure. Toward the end of Alexander Yannai's life, when the latter was already sick, it was obvious to all that his internal policy was a total failure, which resulted in civil war (*War* 1.91-8; *Ant.* 13.372-83). When Shelamzion eventually ascended the throne, she completely reversed the policies of her husband, and for a while curbed the crisis (*War* 1.110-2; *Ant.* 13.405-9).[82] If this policy change was anticipated by the author of *Judith*, his/her writing in the service of the prospective queen is better understood.

c. Esther

The Book of Esther is the only one of the three books that directly mentions the topic of queenship. Even Queen Esther, however, is queen only by virtue of her marriage to the king; but this is no less true for Queen Shelamzion (and for the Egyptian queens mentioned above), and therefore does not diminish the propaganda value of Esther. The arguments against Esther being intended as a feminist manifesto, however, go far beyond this formal objection, and so should be taken very seriously. When scholars first analyzed the book of Esther from a feminist perspective, they found it disappointing, to say the least. The initial feminist thesis rejected Esther and instead upheld Vashti as a role model. Thus Alice Laffey claimed that

> ... feminists point not to Vashti's disobedience but to her courage ... Vashti never speaks but her actions speak loud and clear: NO! She will not become the sexual object of drunken men.[83]

Over and against "feminist" Queen Vashti, of Queen Esther, Esther Fuchs wrote

> ... Esther personif[ies] the reinstitution of patriarchal order. Only by reenacting the roles assigned to them by the patriarchal system as wives or mothers can women become national heroines ... These are not stories of women but stories of female role models determined and fostered by strongly developed patriarchal ideology ...[84]

In the meantime, however, the pendulum has swung in the other direction and an antithesis has emerged which asserts rather that Esther can and should serve as a feminist model. Thus, Rivkah Lubitch writes of her:

> From a systematic study of the verses in the *Megillah* which refer to Esther it is clear that she combines two very different personalities in one woman ... Esther of the beginning of the *Megillah* plays the typical feminine role. Yet at a certain point in the story ... she

---

[82] And see above, chapter 1.

[83] Alice L. Laffey, *An Introduction to the Old Testament: A Feminist Perspective* (Philadelphia 1988) 211.

[84] Esther Fuchs, "Status and Role of Female Heroines in the Biblical Narrative," *Mankind Quarterly* 23 (1982) 158-9.

'snaps' out of the dream world she has been in, and assumes a role which is good for any feminist. Esther 1 is passive, obedient, dependent and silent. Esther 2 is active, assertive, tactful, independent and holds political power in the real world.[85]

How she does this is further described by Susan Niditch:

> Esther ... finally becomes an independent wisdom heroine ... [her] cleverness emerges in the way she employs womanly wiles to seduce Haman and Ahasuerus ... [she] contrasts with rash Vashti, who would insolently and overtly dare to challenge a king.[86]

Sidnie White congratulates Esther in similar style: "Her conduct throughout the story has been a masterpiece of feminine skill. From beginning to end she does not make a misstep."[87] A synthesis of these two approaches sees them as complementing one another. Esther is intentionally portrayed as feminine, obedient and weak. She is, however, never viewed as pompous, stupid and narcissistic like King Ahaseurus, her husband.[88] Much like Judith, she does not rise to prominence in order to upset the patriarchal order of the kingdom; her mission is simply to intervene in time of crisis. It is important, however, to note that, as the king's wife, she is best situated to do this. It requires courage, cunning, wit and charm; and she has them all. More than that, however, she has the opportunity. Or in Bruce Jone's words:

> Mordecai's question in 4:14: 'And who knows whether you have come to dominion for a time like this?' indicates that Esther is in the key position now. Mordecai cannot save the Jews ... However, Esther can. She is in a position to exercise her influence on their behalf.[89]

An intelligent, talented king's wife can, better than any man (including her no-less talented uncle Mordechai), overcome a severe crisis. The king's offer to give Esther half of his kingdom (5:3; 6; 7:2) should, according to our author, be taken literally.[90] The king's widow, if she is wise and just, is his best heir.[91]

---

[85] Rivkah Lubitch, "A Feminist Look at Esther," *Judaism* 42 (1993) 438.

[86] Niditch, "Esther," 39.

[87] White, "Esther," 173.

[88] On the portrayal of Ahaseurus as such, see: Radday, "Humour."

[89] B. W. Jones, "Two Misconceptions about the Book of Esther," *CBQ* 39 (1977) 176.

[90] As inspiration for this idea, see Wyler, "Esther," 133.

[91] In view of this, Esther's marriage to, and sexual relations with the uncircumcised (which has been a problem to all moralist writers on Esther, beginning with the composer of the Greek additions) was for the author not a major problem. The king was an imaginary king, part of an imaginary history. The addition of an apology on Esther's part when the book was translated into Greek may have been the result of the fact that this version of the book was intended for Diaspora Jews, and should, therefore, not seem to recommend mixed-marriages (even with kings).

5. Conclusion

Esther *Judith* and *Susanna* are contributions to the theoretical debate on the nature of women and their competence as political leaders. The books do not openly promote women's leadership, nor are they revolutionary in nature. Yet they do question some of the suppositions of their day on the "natural order", in which man should rule over women. Because the Colophon to the Greek Book of Esther mentions the date 76-77 BCE, just one year before the coronation of Queen Shelamzion in Jerusalem, it may be suggested that certainly Esther (and with it Purim) was created as propaganda for this queen's reign. Because of formal and ideological similarities between Esther and the books of *Judith* and *Susanna*, I have suggested here that all three can be seen as serving that purpose.

Chapter Five

"Wickedness Comes from Women"
(Ben Sira 42:13)
Ben Sira's Misogyny and its Reception by the Babylonian Talmud

The Book of *Ben Sira*, an early Jewish composition from the second century BCE, enjoyed in its day and in the centuries that followed an unprecedented distribution among Jews, compared to other Jewish books that were not canonized. Not only were Hebrew manuscripts of *Ben Sira* found in Qumran (first century BCE), Masada (first century CE) and the Cairo Genizah (ninth century CE), i.e. in practically every Jewish literary cache of antiquity,[1] but it is also quoted as scripture in various works of the rabbinic corpus[2] and it enjoyed a long and colorful transformation in the middle ages.[3] In view of the fate of other books belonging to the same *milieu* as *Ben Sira*, we may be justified in inquiring how this book managed to achieve such an unusual status. This study is an attempt to explain the fame this book attained in one rabbinic circle—the Babylonian Talmud. This will be done with an eye on the traditions from *Ben Sira* preserved and treasured therein.

"*Ben Sira*'s views about women are well known and have been discussed often" wrote Jonas C. Greenfield in his 1990 article about the rendering of a *Ben Sira* text on daughters in the Babylonian Talmud.[4] This text is one of the most virulent diatribes on the burdens of fathering daughters found anywhere in Jewish literature. However, throughout his entire paper, Greenfield totally ignores *Ben Sira*'s disparaging attitude, or its reception by the Babylonian rabbis. This approach is quite surprising in light of the fact that Greenfield

---

[1] On the various manuscripts, see: Israeli Academy of Language, *The Historical Dictionary of the Hebrew Language: The Book of Ben Sira: Text, Concordance and an Analysis of the Vocabulary* (Jerusalem 1973) xi-xix [Hebrew].

[2] See particularly, M. Z. Segal, *The Complete Book of Ben Sira* (Jerusalem 1972) 37-42 [Hebrew].

[3] See E. Yasif, *The Tales of Ben Sira in the Middle Ages: A Critical Text and Literary Studies* (Jerusalem 1984) [Hebrew].

[4] "*Ben Sira 42.9-10 and its Talmudic Paraphrase*," in P. R. Davies and R. T. White (eds.), *A Tribute to Geza Vermes: Essays on Jewish and Christian Literature and History* (*JSOT Supplement Series* 100; Sheffield 1990) 167-73. Quotation from p. 167.

discusses a text of four (or seven) verses which is reproduced in the
Babylonian Talmud with considerable accuracy, and he concedes that no
"other quotations from *Ben Sira* extant in rabbinic literature lend themselves
to this sort of analysis ..."[5] Greenfield's article is a masterpiece of textual
analysis, and a good example of the interest of scholars in form rather than
substance. The question I will be asking here is exactly the one Greenfield
overlooked, namely why, of all the verses of *Ben Sira*, have these and (as I
will presently show) others of a similar nature been preserved by the
Babylonian Talmud?

"*Ben Sira*'s View of Women" is the name of a book by Warren C.
Trenchard published in 1982. Like Greenfield's article, it is primarily a
text-critical work, concerned with the study of verses, traditions and sources.
Unlike Greenfield, however, for Trenchard text criticism was a means rather
than an end. He was interested in the wider question: what was *Ben Sira*'s
attitude to women? And he sums up the issue as follows:

> *Ben Sira* is more than passively interested in women. It is a topic that reflects his personal
> feelings, not merely an environmental phenomenon. *Ben Sira* is often not content to let
> traditional material about women, whether positive or negative, stand unaltered in his text.
> When he edits such material he does so in a negative direction. He deals with negative
> topics about women that are not contained in the biblical wisdom or other literature. He
> makes remarks about women that are among the most obscene and negative in ancient lit-
> erature. He shows himself to be negative to women, no matter what kind of woman he
> discusses ... We may justifiably conclude, therefore, that *Ben Sira* exhibits a personal,
> negative bias against women.[6]

My paper is not a new study about *Ben Sira*'s attitude to women. It takes for
granted the results of Trenchard's investigation and consequently that *Ben
Sira* himself was a relentless misogynist. Often, instead of reformulating
Trenchard's earlier claims, I simply endorse them. Trenchard, however, had
specifically stated that his conclusions pertain to *Ben Sira* alone and do not
reflect his time and contemporaries: "*Ben Sira* is *personally* negative toward
women"[7] wrote Trenchard. If that were true, it would be of little importance
that a certain scholar in the second century BCE, who composed a book of
popular wisdom, hated women. Consequently, placing *Ben Sira* in context
became the aim of another important scholarly work.

With the help of the concepts "honor and shame," applied to Mediterranean
societies in anthropological studies, Claudia Camp has attempted to
demonstrate the close connection between *Ben Sira*'s self-esteem, his

---

[5] *Ibid.*, 171.

[6] W. C. Trenchard, *Ben Sira's View of Women: A Literary Analysis* (*Brown Judaic Studies*
38; Chico CA 1982) 172-3.

[7] *Ibid.*, 2.

"honor," and his control of his household—primarily his money and the womenfolk therein—to the end of avoiding "shame." And she concludes:

> The issue is ... that both money and women are overdetermined symbols of male honor, which has to do ... with the needs for external signs of control: they are the sigla of manliness. Such signs have become the *sine qua non* of contemporary Mediterranean anthropology. Consequently we might be able to understand *Ben Sira*'s shrill, sometimes virulent instruction on women to be no more than an expression of the culture in which he lives ...[8]

In Camp's opinion, therefore, far from being the result of *Ben Sira*'s personal bias, his sentiments on women are very typical of the society in which he lived. I endorse Camp's conclusions regarding the social background against which *Ben Sira* wrote his book just as I endorse Trenchard's conclusions regarding his personal bias. The object of this work, however, is to go one step further and inquire not only into the reasons why *Ben Sira* found himself disparaging women, but also into how these statements were received by later generations. An understanding of their reception will go far to explain why certain circles in Judaism perceived "women" as an abstract concept.

According to Trenchard, 105 verses in *Ben Sira*, namely 7% of the whole, are devoted to women.[9] Thus "woman" is not really the major topic of the book. Nevertheless, compared to books written in circles close to *Ben Sira* in attitude and outlook, such as Proverbs and Ecclesiastes, 7% is not an insignificant percentage.[10] The question I am interested in answering here is how these particular verses affected *Ben Sira*'s popularity and transmission. This I have tested by examining the verses of *Ben Sira* preserved in the Babylonian Talmud.

The book of *Ben Sira* is mentioned seven times in the text of the Babylonian Talmud (1. *bHagigah* 13a; 2. *bYevamot* 63b; 3. *bKetubbot* 110b; 4. *bBava Batra* 98b; 5. *Ibid.*, 146a; 6. *bSanhedrin* 100b; 7. *bNiddah* 16b). The most lengthy discussion and quotations appear in *bSanhedrin* 100b, and some of this text is repeated in *bYevamot* 63b, *bKetubbot* 110b and *bBava Batra*

---

[8] Claudia V. Camp, "Understanding a Patriarchy: Women in Second Century Jerusalem Through the Eyes of *Ben Sira*," in Amy-Jill Levine (ed.), *'Women Like This': New Perspectives on Jewish Women in the Greco-Roman World* (Atlanta 1991) 1-40. The quotation is on p. 38.

[9] Trenchard, *Ben Sira*, 1.

[10] One work which requires special attention in this context is the Qumranic *Wiles of the Wicked Woman* (4Q184, see J. M. Allegro, "'The Wiles of the Wicked Woman': A Sapiential Work from Qumran's Fourth Cave," *PEQ* 96 [1964] 53-5). In my opinion, since this is a typical Second Temple composition, it supports rather than contradicts the sentence I have written above, and only gives further substance to Camp's argument. And see further J. Licht, "The Wiles of the Wicked Woman," in B. Uffenheimer (ed.), *Bible and Jewish History: Studies in Bible and Jewish History Dedicated to the Memory of Jacob Liver* (Tel Aviv 1971) 289-96 [Hebrew].

146a. This fact narrows down the actual individual quotations from *Ben Sira* considerably, leaving them at a total of four. These four are also not evenly divided, for while *bSanhedrin* quotes (depending on one's interpretation regarding the division of lines) at least 26 verses, *bHagigah* 13a and *bBava Batra* 98b each quote but one verse and *bNiddah* 16b quotes three. All in all, therefore, the Babylonian Talmud contains 31 verses from *Ben Sira*. Of these, 13 (or 40%) refer to women. This is no longer the 7% found in the Book of *Ben Sira* itself. It is a much larger percentage, indicating that *Ben Sira*'s teachings about women had rendered this book exceptionally popular (at least in Babylonia). However, these figures tell only part of the story, primarily because not all the verses assigned to *Ben Sira* by the Talmud are authentic quotations from that book. However, eight of the 12 about women are, and some of the others are close renderings. Secondly, authentic *Ben Sira* traditions are cited elsewhere in the Babylonian Talmud without direct reference to their source, and women are the topic of some of these as well. In order to further substantiate the evidence gleaned from these figures we must first of all discuss in full the passage that contains this repository of 12 verses, namely *bSanhedrin* 100b.

1. bSanhedrin 100b

The text of *bSanhedrin* 100b is a comment on *mSanhedrin* 10:1, which states explicitly that anyone who reads the "external books (ספרים חיצונײם)," namely the books which were not canonized, forfeits his share in the world to come. It is the ultimate discussion in the Babylonian Talmud of the reasons why *Ben Sira*, a popular and well-liked book, was not incorporated into the Hebrew canon. The discussants of this text are Rav Yosef and Abbayye, fourth generation amoraim of the fourth century, who display thorough knowledge of the subject matter. They begin by inquiring into the reason why the book was rejected, and Abbayye suggests a number of verses which could have accounted for this. The first two verses run as follows:

1. Do not skin a *galdan* (i.e. a fish) from its ears   So as not to waste its skin
2. But [rather] broil it on flames   And eat it with two loaves.

This quotation, which is cited in Aramaic in the Talmud, although *Ben Sira* was beyond doubt written in Hebrew, is not found in the text of *Ben Sira* available to us today—either in its Hebrew versions or in its Greek or in its Syriac renditions. It therefore remains something of a mystery where these verses (and some others that follow) came from. It is interesting to note that this inauthentic tradition does not, on its face, have anything to do with women. However, Abbayye, in explaining why these verses (which seem to be dealing with the proper way to consume food) are not the reason why *Ben*

Sira was rejected, interprets them in a way that suddenly makes them relevant to the second sex. First, he maintains that the Bible also, like these verses, warns against unnecessary waste of natural resources (Deuteronomy 20:29). However, he doubts whether this advice should be taken literally, and prefers to interpret it metaphorically, as referring to sexual intercourse. In rabbinic literature, as elsewhere, food is often used metaphorically to denote sex. In some rabbinic traditions women and sex are explicitly compared to meat and fish (*bYoma* 75a; *bNedarim* 20b). Accordingly, Abbayye understands *Ben Sira*'s advice as a warning against engaging in "unnatural" sexual practices. Whether this interpretation is consistent with *Ben Sira*'s own teaching is unclear. However this seems likely, since most of the latter's advice on women carries a high, moral tone, and since "one of life's few relational dimensions [*Ben Sira*] can control is his own sexuality. Regulation of sexual activity within the patriarchal family was always part of the Israelite effort to maintain social cohesion. But rarely, if ever, in Hebrew Scripture does one find such intense concern with *man's* personal sexual control."[11] Although *Ben Sira* himself never actually refers to forms of sexual activity he finds permissible, the Babylonian rabbis could well assume he would have approved of such an interpretation. Therefore, even though this text, on its face, does not appear to connote relations between men and women, the rabbis' inclination to interpret it this way suggests that they expected *Ben Sira* to dwell on the subject.

The next quotation from *Ben Sira* confirms this expectation. It is a long one, constituting 4 verses in Hebrew and all of them, excluding the last, short one, are indeed quotations from the Book of *Ben Sira* available to us:

3. A daughter to a father is a worthless treasure   For fear of her he loses sleep at night
4. In her minority, lest she be seduced   In her youth, lest she play the harlot
5. When attaining adulthood, lest she not marry   If married, lest she have no offspring
6. When old, lest she engage in witchcraft.

A text very similar to this one is found toward the end of the book, in *Ben Sira* 42:9-10.[12] On these verses in the original composition Trenchard had commented:

We have ... seen how three intricately constructed distichs ... have been added by *Ben Sira* to a rather general traditional statement of a father's sleepless worry over his daughter. A daughter will cause him worry whether she is married or not. His central problem is to get her married and keep her married. Her sexual purity and fidelity, along with her child-bearing in the proper setting, are necessary for the marital state which he wants her to have. But ... the father is really concerned that as long as a daughter remains unmarried she is a financial burden to him. Furthermore, he will fall beneath this burden again if, for

---

[11] Camp, "Patriarchy," 20.

[12] For a detailed analysis of the two, see Greenfield, "*Ben Sira* 42.9-10."

whatever reason, his married daughter was divorced by her husband and sent back to his home.[13]

Little need be added to this. The Talmud's quotation is relatively long, admirably close to the original, and deviates from it in substance only to add that even when a daughter is happily married and attains old age, the father's troubles are never over, because old women are prone to witchcraft, which is an offense second only in its dimensions to adultery.[14]

The situation of this text in the Book of *Ben Sira* further lends the text a special importance, as Camp had noted:

> *Ben Sira*'s poem on two kinds of shame in 41:14-42:8 ... provides a well integrated summary to his book's formal instruction. Appropriately, then, this poem stands almost—but not quite!—immediately preceding what may be considered the book's two-fold *finale*, the praise of Yahweh (42:15-43:33) and the praise of famous men (44:1-50:21). But one small pericope is unaccounted for: the poem on daughters in 42:9-14 intercedes between the shame-poem and the Yahweh-hymn. Is this an afterthought? I propose it is anything but. Occurring immediately after the summary lesson on shame, and just before *Ben Sira* "turns up the music" to praise the works of the Lord and the everlasting name wisdom bestows, the passage indicates one last time the most dangerous obstacle on a man's path to honor/glory. It is as if, in *Ben Sira*'s drive to master life amid anxiety and arbitrary reversals of fortune, women—especially as sexual beings—epitomize all that is potentially out of control.[15]

Thus stated, it becomes clear that not only the quantity of references to women in *Ben Sira*, but the quality thereof, is equally important. Camp's assertion makes *Ben Sira*'s attitude to women that much more potent in the original composition than is suggested by the mere 7% it occupies. This fact seems not to have been totally lost on the Babylonian rabbis. Thus immediately after quoting the above cited verses, Abbayye assures us that it is not because of these that the book was rejected, since the rabbis themselves are known to have uttered the aphorism: "The world cannot survive without males and females. [Nevertheless] blessed is he whose offspring are male, woe to him whose offspring are female."

Abbayye now suggests that another verse in *Ben Sira* accounts for the book's rejection. This text is likewise in Aramaic, but a close Hebrew version of it is found in *Ben Sira* (30.23).

7. Let no pain enter your heart   For it has slain brave men

Abbayye then dismisses this verse too as the reason for the book's rejection, since a similar idea is voiced in the biblical book of Proverbs (12:24) and

---

[13] Trenchard, *Ben Sira*, 151.

[14] See my *Jewish Women in Greco-Roman Palestine: An Inquiry into Image and Status* (*Texte und Studien zum antiken Judentum* 44; Tübingen 1995) 222.

[15] Camp, "Patriarchy," 35-6.

moves on to the verse that follows next, considering whether it could be the culprit. This verse is in Hebrew and also has a parallel in *Ben Sira* (11:29):

8. Close your house to many	And bring not all therein

This verse too is rejected as the cause of *Ben Sira*'s disgrace. Finally, Abbayye produces another Aramaic text, which is not found in the *Ben Sira* available to us, but which he claims is the reason why the book was not canonized. And had these verses indeed been found in *Ben Sira*, their nonsensical character should certainly have rendered the book unsuitable as a serious work of wisdom:

9. A thin bearded man is wise	A thick bearded man is stupid
10. He who blows in his cup is not thirsty	He who says: With what shall I eat bread, his bread turns away from him
11. He who has a parting in his beard,	The whole world cannot undo him

Abbayye finds it unnecessary to dwell on the reasons why these verses render *Ben Sira* a valueless composition, but now his colleague, Rav Yosef, interposes to state that despite its rejection, the Book of *Ben Sira* does include various passages that commend it to the reader and are worthy of conservation. Not surprisingly, these open with a selection of verses about women/wives.

12. A good woman/wife is a good gift	She shall be placed in the bosom of a God fearing man

This verse appears as the third line in a poem on the "good wife" in *Ben Sira* (26:3). Contrary to his opinion of daughters, *Ben Sira* seems to have been aware of the existence of good wives as well as bad ones. There are minor differences between the Hebrew text of *Ben Sira* and the Talmudic version. Instead of "gift (מתנה)" the Hebrew has "portion (מנה)." Likewise, instead of "bosom (חיק)," Hebrew *Ben Sira* has "lot (חלק)." Both alterations result from a change in a single letter, but the Greek for both (μερίς; μερίδι) confirms the primacy of the Hebrew manuscript. The Babylonian version may, therefore, denote a shift of emphasis. Or as Camp suggested: "... retaining the Hebrew Ms C reading (as 'portion' or 'share') emphasizes the material gains the husband hopes to have from his (wife)."[16] Trenchard understood it no differently: "... *Ben Sira* mentions a good wife in the context of her husband, here a good husband. In effect he receives her as a piece of desired property."[17] This economic emphasis is somewhat softened in the Babylonian

---

[16] *Ibid.*, 24.

[17] Trenchard, *Ben Sira*, 13.

version. This text can therefore be considered only slightly less hostile to women than its source or than the rest of the material cited in the Talmud.

The Talmud, having cited this verse, now, for the sake of symmetry, presents a verse about the bad wife:

13. A bad woman/wife is a like leprosy to her husband

Though rather similar to much of what *Ben Sira* has to say on bad wives, like for example 26:7 ("... a bad woman/wife / he who marries her clutches a scorpion"), this verse has no direct parallel in the extant text of *Ben Sira*. Nevertheless, the atmosphere of *Ben Sira* is present in this verse, for, as Trenchard asserts: "*Ben Sira* goes beyond the Old Testament ... when he employs the term אשה רעה as a broad description of a bad wife. This is not to say that the term originated with him, but it is sufficiently used by him in contrast with the Old Testament that we can safely claim it to be characteristic of his writing."[18] For this reason it is interesting to note that the Munich Ms. of the Babylonian Talmud has here a longer section on the bad wife, which is closer to the original composition:

A bad woman/wife is a bad gift   She shall be placed in the bosom of a wicked man

This is reminiscent of verse 26:25:

A wicked woman will be allotted to a fool   And a virtuous one allotted to a God fearing
                                              man

In light of this addition, which has, for some reason, been dropped by the printed editions, we can safely assume that the Talmud's digression on the wicked wife is no less based on *Ben Sira* than its citation of verses on the good one.

The same is true for the next talmudic verse, which seems no longer to contain an ancient wisdom formula. The question at the beginning of the verse is posed in Aramaic, and the second part, an answer and a piece of advice, appears rather to be a contemporary solution to the evils described by *Ben Sira*:

14. How shall he be cured? He shall remove her from his house And be cured of his leprosy[19]

---

[18] *Ibid.*, 63.

[19] It is interesting to note, with S. Schechter, ("The Quotations from Ecclesiasticus in Rabbinic Literature," *JQR* [O.S.] 3 [1891] 700) that according to some later, but perhaps more reliable rabbinic sources, the whole section (after the *Ben Sira* verse quoted above which is found in mss. but not in the printed version of the Talmud) "A bad woman/wife is a like leprosy to her husband. How shall he be cured? He shall remove her from his house / and

The rabbis, therefore, recommend that a bad woman be divorced by her husband. Despite the prosaic (i.e. non-poetic) character of this verse, the idea contained therein comes directly from *Ben Sira*. In 25:25-6 *Ben Sira* advises:

Do not allow water an outlet   Or sovereignty to a bad woman/wife
If she refuses to walk by your side   Cut her away from your flesh.

Although the medium here above is not *Ben Sira*, the message certainly is! On this too Trenchard had commented: "*Ben Sira*'s call for divorce in the face of a wife's arrogant disdain for her husband's authority stands in stark contrast to the material of Deuteronomy. He counsels the dissolution of the marriage union on grounds far less serious than those found in his national tradition."[20] The idea that a bad wife should be divorced is, of course, not so ingenious and could be reached by many people. The fact that the Babylonians assign such an opinion to *Ben Sira*, and that he indeed held just that one, however, seems to me no mere coincidence.

From this digression on the subject of the bad wife, the Babylonians now return to the discussion of the good wife:

15. A beautiful woman—happy is her husband   The number of his days are doubled

In our version of the book of *Ben Sira* this verse appears in the same poem about the good wife as verse 14 cited above, but two verses earlier (26:1). The striking difference between the two versions is the description of the woman who gives her husband longevity. According to *Ben Sira* she should be "good." According to the Talmud, she should be "beautiful." Nevertheless, the Talmud is not far off the mark in interpreting *Ben Sira* here, since further down in chapter 26, *Ben Sira* does indeed interpret a good woman to be a good-looking one:

26:13: A woman's charm will delight her husband And her intelligence puts flesh on
    his bones

26:16-8: The sun shines in heaven above   A wife's beauty in the holy of holies
    of a man
A candle burns on the sacred lamp   A face is beautiful on a tall figure.
Golden pillars are supported by silver bases   Fair legs by secure heels

On *Ben Sira*'s comment on the beautiful woman Trenchard stated that "The emphasis in vv. 16-8 is on a woman's eye appeal and not on her moral appeal. The context in which she is lauded is that of her home ... This does not suggest that she is beautiful because she has efficiently or aesthetically

---

be cured of his leprosy" is in fact a quotation from Rabbi (Judah the Patriarch) or Abbayye, but not from *Ben Sira* itself.

[20] Trenchard, *Ben Sira*, 85-6.

arranged her home. Rather it is merely the setting in which she is being viewed."[21] And he concludes: "*Ben Sira* makes glowing and complimentary statements about a wife's beauty. However he is not so much concerned about her as a woman, as he is about her appearance to others, particularly to her husband."[22] This conclusion, I believe, becomes even more relevant in the rendition of *Ben Sira* by the Babylonian rabbis in the verse under discussion.

From chapters 25-6 of *Ben Sira*, the Babylonian editor now turns to chapter 9. In this chapter *Ben Sira* lists women with whom it is inadvisable for a sensible man to mix, for fear of temptation. The same message is found in the Talmud, although its list is rather more condensed:

16. Close your eyes to a handsome woman   For fear of falling in her net
17. Do not recline with her husband to drink wine and ale
18. For by a woman's beauty many were corrupted, "Yea, all her slain are a mighty host"
                                                                        (Proverbs 7:26)

The first part of the first verse is from *Ben Sira* 9:8 and the second is from *Ben Sira* 9:3. The second verse corresponds to *Ben Sira* 9:9 and the third is again taken from *Ben Sira* 9:8. *Ben Sira*'s original list of women to be avoided consisted of the stranger, the prostitute, the musician, the virgin and the married women. This list is considered one of the most telling verses in the original book, reflecting to a large measure, the society frequented by the author. Or, in the words of Camp: "... as is evident ... the sage regularly attends banquets, and it is here that entanglements with performers, as well as the arousal of reclining (and whatever else!) at table with married women arise."[23] If, therefore, *Ben Sira*'s list of dangerous women is closely culture bound, it should come as no surprise that the Babylonian Talmud, some 600 years later, and many thousands of miles away, condensed it into the one feminine aspect whose dangerous attraction does not change over time and place—namely beauty. Women's beauty remains the one temptation a man should always heed.

An interesting question is how to reconstruct the original version of verse 17. The version in the Talmud ("do not recline with her husband") corresponds exactly with Ms. A of *Ben Sira* from the Cairo Genizah. However, the Greek version, the Syriac, and apparently some ms. witnesses in the Talmud itself suggest another version, namely "Do not recline with *her*, etc."[24] It seems to me that this is another culture-bound alteration of the original (an alteration made either in the transmission of the Book of *Ben Sira* itself, or by the authors of the Talmud, or by later generations in both),

---

[21] *Ibid.*, 17.

[22] *Ibid.*, 18.

[23] Camp, "Patriarchy," 21.

[24] E.g. Schechter, "Ecclesiasticus," 700; cf. Trenchard, *Ben Sira*, 273-4, n. 121.

because *Ben Sira* described a social situation where men and women ate, drank and conversed *together* in a banquet setting, a situation which was simply incomprehensible to later generations.

The Babylonian treatment of the last verse is very interesting. *Ben Sira* in verse 9:8 makes the following observation:

Close your eyes to a handsome woman   And look not at beauty that is not yours
By a woman many were corrupted   And her lovers were consumed by fire

This last verse is clearly a paraphrase made by *Ben Sira* of a similar verse in the book of Proverbs (7:26):

For many a victim has [the loose woman] laid low   Yea, all her slain are a mighty host

The rabbis obviously noticed this fact, for their rendition of the second half of *Ben Sira*'s verse has restored the original verse from Proverbs.

Of these verses in *Ben Sira,* Trenchard observed: "In this section *Ben Sira* views woman as a sex object. Although she is not pictured here actually committing adultery, she is nevertheless presented in the light of that potential. In fact *Ben Sira* implies that illicit sexual activity is the probable result of a man's gazing at a beautiful, married woman or reveling with her at a banquet."[25] It seems to me that these observations are correct and that the Babylonian Talmud chose to cite these version precisely because they conveyed this message.

Finally, and still on this topic, the Babylonians now quote another verse from the original Ben Sira:

19. Many are the wounds [inflicted by] peddlers   Who promote unchastity as a spark
                                                  lights an ember

The first part of this verse is found in *Ben Sira* 11:29b, and the last part of the second ("a spark lights an ember") is taken from 11:32, but the combination of the two with the theme of unchastity is a talmudic invention—as it were, a sort of *midrash* on the reasons for the insertion of the first part. *Ben Sira* warns his readers of the dangers which wandering peddlers bring to a man's home. This could be interpreted in any number of ways. For example, it could be understood as referring to their cheating, stealing, bringing dirt and disease into the house etc. However, the Babylonian Talmud, in its one-track mind, interprets the peddler as a potential adulterer of whom the husband should take heed. This is therefore a second instance in which the Babylonian Talmud over-interprets *Ben Sira* with regard to women.

From here on, the Talmud cites seven verses claimed to come from *Ben Sira,* and which, with one exception, do not refer to women. Not all these

---

25 Trenchard, *ibid.*, 114.

verses, however, are actually present in the original composition. The talmudic text begins with verses that connect with the one previously cited, as they are also found in chapter 11 of *Ben Sira*:

20. As a basket full of birds   Their houses are full of treachery
21. Close your house to many   And bring not all therein

The first verse in this text is taken from *Ben Sira* 11:29, which is in turn a direct quotation from Jeremiah 5:27. The second verse is also from *Ben Sira* 11:29, and appears in the original just before the preceding two. It in fact repeats one of the verses cited previously by Abbayye as possible grounds for rejecting *Ben Sira*. All three verses evolve around the theme of keeping one's privacy—a topic much cherished by *Ben Sira*. Privacy is important because it guards a man from making a public spectacle of himself and becoming the subject of gossip and ridicule. This is the theme that connects this cluster to the next one in Rav Yosef's list:

22. Many shall be your well-wishers   [But] reveal your secret to one in a thousand

This verse is taken from *Ben Sira* 6:6. The next verse, clearly connected with this one, is not found in our *Ben Sira*, and once again it is closely related to the theme of women and of men's control over them. Interestingly, this one is actually a biblical quotation from the prophetic book of Micah (7:5).

23. From her who lies in your bosom   Guard the doors of your mouth

In Micah this verse is incorporated into a long description of the prophet's time, when all is corrupted and no one can be trusted. Thus, the prophet's advice to avoid revealing one's secrets to one's wife is preceded by similar injunctions not to trust a friend or a great man and followed by an explanation, that *in these hard times* sons betray their fathers and daughters their mothers. Cited here out of context, this verse, when assigned to *Ben Sira*, fits neatly with the theme of preservation of one's privacy recommended in the previous verse and is extended to include one's own wife. Not only should *strangers* not be told of a man's plans, successes and misfortunes—neither should his *wife*. Unlike Micah, where this situation is lamented, here it is applauded. Intimacy between husband and wife is ruled out. This is another case where the Babylonians' expectation that *Ben Sira* will make statements on the danger posed by women to their husbands results in their adducing a verse of the same kind (this time a biblical verse) and assigning it to him.

Finally, the Babylonian rabbis produce another poem of popular wisdom, which *Ben Sira* could theoretically have uttered, and which they assign to him, and yet it is not found in the text of *Ben Sira* that we have.

24. Do not fret about tomorrow's hardships	"For you know not what a day may bring forth" (Proverbs 27:1)
25. For he may be gone tomorrow	And thus frets over a world not his
26. For all the days of a pauper are evil	*Ben Sira* says: His nights as well

Thus ends the longest discussion of the Book of *Ben Sira* in rabbinic literature.

Some statistics are of interest here before we move on. Of the 26 verses in this text, twelve (1, 2, 6, 9, 10, 11, 13, 14, 23, 24, 25, 26) are not authentic, and of these, five (1, 2, 9, 10, 11) do not even fit the general tenor of the Book of *Ben Sira*. None of these latter deals with women. There are thirteen verses on women in this text, namely 50% of the whole. Of the spurious verses, only four (33%) refer to them. Eight out of the thirteen verses that do not directly refer to women (60%) are not in fact from the book of *Ben Sira*. Of the fourteen authentic verses, 9 (64%) are on women. This leads to the conclusion that when verses concerning women are cited from *Ben Sira,* the chances that the sages will get them right are twice as high as on any other topic; and this indicates how closely they read those particular verses.

Finally, it is interesting to note that in three instances the rabbis add (restrictive) references to women where *Ben Sira* refrained from doing so: verses 1 and 2, which are spurious and appear to deal with fish are interpreted by the rabbis as referring to sexual intercourse; verse 19, which does appear in *Ben Sira* but has no relation to women is made in the Babylonian Talmud to refer to adultery; and verse 23, which is a biblical verse not found in *Ben Sira* at all (though certainly fitting his agenda) expresses a piece of popular wisdom about concealing one's secrets from one's wife.

Verses from this text are further quoted elsewhere in the Babylonian Talmud. Verse 26, which, as stated above, is not an authentic *Ben Sira* verse, appears in *bKetubbot* 110b and at *bBava Batra* 146a. However, the longest and most detailed repetition is found at *bYevamot* 63b, in a *aggadic sugya* dealing with marriage and its blessings and curses. *bYevamot* 62b opens the discussion with the famous saying (often cited by Jewish apologists): "Said Rav Hanilai, A man who has no wife is without happiness, without blessing, without goodness ... in the West (i.e. Palestine) they say, without Torah, without a wall ..." and continues with such sayings as "a man should love his wife like his own body and respect her more than his own body ..." However, at the end of page 63a the rabbis quote Ecclesiastes in his famous saying "I found more bitter than death the woman," (7:26) which is followed by a story about the tiresome wife of Rabbi Hiyya. At the top of page 63b the rabbis resort to a discussion of the bad wife. Further down Rava is quoted as stating: "It is a good deed (מצווה) to divorce a bad wife." In light of this advise the rabbis raise the problem of the woman who has an expensive marriage settlement. Divorce from such a woman entails economic hardship for her husband. After a discussion of these difficulties and a long digression, finally the sages refer us to the Book of *Ben Sira* and quote verses 12-20 from *bSanhedrin* 100b, all of them dealing with women (followed by verses 24-25 and then 21-22). Thus the bulk of this material about women is actually quoted with approval twice in the Talmud.

2. Other References

In his book on Ben Sira, Segal divided the quotations from Ben Sira found in the Talmud into three categories: attributed quotations (like the ones discussed thus far); unattributed quotations, namely citation of actual verses from Ben Sira that are not attributed to him by the rabbis; and allusions to ideas in which the Talmud was influenced by Ben Sira although there is neither a direct quotation, nor a reference to the book.[26] This last category I have found not very useful, for like the Babylonian Talmud, Ben Sira is full of popular wisdom and, once a search for general similarities begins, they can be found almost everywhere. I therefore confine myself to the first two categories.

a. Attributed Sayings

Aside from the long discussion in bSanhedrin 100b and quotations of portions of this elsewhere, there are only three other direct citations of *Ben Sira* in the entire Babylonian Talmud. Of these, only one is authentic (*bHagigah* 13a; cf. *Ben Sira* 3:21). The quotation as well as its context are here carried over from the Palestinian Talmud (*yHagigah* 2:1, 77c). This is significant, because it indicates that the Babylonian rabbis did not, in this case, refer to the book itself, but rather to its citation within a received tradition. The two quotations (in the Babylonian and the Palestinian Talmudim) are not very similar to one another and not very close to the original (of which two, slightly different versions exist). The verse in question does not deal with women. Of the other two attributed quotations, one is a complete invention (*bNiddah* 16b) and the other (*bBava Batra* 98b) is somewhat reminiscent of *Ben Sira* 11:8. These two likewise do not deal with women. This pattern, however, repeats the one we saw above, in which inauthentic verses are far more likely to involve subjects other than women. Even if we concede 15 authentic *Ben Sira* traditions in the Talmud, the percentage of verses that show an interest in women is not substantially lowered (60%).

b. Unattributed Sayings

Segal collected five pericopae which are clearly quotations from *Ben Sira* in the Babylonian Talmud, even though they are not treated as such by the rabbis themselves (*bPesahim* 113b, cf. *Ben Sira* 25:2; *bShabbat* 11a, cf. *Ben Sira*

---

[26] Segal, *Ben Sira*, 38; 41-2.

25:13-4; *bEruvin* 54a, cf. *Ben Sira* 14:11-2; *bBava Qama* 92b, cf. *Ben Sira* 13:15; *bBava Metzia* 112a, cf. *Ben Sira* 34:27). Of these five, only one comprises a virulent *Ben Sira* contribution to the misogynist maxims of the Babylonian Talmud:

1. Any disease rather than intestinal disease Any pain rather than pains of the heart
2. Any ache rather than a head-ache   Any wickedness rather than the wickedness of women (*bShabbat* 11a).

The parallel text in *Ben Sira* is 25:13-4. The order is somewhat different but the message is basically the same.

Any blow rather than a blow to the heart   Any wickedness rather than the wickedness of a woman
Any attack rather than an attack of a hater Any vengeance rather than vengeance of an enemy

Clearly the Babylonian rabbis have here altered the suffering *Ben Sira* describes from spiritual to physical. The only verse they have kept intact is the one about the woman. Furthermore, the Talmud has rearranged the order of the verses, so that when viewed as proceeding from bad to worse, the verse about the woman is presented as the culmination. It appears, therefore, that from a varied *Ben Sira* verse, dealing with a complex topic, the rabbis remembered best the part in which he referred to women. However, this emphasis does not seem to be inaccurate, because these verses in *Ben Sira* are incorporated at the beginning of eleven verses devoted to the bad woman, which end with *Ben Sira* accusing women of responsibility for bringing death to the world,[27] and with his advice, cited above, that a bad wife should be divorced.

Although this is the only unattributed text taken from *Ben Sira* which refers to women, the Babylonians, following the same tendency we encountered above, add a reference to women in another unattributed text: *bPesahim* 113b. Verse 25:2 from *Ben Sira* runs as follows:

Three species I despise   And their lives are abominable to me
A proud pauper;   A cheating rich man;   And a lecherous old man

The Babylonian version runs thus:

Four are insufferable to the mind   And these are they:
A proud pauper;   a cheating wealthy man;   A lecherous old man;
And a civil servant (פרנס) who lords it over the public for naught.
Some say: Also he who divorces his wife once and twice and takes her back.

---

27 And here I take exception to J. Levison's views in his "Is Eve to Blame? A Contextual Analysis of Sirach 25:24," *CBQ* 47 (1985) 617-23, that *Ben Sira* was saying less than this.

This text has preserved *Ben Sira*'s version admirably, but the Babylonian rabbis have chosen to embellish it by adding a fourth example to *Ben Sira*'s three. Then they suggest that there is yet a fifth one. I believe this indicates that even while they do not claim *Ben Sira* here as the authority, they are well aware that the last remark, about a man divorcing his wife and taking her back, is not found in any original version of this verse. Nevertheless, they believe it fits an original agenda. I have no doubt that *Ben Sira*, in his pious posture, would approve of this addition, since he could hardly consider a repeated divorce and remarriage as anything but lechery.

Excursus: The Reception of Ben Sira in other Rabbinic Circles

Ben Sira is cited (attributed or unattributed, authentically or spuriously, in Hebrew or in Aramaic) in many other rabbinic compositions, usually assigned to Palestine: the Palestinian Talmud, *Genesis Rabbah, Leviticus Rabbah, Tanhuma, Avot de Rabbi Nathan* etc. It is even cited (unattributed) in the Mishnah (*mAvot* 4:4). None of these, as far as I can tell, is a verse about women. This, in my opinion, points to the very different interest in *Ben Sira* displayed in Babylonia on the one hand, and in Palestine on the other. Why the Palestinians were less interested in Ben Sira's views on women (or why the Babylonians were so much more interested in them) is a difficult question to answer and will not be attempted here.

3. Conclusions

The conclusion that springs from this foregoing survey is that *Ben Sira* was, for the Babylonian rabbis, a very popular book, above all because of what it had to say about women. Since it is well known that *Ben Sira* was anything but an admirer of women, this discovery naturally leads us to deduce that the editors of the Babylonian Talmud shared his opinions. They cherished *Ben Sira* because he condensed in his wisdom rhetoric their own ideas about members of the "other" sex and because they could support their blatantly misogynistic assertions by appealing to a great sage of the distant past. This conclusion, based on facts and figures, is intended neither to laud, nor to disparage the Babylonian rabbis. If scholars of rabbinics ignore my assessment, because of its unfavorable conclusions, or if, for the same reason, "rabbi bashers"[28] us it, my readers will have missed the point of this inquiry, which was not written in order to denounce the Babylonian Talmud. This article is a true historical inquiry which seeks, in the face of post-modern

---

[28] For this expression, see Judith Hauptman, "Maternal Dissent: Women and Procreation in the Mishnah," *Tikkun* 6/6 (1991) 81.

skepticism, to understand what was really happening at that time. In the neglected realm of women studies, many such works have yet to be written. In this discussion of *Ben Sira*, the conclusions are not favorable for the Babylonian rabbis, but I think this is only one side of the coin, and in another chapter I shall show very different results when comparing what the Babylonian rabbis said with what others did about a certain woman.[29] Furthermore, I do not believe that the Babylonian Talmud speaks with one voice; and the following discussion of one final episode will demonstrate that even regarding *Ben Sira* itself, the editors of the Babylonian Talmud were not above laughing at their own prejudices.

4. A Note on Yalta and Ben Sira

In light of what we have seen above, namely that sayings from *Ben Sira* are sometimes cited by the Babylonian Talmud in Aramaic, that verses from different chapters are sometimes combined together, that they are sometimes unattributed, and that *Ben Sira's* interest in women became the major reason for the preservation of that book in that part of the world, one last episode recorded in the Babylonian Talmud (which Segal missed, but which I am sure is a quotation from *Ben Sira*) should not be overlooked in the present study.

In the Babylonian Talmud, a woman named Yalta is mentioned seven times. The following is perhaps the most famous, and certainly the most colorful story about her:

> In a *baraita* it says: Ten things were said about a cup [of wine] that is blessed: ... and he sends it to the members of his household as a gift ... so that his wife [may] be blessed. Ulla visited Rav Nahman. [Ulla] ate and said the blessing over the food. He gave the cup he blessed to Rav Nahman. Rav Nahman said to him: Can you send a cup that was blessed to Yalta? He said to him: The fruit of a woman's womb (literally stomach) is blessed only through the fruit of the man's stomach ... Yalta heard this. She got up in a rage, went to the wine cellar and broke four hundred jars of wine. Said Rav Nahman: Will you send her another cup? [Ulla] sent to her: All this is a goblet of blessing. She sent to him: Rumors (מילי) come from peddlers (מחדורי) and lice (כלמי) from rags (סמרטוטי) (*bBerakhot* 51a-b).

Aside from the opening *baraita*, this entire episode is related in Aramaic. It is a story about a wandering sage from Palestine (Ulla) who used to transmit traditions between Palestine and Babylonia, and his visit to an important sage in Babylonia—Rav Nahman. In the course of this visit Ulla insulted a close woman friend of Rav Nahman—Yalta.[30] This episode has been convincingly discussed by Rachel Adler, and I cannot improve on her description:

---

[29] See chapter 6, below.

[30] That she is not Nahman's wife, I have argued elsewhere, see my *Mine and Yours are Hers: Retrieving Women's History from Rabbinic Literature* (Leiden 1997) 121-9.

Ulla maintains that women should not have direct access to the cup of blessing because the blessing it represents is fertility and ... fertility belongs to men ... In Ulla's biological metaphor, male potency is conflated and fused both with spiritual blessing and with social dominance. By analogy, just as a woman cannot be fertile through any act of her own so too they cannot be blessed through any act of their own, but only through the agency of men acting for and upon them ... Given the existence of other interpretations in texts which include women in the ceremony, we might ask why Ulla is bent upon reducing Yalta to a womb. Perhaps he is compensating for other disparities. Yalta, daughter of the fabulously wealthy leader of the Jews in Babylonia, is Ulla's superior both in affluence and in lineage. The only thing that Ulla has which Yalta does not is the appendage around which he and his sources have been creating a satisfactory structure. Small wonder that Yalta heads for the wine storage to castrate Ulla symbolically four hundred time, shattering the containers and spilling out the sanctifiable liquid, whose blessing, according to Ulla, is a man's prerogative to dispense.

In the final incident, Ulla, urged by Rabbi (*sic*) Nahman, sends Yalta another cup with the message: "All this is a goblet (נבגא) of blessing," which Rashi paraphrases: "All the wine in the pitcher is like a cup of blessing; drink from it." Yalta, daughter of a scholarly family, recognizes this as chicanery. Ulla betrays the lesser holiness of the cup by using a term which is never used in any other context to signify a cup of blessing ... A *navga* of blessing bears the same resemblance to a *kasa* of blessing as "a holly cabinet" does to a "holy ark." It is the same object with the mystery of sanctity removed from it.

Yalta decodes the manipulation, just as she had decoded the original insult, and mocks its perpetrator—Ulla, the traveler between the Palestinian and Babylonian academies, must be telling her a traveler's tale! Flinging his contempt for women back in his face, she declares that it is Ulla himself who is disgusting. His offer of wine from the unsanctified pitcher is like a beggar offering his lice, a worthless and repulsive gift from a giver of nothing to give.[31]

What Adler, like Segal, has failed to notice is that Yalta's last words are not her own, but are in fact rather a complex citation of *Ben Sira*. *Ben Sira* 42:13 runs as follows:

> From a garment (בגד) comes moth (עש, סס) And from a woman the wickedness of women.

Trenchard writes

> Moth is a frequent Old Testament symbol of destructiveness. It retains its negative connotation in our text as well. However, here the emphasis is not on the damage done by moth to the cloth but on its emergence from the cloth. This statement may reflect the ancient idea of spontaneous generation ... *Ben Sira* wishes to suggest that, as moths come from garments, so also wickedness comes from women ... The relationship between women and wickedness or evil is common in *Ben Sira*.[32]

No less interesting is the fact that this verse is followed by probably the most damning statement about women *Ben Sira* ever made "Better is the

---

[31] Rachel Adler, "Feminist Folktales of Justice: Robert Cover as a Resource for the Renewal of Halakhah," *Conservative Judaism* 45/3 (1993) 50-2.

[32] Trenchard, *Ben Sira*, 157.

wickedness of men than the goodness of women." Certainly in the original composition the metaphor of the moth and women was intended to convey a very negative message about women.

In the translation of this saying into Aramaic in the Yalta story, the garments have become rags and the moth, lice. but the metaphor remains the same—in and of themselves clothes have the power to generate creeping and crawling creatures. They look externally attractive but they possess a hidden repulsive quality. In *Ben Sira* this metaphor is applied to women. They, like clothes may look attractive, but they are inherently repulsive. I have no doubt that Yalta, or at any rate the author of this tradition about Yalta, knew the original verse from *Ben Sira* and its allusion to women. This stands to reason from the evidence gathered in the foregoing pages about the attraction *Ben Sira*'s attitude to women had exerted on the Babylonian rabbis. The verses about daughters discussed above (*bSanhedrin* 100b, vs. 3-6), which the Babylonian Talmud cites with approval, come from the same poem as this one in *Ben Sira*. However, talmudic acquaintance with this *Ben Sira* verse is also evident, I believe, from the reversal it has undergone in this story. In the original the metaphor is applied by a man (Ben Sira) to women. In this story, it is applied by a woman (Yalta) to a certain class of men. Just as rags generate lice, so too peddlers disseminate rumors. Obviously Yalta refers here to Ulla's profession—that of a wandering rabbi who transmits traditions between Palestine and Babylonia. His occupation resembles most closely that of a wandering peddler.

However, it seems to me beyond doubt that mention of peddlers contains another subtle reference to *Ben Sira*. As we saw above, *Ben Sira* 11:29 had stated clearly: "Many are the wounds [inflicted] by peddlers." By this he probably referred to the hardships of a small householder, who is hard pressed to distinguish between the truly needy, whom he is obliged to support, and the rogues and cheats who surround him, and whom it is his duty to denounce. Or in the words of Camp: "*Ben Sira*'s advice in 11:29-12:6 to know well the person whom you financially support so that you will do good only to the just and not the sinner ... emerges as a moralizing rationalization for the protection of one's honor along with one's possessions."[33] The Babylonian Talmud, however, has interpreted the "wounds inflicted by peddlers" as specifically referring to their propensity to commit adultery with the mistress of the house. The author of the Yalta story obviously knew this Babylonian interpretation, for here, as in the other half of this verse, a reversal is evident: peddlers are dangerous not because they can corrupt the chastity of the women of the house, but rather because they can destroy their good name and reputation. They bear tales to the master of the house and influence adversely his opinion of his female relatives.

---

[33] Camp, "Patriarchy," 17.

The story of Yalta is obviously told from her perspective. Although her capricious action in breaking the wine jars is not complimentary, the fact that the author gives her the last word indicates that s/he wanted the reader to identify with the insulted woman. The story, therefore, bears testimony to a certain ambivalence in the Talmud about the teachings of *Ben Sira* on women. On the one hand, these sayings were recited and transmitted more than any other part of his wisdom, but on the other hand they must have engendered some uneasiness, as is suggested by Yalta's enigmatic answer to Ulla, which turns *Ben Sira*'s wisdom on women on its head.

Chapter Six

"Beruriah Has Spoken Well"
(*tKelim Bava Metzia* 1:6)
The Historical Beruriah and Her Transformation in the Rabbinic Corpora

No little courage is required in order to engage in a new study of the Beruriah traditions, in view of the fact that much has been written in recent years about her by such prominent talmudists as David Goodblatt and Daniel Boyarin,[1] and such important Jewish feminists as Rachel Adler.[2] Beruriah, the one woman in rabbinic literature who has an opinion on anything, who argues with men (including her husband) as though they were her equals, who teaches others how to read scripture and how to interpret rabbinic dicta—Beruriah is an anomaly, and a welcome one for feminists. She can be hailed as proof of what women could and should do in Judaism. She could be mourned as an example of women's marginality and the limitations imposed on even the most talented among them. All this has been done before. Was there really a Beruriah, however, or was she no more than a metaphor? And if her story is only a parable, how and why did such a parable arise? I venture into this field only because I believe that the question of the historical figure of Beruriah and the way she influenced her myth has been totally ignored and it seems something can be added to the ongoing debate by exposing it and by proceeding to chart Beruriah's development through the various realms of rabbinic literature.

At the risk of being charged with blasphemy, I would suggest that the quest for the historical Beruriah resembles in some respects the quest for the historical Jesus. All we know about her comes from sources dated to some time after her death, and although they all claim to represent the same strain of Judaism—rabbinic Judaism—Beruriah is represented very differently in the older tannaitic Palestinian layer, in the later amoraic Babylonian layer and elsewhere. This creates a situation where the historian is inclined either to

---

[1] D. Goodblatt, "The Beruriah Traditions," *JJS* 26 (1975) 68-85; D. Boyarin, *Carnal Israel: Reading Sex in Talmudic Culture* (Berkeley 1993) 167-96.

[2] Rachel Adler, "The Virgin in the Brothel and Other Anomalies: Character and Context in the Legend of Beruriah," *Tikkun* 3/6 (1988) 28-32; 102-5; and see also my "The Quest for the Historical Beruriah, Rachel and Imma Shalom," *AJS Review* 22 (1997) 1-17.

believe everything,[3] or to doubt everything.[4] Following the fine methodologies developed by various scholars of synoptic traditions in both Judaism and Christianity, however, permits a more nuanced view of the sources.

This study is divided into two parts. In the first I attempt to show what we can know about the historical Beruriah. The second is a journey in which we accompany the historical figure into the realm of fantasy and myth and chart her transformation in the process. In sum, this is a study of rabbinic sources and their attitude to women and gender.

1. Beruriah of the Tosefta

The investigation of Beruriah should begin with the evidence found in the earlier tannaitic strata. Beruriah is mentioned by name only once in the entire tannaitic corpus—in the Tosefta. The reference to her runs as follows:

> A Claustra (קלוסטרה i.e. door hinge), Rabbi Tarfon declares unclean and the sages declare clean. And Beruriah says: One may let it fall from the doorway and may hang it on the next [doorway] on Sabbath. These things were said before Rabbi Joshua (or alternatively: hangs it on the next [doorway]. On Sabbath these things were said before Rabbi Joshua— שומטה מן הפתח [פסח] זה ותולה בחברתו בשבת נאמרו דברים לפני ר׳ יהושע). He said: Beruriah has spoken well (*tKelim Bava Metzia* 1:6).

This tradition does not particularly stand out in the Tosefta. It is preceded and followed by scores of traditions formulated in more or less the same way, namely, a sage, mentioned by name, utters a statement about the correct procedure or ruling to the best of his knowledge. The only anomaly in this tradition is the gender of the transmitter. This, and another tradition also in the Tosefta (assigned to the daughter of Hananiah ben Tardion) are the only two in the entire tannaitic legal corpus said to have been transmitted by women. A look at this second tradition is certainly instructive in this context:

> From what time does an oven become unclean? ... Rabban Shimeon ben Gamaliel said in the name of Rabbi Shila: If it was plastered in a state of purity, and became unclean, from when is it pure? Said Rabbi Halafta of Kefar Hananiah: I asked Shimeon ben Hananiah who asked Rabbi Hananiah ben Tardion's son and he said: From the time when it is removed from its place. And his daughter said: From the time when it is disassembled. When these things were said before Rabbi Judah ben Bava he said: His daughter has spoken better than his son (*tKelim Bava Qama* 4:17).

The two traditions look strikingly similar. They both deal with the ritual status of objects (a door hinge, an oven) under changing circumstances. The traditions are found in the Division of Purities, the most complex and least

---

[3] See e.g. L. Swidler, "Beruriah: Her Word Became Law," *Lilith* 3 (1977) 9-12.

[4] Goodblatt, "Beruriah."

studied of the six divisions according to which rabbinic literature is organized. The tradition about the correct procedure regarding the door hinge is assigned by the Tosefta to Beruriah. Her explanation (whatever it means[5]) is then lauded by an important sage—Rabbi Joshua, who is, by all accounts, none other than Rabbi Joshua ben Hananiah, the renowned disciple of Rabban Yohanan ben Zakkai. The tradition about the correct procedure regarding the oven is assigned to the daughter of Rabbi Hananiah ben Tardion. Her explanation is then also lauded by an important sage—Rabbi Judah ben Bava, one of the famous martyrs of the Bar Kokhba revolt. In this last respect, the two traditions resemble one another, but do not resemble most other *halakhic* traditions, perhaps suggesting that the gender of the transmitters made it necessary to specify that a higher authority sanctioned them.

In light of later speculations in rabbinic literature, specifically identifying Beruriah with the daughter of Rabbi Hananiah ben Tardion, it is relevant to inquire whether these two traditions indicate that the two women featuring in them are one and the same. I believe not, and not merely because the sources do not identify them explicitly. There are also traditional rabbinic dating techniques to be taken into account. Since we know nothing from tannaitic literature about the identity of Beruriah, one must investigate the persons mentioned in proximity to her. Traditionally, much of the historical information gleaned from rabbinic literature has been procured by this method. In recent years this relative periodization has come under sharp criticism. Scholars claim that names may have been fabricated, invented, misspelled or misquoted.[6] In other words, the most skeptical scholars deny the validity of this system. However, in my opinion, there is evidence enough in rabbinic literature to prove that the rabbis themselves abided by it, and the choice of names appended to traditions, even when fictitious, was intended, *inter alia* to date them. I will not inquire here whether the assigned traditions are authentic, but will simply demonstrate that a comparison of manuscripts indicates that developments in the figure of Beruriah in later rabbinic corpora, caused problems for the rabbis because of the names previous generations had tagged to this tradition, and so they attempted to alter them. Such evidence lends greater credence to the original names (and thus the original dating) suggested by the rabbis.

The daughter of Hananiah ben Tardion is easy to date. Her father is mentioned in an early tannaitic midrash as a martyr in the aftermath of the Bar Kokhba revolt (*Sifre Deuteronomy* 307). She herself is probably mentioned in

---

[5] For a fine explanation of this tradition see now Judith Z. Abrams, *The Women of the Talmud* (Northvale NJ 1995) 2-6.

[6] J. Neusner, *In Search of Talmudic Biography: The Problem of the Attributed Saying* (*Brown Judaic Studies* 70; Chico CA 1984). Even Neusner concedes that legal attributed sayings have more to recommend themselves: "The legal sayings do seem to wish to preserve a uniformity of viewpoint or principle, so far as can be demonstrated" *ibid.*, 133.

the same tradition, although not as a *halakhic* expert but rather as an expert in Scripture. The daughter of Hananiah ben Tardion was, therefore, alive ca. 135 CE. Rabbi Judah ben Bava, who authenticates her tradition, was also a Bar Kokhba martyr (*bSanhedrin* 14a; cf. *tSotah* 13:4). The daughter could have transmitted her tradition several years before the Bar Kokhba revolt, namely the late 120s / early 130s. The case of Beruriah is very different. The authority who endorses her ruling is Rabbi Joshua ben Hananiah, who was already an adult in 70 CE, since he is associated with Rabban Yohanan ben Zakkai in the earliest traditions (and in later ones is identified as one of the students who escaped from Jerusalem with him),[7] and also preserves some traditions from the time of the Temple itself. Exactly when he died is not altogether clear, but he was certainly no longer alive when the Bar Kokhba revolt broke out (although traditions maintain that he was still around when Hadrian ascended the throne in 117 CE, 47 years after the destruction of the Temple—*Genesis Rabbah* 10:3; 13:9; 28:3; 78:1). In order for Beruriah to have gained Joshua's good opinion, she would have had to deliver her ruling at least two decades earlier than the time when Rabbi Hananiah ben Tardion's daughter gave hers. While this is not chronologically impossible for the same woman, it would suggest that Beruriah was no longer a young woman during the Bar Kokhba revolt; but this contradicts other traditions about her stemming from the same circles that suggest the identification of the two, namely the Babylonian Talmud. Since the readers of the sources themselves realized this chronological discrepancy, one Tosefta manuscript has Rabbi Judah authorizing Beruriah's tradition.[8] However, as we shall see presently, the reading "Joshua" is older and can hardly be contested. I therefore conclude that a neutral reading of the Tosefta text would not lead to an identification of the two women.

Let us now return to the Beruriah tradition in the Tosefta. Is it a reliable historical record? I believe the answer to this question is in the affirmative. It is almost impossible to deny its authenticity because (a) it is not a strictly literary composition and (b) it deals with issues that are of little interest to anybody, even to Jews. The main question to pose is, therefore, who would be interested in fabricating such a tradition in the first place? Even more importantly, however, if this tradition does not record a historical occurrence but an imaginary one, who would invent a woman tradent? On the strength of these arguments, I think we may conclude that the tradition is authentic, and that there was, once upon a time, a woman by the name of Beruriah who found herself, as the result of unknown social circumstances, in a position to

---

[7] On these traditions, see primarily G. Alon, *Jews and Judaism in the Classical World* (translation I. Abrahams; Jerusalem 1977) 269-313.

[8] The Erfurt Ms. on which Zuckermandel's Tosefta edition is based, but see his *apparatus criticus* for the Vienna Ms. p. 579. On the primacy of the Vienna Ms. here as elsewhere, see S. Lieberman, *Tosefeth Rishonim* 3 (Jerusalem 1939) 35 [Hebrew].

instruct the sages about a matter of purity. Her ruling was duly recorded. This, I believe, is where history ends. The rest is speculation. Nevertheless, some further observations may be added here before taking on the question, how others received this tradition.

In the first place, it is of no small consequence that a woman, even if we know nothing else about her, achieved the position of influence described above. For a woman to know better than a man the *minutiae* of ritual purity, she would have had to be learned indeed.[9] She could, perhaps study in the kitchen while making the fire, cooking, washing the dishes and drawing water, but this is hardly likely, and if it were so, could hardly explain how the tradition came to be incorporated into the Tosefta. For this to happen, Beruriah would have had to pronounce her learned conclusion from the benches of the study house. And if she did, was she the only woman there? Or perhaps she (and the daughter of Hananiah ben Tardion) were the only one(s) recorded? Were there any study-houses where women could be found? Perhaps that of Rabbi Joshua ben Hananiah? Did they study with the men or did they study separately? And if they studied separately, who would have recorded this Beruriah tradition? Obviously all this is beyond historical fact and deep in the realm of speculation, but in light of the tradition itself, this speculation is not so farfetched.

With this in mind we may move on to inquire how this unusual phenomenon of women transmitting halakhah was tackled by later rabbinic generations.

2. Beruriah of the Mishnah

Beruriah is not mentioned by name in the Mishnah, but this is no accident of transmission. We know this, because Beruriah's ruling, the one found in the Tosefta, is indeed found in the Mishnah:

> A claustra is unclean ... And the claustra—Rabbi Joshua says: One lets it fall from the doorway and hangs it on the next on Sabbath. Rabbi Tarfon says: It is like all other vessels and may be removed in the courtyard (*mKelim* 11:4).

Tractate *Kelim* in the Mishnah is about a third of the size of its counterpart in the Tosefta. This is not surprising, because the Tosefta includes much material which was excluded by the editors of the Mishnah.[10] Nevertheless, Beruriah's

---

[9] Contra Goodblatt, "Beruriah," 83.

[10] This is not the place to discuss the primacy of the Mishnah or Tosefta. I have discussed the issue at some length in my book, *Mine and Yours are Hers: Retrieving Jewish Women's History from Rabbinic Literature* (Leiden 1997) 55-7 as regards issues pertaining to women. My conclusion there, that the Tosefta holds much unedited material rejected by the Mishnah,

insignificant ruling was deemed important enough to include in the reduced but more highly valued canon of the Mishnah. However, while her ruling was deemed worthy, Beruriah herself was not. Rabbi Joshua, who in the Tosefta does no more than praise the talented woman for her eloquence, is now assigned authorship of the ruling. The primacy of the Mishnah version over the Tosefta in this instance is ruled out by the principle of *lectio difficilior* in its most blatant manifestation. It is easy to explain how the ruling of the insignificant, almost anonymous Beruriah of the Tosefta would be assigned to the important sage Rabbi Joshua. A reverse procedure would be unheard of. Therefore, unless the tradition was indeed genuinely Beruriah's, it is practically impossible to explain how or why anyone would (falsely) assign it to her.

The Mishnah's reaction to Beruriah's ruling can, therefore, be considered as the first instance in which editors of rabbinic literature had to contend with the rather surprising and very uncomfortable fact, that a woman's words (whatever their real, as opposed to ideal position in rabbinic circles was) had actually invaded the sacred male space of Torah. When the editors of the Mishnah had to decide what to do with Beruriah's ruling, they decided it was too valuable to lose, but at the same time the finished product of the editorial activity—the Mishnah—was designed to uphold the ideal world of learning, in which women had no place. Beruriah was, therefore, edited out.

Excursus: Beruriah of the Palestinian Talmud

The editors of the Palestinian Talmud, who flourished some 200 years after those of the Mishnah, saw no reason to improve on their predecessors' handling of the Beruriah tradition. Since Beruriah was edited out of the Mishnah, there is absolutely no mention of her in the entire extant Palestinian Talmud. Nevertheless, it is important to emphasize that no Palestinian Talmud for most of the Division of Purities has been preserved. This deprives us of a talmudic discussion of the relevant passage in tractate *Kelim*. If there had once existed a talmudic discussion of that tractate, we might expect to find Beruriah mentioned there. However, it is doubtful whether there ever was a Palestinian Talmud for these tractates,[11] and in the present state of our knowledge, any other suggestion would be mere speculation.

---

holds here too. And see also bibliography for Judith Hauptman's discussion of this topic, above, chapter 1, n. 71.

[11] See L. I. Rabinowitz, "Talmud, Jerusalem," in *Encyclopedia Judaica* 15 (Jerusalem 1971) 774.

3. *Beruriah of the Babylonian Talmud*

The Babylonian Talmud likewise lacks a commentary on the mishnaic Division of Purities; and in light of the negligible historical evidence on Beruriah found in the Tosefta and the attempt of the mishnaic editors to suppress even this limited information, the emergence of Beruriah as the ideal rabbinic scholar in the Babylonian Talmud is indeed striking. She is mentioned in the Babylonian Talmud in four separate places, of which two are collections of her sayings (*bBerakhot* 10a; *bEruvin* 53b-54a), the third is a proclamation of her great scholarship (*bPesahim* 62b) and the fourth is a legend, replete with folkoristic motifs.

a. *bPesahim 62b*

In *bPesahim* Beruriah is hailed as a great sage:

> Rabbi Yohanan ... said: Beruriah the daughter of Hananiah ben Tardion and the wife of Rabbi Meir learnt three hundred traditions in a day from three hundred masters ... (*bPesahim* 62b)

This proclamation of Rabbi Yohanan is made in response to a demand by a student to be taught the *Book of Genealogies* in an extremely short time. Rabbi Yohanan objects to teaching him the book, and when indicating to him the futility of his endeavor, Rabbi Yohanan mentions as an ultimate example of serious scholarship the woman Beruriah. Why the Babylonians chose to introduce Beruriah here rather than any number of male sages who frequented the academies during her time, earlier or later, remains in the present context obscure. That it is indeed a Babylonian choice rather than an authentic, ancient tradition can be deduced from the fact that a parallel Palestinian text tells the same story, of the same student and Rabbi Yohanan, but fails to mention Beruriah (*yPesahim* 5:3, 32a-b).[12]

How, then, did such a Beruriah come into existence? One may suggest that the Beruriah of the Babylonian Talmud is constructed out of ancient, authentic traditions which the sages of Babylonia received orally and incorporated into their writings. Therefore, in two of the Beruriah traditions (the one cited above and also *bAvodah Zarah* 18b) Beruriah is identified with the (aforementioned) daughter of Rabbi Hananiah ben Tardion and also supplied with a husband—Rabbi Meir. However, is this a received, authentic tradition? Goodblatt has, in my opinion, proved sufficiently[13] that the family connections mentioned could hardly be based on authentic data since they contradict other information, available elsewhere; and in light of the

---

[12] I am well aware, of course, that the other possibility, namely that Beruriah's name was erased in the Palestinian version, is also possible, and is, in light of what has been demonstrated with regard to the Mishnah, actually rather probable.

[13] "Beruriah," 68-77.

Babylonian Talmud's flair for creating fictitious family relations for its heroes,[14] this relationship should be considered as no more than a literary invention. The conflation was, apparently, necessary for the Babylonian editors so as to reduce to the bare minimum the number of learned women mentioned in rabbinic literature. It seems to me, therefore, that *bPesahim* 62b thereby demonstrates the extent to which the Beruriah tradition influenced and inspired the authors of the Babylonian Talmud.

b. bBerakhot 10a

A stronger indication that the Babylonian Talmud did not preserve authentic Beruriah traditions, but rather created them as it went along is found in this passage in *bBerakhot*:

> Certain bandits who were in the neighborhood of Rabbi Meir troubled him much. He prayed that they might die. Beruriah his wife said to him: Do you base your prayer on what is written: "Let sins cease" (Psalms 104:35)? Is "sinners" written? "Sins" is written. Furthermore, cast your eyes to the end of the verse "and they are wicked no more". Since sins will cease, they will be wicked no more. He prayed for them and they repented (*bBerakhot* 10a).

In this tradition, Beruriah's proficiency in scripture and deep understanding of it allows her to instruct her husband, Rabbi Meir, one of the greatest scholars of the day, and prevent him from erring. This tradition certainly asserts that Beruriah is highly educated, tactful and compassionate. She comes out of this tradition as a winner in a contest that she was probably disqualified from entering in the first place. Like the previous tradition, this one is also all praise. No negative undertones can be detected, and indeed it seems a mystery why Rabbi Meir's wife (and not his teacher, his colleague, or even his student) is the one who corrects him. This mystery is, to a certain extent, resolved when compared with another tradition preserved in the Babylonian Talmud.

> [Abba Hilqiah said]: There were once bandits in our neighborhood. I prayed that they might die, but [my wife] prayed that they would repent (*bTaanit* 23b).

This is a tradition about a very different sort of couple—the miracle rain-maker Abba Hilqiah and his pious but nameless wife. The sages approach Abba Hilqiah in the hope that he may bring rain to counter a drought. The sage and his wife go up to his roof and pray. When rain indeed comes, it appears from the wife's quarter. The story Abba Hilqiah relates, and which is quoted above, is a response to the question why it was the wife rather

---

[14] S. Safrai, "The Tales of the Sages in Palestinian Tradition and the Babylonian Talmud," in J. Heinemann and D. Noy (eds.), *Studies in Aggadah and Folk-Literature* (*Scripta Hierosolymitana* 22; Jerusalem 1971) 229-32.

than he who had brought the rain. It therefore seems clear that the rabbis of Babylonia retained in their repository of tales a story of a wife who bested her husband on the question of how to deal with criminal neighbors. The two reworkings of the story presented above fulfill two different functions—the latter is the account of simple pious people who tackle criminal neighbors, the former of a couple of sages approaching the same problem. The story, however, seems older than the two reworkings, for had it been an authentic, ancient Beruriah tradition, it is unlikely that it would have been reworked for the edification of Abba Hilqiah's wife.[15] This, in my opinion, proves satisfactorily that the Beruriah traditions of the Babylonian Talmud are literary creations formulated in Babylonian circles in order to fit their agenda. What was their agenda? Although Beruriah appears in only a few places in the Babylonian Talmud, her presence there is incomparably more powerful than the harmless tradition preserved in her name in the Tosefta. Next to the traditions cited above, the best example of this is the mention of Beruriah in tractate *Eruvin* of the Talmud. This tradition will now be discussed within the context of its *sugya*.

c. bEruvin 53a-54a

Talmudists are forever warning us not to isolate talmudic traditions from their wider context. Although the cynical conversation between Rabbi Yose the Galilean and Beruriah, in which the latter beats and humiliates the former has been discussed by all who have deemed the Beruriah traditions worth investigating, the wider context of this specific tradition has been practically ignored. It seems to me, however, that a close reading of the entire *sugya* has much to commend itself to those who wish to understand the Beruriah traditions within the framework of the Babylonian houses of study.

The *gemara* on page 53a, which opens the commentary on chapter 4 of the mishnaic tractate *Eruvin,* consists of a long *aggadic sugya* designed to convey to the reader the importance and bounty of Torah study. It begins with a dispute between the two great Yeshiva heads Rav and Shmuel on the spelling of the mishnaic word *me'abrin* and the implications of spelling it with an *Ayin* (ע) or an *Aleph* (א). This is followed by three other disagreements between Rav and Shmuel, but the dispute on the spelling of the word is taken up again with a comment by Rabbi Yohanan about his days of study with Rabbi Oshaya, which suggests that the use of *Aleph* represents the Palestinian spelling, perhaps because in Palestine the gutturals had fallen into disuse in this period, as is evident from elsewhere.[16] This statement is followed by a number of stories of various rabbis about their years of study with various

---

[15] And on this see further in my *Mine and Yours*, 288.

[16] For a thorough study of the topic, including this text, see Y. Kutscher, *Hebrew and Aramaic Studies* (Jerusalem 1977) 209-26 [Hebrew].

sages, but the topic of the pronunciation of Hebrew and Aramaic words in Palestine is resumed at the bottom of page 53a. We are informed that the Judaeans observed correct pronunciation and thereby succeeded in preserving their Torah, while in Galilee the correct pronunciation was neglected and so their Torah was lost. The statement is followed by a number of examples. The first tells of the perfect, almost poetic metaphors of a Judaean. This is followed by a story about a Galilean who asks for something, but his pronunciation is so vague that he is addressed by his fellows with the derogatory appellation "Galilean Fool," and he is then shown how the word he had used and the way he had uttered it could be understood as four different things. This story is then followed by episodes about two women (who, incidentally are not specifically identified as Galilean). In both episodes the pronunciation of these women is so garbled that, despite their innocent intentions, the first insults her neighbor and the second a judge. All three episodes are extremely difficult to translate into English, because they deal specifically with ancient Hebrew and Aramaic dialects and the confusion they caused even among the very people who spoke them.

Gender issues underlie these two last stories. It is subtly suggested that Galilean women's speech, more than that of Galilean men, is garbled and is thus a legitimate topic for ridicule. Now however the *sugya* takes a surprising turn, for the following stories do not continue to dwell on the issue of Galilean pronunciation, but rather seek to right the wronged women, who may have been insulted by the two jokes just cracked at their expense. Surprisingly, the next story again involves a woman, but not a freeborn, Jewish woman (albeit a foolish and inarticulate Galilean). Rather, it is about a (non-Jewish?) slave woman (albeit in the service of Rabbi Judah the Patriarch) who engages in wisdom language:

> When Rabbi's maidservant engaged in wisdom speech (לשון חכמה), she would say: The ladle has hit the jar (i.e. there is no more wine), let the eagles soar to their nests (i.e. let the students return home). And when she wanted them to stay she would say to them: The lid shall be removed from her friend (i.e. let us open another jar) and the ladle shall float in the jar like a ship on the sea (*bEruvin* 53b).

The introduction of Rabbi's maidservant into the debate is inexplicable in any other light except the one suggested above. She speaks in double meanings intentionally, but is praised rather than derided for it. It indicates that women are not just inarticulate fools, who end up saying the opposite of what they mean, but can also be wise and say one thing as an intentional metaphor for something else. The class of the speaker also indicates that not only is gender not the decisive factor in of a person's capacity for wisdom, neither is social status. Rabbi's maidservant is one of three individuals who engage in "wisdom speech." The other two are the rather obscure Rabbi Yose ben Asyan on the one hand and the very well known Rabbi Abbahu on the other.

Both of these rabbis also use metaphors and double meanings in their speech. Rabbi's maidservant is, therefore, presented in very good company. Her ability to use "wisdom speech" matches that of rabbis.

Reinforcing this decidedly favorable presentation of Rabbi's maidservant is the next episode in the *sugya*, which says loud and clear that gender and age are no impediments to acquiring wisdom:

> Said Rabbi Joshua: Never have I been defeated except by a woman, a boy and a girl. By a woman, how? One time I was residing with a certain innkeeper and she cooked me some beans. On the first day I ate them and left nothing. On the second day I left nothing. On the third day she over-salted them. Having tasted them, I withdrew my hand from them. Said the woman to me: Rabbi, why are you not eating? I said: I have already eaten earlier. She said: [If that were so], you should not have eaten bread either. She said to me: My master, is it possible that you did not leave a *peah* (i.e. leftover for charity) in the first meals, for the sages said: A *peah* must not be left in a pot [and you have left a *peah* here because they said]: a *peah* must be left on a plate? (*bEruvin* 53b).

This tradition tells how, as a result of an embarrassing situation, in which a sage does not want to insult a woman about her poor cooking, he comes out bested by her in matters of Jewish law. The woman, it turns out, can cite to the sage a rabbinic law he does not know (and neither do we from any other rabbinic source). A woman can, therefore, like any male sage, put a halakhic spin on a normal human encounter. The tradition then goes on:

> By a girl, how? Once I was walking on my way and I saw a path traversing a field and I took it. One girl said to me: Is this not a field? I said to her: Is this not a trodden path? Said she to me: Bandits like you trod it.

This case does not show that a girl has greater wisdom in the law than a sage. It shows only how in her commonsense (and in her sense of decency) the girl overcame the sage's argument. The tradition about the girl is supplemented by the tradition about the boy:

> A boy, how? Once I was walking on my way and I saw a boy sitting at a crossroads. I asked him: By which road shall we go to that city? He said to me: This one is short and long and this one is long and short. And I took the short and long one. When I came to the city I discovered it was surrounded by gardens and orchards and I went back. I said to him: My son, did you not say that it is short? He said to me: But did I not say that it was long. I kissed him on his head and said to him: Blessed are you O Israel, that all of you are very wise, from the greatest to the least.

This tradition also refers to a road. The boy also bests Rabbi Joshua in matters of common sense rather than law. Even though the boy's behavior could be interpreted as disrespect for the sage, Rabbi Joshua is impressed by the wit of the boy rather than his youthful prank. Young boys, young girls and women, all of them disdained by society as greatly inferior in wisdom to sages, are singled out by this tradition as wise. However, the tradition about the boy ends somewhat differently. The sage kisses the boy on his head and blesses him. Naturally, had he reacted in a similar fashion to the wisdom of the woman or the girl, his action would have been interpreted as indecent, even lecherous. Yet, not just the physical gesture (which, if present, would have been interpreted as inappropriate) is missing, but also the blessing. This would perhaps suggest that while wise boys have a future in the world of the sages it is not so with wise women and girls.

Rabbi Joshua's tradition is followed by two traditions about Beruriah:

> Rabbi Yose the Galilean was walking along the road. He met Beruriah. He said to her: By which road shall we go to Lod (באיזה דרך נלך ללוד)? She said to him: Galilean fool! Did not the Sages say: "Do not talk too much with a woman" (*mAvot* 1:5)? You should have said: By which to Lod (באיזה ללוד)? (*bEruvin* 53a).

The immediate reason for the insertion of this tradition at this point is the almost identical manner in which Rabbi Yose the Galilean addresses Beruriah and Rabbi Joshua addresses the boy in the preceding tradition: "By which way shall we go to ..." However, aside from this formal similarity, there is at least one other intertext that connects this tradition to the previous ones—namely the negative appellation Beruriah reserves for Rabbi Yose: "Galilean fool." The reader will recall that at the beginning of this chain of traditions this very same title was applied to a person from Galilee who had mispronounced his words. It had than been followed by similar and even more derisive stories about two (apparently Galilean) women. However, in light of the trend in this *sugya* to counter a negative approach to women as sillier than men, the Beruriah tradition here contains in a few words this very powerful message. Rachel Adler writes:

> The story is laden with ironies. Rabbi Yose, fearing that a superfluous pleasantry will open him to lust, rudely asks directions without a greeting. Beruriah obligingly demonstrates how he might have made the conversation briefer yet, thereby prolonging their contact. Not only must Rabbi Yose converse with a woman, he must be rebuked by her, not only rebuked but taught Torah, and not just any Torah but precisely the dictum he had been trying so zealously to observe."[17]

However, recording this story here, together with the others we have seen, renders redundant the contents of the dictum about which Beruriah instructs Rabbi Yose. The *sugya* suggests that it is in fact very fruitful to converse with a wise woman. At this point in the *sugya* the editors have made their point—wisdom is an inborn rather than an acquired trait. Women, children, slaves, even female slaves may posses it from birth. Dicta claiming the opposite are ridiculous. Beruriah, the great female sage, is introduced in order to demonstrate this claim at its most blatant extreme. Other women's wisdom—

---

[17] Adler, "Virgin in the Brothel," 30.

Rabbi's maidservant, the innkeeper and the girl—had been measured against that of men who are reputed as great sages. Beruriah's is measured against the stupidity of one of similar renown, rendering her victory that much greater. The message the Babylonian Talmud has been formulating in these lines runs, as Boyarin would have it, contrary to the hegemonic rabbinic discourse, and reveals a "sub-version."[18] Naturally it is safely tucked away between heaps of other traditions, which shield it from the undiscerning reader.

In the final analysis, however, the ridicule of certain groups, of certain localities, or of a certain gender, which opened the *sugya*, but which was then refuted, wins the day. The revolutionary message of equality in face of wisdom, which has developed to a crescendo now starts to recede to the more conventional view espoused in rabbinic circles, namely that wisdom manifests itself in Torah study in the study house, being, therefore, reserved for freeborn Jewish males. The next tradition featuring Beruriah leads to that path:

> Beruriah met a student who was studying silently. She kicked him and said to him: Is it not written: "ordered in all things and secure" (2 Samuel 23:5)? If [the Torah] is ordered in all of your two hundred and forty eight limbs it is secured; but if it is not, it is not secured (*bEruvin* 53b-54a).

The Beruriah of the previous tradition is herself its subject. She is a female sage whose mere presence is designed to counter the rabbinic dictum she is teaching. In this tradition, although Beruriah is still present, the subject of learning becomes the *leitmotiv* of the following anecdotes, namely the necessity to exert oneself in the study of Torah. Beruriah here is represented as a rather impatient master who teaches her students by violent means. On the one hand, it presents Beruriah, a woman, uncritically as a teacher in the study house just like any other teacher (and somewhat like her neutral portrayal in the Tosefta as stating a halakhic ruling); on the other hand, gender no longer is an issue. The principle Beruriah teaches her student becomes paramount. The *sugya* moves on to discuss various forms of Torah study. The next tradition tells of a student of Rabbi Eliezer who also learnt in silence to his detriment. Then another tradition tells of another student of Rabbi Eliezer who erred in another way, and is followed by several about rabbis and their students. These stories are followed by a number of rabbinic homilies about the desirability of Torah study, and, as in the Beruriah tradition, about how to behave in order to preserve one's Torah. All these homilies, like Beruriah's lesson to the silent student, are embroidered with biblical verses. These sayings and anecdotes continue into page 54b. Further on, the subject changes slightly, and is now concerned with the proper process of Torah transmission. An example is brought from the case of Moses, Aaron, Aaron's sons and the elders of Israel, in order to demonstrate the right procedure. The Torah is

---

[18] *Carnal Israel*, 241-2.

transmitted from males to males. Naturally no women are mentioned. The very last part of the *sugya* discusses the verse "It is not in heaven" (Deuteronomy 30:12) as referring to the Torah. This verse could have been interpreted to mean that the Torah is within reach of all, as is in fact implied half way through the *sugya*. However, this line of interpretation is not taken up:

> Rabbi Yohanan said: "It is not in heaven"—It is not found in rowdy people, "Neither is it beyond the sea" —nor among merchants and peddlers (*bEruvin* 55a).

The last tradition in the *sugya*, therefore, limits significantly the categories of persons who acquire Torah. The same Rabbi Yohanan who (in another tradition cited above) praised Beruriah for her prolific knowledge of Torah, states here that Torah is not to be found in the uncultured, in merchants and in peddlers. This ending is quite surprising, in light of the general trend of the *sugya*, which seems to suggest that true sagacity is dictated by neither gender nor age nor social status. The revolutionary impulse, that had raised its head in the center of the talmudic passage discussed here, has by now been tamed. After reading two densely packed talmudic pages full of traditions about the desirability of Torah study, all transmitted by men, and about teachers and students, all of them male, the reader may by now have forgotten one of the basic claims of this *sugya* about the inclusiveness of wisdom. Rabbi Yohanan may be allowed to utter a bit of conventional wisdom about the exclusivity of Torah study.

So what has the use of Beruriah achieved? The entire *sugya*, aside from its obvious preoccupation with Torah study, succeeds in conveying an unconventional message about the equality of men and women in the division of wisdom. Many anecdotes about women who fulfill this expectation could have been presented but no collection is complete in the view of the Babylonians without incorporating into it Beruriah, who in their eyes succeeded in achieving that ultimate goal. Here, even more than in the traditions discussed above, Beruriah emerges as the ultimate sage.

The three Babylonian Beruriah traditions discussed above leave one with an inescapable feeling that the Babylonians created a repository of traditions about Beruriah, presenting her in this light, namely as a great sage. The sage Beruriah was not treated with scorn—on the contrary, she was sympathetically and condescendingly received. The Babylonian rabbis drew on the Beruriah traditions occasionally when their contents fit into the *sugya* they were editing, and when they wanted to make an unexpected remark about gender. Both Boyarin and Goodblatt had pondered over this unique phenomenon, and both attempted to explain it against the historical background of Jewish Babylonia, which produced the Babylonian Talmud. However, interestingly, while Goodblatt concluded that "Beruriah was an exception to the rule regarding the degree of education of women in rabbinic society .... the background of this exception is Sassanian Babylonia, not Roman Palestine,"[19] Boyarin views the texts as saying quite the opposite: "in both (Babylonia and Palestine) she is atypical, but only in one (Babylonia) she becomes a scandal."[20] I think, however, that from the evidence at hand no such conclusions are warranted. The Beruriah of the Mishnah and the Beruriah of the Babylonian Talmud simply reflect two different reactions to the one piece of historical information about Beruriah, namely the tradition in her name in the Tosefta. For both she is an anomaly, and both overreact to the (historical) Beruriah of the Tosefta. However, while the mishnaic rabbis preferred to eliminate all memory of her, the Babylonians chose, conversely to blow up her scholarship out of all proportion, making Beruriah into a grotesque fantasy. This too would ensure that Beruriah the scholar would remain an anomaly.

4. Rashi's Beruriah

Many centuries after the editing of the Babylonian Talmud, in quite a different locale (medieval France), the great Jewish scholar Rashi wrote a commentary on the Babylonian Talmud. At one point, responding to an obscure reference to "the Beruriah Incident," Rashi inserted the following tale:

> Once [Beruriah] mocked the sages saying, "Women are light-headed". [Rabbi Meir] said to her: By your life, you will eventually affirm their words. He instructed one of his disciples to seduce her. [The student] urged her for many days until she consented. When the matter became known to her she hanged herself, and Rabbi Meir fled in disgrace (Rashi to *bAvodah Zarah* 18b).[21]

Contrary to Rachel Adler and Daniel Boyarin, I see no reason at all to assign this tradition to a lost Babylonian text. Rather, in my opinion, it is Rashi's personal contribution to the Beruriah traditions, and therefore, also to the debate about women's position *vis-à-vis* wisdom and learning. Rashi obviously represents in this text the society he lived in and its views and prejudices with regard to women. However, just as I believe that Beruriah of the Babylonian Talmud taught us little of women of the talmudic *milieu*, and much about the Talmud's reaction to the isolated and unusual *baraita* about Beruriah preserved in the Tosefta, so too, this tradition is, in my opinion, Rashi's reaction to the much expanded and inflated Beruriah of the Babylonian Talmud. It should be remembered that we know little of Rashi's familiarity with the Tosefta, and we have no way of knowing whether he

---

[19] Goodblatt, "Beruriah," 85.

[20] Boyarin, *Carnal Israel*, 189.

[21] On Rashi's stories of this sort, see my *Mine and Yours*, 63-73.

knew anything of the original Beruriah tradition.[22] There is little doubt, however, that he knew a lot about the accomplished Beruriah of the Babylonian Talmud, and that he did not like her.

I believe we can easily unpack Rashi's agenda if we follow his talmudic reasoning closely, but in order to do so we must first inspect the talmudic text on which he commented when he told the story of Beruriah. In tractate *Avodah Zarah* of the Babylonian Talmud, in a *sugya* that deals with cooperation with heretics and idol worshippers, a number of stories tell of the connection between heresy and prostitution. These lead up to the story of the martyrdom of Hananiah ben Tardion. This story is based on an old tannaitic tradition:

> When Rabbi Hananiah ben Tardion was arrested, it was decreed that he be burnt with his [Torah] book ... they told his wife: It has been decreed that your husband be burnt and you executed .... they told his daughter: It has been decreed that your father be burnt and your mother executed and you be forced to do work ... (*Sifre Deuteronomy* 307)

What this last part of the tradition (namely working) refers to exactly is not clear, but in the Babylonian Talmud it was altered to fit the wider context of the *sugya* into which it was incorporated: "It was decreed that [Hananiah ben Tardion] be burnt and his wife be executed and his daughter be placed in a brothel" (*bAvodah Zarah* 17b). This indeed is the ultimate test of a pious woman. Is this what Beruriah, whom the Babylonian Talmud generally identifies with the daughter of Rabbi Hananiah ben Tardion, was made to suffer? The Babylonian Talmud elegantly sidetracks this embarrassment:

> Beruriah, the wife of Rabbi Meir, was the daughter of Hananiah ben Tardion. She said to him: It is shameful for me that my sister sits in a brothel (*bAvodah Zarah* 18a).

It was, thus, not Beruriah who underwent the degrading ordeal of reduction to prostitution, but rather her sister. Following this statement by Beruriah, Rabbi Meir sets out on a rescue mission and delivers the sister from her fate worse than death. However, somewhere along the way something goes wrong and Rabbi Meir is forced to flee to Babylonia as a result of this escapade. On this the Talmud comments: "Some say [his flight] resulted from this incident and some say it resulted from the Beruriah incident" (*bAvodah Zarah* 18b). We are now left with the difficult question, what exactly is meant by the "Beruriah incident." The Talmud obviously decided it was superfluous to spell it out. Most scholars, inspired by Rashi's tale, think that the Talmud refrained from telling it because the story was well known, perhaps coincided with the one told by Rashi, and in any event was not very complimentary to Beruriah. However, if we put Rashi's commentary aside for a minute, we can

---

[22] On Rashi's familiarity with the Tosefta, see Y. L. Hacohen Maimon, "Rashi," in *idem* (ed.), *Sefer Rashi* (Jerusalem 1956) 108-14 [Hebrew].

see that the Talmud itself is most likely telling us what the "Beruriah incident" actually was. The Talmud has just told us how Rabbi Meir saved a daughter of Rabbi Hananiah ben Tardion from prostitution in a Roman brothel, and was forced to flee as a result. That daughter was specifically identified as another daughter—not Beruriah. However, up to this point (and as Goodblatt has plainly shown[23]) we have been led by the Babylonian Talmud to understand that Hananiah ben Tardion had but one learned daughter, namely Beruriah. It is quite likely that when the Talmud contrasts "this incident" with the "Beruriah incident" it is subtly suggesting that the original story of the daughter in the brothel was told about Beruriah and that out of respect for her the Talmud chose to conceal this fact.

My conjecture may be supported by a literary parallel not too far removed in time. In *Antiquities* (19:356-357), Josephus tells us that on King Agrippa's death the Caesarian mob attacked his palace, carried off the statues of his three daughters to the nearest brothel and did to them "things too indecent to be reported." Centuries later the Byzantine monk Photius told this same story differently: "For no other reason than their crazy rage, the Sebasteans kidnapped them (i.e. the daughters themselves) suddenly, shut them up in a house of prostitution and subjected them to all the outrages that one could mention, and others that are unmentionable" (*Bibliotheke* 238 [316b]). To what extent Photius was reporting actual facts is difficult to say. Either he used an edition of Josephus different from the one we now have, or he made the story more juicy than his source. Either way, this example indicates that the presence of respectable women in brothels was unacceptable to some historians or storytellers and they felt that the identity of a heroine who underwent such an ordeal was better disguised.

Let us now return to Rashi. In light of the fact that the entire *sugya* in the Babylonian Talmud associates religious transgression with sexual transgressions, it should come as no surprise that Rashi has also decided to present "the Beruriah incident" as a sexual offense. Beruriah may be a great scholar, but like all women she is prone to sexual license; and her behavior with Rabbi Meir's student is proof enough that the freedom she enjoyed because of her scholarship was undeserved.

However, for the retelling of "the Beruriah incident" Rashi used a different talmudic intertext, namely *bQiddushin* 80b-81b. Several strands in Rashi's story point squarely in that direction, beginning with the rabbinic dictum Beruriah mocks, namely the assertion that "women are light-headed." As we have seen above, the Babylonian Talmud indeed presents Beruriah as criticizing the rabbis' injunction, "do not converse too much with a woman." But while this last statement is well known, and found in the most important collection of rabbinic maxims in the Mishnah, tractate *Avot*, the statement that

---

[23] "Beruriah," 73-5.

women are light-headed is far more obscure, appearing only once under the enigmatic heading "*Tanna de Vei Eliyahu*"[24] in *bQiddushin* 80b. The statement follows a mishnaic injunction that suggests that a man is forbidden to spend time alone with two women but a woman is allowed to spend time alone with two men.[25] The Babylonian rabbis immediately inquire how is that possible and then come up with the seemingly early tannaitic explanation that "women are light-headed." In other words, it is not safe for a man to associate with two women for they will immediately seduce him. For a woman, however, it is considered safe to spend time with two men, because they are not light-headed and so will not seduce her. This explanation is than followed by a learned discussion about the logic of this statement, coming up with surprising and, occasionally, diametrically opposed conclusions particularly as regards the second part of the mishnaic argument. For example, we are told about two famous rabbis, Rav and Rav Yehudah, who

> were walking along the way. A woman was walking before them. Said Rav to Rav Judah: Lift your legs up in the face of hell (גיהנם). Said [Rav Judah] to him: But did you not say that it is allowed [for a woman to be alone with two men] in case of trustworthy people (כשרים). Said Rav to him: Did I say trustworthy people such as you and myself? (*bQiddushin* 81a).

This suggests that the Babylonian rabbis were well aware that a woman in the company of several men was no less (and perhaps more) in danger of seduction, or even rape than the other way around. This is further emphasized by a story which brings the situation *ad absurdum*:

> There was a case of a woman [who pretended to be dead] and was taken out [of the house] on a bier by ten men [supposedly to bury her but in reality in order to engage in sex] (*bQiddushin* 80b).

This is clearly a case where the men, as much as woman, cannot be trusted.

The learned discussion continues with disputes on several issues, but then evolves into a series of stories whose main aim is to show the sexual promiscuity of men rather than women. And not just any men, but exceptionally pious ones, even rabbis. We are told, for example, of Amram the Pious that

---

[24] The exact nature of "*Tanna de Vei Eliyahu*," of the Babylonian Talmud and its relationship to the composition known as *Seder Eliyahu* is disputed and enigmatic. For one opinion see: M. Margaliot, "On the Antiquity of Seder Eliyahu," in M. D. Kassuto, J. Klausner, and J. Guttman (eds.), *Sefer Asaf* (Jerusalem 1973) 370-90 [Hebrew]. Unfortunately, Margaliot's treatment of the text in question (p. 375) is less than satisfactory.

[25] For a detailed discussion of these texts, see Judith Hauptman, *Rereading the Rabbis: A Woman's Voice* (Boulder CO, 1997) 38-45.

women captives were brought to Nehardea. They brought them to the house of Rav Amram the Pious. They removed the ladder from below [so that even if he desired these women they would be beyond his reach]. But when one of them passed by, a light fell on her from the opening in the roof. Rav Amram snatched the ladder which ten men could not lift, placed it and climbed. When he was half way up he stopped and cried out loud: Amram's house is on fire. The rabbis came and said to him: We have shamed you. Said Amram to them: It is preferable that you shame me in this world than in the next (*bQiddushin* 81a).

Pious or not, Rav Amram could not withstand sexual enticement without the help of friends. This story obviously shows that even the most pious are prone to sexual temptation and should not rely on their strong character, but should take every precaution to avoid unnecessary closeness and familiarity with women.

However, from our point of view, the apex of the *sugya* is the story told of Rabbi Meir, Beruriah's husband:

Rabbi Meir used to scoff at transgressors. One day Satan appeared to him in the guise of a woman on the opposite bank of the river. There was no ferry so [Meir] seized the rope and proceeded across. When he had reached half way along the rope [Satan] let him go, saying: Had they not proclaimed in Heaven, take heed of Rabbi Meir and his learning, I would have valued your life at two nickels (*bQiddushin* 81a).

The similarity between this episode and the one Rashi tells about Beruriah is striking. Both Beruriah and Meir were seduced as part of a test, but as Adler had commented,

having a place in the rabbinic authority structure ... entitles one to the help of Heaven when ones own defenses against temptation have proven inadequate. Hence the rabbi [is] rescued. By contrast, no heavenly voice protects Beruriah by proclaiming: 'Take heed of Beruriah and her learning.' Like the virgin in the brothel, she is judged by more stringent standards, but, unlike the virgin, Beruriah will fail the chastity test.[26]

Nothing less than her death can satisfy this storyteller.

It seems to me that Rashi had used the Meir story in creating the "Beruriah incident." His version is constructed of building blocks taken from *bQiddushin* 80b-81b,[27] but has, to a certain extent, missed the Babylonian Talmud's subtle criticism of the tannaitic expression "women are light-headed." The Babylonian editors composed an entire *sugya* designed to undermine the idea that women are more light-headed than men. To that end they collected a large variety of stories which tell of men's fallibility. Here again, Boyarin's principle of a "counter-voice"[28] is at work. Rashi has taken the saying which the Babylonians contest and the sort of stories this *sugya*

---

[26] "Virgin in the Brothel," 104.

[27] See my *Mine and Yours*, 70-1.

[28] See e.g. *Carnal Israel*, 113.

tells, and applied them both to Beruriah. The story of Beruriah, in contrast with the *sugya* in *Qiddushin* confirms rather than denies the veracity of the statement that women are light-headed. This, I believe, is how Rashi's "Beruriah incident," which now looms large over any serious discussion of the Beruriah traditions, came into being.

5. Conclusion

In concluding this chapter, it is important to retrace our steps, much like an archaeologist, from the latest to the earliest layers. Beruriah as she emerges today—a fine sage but a promiscuous woman who cannot transcend her sex in pursuit of learning—is not the Beruriah Rashi knew. Rashi was confronted with an ideal scholar woman who had overcome the limitations imposed on those of her gender. His obvious misogyny made it impossible for him to accept her as such. It is to Rashi that we owe the blemished traits of Beruriah's character.

Similarly, the Beruriah Rashi "met"—an accomplished woman scholar in no way resembling those of her gender—was not the Beruriah encountered by the Babylonian rabbis. The latter felt it necessary to embellish Beruriah in this way because a dim reflection of the woman (or perhaps two women), who left a mark on the tannaitic legal scene, perplexed them. If there ever was a woman, the Babylonians reasoned, who had sat in the study house and transmitted legal traditions, she must have been unique. She must have been perfect. None of the weaknesses of her sex could have tarnished her soul. In this fashion they molded their legendary wonder-woman.

The dim reflection the Babylonians (and incidentally also the editors of the Mishnah) encountered is, however, the only visible trace of a real woman, Beruriah, who had once discoursed with members of the rabbinic circle on matters of purity laws which were of interest to them. Whether she was absolutely unique or rather more commonplace (as perhaps the tradition about the daughter of Rabbi Hananiah ben Tardion suggests) remains uncertain. That such a woman actually existed seems beyond doubt.

Therefore, even though the stories of Beruriah in the Babylonian Talmud are highly literary compositions, and it is very unlikely that they reflect any real event in Beruriah's life, since Beruriah is a historical figure, they may not be telling the facts of her life, but they are certainly making an educated guess as to what that life would have been like. We, as historians, may attempt similar imaginary reconstructions, but it is doubtful whether our guesses would be closer to the mark than theirs, or that we will be any closer to grasping the historical woman. In any event, in essence, our possible reconstruction would not be too far removed from the one the Babylonians made.

Chapter Seven

"Bone of My Bones" (Genesis 2:23)
The Use of Skeletal Remains for the Study of
Gender and Social History*

In the late 1960s, when Giv'at Hamivtar in Jerusalem was singled out as a building site, several salvage excavations were carried out on location, particularly in burial caves, which were discovered there as elsewhere over Jerusalem. In 1970, Nicko Haas published in the *Israel Exploration Journal* the results of an investigation of the skeletal remains of Jews buried in three of these caves.[1] Their ethnicity was determined by the Hebrew and Aramaic inscriptions discovered in association with the remains. Haas' publication became famous immediately, because it contained a report on the unusual discovery of the first skeletal evidence for the practice of crucifixion at the time.[2] However, for the social historian the interest in crucifixion is only minor, and Haas' model publication contains a wealth of information on a wide array of social phenomena, which were overshadowed by the crucifix. I would like to use data obtainable from this burial cave as a starting point for some observations on the use of statistics for demographic evaluation, which can be of great significance for the ancient historian.

The caves on Giv'at Hamivtar, which Haas examined, were relatively undisturbed. "In general skeletal remains recovered from ossuaries in the Jerusalem area are poorly preserved" wrote the physical anthropologist Patricia Smith in a report from 1977. This she attributed to the damp environment and then added: "An additional complication results from the fact that the collection of bones for placement in the ossuaries was apparently performed somewhat haphazardly. Thus parts of the skeletons are commonly missing, while bones from other individuals, and sometimes even animals, are

---

* This paper was first presented in a conference held in Bar Ilan University, Israel "Application of the Social Sciences in the Study of Judaism in Antiquity" 1996, in honor of Prof. Mary Douglas. I thank Prof. Albert Baumgarten of Bar Ilan University for inviting me to participate in the conference. Prof. Anna Belfer-Cohen of the Archaeology Department at the Hebrew University read an early draft of this paper and I thank her for her comments.

[1] N. Haas, "Anthropological Observations on the Skeletal Remains from Giv'at ha-Mivtar," *IEJ* 20 (1970) 38-59.

[2] In my opinion, works like M. Hengel *Crucifixion in the Ancient World and the Folly of the Message of the Cross* (Philadelphia 1977) were prompted by this discovery.

too frequently found in apparently intact ossuaries."[3] Luckily this was not the case with most of the remains from Giv'at Hamivtar. Haas could identify 35 individuals, which, he observed, comprised 11 males, 12 females and 12 (34%) children (whose sex, unfortunately, cannot be determined).

Our statistical-demographic observations can start here. We may begin by inquiring, to what extent are these remains representative of Jerusalem's population at the end of the Second Temple Period? If we find them adequate, we may learn even from this limited data about the ratios between the male and female Jewish population, and the rate of child mortality.

Statistical data is obtained by two methods. The one is global; information about the entire population is collected and then analyzed according to various criteria in order to determine patterns and trends of behavior. Modern western societies are well organized for such studies. State controlled registration of birth, deaths, marriages and divorces contribute to the creation of a complete corpus of "vital statistics," as these are called.[4] Large computer databases simplify the process. These are stored in various government bureaus, as well as public service institutions such as banks, schools and hospitals. This information is collected and employed primarily for legal purposes but may also be computed and displayed numerically for predictions that allow future policy making and economic and health planning. These data bases are clearly not compiled for the historian's benefit, and her employment of them is of a thoroughly secondary nature. Yet historians of modern times, studying the last two centuries, have made extensive use of such data, and have arrived at fascinating and accurate historical conclusions on this basis. For example, in her book *Gender and Assimilation*, Paula Hyman was able to show, from the complete records of the Orthodox church in Lithuania, that Jewish women converted to Christianity in far larger numbers than men.[5] Obviously such figures have important implications for social historians; but this kind of statistics is unavailable to the historian of the ancient past.

In the ancient world, registration was often carried out for taxation purposes. Thus we know that in the year 6 CE, when creating a Roman province in Judaea, the Romans carried out a census in which all the Jews of the land were registered, together with their property and income. Yet this register is one of the many documents which have not come down to us from antiquity. Census returns from Roman Egypt, of the sort that would have been produced by Palestinian Jews at the same time, have, however, been preserved on papyrus and are being used by historians in the reconstruction of

---

[3] Patricia Smith, "The Human Skeletal Remains from the Abba Cave," *IEJ* 27 (1977) 121.

[4] Handbook of Vital Statistic Method, *Studies in Method* ... Series F no. 7 (United Nations: New York 1955).

[5] Paula E. Hyman, *Gender and Assimilation in Modern Jewish History* (Seattle 1995) 73-4.

Roman Egyptian demography.[6] In this, as in other areas, historians of Hellenistic-Roman Egypt are lucky, because the dry climate of the land has preserved for them much material lost elsewhere. While it is true that documents written on perishable material were also preserved in the Judaean Desert, that area was not an administrative center and the documents it yielded came from peripheral groups and refugees.[7] Even the membership register of the Qumran sect, referred to in the literary documents of the sect, was not found among the Dead Sea Scrolls.

Thus, in the absence of an entire corpus, one needs to resort to the second statistical tool, namely the sample. "Sampling consists of selecting some part of a population to observe, so that one may estimate something about the whole population."[8] The statistic theory of sampling is based on the law of probability, which maintains that while individual behavior is unpredictable, the behavior of many follows a pattern, which may be quantitatively defined. "For example: in the science of genetics it is uncertain whether an offspring will be male or female, but in the long run it is known approximately what percent of offspring will be male and what percent will be female."[9] Thus, a controlled sample representing a larger population will, theoretically, display behavioral characteristics of the whole. Modern public opinion polls are based on this theory. However, its effectiveness is uncertain even under ideal conditions, where the sample can be carefully selected. Obviously the difficulties are compounded in the application of similar methods to ancient data, where the sample is always random rather than controlled. We cannot know how the 35 individuals of Giv'at Hamivtar came to be buried where they were. Did they belong to one family? Where they "average" Jerusalemites? Do they represent one class rather than another? Thus, perhaps, the division between the sexes, or the figures for child mortality suggested by this sample represent only one sector of society. But if so, which sector? In the face of these difficulties, the ancient demographer Roger Bagnall suggests that "Many different data sets must be compared in order

---

[6] R. S. Bagnall, and B. W. Frier, *The Demography of Roman Egypt* (Cambridge 1994). Ancient historians on the whole are deprived compared to modern and even medieval historians where quantitative data is involved. See e.g. Beryl Rawson, "From 'Daily Life' to 'Demography'," in R. Hawley and B. Levick (eds.), *Women in Antiquity: New Assessments* (London 1995) 1-20.

[7] Thus three census returns from the Roman census of the province of Arabia in 127-8 CE were discovered among the documents in the Judaean Desert, see Hannah M. Cotton, W. E. H. Cockel, F. G. B. Millar, "The Papyrology of the Roman Near East: A Survey," *JRS* 85 (1995) 223-4 (nos. 177-9), but these could hardly serve as statistical data. Perhaps the newly discovered Petra papyri (*ibid.*, 215) will be more helpful in this respect, but the Jewish element in this find will, by necessity, be limited.

[8] S. K. Thompson, *Sampling* (New York 1992) 1.

[9] A. M. Mood, F. A. Graybill and D. C. Boes, *Introduction to the Theory of Statistics* (1974) 2.

that inevitable errors may cancel one another out, for it would be extremely
unlikely that they should all tend in the same direction."[10] If we make the
claim that Haas' 23 adults to 12 children represents the usual child mortality
ratio (34%) in Second Temple Jewish Jerusalem, we should corroborate it,
according to Bagnall, from other sets of data.

Can we do this? On the face of it the answer tends to be "why not?" The
Giv'at Hamivtar caves are three out of over 750 similar finds from
Jerusalem.[11] Is it not possible for scholars to conduct similar investigations in
the other caves? The answer is, to date, a qualified "no." The quotation from
Patricia Smith above supplies one reason for this. Another is given by Haas
himself: "Our anthropological work was hampered by circumstances beyond
our control which allowed only four weeks for the examination of the remains
before their modern reburial. This necessitated emergency manipulations and
precluded proper ... recording."[12] Haas had four weeks; he complains but he
was lucky. In fact, Haas' report is one of only eight complete or partial
skeletal reports on ossuary caves from Jerusalem that are available to the
historian (see Table 1 at end of chapter).[13] This figure is clearly not large
enough for accurate sampling. The situation, however, is not as hopeless as it
would appear at first sight, because other skeletal finds pertaining to Jews are
also available: remains from Hellenistic Jewish tombs (slightly earlier and
containing no ossuaries) have been reported from Ein Gedi and Jerusalem;
some skeletal information from Qumran and neighboring sites has become
available; skeletal remains of Jewish individuals who died as refugees in the
Judaean Desert in the aftermath of the Bar Kokhba Revolt (135 CE) have also
been investigated.[14] All these substantially enlarge the sample under study

---

[10] R. S. Bagnall, *Reading Papyri, Writing Ancient History* (London 1995) 75.

[11] A. Kloner, *The Necropolis of Jerusalem in the Second Temple Period* (Unpublished
Ph.D. Thesis, Hebrew University; Jerusalem 1980) 1 [Hebrew].

[12] Haas, "Observations," 39.

[13] The others are 1. B. Arensburg and Y. Rak, "Skeletal Remains of an Ancient Jewish
Population from French Hill, Jerusalem," *BASOR* 219 (1975), 69-71; 2. Smith, "The Abba
Cave," 122-3; 3. Rachel Hachlili, and Patricia Smith, "The Genealogy of the Goliath Family,"
BASOR 235 (1979) 67-70; 4. J. Zias, "Human Skeletal Remains from the Mount Scopus
Tomb," *Atiqot* 21 (1992 - English Series) 97-103; 5. J. Zias, "Human Skeletal Remains from
the 'Caiphas' Tomb," *ibid.*, 78-80; 6. J. Zias, "Anthropological Analysis of Human Skeletal
Remains," in G. Avni and Z. Greenhut (eds.), *The Akeldama Tombs* (IAA Reports 1;
Jerusalem 1996) 117-20. A partial report is available in A. Kloner, "A Burial Cave of the
Second Temple Period at Giv'at Hamivtar, Jerusalem," in A. Oppenheimer, U. Rappaport and
M. Stern (eds.), *Jerusalem in the Second Temple Period: Abraham Schalit Memorial Volume*
(Jerusalem 1980) 191-224 [Hebrew].

[14] These reports include, 1. H. Nathan, "The Skeletal Material from Nahal Hever," *Atiqot*
3 (1961) 165-175 [Hebrew] (this report refers to the finds of Aharoni in Nahal Hever, see his
"The Caves of Nahal Hever," *ibid.*, 148-62); 2. B. Arensburg, M. S. Goldstein, H. Nathan,
and Y. Rak, "Skeletal Remains of Jews from the Hellenistic and Roman Periods in Israel,
(Pathology)," *Bulletins et memoires de la Societe d'anthropologie de Paris* 8 (1981) 11-24

(see Table 2 at end of chapter). With Bagnall's recommendation in mind, we may proceed to test against other sets of data each statistical datum we deduce from Haas' report. Let us begin with the issue of child mortality.

1. Infant Mortality

"Infant Mortality" reports the United Nation Handbook of Vital Statistic Method "is perhaps the most sensitive index of the effectiveness of health and sanitation."[15] In Haas' report the 12 children compared to the 23 adults constitute 34% of the population. In other words 34% of the population died before reaching adulthood. Is this normal? Is it typical of the Jewish population of Jerusalem? The sequence of discoveries in ossuary tombs and the chronology of their publication is an excellent indication of the importance of Bagnall's caveat.

Shortly after Haas' publication, Baruch Arensburg and Yoel Rak published the skeletal finds from an ossuary cave in the French Hill Jerusalem. This is what they wrote about child mortality:

> The total number of adult individuals (70%) is very high if we consider a historic population, In contrast the 30% of immature individuals is extremely low and unexpected, as the reverse situation is usually found in historic sites ... This fact, and the presence of very old people here as well as in similar sites in Jerusalem indicates that an active demographic change induced this abnormal distribution of age. We suggest that a specific way of life and social organization was responsible for this highly significant distribution pattern of ages in the French Hill grave.[16]

In other words the authors, basing their finds on two reports, theirs and Haas', arrived at far-reaching conclusions about Jewish practice, perhaps implying that observation of the Jewish purity commandments provided better sanitation, and abiding by *kashrut* laws a healthier diet.

(this report refers to the finds of Avigad in Nahal David: N. Avigad, "Expedition A: Nahal David," *IEJ* 12 [1962] 181-3; and of Yadin's in Nahal Hever: Y. Yadin, "Expedition D," *IEJ* 11 [1961] 37-8); 3. Patricia Smith and J. Zias, "Skeletal Remains from the Late Hellenistic French Hill Tomb," *IEJ* 30 (1980) 109-15; 4. B. Arensburg and Anna Belfer-Cohen, "Preliminary Report on the Skeletal Remains from the 'En Gedi Tombs," *Atiqot* 24 (1994) 12*-14*; R. de Vaux, "Fouille au Khirbet Qumrân: Rapport Préliminaire," *RB* 60 (1953) 103; "Fouilles de Khirbet Qumrân," *RB* 63 (1956) 569-71; S. H. Steckoll, "Preliminary Excavation Report in the Qumran Cemetery," *RQ* 6 (1968) 335; P. Bar-Adon, "Another Settlement of the Judaean Desert Sect at En el-Ghuweir on the Shores of the Dead Sea," *BASOR* 227 (1977) 12-7.

[15] P. 15.

[16] Arensburg and Rak, "French Hill," 69.

Other finds, however, tended to upset this rather surprising discovery. Five years later, Patricia Smith and Joe Zias wrote, concerning another cave with a very low child mortality rate, as follows:

> Arensburg and Rak suggested that the low figure of 30% child mortality ... is perhaps indicative of different cultural traditions regarding health care, since non-Jews of the same period had a higher rate of infant mortality. However this finding could just as easily reflect differences in economic situation that would have directly affected the family's ability to provide its members with better nutrition and healthcare. The findings at Meiron seem to confirm this, as 47% of the individuals at that village site died before the age of eighteen.[17]

At Meiron a Jewish tomb from the 1st to 4th centuries CE yielded 197 individuals. This tomb is slightly later than the material surveyed here and is therefore not included in the sample under investigation.[18] However, because Smith and Zias themselves investigated it, it helped them correct earlier views on the uniqueness of Jewish life expectancy. As we shall see, this was only one stage in the process.

In 1992 Joe Zias published the finds from two additional ossuary burials from Jerusalem. On one of these he wrote:

> 30% of the population died between birth and four years of age. A further 17% did not reach the age of 18. While other published reports for the period cite lower figures, this is the percentage noted for the ancient Jewish site of Meiron, and probably reflects the high child mortality prevalent at the time.[19]

In other words, Zias' finds suggested to him that it was perhaps unwise to theorize about superior Jewish health and hygiene, when the findings were beginning to turn in another direction.

The most depressing results for Jewish child survival, however, came from the second cave Zias investigated that year, which is the now famous Caiaphas cave identified as the burial ground of the high priestly family of that name. Zias wrote on the human remains of this cave as follows:

> Undoubtedly the most striking fact emerging from the analysis of the material is the high mortality (68%) of infants, children and sub-adults ... the reason for this abnormally high mortality rate in this burial is unknown ...

Statistically, this cave could be interpreted as a corrective for the misinterpretation of Jewish child mortality rates reached by comparison with other caves. It could be viewed as an indication that the Jews suffered a rate

---

[17] Smith, Zias, "Hellenistic French Hill," 114.

[18] Patricia Smith, Elizabeth Bornemann, and J. Zias, "The Skeletal Remains," in E. M. Meyers, J. F. Strange and Carol L. Meyers (eds.), *Excavations at Ancient Meiron, Upper Galilee, Israel 1971-2* (Cambridge MA 1981) 110-8.

[19] Zias, "Mount Scopus," 97.

of child mortality no lower than their gentile neighbors. In some caves we find fewer cases of infant dead and in others more. Together they represent an average similar to that found in non-Jewish Greco-Roman burial sites. Zias, however, tried to explain this find historically: "The severe drought in Jerusalem between 41 and 48 CE ... may have been responsible for the unusually high mortality represented here ..."; and he concludes: "It has been postulated that high social status should be expressed in lower mortality rates ... the evidence presented here, in what appears to be the tomb of the high priestly family of Caiaphas, suggests that the relative wealth of the family did not confer any significant health advantages ..."[20]

In light of the glimpses which scholars get from these very partial reports, we can adduce the results from my computed data base, compiled from all 8 ossuary reports. It yielded, 176 children to 227 adults, namely a child-mortality rate of 44% (see Table 1). While this is admittedly lower than the figures given for the non-Jewish population, the difference is not very striking. Does it tend to reflect the real situation among the Jews or will further finds tilt the results further in the direction of their non-Jewish neighbors? At this point we can only speculate.

Non-ossuary finds of Jewish skeletal remains from the same period, however, are also available to the historian for comparison, and these tend to confirm the anthropologists' early suspicions because they do bring down the child-mortality figure—315 children to 491 adults—to 39%. This figure is substantially lower than that for contemporary non-Jews. It could indeed be explained as confirming the anthropologists' suspicion that Jews lived a healthier life than their neighbors did.[21] But before adopting such conclusions one should inquire about other possible intrusions in the sample. This figure, moreover, seems to be biased. For example, in the Hellenistic tombs from Ein Gedi, out of 99 skeletons examined, only 23 belonged to children below 17 years of age. The skeletons in Ein Gedi were discovered in 4 caves, but their distribution by cave is not reported anywhere. Perhaps in some caves no children were buried at all? This could also suggest something about the population that was buried in these graves. Not only are children rare, women are also under-represented (32/44), and more than 50% are under 25 years of age. Perhaps these were tombs of hired laborers who resided in Ein Gedi and operated the balsam industry at the site. If so, these were not families, and therefore do not represent a normal population.[22] In Qumran likewise, only a

---

[20] Zias, "'Caiphas' Tomb," 79.

[21] For figures on non-Jews (Greeks) see J. L. Angel, "Ecology and Population in the Eastern Mediterranean," *World Archaeology* 4 (1972) 88-105, and see especially Table on pp. 95-6.

[22] Compared with the excavations at burial caves in Ein Gedi published in 1994, these conclusions are not confirmed. However, most of the burial ground of 1994 is located in Nahal Arugot, south of Ein Gedi, whereas most of Avigad's early excavations were carried

small number of children were buried. This phenomenon will be discussed below in some detail.

Even so, 39% is still higher than the 34% Haas presented from his cave. Thus the investigation carried out here has indicated us on the course we should take toward correcting the data available from Haas' work. The questions generated by his report are of great importance, but answers should be given with reference to additional data.

2. The Sex Ratio: Exposure and Neglect

Let us now turn to Haas' other figures, namely those pertaining to sex ratio. The sex ratio is an important index for the study of ancient demography. In their book "Too Many Women?" Marcia Guttentag and Paul Secord have demonstrated ways in which unequal numbers of members of the opposite sex have influenced the face of societies past and present.[23] In Haas' report we find 12 Females and 11 males. Since the sex of the children in Haas' report cannot be determined, we must allow that 11 to 12 is the ratio in the adult population. If the finds are representative of Jewish society, they imply a slightly higher percentage of females in the adult Jewish population. This fits well with modern statistics, which suggest that more boys come into the world than girls (at a ratio of 105/100), but that slightly more females survive into adulthood. Of course many factors contribute toward differences in sex ratios between ancient and modern societies. Wars take a high toll of the numbers of men. Nutrition is a factor that cannot be ignored. In some societies, men are better fed than women. Naturally this takes its toll. Death in childbirth has, until modern times, been a serious risk for women. The anthropologists who provided the data for my study were not interested in the sex ratio question. But awareness of it urges the historian to translate his data into figures.

Historians of antiquity have been interested in the sex-ratio question because of the particular form of family planning current in the Hellenistic-Roman world, of which Palestine was a part—infanticide and/or child exposure. "One of the reasons why Romans relied heavily on child exposure to control population," wrote Harris, "was that, unlike contraception or abortion, it permitted them to choose the sex of the child"[24] to be left alive. This method definitely favored male children. Several scholars have shown

---

out in a burial ground in Nahal David, north of Ein Gedi. See G. Hadas, "Nine Tombs of the Second Temple Period at 'En Gedi," *Atiqot* 24 (1994) 1-2. The one tomb Hadas excavated in Nahal David yielded no bones, see Arensburg and Belfer-Cohen, "'En Gedi," 13*.

[23] Marcia Guttentag and Paul F. Secord, *Too Many Women: The Sex Ratio Question* (Beverly Hills 1983).

[24] W. V. Harris, "Child Exposure in the Roman Empire," *JRS* 84 (1994) 11.

that female infanticide and exposure in ancient Greece and Rome were very widespread.[25]

Most scholars, however, tend to stress that in the case of the Jews, this factor should not be considered in calculating the sex ratio, because all ancient non-Jewish sources proclaim with awe the fact that Jews did not practice infanticide or child exposure. Jewish sources, moreover, repeatedly condemn such practices. This premise, however, should be approached with some caution. The information about the social behavior of Jews with relation to child rearing is actually based on the statements of two outsiders and two Jews.

The first outsider, Hecataeus of Abdera, a Greek historian who lived only shortly after the East had come under the sway of Greek influence, is hardly a reliable source for the question that interests us. His description of the Jews as raising all their children, should be viewed as his anthropological observation of a group whose anomalies are described by reference to the social behavior of the observer's own group, the latter serving as the norm.[26] However, even if Hecataeus' observations are correct, they are very early and can hardly be used as evidence for the Roman period (three centuries later), when the Haas' cave was unearthed. By the time this burial site came into use, the Jews were heavily influenced by Greek and Roman mores.

The second outside observer who lived close to the time when the finds from Giv'at Hamivtar were deposited, was the Roman historian Tacitus, of the early second century CE. He too claimed that the Jews refrain from killing newborn babies.[27] In our context, however, it is instructive to note that, when describing Jewish practices, Tacitus is heavily dependent on older sources, particularly those of Alexandrian Greek-Hellenistic circles, who may actually have used Hecataeus as their source of information on Jewish behavior with respect to child-rearing. Thus, Tacitus does not seem to be a first-hand observer for his information.

The other two sources on this topic are Josephus and Philo. As Jews, they are internal sources, but perhaps for this very reason should be treated with even greater caution. They are both apologists, and at a time when child exposure was coming under public censorship in the Roman Empire,[28] it would have been expedient to describe the Jews as acting in accordance with moral codes that are indeed cornerstones of their religious doctrine. No

---

[25] For a quantitative analysis of a Greek document to this end, see Sarah B. Pomeroy, "Infanticide in Hellenistic Greece," in Averil Cameron and Amélie Kuhrt (eds.), *Images of Women in Antiquity* (Detroit 1985) 207-22. For a quantitative analysis of Roman-Egyptian material see Bagnall and Frier, *Demography*, 151-3; 156-9.

[26] For Hecataeus, see M. Stern, *Greek and Latin Authors on Jews and Judaism* 1 (Jerusalem 1974) 27. The English translation is on p. 29.

[27] *Ibid.* 2, 1980, 19, English on p. 26.

[28] See Harris, "Child Exposure," 15-7.

normative Jewish document recognizes the possibility of abandoning or killing newborns. This of course does not mean that Jews never exposed infants, and Hellenistic and Roman patterns of behavior could hardly have passed them by unnoticed. Thus, Adele Reinhartz points out that Philo's vehement protest against the practice of child exposure (particularly with reference to the biblical story of Moses in the bulrushes) may well be directed at his fellow Jews rather than at foreigners.[29] But that may perhaps have been truer for Alexandria than it was for Jerusalem.

In any case, even though Jews never spoke respectfully, or even indifferently about child exposure, they certainly made no secret of their preference for male children. As early as the second century BCE, we find in the writings of Ben Sira concerning the birth of a daughter: "It is a disgrace to be the father of an ignorant son, and to have a daughter [any daughter] is a disadvantage" (22:3). Further, he advises the father: "If you have daughters ... do not look favorably upon them" (7.24). What does "looking favorably" on someone actually mean? It could mean that Ben Sira is imparting a piece of didactic advice, to the father, but, as we shall presently see, if translated into action it might have had grave consequences. Rabbinic literature is reputed to have preserved similar maxims. Thus, they say: "The world cannot survive without males and females. [Nevertheless] blessed is he whose offspring are male, woe to him whose offspring are female" (*bSanhedrin* 100b). In addition, rabbinic texts allow fathers not to provide for their daughters as they do for their sons. Here is a text from the Mishnah:

> This is the midrash Rabbi Eleazar ben Azariah expounded before the sages in the vineyard at Yavneh: 'sons inherit and daughters receive maintenance'—just as sons inherit only after the death of their father, so daughters receive maintenance only after the death of their father (*mKetubbot* 4:6).

Given that this text is interpreting a rabbinic injunction, it was obviously constructed as a theoretical exercise of rabbinic exegesis. But another text from rabbinic literature suggests that it must have been taken seriously in some circles. Thus we read "In Usha it was decreed that a father must maintain both his sons and his daughters while they are minors" (*bKetubbot* 49b). Rabbinic decrees are, by and large, emergency measures, taken in the face of disasters. This decree is designated an Ushan decree, and it is well known that the rabbis convened at Usha after the Bar Kokhba revolt. This may suggest that, in the face of economic hardship which ensued after that war, neglect of daughters prevailed and the rabbis saw fit to countermand it among their constituents. However, some scholars claim that the Ushan decrees should be dated to later than that post-war period,[30] and this would

---

[29] Adele Reinhartz, "Philo on Infanticide," *The Studia Philonica Annual* 4 (1992) 42-58.

[30] See G. Alon, *The Jews in their Land in the Talmudic Age (70-640 CE)* 2 (Jerusalem 1984) 730.

suggest that neglect of female daughters was more widespread than we would have supposed had it occurred only as a result of the hardships of war.[31]

"Children may die from neglect as well as violence" claimed Harris, in regard to the Roman empire as a whole, and he went on to say that "given the higher value that was ascribed to boys, it is likely that some female children suffered the fatal results of neglect."[32] It is interesting to note that of the twelve child skeletons that Haas examined in the Giv'at Hamivtar cave, three (one three months old, one three years old and one seven years old) had evidently died of malnutrition. Haas' malnutrition cases happen to be the only reported cases available to the historian of Second Temple Judaism. Because the starved children were found in the context of an organized burial, their death could be viewed as normal. If external political factors are removed, we need to inquire who would die of malnutrition under normal circumstances? Boy? Girls? Both? When Haas conducted his study, it was impossible to determine whether these dead children were male or female. Developments in the study of paleogenetics make it possible to answer that question, based on paleo-DNA analysis. Of course in the case of Giv'at Hamivtar, this is too late. In the absence of such methods, in order to answer the question posed above, we may refer to one very suggestive set of data. Usually anthropologists refrain from determining the sex of individuals less than 17 years old, but in the report from the Jewish tomb at Meiron mentioned above the investigators were able to determine the sex of children between 13 and 18. It is therefore striking to observe that of the 11 children who died between these ages, 10 were identified as female, and only one as male.[33] If this report is to be believed, many more girls died in childhood than boys. Did some of them die of malnutrition? For now the case must rest there.

If more girls than boys did die during childhood, this finding should reflect on the adult population. Here the sex ratio becomes vital. It is important to discover whether the sample of the adult Jewish population of Second Temple Palestine yields more males than females. Haas' cave certainly did not suggest this. Nor do the results from the total number of skeletons observed from ossuary tombs confirm such a suspicion. In fact the finds are strikingly even—77 males and 78 females. However, addition of the other datable individuals from the period under discussion does suggest that more girls than boys died in childhood. The sex ratio is 226 males to 182 females (see Table 2), namely when sex becomes discernible, boys greatly outnumber girls.

---

[31] Earlier rabbinic references also support this assertion, see e.g. *tKetubbot* 4:8.

[32] Harris, *ibid.*, 3.

[33] Smith et al., *Meiron*, 111.

Excursus: The Case of Qumran

Naturally, since the ossuary finds disagree with the other finds, we must subject our sample to further scrutiny, since the inconsistencies may reflect no more than the society which produced the skeletons, which was, perhaps, not as balanced as the ossuary population from Jerusalem. One such segment of the investigated population, the skeletons from Qumran, would, according to most scholars, contribute toward such an imbalance, since the cemetery at that site served the celibate male Essene population. Thus a short digression is desirable in order to clarify this issue.

Were the members of the Dead Sea Sect identical with the male community of Essenes? There are various reasons for rejecting this hypothesis, not the least of which are the finds from the Qumran cemetery. In his Schweich lectures in 1973, de Vaux, the excavator of Qumran reported that "Twenty six .. tombs have been excavated" and he goes on to report that "apart from some instances which were uncertain due to the bad state of preservation of the bones, all the skeletons ... are male." He did concede however, that "the rectangular grave, which is abnormal in type and situated apart from the rows, contained a female skeleton" and that "in the extensions of the cemetery over the hillocks to the east, four of the six skeletons examined are of women while one is a child."[34] De Vaux sincerely believed that the Qumran sect was to be identified with the Essenes, and thus he wrote "This [namely that women were not buried in the main cemetery] may indicate that women were not members of the community, or at any rate not in the same sense as the men buried in the main cemetery."[35] The way this sentence is formulated indicates, I believe, the difficulties de Vaux encountered in harmonizing his finds with his perceptions. But even so, de Vaux was not revealing to his readers all the facts. In 1953, when he published the first report of his Qumran finds in the journal *Revue Biblique*, de Vaux reported his initial excavations of 11 tombs at the central cemetery of Qumran. Nine skeletons, according to this report, were sent to the Musée de l'Homme in Paris for examination, and the results indicated that the skeletons consisted of "*plusieurs femmes* (many women)."[36]

How many the "many" comprised de Vaux refrained from stating. In general he seems to have been displeased with these results. In his 1956 report the skeletons were placed in the hands of someone else—Dr. Kurth of Göttingen—who was, apparently, willing to deliver the required results. Kurth told de Vaux that of the 20 individuals he examined, those whose sex he could determine were male. He was, however, reluctant to pass judgment on the

---

[34] R. de Vaux, *Archaeology and the Dead Sea Scrolls* (Oxford 1973) 46-47.

[35] *Ibid.*, 129.

[36] de Vaux, "Fouilles," (1953) 103. On the theoretical basis for the problems encountered here see also Miriam Peskowitz, "The Gendering of Burial; the Burial of Gender: Notes from Roman Period Archaeology," *JSQ* 4 (1997) 105-24.

sexual identity of five individuals. De Vaux published them as "*Homme* (?)." Quantitative results based on all of de Vaux' finds reveal 9 women, 17 men and 4 children. In the final analysis, this is not such an enormous bias against women.

Furthermore, De Vaux was not the only person who excavated the cemetery of Qumran. In a short note from 1967, Steckoll reported nine graves—six being those of males, and three of females.[37] In 1977 Pesah Bar-Adon published the finds from En el-Ghuweir (near Ein Feshkah), another settlement of the Dead Sea Sect. The tombs yielded 6 women, 13 men and one child.[38] Both of these finds confirm the sex ratio painstakingly extracted from the secret codes of de Vaux, and a conjunction of all together suggest that in the Qumran community men outnumbered women at a rate of 2:1, but there were certainly many women (and some children) around.

The addition of this small community to our general sample does not drastically bias it against women. Its greater importance is in calling into question the identity of the Dead Sea Sect with the Essenes.

3. Gender and Age at Death

Still on the sex-ratio and back to Haas' report, a close look at the age of the adult population in this sample shows that a biased pattern favoring boys continues into adulthood. Of the 11 males reported by Haas, two died over 60 years old and five between the ages of 40 and 50; but no female over 50 years old is reported, and only two had lived beyond the age of 40. Eight of the women died between the ages of 20 and 40, while only two men died in that age range. Evidently, in this sample women's life expectancy was considerably lower than a man's was.

Is this finding representative of the larger society? In order to test this, we need a control sample. For this I propose Hachlili and Smith's report on a Jewish family burial from the same period found in Jericho, and Joe Zias' report of a burial cave from Mount Scopus.[39] In the Jericho cave, where 30 skeletons were examined, the ratio between the sexes is reversed and drastically decreases the number of females—7 females versus 11 males. The ages of the interred are not easily discernible but again two of the men are said to be about 60, while the same is said of only one women, whose gender is doubtful. Four men are said to be around 50, but only one woman is said to have reached this age. And even though males considerably outnumbered females in this cave, two of the women but only one man are said to have died

---

[37] Steckoll, "Qumran," 335.

[38] Bar Adon,"En el-Ghuweir," 16.

[39] Hachlili and Smith, "The Goliath Family"; Zias, "Mount Scopus."

in their early twenties. Joe Zias' finds from Mount Scopus again favor females in his sex ratio (12/8) but the pattern of life expectancy for women is the same. Of those women whose ages could be discerned, six died in their 20s or earlier, while only one man died so young (and he died a violent death—see below). All other men whose age could be determined (six) died over 30 while only two women reached that age.[40]

This suggests that while the sex ratio is not constant between these samples, the pattern of women dying younger than men is consistent. This fact has finally been noted by the anthropologists Baruch Arensburg and Anna Belfer Cohen, who in a 1994 report of Hellenistic tombs from Ein Gedi, commented: "Estimates of age of death ... point to a greater average life span among males."[41] The facts are stated but no explanation is offered. Historians, I think, are expected to fill in this gap.

4. Violence of War or Violence in the Family?

One of the most spectacular features of Haas' report is the number of people interred in these caves who died a violent death (not including the three infants who died of malnutrition and the woman who died in childbirth, who will be discussed below). Aside from the crucified individual, two adults, a male youth (16 years old) and a female (24 years old), seem to have died of burning, one woman died of a mace blow and one child of an arrow wound in the back of the head. Had all these finds been concentrated in one cave, indicating a family burial, we could assume that these five individuals died in a violent encounter. Perhaps they were rebels, who used their house as a stand against the Romans sometime during the first century. An arrow shot at the house penetrated a child's head. A Roman soldier clubbed a woman who tried to fend off the attack. Finally the house was burnt. Two people who remained in it died in the fire. One member of the family was captured by the Romans and crucified. Relatives of the family brought them to burial. This is perhaps not a typical Jewish family, but is certainly an interesting one and could join the Jewish pantheon of freedom fighters toward the end of the Second Temple Period.

I suspect, however, that, this reconstruction is more romantic than tenable. The male youth and the woman who died of fire were found in two different

---

[40] The figures quoted here are based on a calculation of the finds in the ossuaries themselves, and not those found in the loculi. I have resorted to this method in order to allow for a more controlled sample. Bones found outside ossuaries could have been deposited at other periods.

[41] Arensburg, Belfer-Cohen, "'En Gedi," 12*.

caves, a fair distance of one kilometer apart.[42] The woman who died from a mace blow, and the crucified man, were found in one of these two caves and the child with the arrow wound in the other. Violent deaths are almost evenly distributed between the two locations.

This high percentage of violent deaths (14%) could be considered mere coincidence, of course, but it could also be telling us something about another aspect of ancient life. Perhaps violent deaths were more common than we imagine today.[43] I would like to check this assertion by comparing our data with finds published by several other physical anthropologists after Haas' report came to light. Patricia Smith published the finds from another burial cave discovered at Giv'at Hamivtar two years after those published by Haas.[44] The cave in question came to be known as the Abba Cave, because of a unique inscription discovered in it, which told of the hardships of a certain Abba, who was exiled to Babylonia and then returned bearing with him the bones of a certain Matthias son of Judah, which he claims to have buried in the same cave.[45] Speculations on the identity of this individual immediately ensued, the most ingenious suggesting that this Matthias was none other than the last Hasmonean king Matthias Antigonus.[46] This conclusion was strongly supported by the initial examination of the skeletal remains of an individual interred in the only (very finely decorated) ossuary discovered in the cave, who, it seems had died of a wound inflicted to his face by a sharp weapon. Matthias Antigonus, we are informed by Josephus, was beheaded by the Romans (*Antiquities* 15.9). For this reason Patricia Smith was very careful when she set out to spoil everybody's fun. This is how she described the injury this person had suffered before death:

[T]he inferior margin of the ramal fragment (=part of the lower jaw) had been cut by a sharp implement in an anterior and medial direction. A fragment of the left ramus ... shows a similar cut surface in a posterior direction ... Assuming that all fragments so far

---

[42] See map in V. Tzaferis, "Jewish Tombs at and Near Giv'at ha-Mivtar," *IEJ* 20 (1970) 19.

[43] The interest in pathology and violence is great among physical anthropologists. For additional cases among Second Temple Jews not discussed here see also: Y. Rak, B. Arensburg and H. Nathan, "Evidence of Violence on Human Bones in Israel, First and Third Century," *PEQ* 108 (1976) 55-8; Steckoll, "Qumran," 334; see also Arensburg and Belfer Cohen, "'En Gedi," 13*: "A decapitation observed in Ein Gedi ... deserved to be mentioned here as similar cases have been found among contemporaneous remains of Jewish individuals from Jerusalem."

[44] Unfortunately no map was ever published with the finds, so it is impossible to locate this cave with relation to the earlier caves discovered in the vicinity. See: V. Tzaferis, "The 'Abba' Burial Cave in Jerusalem," *Atiqot* 7 (1977; Hebrew Series) 61-4.

[45] See E. S. Rosenthal, "The Giv'at ha-Mivtar Inscription," *IEJ* 23 (1973) 72-81; J. Naveh, "An Aramaic Tomb Inscription Written in Paleo-Hebrew Script," *IEJ* 23 (1973) 82-91.

[46] I. M. Grintz, "The Giv'at Hamivtar Inscription: A Historical Interpretation," *Sinai* 75 (1974) 20-3 [Hebrew]. And see also chapter 8, below.

described belong to the same individual, the direction of the cuts suggests that two separate cuts were made, one on each side of the jaw ...The sharp surface of the cut surfaces indicates that the cuts were made with a sword rather than an ax ... either during life or very soon after death ... Since the ... blows passed through the mandible and must have sheared off part of the face, it would seem likely either that the victim was moving at the time, for instance in battle, in an attempt to dodge the blow, or that the executioner was rather inept.[47]

But Smith's doubts about this being a death by execution actually relied more on her other, more startling conclusion, that the person who suffered this violent death was in fact a woman. Smith really felt bad about this discovery for she adds, rather apologetically that "The identification of the remains of the individual with the cut mandible ... as female and elderly was confirmed by independent observations made by another anthropologist."[48]

This female who had suffered a violent death thus resembles closely the woman whom Haas described as having died from a mace blow. Therefore, instead of harboring romantic views about freedom fighters at every new find turned up by the archaeologist's hoe, perhaps we should identify these two cases as deaths by family violence. These two women may have been killed by their husbands.

Other reports of violent deaths appeared subsequently. Thus, in a special article devoted to violent deaths, Zias described "one woman (aged 50-60) [who] was struck by a sharp instrument which cleanly sheared the distal end of the right humerus ... the individual probably died from the attack."[49] Another woman, described by Joseph Zias in the cave from Mount Scopus, is said to have suffered a fracture of the skull as a result from a blow to the head; but she recovered from it.[50] Another individual from this cave is said to have died from a series of violent injuries, such as severing of an arm, blows to the face with a sharp instrument etc. When describing this individual, Zias commented: "The mutilated individual found in Ossuary 18 is an adult male, of slight build, 18-21 years old ..."[51] However, interestingly, in the Table reporting the finds from the ossuaries the sex of the adult in Ossuary 18 is described as "undetermined," i.e. the anthropologist could not decide whether he was male or female. I wonder whether the scholar's romantic ideas about freedom fighters and gang warfare have not clouded his judgment here. Thus, despite Zias' claim that "According to written sources, violence was common

---

[47] Smith, "Abba Cave," 122-3.

[48] *Ibid.,* 124.

[49] J. Zias, "Anthropological Evidence of Interpersonal Violence in First Century A.D. Jerusalem," *Current Anthropology* 24 (1983) 233. The remains came from a cave that was not properly published and no complete skeletal record is available. For the present, see: L. Y. Rahmani, *A Catalogue of Jewish Ossuaries in the Collections of the State of Israel* (Jerusalem 1994) ossuaries 691-98.

[50] Zias, "Mount Scopus," 99.

[51] See, *ibid.,* 101.

in the Roman period ...,"[52] this case also need not be interpreted as death by the hand of the Roman enemy. After all, the wounds do not give the impression of an execution. If the identification of the person as male is incorrect, perhaps this was yet another woman who died a violent death at the hands of a family member.

Admittedly, these are grave accusations. Jewish sources of the time (and later) are conspicuously silent on this issue. Women who die in a domestic setting are not generally reported. Only one Talmudic story I know tells of a husband killing his wife—the story is about an innkeeper, named Kidor, who tried to rob some rabbis staying at his institution. His wife secretly returned their money, and when he found her out he killed her (*bYoma* 83b). It is therefore important to note regarding this case, that the facts are told dispassionately. Although the rabbis are reputed as miracle makers, and the wife obviously helped them, they do not intercede on her behalf. Her death troubles them not at all. This does not suggest that wife abuse was rare but rather that it was so common it was hardly worth mentioning. Obviously, with our very limited sample, we can say nothing about percentages and averages, but a chance comment by demographic anthropologists who discussed the finds from ancient cemeteries on this topic may suggest that we see here only the tip of the iceberg. Thus wrote Alan Swedlund and George Armelagos: "In the study of Nubian Skeletons, there was a dramatic increase in the fractured bones in females from the Christian period (A.D. 550), which may indicate the low status of females within this culture."[53] Swedlund and Armelagos were discussing large-scale excavations, in which scores of skeletons were studied. They were writing in the mid-seventies, when questions of social history like those discussed here were only just beginning to be probed. The fact that they could make an observation like the above suggests that the issue could and should be studied further.

5. Death in Childbirth

Another unique find which came up in Haas' report was the first example of a female skeleton in the very process of childbirth, the bones of the fetus still caught in the pelvic bones of the mother. "High maternal mortality rates" writes the United Nation Handbook of Vital Statistic Method "suggest a need for further study, not only of the causes of maternal mortality, which is a medical research problem, but of the circumstances under which these deaths

---

[52] "Interpersonal Violence," 233.

[53] A. C. Swedlund, and G. J. Armelagos, "Paleodemographic Studies," in *Demographic Anthropology* (Dubuque, IA 1976) 44.

take place."[54] The case discussed here is unique because it provided unequivocal proof,[55] corroborated both by the skeletal remains and the ossuary inscription, that the woman died in childbirth.[56] The skeletal remains, aside from indicating that many more women than men died during child-bearing years, cannot normally pinpoint childbirth as the cause of death. Inscriptions are not very helpful either. Aside from the inscription from Giv'at Hamivtar, only one Jewish inscription from Byblos in Lebanon (*CII* 874) and three inscriptions from Egypt (*CII* 1481, 1515, 1530) can be interpreted this way. Another criterion, namely burial together with a (newborn) child, attested both by inscriptional evidence and skeletal remains, is inconclusive. Much as we would like to be informed on the figures governing death in childbirth, particularly because of the intriguing Giv'at Hamivtar find, this topic remains numerically inaccessible. Many women died in childbirth, but we do not know how many, and have no means of even vaguely calculating or estimating the figure.[57]

6. Gender and Inscriptions

Finally, this last case has pointed us in a new direction not yet explored. The inscription on the ossuary confirmed death in childbirth. Up to this point I have approached the issue under discussion here in a manner somewhat commensurate with methods usually employed by prehistorians, namely scholars of periods and peoples that have left no written record. Here, of course, the case is different. Most of the important statistical studies carried out on ancient populations, such as Bagnall's model work on Roman Egypt, are based on written records, primarily, as mentioned above, census returns. Hopkin, based on hundreds of burial inscriptions mentioning data of this sort, carried out an important study on the age of Roman girls at marriage.[58] Further refinement of this method was suggested by Shaw, who investigated

---

[54] P. 16.

[55] For a similar, though non-Jewish case, excavated in Israel, see J. Seligman, J. Zais and H. Stark, "Late Hellenistic and Byzantine Burial Caves at Giv't Sharet, Bet Shemesh," *Atiqot* 29 (1996) 47 and see also J. Zias, "Canabis Sativa (Hashish) as an Effective Medication in Antiquity: The Anthropological Evidence," in S. Campbell and A. Green (eds.), *The Archaeology of the Dead in the Ancient Near East* (Oxford 1995) 232-4.

[56] On the inscription, see Naveh, "Giv'at ha-Mivtar," 36-7.

[57] And see my comments in *Jewish Women in Greco-Roman Palestine* (*Texte und Studien zum antiken Judentum* 44; Tübingen 1995), 117-9.

[58] K. M. Hopkins, "The Age of Roman Girls at Marriage," *Population Studies* 18 (1964-5) 309-27.

the relationship of the commemorators of the buried woman (parents or husband) as an indication of the woman's marital status.[59]

A comparison of the Jewish Palestinian inscriptions with those of their neighbors proves disappointing. No inscription from Palestine ever mentions the age of a girl at marriage and no ossuary inscription ever names the person who set up the tomb or the inscription. The same is true for other forms of data. Only 7 Jewish inscriptions that I know from Palestine provide the age of the deceased at death.[60] None of these were found on Jerusalem ossuaries. The only data these inscriptions may provide is the sex ratio, and here too the ossuaries prove disappointing.

Thus, in Haas' cave, while the skeleton ratio between males and females is 11 to 12, the ratio of males to females commemorated by inscriptions is 5 to 3. Thus, while the female skeletons outnumber the males, commemorated males outnumber commemorated females. This pattern tends to repeat itself elsewhere. If we were to rely on the evidence of the inscriptions, we would get a very distorted sex ratio record.[61]

7. Conclusions

Historians are defined by the fact that they obtain their data from written sources. History is defined as the period commencing with the human mastery of the craft of writing and reading. Yet history is, at the same time, the story of the human race. Basically it is interested in everything people were and did, and how that combination shaped the past. Thus, definitions aside, historians should be able to rely in their studies on every available bit of information. This information can be obtained by traditional historical methods, but it can also be obtained by methods developed in other disciplines with purposes very different from those of the historian. Demographic data is one such source of information. The study of human demography is closely tied to statistic research. It relies first and foremost on a large database. Ancient demography is traditionally studied with the assistance of a variety of written documents that record certain aspects of the past. Historians of Second Temple Judaism have no such records at their disposal. However, they do not need to despair. Methods employed in the study of prehistoric or non-literary societies—namely the study of skeletal remains—can be applied to their

---

[59] B. D. Shaw, "The Age of Roman Girls at Marriage," *JRS* 77 (1987) 30-46.

[60] J. B. Frey, *CII* 2 (Rome 1952) nos. 891, 984, 986, 1169; M. Schwabe, "Notes on the History of Tiberias: An Epigraphical Study," in M. Schwabe, J. Guttman (eds.), *In Memoriam Iohannis Lewy* (Jerusalem 1949) nos. 7, 8 (9); N. Avigad, *Beth She'arim* 3 (Jerusalem 1976) 242 (no. 15); 251 (no. 26).

[61] See my "Notes on the Distribution of Women's Names in Palestine in the Second Temple and Mishnaic Periods," *JJS* 40 (1989) 188-9.

studies in order to create a reliable database and extract from it intriguing historical information. There are, however, pitfalls everywhere. The reliability of the sample should continuously be brought into question, but the basic method is a good one and the results it produces are well worth the effort.

Table 1: The Ossuaries

Publication	Males	Females	Children	Undetermined
1. Haas 1970	11	12	12	-
2. Rak 1975	12	8	12	-
3. Smith 1977	1	1	-	-
4. Smith 1979	15	9	16	14
5. Kloner 1981	2	3	7	7
6. Zias 1992a	13	6	42	3
7. Zias 1992b	15	24	39	9
8. Zias 1996	8	15	48	37
Total	77	78	176=44%	72

1. Haas, "Giv'at Hamivtar."
2. Arensburg and Rak, "French Hill, Jerusalem."
3. Smith, "The Abba Cave."
4. Hachlili, and Smith, "The Goliath Family."
5. Kloner, "Giv'at Hamivtar, Jerusalem."
6. Zias, "'Caiphas' Tomb."
7. Zias, "Mount Scopus.
8. Zias, *The Akeldama Tombs.*

Table 2: Other Finds

Location	Males	Females	Children	Undetermined
French Hill Hellenistic	10	8	10	5
Ein Gedi Avigad 1962	44	32	23	-
Ein Gedi Hadas 1994	52	27	77	1
Nahal Hever Horror Cave	5	5	10	1
Nahal Hever Letter Cave	4	10	14	-
Qumran	24	11	5	4
Ein al-Ghuweir	13	6	1	-
Total	152	99	140=34.8%	11
Total of both Tables	229	177	316=39%	83

1. Nathan, "Nahal Hever."
2. Arensburg, Goldstein, Nathan and Rak, "Hellenistic and Roman Periods in Israel."
3. Smith and Zias, "Hellenistic French Hill Tomb."
4. Arensburg and Belfer-Cohen, "'En Gedi Tombs."
5. de Vaux, "Khirbet Qumrân" (1953); "Khirbet Qumrân" (1956).
6. Steckoll, "Qumran Cemetery."
7. Bar-Adon, "En el-Ghuweir."

Part 3

Women and the Judaean Desert Papyri

Chapter Eight

Julia Crispina
A Herodian Princess in the Babatha Archive

One of the exciting tasks of the historian is to piece together information gathered from various sources in order to arrive at a more complete historical picture. This is especially true for the study of antiquity, where the sources are so rare, and it is particularly important in the case of women, who are even less conspicuous. This study will attempt to identify Julia Crispina, mentioned in the papyri of the Babatha archive from the Judaean Desert,[1] with a historical figure. In so doing, not only will material be added to women's history in the Roman period in general, but our corpus of Jewish women, which is small by any standard, will be enriched.[2] New Jewish women can teach us more about their history, showing us nuances and new venues of research.[3]

Attempts to identify epigraphical, papyrological or numismatic figures with historical persons mentioned in the literary sources are not always successful. And while a sound identification can assist the reconstruction of history,[4] a

---

[1] N. Lewis, *The Documents from the Bar Kokhba Period in the Cave of the Letters, Greek Papyri* (Jerusalem 1989) 90-1; 108-10. These documents will henceforth be referred to as *P. Yadin.*

[2] See my "Notes on the Distribution of Jewish Women's Names in Palestine in the Second Temple and Mishnaic Periods," *JJS* 40 (1989) 193-200; and see also my *Mine and Yours are Hers: Retrieving Women's History from Rabbinic Literature* (Leiden 1997) 311-8.

[3] Another example for such a woman retrieved for Jewish history in the Greco-Roman period is my "Matrona and Rabbi Jose: An Alternative Interpretation," *JSJ* 25 (1994) 18-51; and see also on this woman, independent of my work, Judith Z. Abrams, *The Women of the Talmud* (Northvale NJ 1995) 17-38.

[4] See, for example, the effect of the Bar Kokhba letters and the discovery that the personal name of the leader of the revolt was Simon, on relating the "Simon Nasi' Israel" coins to this revolt (J. T. Milik, "Une Lettre de Siméon Bar Kokheba," *RB* 60 [1953] 277-82). Prior to this discovery such coins were attributed to either Simon the Hasmonean of the Second Century BCE Jewish revolt against the Seleucids or to Simon ben Gamaliel of the 66-70 CE Jewish revolt against Rome, or to his contemporary Simon bar Giora; see: F. W. Madden, *History of Jewish Coinage* (London 1864; republished New York 1967) 161-82. The only "Simon Nasi' Israel" coins assigned by him to Bar Kokhba were those minted on Roman coins postdating the Jewish revolt of 66-70 CE (pp. 203-10). The state of research is summed up at this stage by Y. Meshorer, *Jewish Coins of the Second Temple Period* (Tel Aviv 1967) 88-110. This decisive identification has, however, given rise to speculation regarding another person

false one can cause confusion in the chronology and understanding of historical events.[5]

This paper, which also sets out to suggest a historical identification, is divided into two parts. The first part spells out the criteria necessary for a sound historical identification and cites examples to illustrate them. The examples will focus on historical identifications made by scholars of the Second-Temple period and subsequent periods, as they coincide chronologically with, and sometimes support the identification of, Julia Crispina that I propose here. In the second part I shall apply these criteria to my suggested identification.

1. The Criteria

a. Chronology

Some inscriptions or papyri are internally dated. Others may be circumstantially dated by reference to the archaeological context in which they were discovered. A sound identification of a person mentioned in a dated document with a historical figure demands that there be no discrepancy in chronology. Two examples will illustrate this point.

i. Two papyri from Egypt mention a certain person named Gaius Julius Alexander, who owned land in Euhemeria in the Arsinoite Nome (modern Fayum).[6] Initially this person had been tentatively identified by M. Rostovzeff[7] as Alexander, King Herod's son by Mariamme the Hasmonean. The editors of the *Corpus Papyrorum Judaicarum*, however, had to reject this identification because of a chronological discrepancy.[8] The documents in which Gaius Julius Alexander is mentioned were issued in 26 and 28-29 CE

---

mentioned on these coins—"Eleazar the Priest." Madden, *ibid.*, 155-6, 161-6, in accordance with his other assumptions, had identified him with Eleazar son of Shimeon of the 66-70 CE Jewish Revolt against Rome. When it became evident that the man should be dated to the Bar-Kokhba revolt, new suggestions were raised, paramount among them being his identification with Rabbi Eleazar the Modaite (of Modi'in[?]), who is mentioned together with Bar Kokhba in *yTaanit* 4:8, 68d-69a, see: G. Alon, *The Jews in their Land in the Talmudic Age* 2 (Jerusalem 1984) 623; S. Safrai, "Eleazar of Modi'in," *Encyclopedia Judaica* 6 (Jerusalem 1971) 603. For doubts regarding this identification see: P. Schäfer, *Der Bar-Kokhba-Aufstand* (*Texte und Studien zum antiken Judentum* 1; Tübingen 1981) 173-4.

[5] See for example: Y. Garfinkel, "The Elyakim Na'ar Yokan Seal Impressions: Sixty Years of Confusion in Biblical Archaeological Research," *BA* 53 (1990) 74-9.

[6] V. A. Tcherikover and A. Fuks, *Corpus Papyrorum Judaicarum* 2 (Cambridge MA 1960) 202-3.

[7] In P. M. Fraser (ed.), *The Social and Economic History of the Roman Empire* (Oxford 1957) 672, n. 45. He was followed by N. Hohlwein, "Euhemreia du Fayoum," *Journal of Juristic Papyrology* 3 (1949) 81.

[8] Tcherikover et al., *CPJ* 2, 200.

respectively, while Alexander, Herod's son, was executed in 7 BCE.[9] The documents were, however, included in the *Corpus* because the name could be assigned to a famous Egyptian Jew, Alexander the alabarch, brother of Philo the philosopher (*Ant.* 18.159, 259; 19.276-7; 20.100), whose son bore the telling name Tiberius Julius Alexander (*War* 2.220, 309, 492-3; 4.616-7; 5.45; 6.237; *Ant.* 20.100).[10] Chronology had been safely settled.

ii. On the other hand, a sound suggestion is that of Fuks, who identifies a certain Marcus Julius Alexander, mentioned on a number of business ostraca from the ports of Berenice and Myos Hormos on the Red Sea, with Marcus, son of the above mentioned alabarch, who, according to Josephus, married princess Berenice, daughter of King Agrippa I (*Ant.* 19.276-7).[11] Josephus reports that when this Marcus died Berenice married her uncle, Herod of Chalcis, and that this happened before her father's death in 44 CE (*Ant. Ibid.*). And indeed, the last ostracon on which Marcus Julius Alexander is mentioned dates from some time between August 43 and August 44 CE. Naturally, new ostraca, bearing later dates, could upset this seemingly sound identification.[12]

b. Geography:
Establishment of the geographical setting of an inscription strengthens the certainty of the identification. Two examples will be cited here to clarify this point.

---

[9] For this date, see: E. Schürer, G. Vermes, F. Millar and M. Black, *The History of the Jewish People in the Age of Jesus Christ* 1 (Edinburgh 1973) 294, n. 18.

[10] Naturally, further doubt could be cast on this identification, if the alabarch's name was in fact Alexander Lysimachus, as some of the Josephus manuscripts of *Ant.* 19.276 indicate. However, it is hard to decide whether this reading should be preferred on grounds of *lectio difficilior*, or discarded as superfluous since it is missing in the better manuscripts.

[11] A. Fuks, "Markus Julius Alexander," *Zion* 13 (1944) 10-7 [Hebrew].

[12] Tcherikover et al. *CPJ* 2, 199, no. 419d. For the chronological analysis see: Fuks, *ibid.*, 15-6. A different chronology is suggested by D. R. Schwartz, *Agrippa I: The Last King of Judaea* (*Texte und Studien zum antiken Judentum* 23; Tübingen 1987) 107-12, who places Agrippa's death in September 43 CE. If Schwartz's chronology is correct, then Fuks' suggestion is impossible. According to Fuks, the last ostracon mentioning Marcus dates to Emperor Claudius' fourth year, i.e. between August 43 and August 44 CE. Even assuming, as Fuks suggested, that this receipt could date to August 43, and that it was issued in Marcus' name very soon after his death, but before it had become known, it is hardly likely that between, say, July and September 43 the news of Marcus' death would have reached Agrippa so that he could arrange for the new widow a marriage with his brother, leaving the King time to attend the September games at Caesarea where he died. Schwartz's arguments for this proposed date are not conclusive. See *ibid.*, n. 6, and appendix 7, 203-7 for other chronological suggestions, placing Agrippa's death in March 44 CE.

i. The name Yair is not rare in the Jewish onomastics of the Second Temple Period,[13] but when an ostracon bearing the inscription "Ben Yair" was discovered in the destruction layer dated to 73 at Masada,[14] it was obvious that he should be identified with Eleazar ben Yair, mentioned by Josephus as the leader of the Sicarii on Masada (*War* 2.447).[15]

ii. When the impressive Jewish cemetery in Western Galilee had been correctly identified with historical Beit She'arim,[16] it was just a matter of time before someone identified the tombs of the Patriarchs in it. Naturally, when the names Simon and Gamaliel appeared together in a burial chamber, they were identified as Judah the Patriarch's two sons, despite the lack of grandeur in the inscriptions and the absence of any titles.[17] Were these two names to appear together in any other geographical context, and in a similar fashion, such an identification would be less than acceptable, but since we know that Rabbi Judah the Patriarch was buried in Beit She'arim (*yKetubbot* 12:3, 35a; *yKelaim* 9:4, 32b, *bKetubbot* 103b), and since Gamaliel is a typical name of the Patriarch's family, and rather rare in other circles,[18] the identification is certainly plausible.[19]

c. Names

Naturally, the two persons proposed for identification should bear the same name, but because a name is not unique it cannot serve as sufficient evidence for identification. In the case of names, therefore, three additional criteria can be employed:

---

[13] Tal Ilan, *The Names of the Jews in Palestine in the Second Temple and Mishnaic Periods: A Statistical Study* (Unpublished MA Thesis; Jerusalem 1984), chapter 2 [Hebrew].

[14] Y. Yadin, *Masada: Herod's Fortress and the Zealots Last Stand* (London 1966) 197; 201.

[15] See Y. Yadin and J. Naveh, *Masada 1: The Aramaic and Hebrew Ostraca and Jar Inscriptions from Masada* (Jerusalem 1989) 28. Naveh makes the proposal that one can alternatively read בני אור "Sons of Light" and in view of other finds relating to the Dead Sea Sect on Masada (Y. Yadin, "The Excavation at Masada: 1963/4 Preliminary Report," *IEJ* 15 [1965] 105-8, and more recently: S. Talmon, "Fragments of Scrolls from Masada," *Eretz Israel* 20 [1989] 278-86 [Hebrew]), such a proposal should not be entirely ruled out.

[16] B. Mazar, *Beth She'arim* 1 (Jerusalem 1973) 7-9.

[17] N. Avigad, *Beth She'arim* 3 (Jerusalem 1976) 65-2.

[18] Ilan, *Statistical Study*.

[19] S. J. D. Cohen ("Epigraphical Rabbis," *JQR* 72 [1981-2] 10, n. 12) claims that there is not enough evidence to warrant this identification, but because of his general thesis in the article it is doubtful whether any evidence would have induced him to accept an identification. For further reservations, see M. Schwabe and B. Lifschitz, *Beth She'arim* 2 (Jerusalem 1974) 148, n. 6.

i. *Rare Name*: A rare name is more likely to support the identification of an epigraphic reference with a historical figure. I shall provide two illustrations.
1. The weight stone with the inscription "Bar-Qatros," discovered by N. Avigad in Jerusalem,[20] is certainly to be identified with the Qatros family mentioned in the Talmud (*bPesahim* 57a) and in Josephus (*Ant.* 19.342[?]).
2. On the other hand, it is very unlikely that Salome the Jewess, mentioned derisively as the "real" mother of the Emperor Claudius, in the famous antisemitic *Acts of the Pagan Martyrs of Alexandria*, is to be identified with Salome the sister of King Herod.[21] Salome was one of the two commonest Jewish female names at the time[22] and could, in this case, serve as a typical Jewish name, having no reference to a specific individual.

ii. *Two Names*: If a certain person is mentioned both by his own name and by that of his father, or by his own name and a family name, this increases the chances that the identification is sound,[23] though in cases where both names are very common, it is by no means definitive, as the following example illustrates.

Y. M. Grinz made an attempted to identify a certain Mattathias, son of Judah, buried in an ossuary found on Giv'at Hamivtar in Jerusalem, with the last Hasmonean king, Mattathias Antigonus, son of (Judah) Aristobulus.[24] This identification, however, is unfounded, for it assumes that Mattathias Antigonus' father must have had the Hebrew name Judah; and even if he did, the popularity and widespread usage of both these Hebrew names argues against a sure identification.[25] The Babylonian Talmud in fact mentions another man, a sage of the same name, Mattathias son of Judah (*bHullin* 67a).

Firm identification of an individual with two names usually requires additional proof from another quarter.[26]

---

[20] *Discovering Jerusalem* (Jerusalem 1980) 129-30.

[21] Tcherikover et al., *CPJ* 2, 80-1, no. 156d, and see above, chapter 3, n. 89.

[22] Ilan, "Distribution of Women's Names," 191-2, 198-9.

[23] N. Avigad, "On the Identification of Persons Mentioned in Hebrew Epigraphic Sources," *Eretz Israel* 19 (1987) 235-7 [Hebrew], has used this criterion, together with title and chronology as the means by which to identify persons mentioned in seals and bullae with persons mentioned in the Hebrew Bible.

[24] "The Giv'at Hamivtar Inscription: A Historical Interpretation," *Sinai* 75 (1974) 20-3 [Hebrew].

[25] See: Tal Ilan, "The Greek Names of the Hasmoneans," *JQR* 78 (1987) 12-3; eadem, "The Names of the Hasmoneans," *Eretz Israel* 19 (1987) 238-41 [Hebrew]. And see also Chapter 7, above.

[26] Ossuaries bearing the inscription "Jesus son of Joseph" have also come up (A. Reifenberg, *Ancient Hebrew Art* [New York 1950] 64; cf. P. Figueras, *Decorated Jewish Ossuaries* [Leiden 1983] 12-3; A. Kloner, "A Tomb with Inscribed Ossuaries in East Talpiyot, Jerusalem," *Atiqot* 29 [1996] 18), although the identification of any of these men with Jesus, the founder of Christianity can only be suggested, in my opinion, as a matter of curiosity and should probably be ruled out because of the popularity of both names at the

iii. *Name and Title*: Identification can be almost certain in the case where the persons identified bear not only the same name, but also the same title. Following are two examples:

1. The ossuary of Nicanor the Gate-maker (ποιήσαντος τὰς θύρας) discovered in Jerusalem by Gladys Dickson in 1903[27] is the best example. Although the name Nicanor is not very common among Jews,[28] an ossuary bearing just this name, with a statement that the man buried in it came from Alexandria, would nevertheless not necessarily have identified the famous wealthy Jew of Alexandria who made gates for the Temple (*mYoma* 3:10, *mMiddot* 2:3; *tYoma* 2:4). The fact, however, that the man buried in the ossuary also bore the title "Gatemaker" makes the identification almost certain.[29]

2. The second case is that of Eliezer ha-Qappar. An inscription was discovered in the Golan Heights, which reads "this is the academy of Rabbi Eliezer ha-Qappar."[30] Although the name Eliezer was extremely common at the time,[31] the rare nickname "ha-Qappar", also borne by one Eliezer, a sage mentioned in rabbinic sources (e.g. *mAvot* 4:21; *tOhilot* 18.18), makes the identification certain. A sage with both a rare nickname and an academy make the identification very plausible.[32]

Some examples can fit into more than one of the categories drawn. Naturally, the more elements in common, the more certain the identification, as the following example shows:

The identification of the Sepulcher of the Kings in Jerusalem with that erected by the Jewish monarchs of Adiabene (*War* 5.55, 119, 147; *Ant.* 20.95; Pausanias, *Description of Greece*, 8.16.5) is almost unquestioned. But the only inscription discovered on a sarcophagus found there bears the unfamiliar

---

time, see: Ilan, "Hasmoneans." See, however, the program on Jesus' death "The Body in Question," aired on the BBC in England in the Easter of 1996.

[27] *PEFQS* 35 (1903) 93; cf. C. Clermont-Ganneau, "Archaeological and Epigraphical Notes on Palestine," *PEFQS* 35 (1903) 125-31.

[28] Ilan, *Statistical Study*, chapter 3.

[29] However, this identification has also been contested, see: P. Roussel, "Nicanor d'Alexandrie et la porte du temple de Jerusalem," *REG* 37 (1924) 79-82; and see also J. Schwartz, "Once More on the Nicanor Gate," *HUCA* 62 (1991) 248-50.

[30] D. Orman, "Jewish Inscriptions from Dabura in the Golan," *Tarbiz* 40 (1971) 406-8 [Hebrew].

[31] Ilan, "Hasmoneans."

[32] Cohen ("Epigraphical Rabbis," 11), contests this identification, but see my critique of his attitude, above n. 19. His remarks would be more fitting in regard to identifications such as S. Safrai, "The Synagogues South of Mt. Judah," *Immanuel* 3 (1973-4) 48-50; D. Orman, "Jewish Inscriptions of the Mishnah and Talmud Period from Qazrin in the Golan," *Tarbiz* 53 (1984) 542-4 [Hebrew].

name Queen Sadan (צדן מלכתא).[33] This name has, therefore, been identified as the Aramaic version of the Greek Helene,[34] the name by which the Adiabenese queen is known (*War* 5.253, 6.355; *Ant.* 20.17-101; *mYoma* 3:10, *mNazir* 3:6, *tYoma* 2:3, *tSukkah* 1:1). Had this name been discovered in another geographical setting, such an identification would have been rightly ridiculed. But it is not only the geographical setting that fits—the royal title "queen" is also convincing.[35]

In almost all the examples cited, doubts have always been raised as to the probability of the identification,[36] and doubts will certainly arise in the case of the identification proposed below. The question is always: which is weightier, the identification or the challenge to its plausibility? Therefore, with these criteria in mind I shall also propose a new historical identification.

2. The Case Study of Julia Crispina

The Greek papyri from the Babatha archive discovered by Yadin some thirty years ago in the Judaean Desert were published in 1989.[37] These documents inform us that the unnamed nephews of Babatha's second husband, designated "the orphans" in the documents, were represented in court in their claims against Babatha by two guardians: one, Besas son of Jesus, a Jew from Ein Gedi titled ἐπίτροπος (*P. Yadin* 20, 23, 24 and 25), and the other a woman, Julia Crispina, termed ἐπίσκοπος (*P. Yadin* 20 and 25).

The image of Julia Crispina had eluded Yadin. He described her and her exploits as follows:

---

[33] See M. Renan, "Nouvelles observations d'épigraphie hébraïque," Journal Asiatique 6 (Serie 6; 1865) 550-60.

[34] For example: M. Lidzbarski, *Handbuch der nordsemitischen Epigraphik* 1 (Weimar 1898) 117.

[35] S. Klein (*Jüdisch-palästinisches Corpus Inscriptionum* [Wien-Berlin 1920] 20) rejects this identification on onomastic grounds, but agrees that the queen mentioned in the inscription is of the same dynasty. His rejection is strange in view of the many other much less plausible identifications which he makes, for example, that of the priests of the Bnei Hezir Inscription with the Boethus priestly family, *ibid.*, 15-6; cf. also 19, 24, 28, 37, 39-42. However, the only other female of this dynasty mentioned by Josephus is a certain Grapte (*War* 4.567) and her name is Persian, so probably she did not have another non-Greek name.

[36] Tcherikover et al., *CPJ* 2, 200; Yadin, Naveh, *Masada 1*, 28; Cohen, "Epigraphical Rabbis," 10, n. 12; Schwabe, Lifschitz, *Beth She'arim* 2, 148, n. 6; Ilan, "Greek Names," 12-3; Roussel, "Nicanor d'Alexandrie," 79-82; J. Schwartz, "Nicanor Gate"; Klein, *Corpus Inscriptionum*, 20. *IEJ* has also been the stage of a hot debate over a proposed identification of this sort. See: B. Z. Rosenfeld, "The 'Boundary of Gezer' Inscriptions and the History of Gezer at the End of the Second Temple Period", *IEJ* 38 (1988) 235-45; R. Reich, "The 'Boundary of Gezer' Inscriptions Again," *IEJ* 40 (1990) 44-6; J. Schwartz, "Once More on the 'Boundary of Gezer' Inscriptions and the History of Gezer and Lydda at the End of the Second Temple Period," *ibid.*, 47-57.

[37] Lewis, *Greek Papyri*. See genealogical charts at the end of this chapter.

Besas appears with a mysterious Roman woman, by the name of Julia Crispina, who is described as *episkopos*, but the documents shed no light on the nature of her "overseership." She appears later in lieu of Besas who is indisposed in a legal dispute with Babata. Professor H. J. Polotsky,[38] when studying these documents, discovered an interesting allusion to a woman of the same name in a document from Fayyum in Egypt, dated 24 July 133, in which she declares her property there. "It would be a strange coincidence indeed" writes Professor Polotsky, "if two women of the same Roman name had been living at about the same time in the same area. The dates would seem to suggest, that after the spread of the Jewish Revolt Julia Crispina broke off her Jewish connections and transferred her activities to Egypt, if indeed they had not extended to Egypt even before."[39]

In the Egyptian document in question, the Roman Julia Crispina is writing a letter to the commander (στρατηγός), the royal scribe (βασιλικός γραμματεύς), the village scribe (κωμογραμματεύς) and the tax registrars (λαογραφοῖ) of a certain village, Dionysias, in the division (μερίς) of Themistes in the Arsinoite Nome, declaring her ownership of two houses with courtyards in the village for taxation purposes.[40]

We may sum up Yadin's queries concerning this Julia Crispina as follows: (1) Why was a Roman Matron serving as guardian of orphans in a place like Ein Gedi, a far outpost of the Empire? (2) What kind of connections with both Egypt and Palestine could such a Roman woman have had? In designating her "the mysterious Julia Crispina,"[41] Yadin assumed that these questions could not be answered.

One detail about Julia Crispina which Yadin had not disclosed, and which he may not even have noticed, but which came up in the final publication of the documents is the mention in the second document (*P. Yadin* 25) of Julia Crispina's father's name: Berenicianus. The name is rather a special one, certainly not Roman, so that the matron bearing it probably belonged to a Hellenized eastern family holding Roman citizenship.

Could one go further and identify this Berenicianus? The Jewish literature of the period records only one person by this name—the son of Queen Berenice from her second husband, King Herod of Chalcis, grandson of

---

[38] "The Greek Papyri from the Cave of the Letters," *IEJ* 12 (1962) 261-2.

[39] Y. Yadin, *Bar Kokhba: Rediscovery of the Legendary Hero of the Second Jewish Revolt against Rome* (Jerusalem 1971) 247-8.

[40] The papyrus can be seen in: *Ägyptische Urkunden aus den Königlichen Museen zu Berlin: Griechische Urkunden* 1 (Berlin, 1895) 57, no. 53. It is designated: *BGU* 53. This old publication contains a handwritten interpretation of the document (no photograph attached). The copying was performed by P. Viereck, and corrections were later suggested by U. Wilcken. The Staatliche Museen in Berlin (previously East Berlin) was kind enough to supply me with a photograph of the original, for which I am very grateful to Dr. G. Peothke of the Papyrus collection. As far as I can tell, Wilcken's readings were indeed correct.

[41] Yadin, *Bar Kokhba*, 247.

Herod the Great (*War* 2.221; *Ant.* 20.104).[42] Her first husband, as noted above, was the Egyptian Jew Marcus, son of Alexander, the alabarch of Alexandria.[43] Can we assume that Julia Crispina was Jewish and that she was the granddaughter of Queen Berenice? In other words, could Julia Crispina be identified as the last Herodian princess in Palestine? The answer to this question depends on how this identification matches the criteria we have outlined above.

a. Chronology

According to Fuks' aforementioned chronology,[44] Queen Berenice was married to King Herod of Chalcis between the years 44 and 48 CE. We are told that she bore him two sons: Hyrcanus and Berenicianus (*War* 2.221; *Ant.* 20.104). Although Berenicianus is mentioned first in both sources, we need not take this as an indication that he was the elder and may assume that he was born any time between 45 and 48 CE. This would make him 22-25 when Jerusalem was destroyed in 70 CE, and when his mother, Queen Berenice, was aspiring to the high position of empress, wife of the emperor designate Flavius Titus (Tacitus, *Histories* 2.2.1; Seutonius, *Titus* 7.1-2; Casius Dio, *Roman History* 66.15.3-5; 18.1; *Epitome de Caesaribus* 10.4-7).[45] If a daughter by the name of Julia Crispina had been born to him, say between 73 and 95 (his twenty-fifth through fiftieth birthday), she would have been somewhere between thirty-six and fifty nine years old when she served as guardian for the orphans at Ein Gedi, and between thirty-seven and sixty when she made her formal declaration of property in Egypt. Chronologically, the scenario is certainly possible.

b. Geography

What was Julia Crispina doing both in Egypt and in Ein Gedi, and how does her presence in these two places support her identification as Berenice's granddaughter? It would not be surprising to find the granddaughter of Queen Berenice owning property in Egypt. As mentioned above, Berenice's first marriage had been into the Jewish-Egyptian financial aristocracy. When her

---

[42] See: Ilan, *Statistical Study*, chapter 3; W. Pape, *Wörterbuch der griechischen Eigennamen* 1 (Braunschweig 1863) 206. Another person, a sophist, by the name of Beronicianus, is mentioned in Eunapius' *Lives of the Sophists* (See: W. C. Wright's English translation [Cambridge MA 1967] 565). The name could be a variant of Berenicianus, but it could also be the male Greek version of the Christian apocryphal name Veronica. The Bronicianus mentioned by Eunapius was still alive when his book was completed, at the end of the fourth century, a detail which is of importance for our dating theory, as will be shown below.

[43] See in this chapter, above.

[44] "Marcus Julius Alexander."

[45] On Berenice see E. Mireaux, *La Riene Bérénice* (Paris 1951); Ruth Jordan, *Berenice* (London 1974), and see chapter 3, above.

husband Marcus died, she could most certainly have inherited land in Egypt. The houses in Julia Crispina's possession are situated in an area densely populated with Jews—the Arsinoite Nome.[46] In fact, if we accept the identification suggested above, of the Gaius Julius Alexander of the papyri with Queen Berenice's first father-in-law, we find that he owned land in the village of Euhemeria, which is situated right next to Dionysias, the village where Julia Crispina owned her houses.[47] Another papyrus may add more, albeit circumstantial information in this matter. This papyrus[48] dating from 136 CE, is from Theadelphia, a third village in the Themistes division, situated west of Euhemeria, the same distance as Dionysias is located east of it.[49] It is a receipt given by the οἰκονομία of the division to one Eudaimon son of Theogis, who had rented land from the οὐσία of a woman by the name of Julia Berenice. Although the editor of the papyrus had noted the fact that this name is identical with that of the Herodian queen,[50] he cautioned against hasty conclusions, since the papyrus dates from 136 CE, obviously some years after the queen's death (last heard of, old and disappointed in 79 CE). Rostovzeff, therefore, suggested that the woman in question was a descendent of the queen,[51] although he states more than once that the estate had originally belonged to Berenice.[52] He based his suggestion on the fact that Julia Berenice in the papyrus is an owner of an οὐσία, an estate granted to favorites of the Julio-Claudian dynasty. The relationship between the imperial family and the Herodians is well known. So, too, is the imperial favor bestowed on the Alexandrian family of Alexander the alabarch into which Berenice married. All papyrological evidence of members of these two families in Egypt is concentrated in the division of Themisthes in the Arsinoite Nome. Julia Berenice of *MS P. Hamb.* 8 could be identified as a second daughter of

---

[46] See for example: Tcherikover et al., *Corpus* 1, 9.

[47] On the geography of the Fayum and the Arsinoite Nome, and on the relations between the two villages one to the other, see: B. P. Grenfell, A. S. Hunt and D. G. Hogarth, *Fayum Towns and Papyri* (London 1900) 10-1; Hohlwein "Euhemeria," 64. A map showing the two villages is found in N. Lewis, *Life in Egypt under Roman Rule* (Oxford 1983) 230-1. Lewis (*Greek Papyri*, 111) makes the mistake of calling Julia Crispina's village "Euhemeria." This mistake can only be understood as a result of Lewis' knowledge of Egyptian-Hellenistic geography and the very close proximity of the two villages, of which Lewis was aware. See, for example his *Life in Egypt*, 24. We know from The Catalogue of the Greek Papyri in the John Rylands Library 126 (Tcherikover et al., *Corpus* 2, 202-3, no. 420b), that the territories of Gaius Julius Alexander in Euhemeria passed into the hands of the Empress Livia at about 27 CE. However, lands owned by the family in the neighboring village, Dionysias, may have remained in Queen Berenice's hands.

[48] MS *P. Hamb.* 8—to be seen in: P. M. Meyer, *Griechische Papyrusurkunden der Hamburger Staats- und Universitätsbibliothek* 1 (Leipzig-Berlin 1911) 27-9, no. 8.

[49] See: Lewis, *Life in Egypt*, 230-1.

[50] Meyer, *Papyrusurkunden*, 27, n. 1.

[51] *Social and Economic History*, 672, no. 43.

[52] *Ibid.*, 293, 295.

Berenicianus, namely Julia Crispina's sister, named after her grandmother. Alternatively another Herodian-Egyptian connection may be proposed. We know that Berenice's sister, Mariamme, was married to Demetrius, alabarch of Alexandria (*Ant.* 20.147). It is, however, uncertain whether he was related at all to the family of the previous alabarch. We also know that Mariamme had a daughter from a previous marriage by the name of Berenice (*Ant.* 20.140). Julia Berenice of *P. Hamb.* 8 could very well be that daughter, or perhaps a descendent of hers.

Somewhat more elusive is the question of Julia Crispina's presence at Ein Gedi on the shore of the Dead Sea. Tentatively, one may assume that her business there stemmed from Herodian ownership of balsam groves. Of Herod's ownership of balsam we are informed elsewhere (*War* 1.361-362[?]; *Ant.* 15.96; Pliny, *Natural History* 12.111).[53] Another piece of circumstantial evidence may help us link Julia Crispina more closely with the balsam trade. Crown property in Judaea duly passed into the hands of the Roman treasury and was later disposed of at its discretion (Pliny, *Natural History* 12.111). A fine example of this is the crown lands of Beit She'arim.[54] From Josephus' *Vita* we learn that Queen Berenice owned fields and granaries there (118-9). At the time of Judah the Patriarch we are informed that these properties had been bestowed on his household by the emperor.[55] Furthermore, we learn also that Rabbi Judah the Patriarch owned balsam groves that he had received from the Roman authorities (*bBerakhot* 43a). We may assume that both parcels of property had originally belonged to the Herodian family. Although Pliny the elder, writing in 75 CE (*Natural History* 12.118), tells us that the balsam groves of Ein Gedi were being cultivated in his day by the *fiscus* (12.112-3), this is no indication that the Romans did not, eventually, hand this property back to their allies, the Herodians. Such a scenario is particularly plausible between 75 and 79 CE, the years when Queen Berenice was influential with Titus. Julia Crispina could have owned these Ein Gedi groves before the Bar Kokhba revolt.

c. Name

I claimed that three criteria help to determine whether the similarity of a name can render an identification possible.

---

[53] See also: Hannah M. Cotton and J. Geiger, *Masada II: The Latin and Greek Documents* (Jerusalem 1989) 68-70, on the balsam trade. Yadin and Naveh (*Masada I*, 47) mention a jar from Masada with the Hebrew inscription "balsam," which had almost certainly been owned by Herod or one of his household.

[54] Mazar, *Beth She'arim*, 5.

[55] S. Safrai, "Beit She'arim in Talmudic Literature," *Eretz Israel* 5 (1958) 206-12 [Hebrew]. See also in this chapter, above.

i. *Title*: Julia Crispina bears a most distinguished title—ἐπίσκοπος (overseer); yet it is not helpful in determining the identification. However, if Julia Crispina is a Herodian princess, this may explain why she bears a title of such authority.

ii. *Two Names*: Here the identification can receive further support. Although the name Crispina is absent from Herodian onomastics, the name Julia should certainly be considered the correct *gentilicum* of the Herodian family. Julius Caesar had bestowed Roman citizenship on Antipater, Herod the Great's father (*War* 1.194; *Ant.* 14.137), and the Herodians had henceforth borne this *nomen*.[56] Therefore, two elements in the name support the identification, both the father's name and the family name.

Further information, albeit circumstantial, should also be noted regarding the name Crispina. The name Crispus appears only once in the Jewish onomastics of the Second Temple Period, but the man who bears it is of interest to us. He is mentioned in Josephus' *Vita* as a member of the conservative Galilean aristocracy and a member of King Agrippa II's party (*Vita* 33), his full name being Julius Crispus. Agrippa II, be it remembered, was Queen Berenice's brother. We can assume that, enjoying such a status, Julius Crispus could easily have married his daughter off to Berenice's son. His daughter would, no doubt, have been called Julia Crispina.

iii. *Rare Name*: In Jewish onomastics and literature, the name Berenicianus is indeed rare. As stated above, it is present only in the name of Queen Berenice's son, and it is on this rarity that I have based our identification. However, we need not assume that Berenicianus of the Babatha archive was Jewish, and once we turn to the international and epigraphic scene the picture concerning this name changes considerably. It is mentioned in numerous inscriptions, as well as in two papyri from Egypt.[57]

---

[56] See, for example: the inscription of Queen Berenice from Athens, where she is designated "Queen Julia Berenice daughter of the Great King Julius Agrippa," W. Dittenberger, *Orientis Graeci Inscriptiones Selectae* 1 (Leipzig 1903) 638-9, no. 428; Agrippa II is probably designated "[Marcus Jul]ius Agrippa" in another inscription: *ibid.*, 632, no. 421.

[57] Here is a full catalogue of the names I have come up with; it is based largely on data provided by Prof. P. M. Fraser, editor of the *Lexicon of Greek Personal Names* (to date three volumes have appeared: Oxford 1987, 1994 and 1997), to whom I am indebted for the information beyond the material found in the published volumes. I also wish to thank Prof. J. Geiger who introduced me to the editor of the lexicon. A. The inscriptions: (1) W. Froehmer, *Les Inscriptions Greques, Musée Impérial du Louvre* (Paris 1865) no. 176; (2) W. H. Waddington, *Inscriptions Grecques et Latines de la Syrie* (Paris 1870) no. 2404; (3) *ibid.*, no. 2547; (4) *ibid.*, no. 2557c; (5) O. Reimann, "Inscriptions Greques provenant du recueil Cyriaque d'Anacone," *Bulletin de correspondence hellènique* 1 (1877) 292; (6) B. Haussoullier, "L'oracle d'Apolon à Claros," *Revue de Philologie* 22 (1898) 260-1; (7) R. Brünnow, "Reisebericht 1898," *Mitteilungen und Nachrichten des Deutschen*

I would like, therefore, to suggest here a radical history for this name. The masculine name Berenicianus is without doubt derived from the feminine Berenice. The name Berenice had been extensively used the world over since the Hellenistic Period. It was the name of Egyptian-Ptolemaic queens[58] and served as a name for a great city in Cyrene and an important port on the Red Sea, as well as other Hellenistic cities. The male name Berenicianus was unheard of until the outspoken Herodian queen decided to name her son after herself. It was most common in the Hellenistic and Roman world and was becoming increasingly popular with the Jews to name women with the feminine version of a male name. Queen Berenice decided to reverse the practice. This Berenicianus may, therefore, be the first in the world. No evidence to the contrary exists.

Both the papyri and eight of the inscriptions are dated, and all mentions of Bereniciani in them post-date our man. A papyrus from Memphis (no. 24 in n. 57), mentioning the rhetor Berenicianus, is dated 135 CE. This rhetor is therefore of the same age or younger than Julia Crispina, thus a generation younger than the Berenicianus we are dealing with. The second papyrus (nos. 26-27), recording two persons by the name of Berenicianus, has been dated to the year 197-8 CE.

Of the eight dated inscriptions, four are precisely dated to 143 CE (no. 20), 199-208 CE (no. 10), 202-3 CE (no. 21) and 249 CE (no. 9). Two others may be dated by implication. No. 19 should be dated to the late third century at the earliest, since it is a typical Christian burial inscription; and no. 23, as suggested by the editor, should be dated to the first half of the third century, given the imperial *cognomen* Antoninus borne by this man.

The dating of inscription no. 4 in n. 57 merits special attention. This inscription was found in the village of Rakhle, at the foot of Mount Hermon, in the vicinity of Chalcis, Queen Berenice's kingdom. Although the word ἔτους (year) is clearly visible on the inscription, as well as the name of the

---

Palästina-Vereins 5 (1899) 87, no. 54; (8) I. Delamarre, *Inscriptionum Graecum* 12 (VII) (Berolini 1908) no. 353; (9) G. Kolbe, *ibid.* 5 (I) (1913) no. 1398.81; (10) J. Kirchner, *ibid.* 2² (1914) n. 2203.61; (11) E. Littman and D. Magie, *Syria: Publications of the Princeton University Archaeological Expedition to Syria in 1904-5 and 1909, Division III: Greek and Latin Inscriptions* (Leiden 1921) no. 435; (12) *ibid.*, no. 765.11; (13-14) *ibid.*, no. 793.4; (15) *ibid.*, no. 797.8; (16) *SEG* 7 (1934) no. 278; (17) *ibid.*, no. 330; (18) *ibid.*, 8 (1937) no. 120; (19) L. Jalabert and R. Monterde, *Inscriptions Grecques et Latines de la Syrie II: Chalcidique et Antiochene* (Paris 1939) no. 324; (20) *ibid.*, no. 556; (21) L. Jalabert, R. Monterde and C. Mondesert, *Inscriptions Grecques et Latines de la Syrie IV: Laodicée Apamene* (Paris 1955) no. 1379; (22) T. Weigand, *Didyma: 2. Teil: Die Inschriften* in A. Rehm (ed.), (Berlin 1958) no. 14; (23) J. P. Rey-Coquais, *Inscriptions Greques et Latines de la Syrie VI: Ba'albek et Beqa'* (Paris 1967) no. 2784 (in Latin); (24) R. Merkelbach and J. Nolle, *Die Inschriften von Ephesos* 6 (Bonn 1980) no. 2039. B. The papyri: (25) *BGU* 136; (26-27) F. G. Kenyon, *Greek Papyri in the British Museum* 3 (London 1907) 61-8.
[58] For a full list, see: U. Wilcken, "Berenike," *Pauly-Wissowa Real-Encyclopädie der klassischen Altertumswissenschaft* 3/1 (Stuttgart 1897) 282-7, nos. 9-14.

Macedonian month Xandikos, the actual figure referring to the year is unclear. In his initial publication,[59] Waddington refrained from suggesting a date. A second publication[60] suggested that the year should read: 344 (δμτ'), although a question mark following the suggestion indicates its tentative nature. If, however, this reading is correct, the question of the era by to which this date is calculated should be considered. In the computerized information provided me by the *Lexicon of Greek Personal Names* this inscription was dated to 32 CE, apparently based on the assumption that the era is that of the Seleucid dynasty, beginning in 312 BCE; but I believe that this interpretation is wrong. The words of the text read as follows: ἔτους δμτ' [Ξ]ανδί[κ]ου, ἐπὶ ἀρχῆς 'Αβιλάνου (the year 344, month Xandikos, in the time of the sovereignty of Abila) i.e. of the Abila calendar. Abila was one of the Greek cities of the Decapolis in Transjordan. According to the coins of this city, the calander of Abila began in the year 63 BCE (with the Roman conquest of the East).[61] If this interpretation is correct, the date of this inscription is 281 CE, and it too post-dates Berenicianus, Berenice's son. All the other inscriptions have been tentatively dated by their publishers to no earlier than the second century.

One Berenicianus, apparently mentioned in two inscriptions, one dated and one undated, may be of special interest. A Gaius Julius Alexander Berenicianus is mentioned on an inscription from Ephesus (no. 5 in n. 57), which was copied in the 15th Century by Cyrique of Anacona and has not been seen since. This Berenicianus could be identified with another man who had served as proconsul of the province Asia in the year 132-3, mentioned in an inscription from Laodicea (no. 6 in n. 57), where he is designated Berenicianus son of Alexander. In 1882[62] Waddington had identified this Berenicianus with the grandson of Alexander, the last Herodian king of

---

[59] Above, n. 57, no. 4.

[60] M. Renan, "Note additionalle à la page 81," *Mémoires de l'Institute Impérial de France: Académie des Inscriptions et Belle Lettres* 26 (1870) 559-60.

[61] See: Y. Meshorer, *City Coins of Eretz Israel and the Decapolis in the Roman Period* (Jerusalem 1985) 78.

[62] W. H. Waddington, "Aux Fastes de la province d'Asie," *Bulletin de correspondance hellènique* 6 (1882) 289-91.

Cilicia (*Ant.* 18.140).[63] If this identification is correct, it is an indication that at least one other of the persons bearing this name was of Herodian stock.[64]

It appears that the name Berenicianus quickly gained popularity in Herodian circles and elsewhere, particularly in the vicinity of Chalcis were Berenice had been queen. Most of the inscriptions with the name Berenicianus are from Syria and Lebanon. These may testify to Berenice's popularity in her own time and her influence thereafter.

3. Discussion

Some justification exists for the proposed identification of Julia Crispina of the Babatha archive as the granddaughter of Queen Berenice. What is gained by this identification? We may now be in a position to solve the two questions raised by Yadin (one of them directly relevant to the issue of women's social position), and gain information in a third field—our knowledge of the post-70 CE Herodians.

i. According to tannaitic Jewish law, it is forbidden for a woman to serve as a guardian to orphans, nor is it even recommended (though it is legal) in the case of their mother (*tTerumah* 1.11; *tBava Batra* 8.17). The case of Jesus, Babatha's son from her first marriage, serves as a good example. Babatha was not his legal guardian. The court at Petra had nominated two men for this purpose, one a Jew and one a Nabatean, as their names—John son of Egla; Abdobdas son of Illouthas—indicate (*P. Yadin* 12, 13, 14, 15, 27).[65] However, one should not expect the Nabatean courts of Petra and Maoza to act according to Jewish law, neither as independent Nabatean courts, nor after Nabatea became the Roman province Arabia in 106. The nomination by these courts of two guardians for the orphans of Joseph, Babatha's second

---

[63] This Alexander's reign is subject to uncertainty. See E. Groag, "Julius (Alexander)," *Pauly-Wissowa Real-Encyclopädie der klassischen Altertumswissenschaft* 10/1 (Stuttgart 1917) 151-2. However, because of the name Berenicianus it has been suggested (*ibid.*, 157-8) that the Gaius Julius Alexander Berenicianus of the Ephesos and Laodicea Inscriptions was a descendant of the Herodian house of Chalcis i.e. the family of Queen Berenice, and not of the Armenian-Asian branch; or alternatively, that his mother too was called Berenice (perhaps the Berenice mentioned in *Ant.* 20.140). This suggestion presumes what I claim, i.e. that Berenicianus, Queen Berenice's son, is thus named after his mother.

[64] Inscription no. 20 of the year 143 could perhaps also be assigned to this person, because, according to a feasible reconstruction, it mentions an Antonius Herod Alexander Bernicianus, son of Alexander. The inscription's location, Antioch, is not far removed from Laodicea. The editor of inscription no. 23 has also suggested a Herodian-Chalcian kinship for its subject. The man's name is Ti[berio] Claudio Antonino C[al]purnio Attic[o] [Iul]io [B]erenic[iano] Ti(beri) Claudi A[ntoni]ni Attici [f(ilio)].

[65] On this issue, see Hannah M. Cotton, "The Guardianship of Jesus son of Babatha: Roman and Local Law in the Province of Arabia," *JRS* 83 (1993) 393-420.

husband's brother, is interesting in this context. Roman law, as well as Jewish law, forbade women from serving as legal guardians. On the contrary, a woman was not expected to appear before a Roman court of law except with a male guardian.[66] Babatha, in her transactions, always followed this procedure (*P. Yadin* 14, 15, 16, 17, 22, 25, 27). The fact that Julia Crispina, a woman, serves as a guardian, an exclusively male obligation in both Jewish and Roman law, is surprising.

The question is not only, how could a court of law under Roman jurisdiction appoint a woman to such a function, but more importantly, what would have induced an obscure Roman matron to accept such an obligation? The other guardian, Besas, was obviously a Jew, as the name of his father (Jesus) indicates. Thus, his inclination to accept the position offered him is understandable as an obligation toward a fellow Jew.

Although the legal question remains unsolved, the present inquiry may enable to understand Julia Crispina's motivation in accepting the appointment. We could understand her interest in the matter if she was a Jew. Her nomination by the court could be seen as a provincial anomaly, but only if she were also wealthy and important. If she was in fact a Herodian, she was both, beside being also public-spirited, assuming that her family connections entailed some obligation toward the Jewish people. The title that she bore, ἐπίσκοπος, may have had nothing to do with the specific obligations of guardian, to which she was nominated. Perhaps it should be understood as an honorific title bestowed upon her in view of her position as successor to the Herodian royal dynasty.

ii. Julia Crispina's presence in Egypt in 133 CE can likewise be explained in this vein. In 132 CE hostilities broke out in Judaea. Julia Crispina, a true Herodian, would not have sided with the Jewish rebels against Rome. In any case, Palestine ceased to be a safe place, so she withdrew to her Egyptian holdings to await the outcome of events. Her letter to the tax officers at her village in Egypt need not indicate an "absentee owner."[67] Rather, it may be an attempt to put her business in order once she had arrived on the scene.

iii. If my suggestion is correct, we also learn that not all Herodians emigrated to Rome after 70 CE. Indeed we know that Queen Berenice herself was asked to leave Rome on one or more occasions.[68] Where did she retire? Did Titus restore her Herodian balsam groves? Can we now add to the Roman, Armenian, Egyptian and Asian post-70 CE Herodians a Judaean branch as

---

[66] Sarah B. Pomeroy, *Goddesses, Whores, Wives and Slaves* (New York 1975) 150-3; and see now Hannah M. Cotton, "The Guardian (Ἐπίτροπος) of a Woman in the Documents from the Judaean Desert," *ZPE* 118 (1996) 267-73.

[67] As suggested by Lewis, *Greek Papyri*, 111.

[68] J. A. Crooke, "Titus and Berenice," *American Journal of Philology* 72 (1951) 162-75.

well?[69] Can we also postulate, on the strength of the Julia Crispina papyrus from Egypt, that after the Bar Kokhba revolt this branch of the Herodian dynasty migrated to Egypt? The evidence adduced in this chapter lends plausibility to that hypothesis.

1. Late Herodian Genealogical Chart

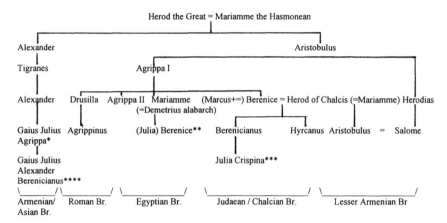

All Herodians with asterix mentioned elsewhere other than Josephus.
*C. Curtius, "Inschriften von Ephesos," *Hermes* 4 (1870) 190-1.
**Perhaps the Julia Berenice mentioned in *P. Hamb.* 8, above, n. 48.
*** *P. Yadin* 20, 25, above n. 1.
****Waddington "Aux Fastes." For an alternative, see Groag, *Pauly-Wissowa* 19, 151-2
+For Marcus' genealogy, see Chart 2 below.
For other possible Herodians, see also: above, n. 64.

2. Genealogical Chart of the Family of Philo of Alexandria

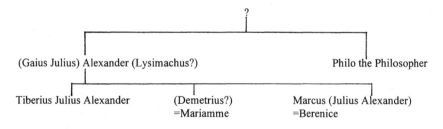

---

[69] See an attempt to draw the complete Herodian genealogy: K. C. Hanson, "The Herodians and the Mediterranean Kinship," *Biblical Theological Bulletin* 19 (1989) 75-84; 142-51. See also: appended genealogical chart.

Chapter Nine

"He Who Eats at his Father-in-Law's in Judaea ... Cannot Bring a Virginity Suit" (*mKetubbot* 1:5) Premarital Cohabitation in the Judaean Desert Papyri and the Mishnah

1. The Marriage Contract of Salome Komaise

The marriage contract of Salome Komaise was first published together with the now famous Babatha archive from the Cave of Letters in Nahal Hever.[1] Yadin discovered this archive, together with other documents, in that cave in the early 1960s.[2] They were deposited in the cave in the aftermath of the Bar Kokhba revolt (135 CE) by Jewish survivors of nearby Ein Gedi, who fled to the desert taking their documents with them. Some of them were actually refugees from Maoza in the province of Arabia. Apparently, they all died in the cave. Recently, Hannah Cotton has convincingly shown that this document should be considered part of the archive of another Jewish woman, Salome Komaise, whose documents had been discovered by Bedouins and sold to French archaeologists in Jerusalem.[3]

The document discussed here is a marriage contract written to Salome Komaise of Maoza by a Jesus son of Menahem. It displays various interesting features that one does not expect to find in a Jewish marriage document, such as a clause in which the husband assumes responsibility for the support of his wife "in accordance with Greek custom (νομῷ Ἑλληνικῷ)"; the presence of a guardian (ἐπίτροπος) who represents the bride, as is customary in Greek documents from the Judaean Desert—but certainly not in Jewish ones; and the size of the bridal settlement (ninety-six *denarii*) does not accord with the Jewish legal tradition of the *ketubbah*, which stipulates two hundred *zuz* for a

---

[1] See in N. Lewis, *The Documents from the Bar Kokhba Period in the Cave of the Letters: Greek Papyri* (Jerusalem 1989) 130-133 = *P. Yadin* 37; and see now its republication in Hannah M. Cotton and Ada Yardeni, *Discoveries in the Judaean Desert* 27 (Oxford 1997) 224-37, where it is designated *XHev/Se* 65.

[2] Y. Yadin, *Bar Kokhba: Rediscovery of the Legendary Hero of the Second Jewish Revolt against Rome* (Jerusalem 1971).

[3] On this discovery and its connection to the discoveries in Nahal Hever, see Cotton and Yardeni, *Discoveries*, 224-37. On the archive of Salome Komaise, see pp. 158-65.

virgin and one hundred for a widow or divorcee (*mKetubbot* 1:2). All these matters have been discussed elsewhere.[4]

Another unusual clause in the document states that "Jesus son of Menahem ... has taken Salome ... to live with her as heretofore (συμβιῶσαι [τὸν ᾽Ιησοῦν μετ᾽] αὐτῆς [ὧς κ]αὶ πρὸ τούτου τοῦ χρόνου)." This statement raises several questions with relation to the nearly universal view of Jewish society and Jewish matrimonial practices during the Roman period as reflected in Jewish sources. This view maintains that girls were kept segregated in their homes before marriage so as to insure that they entered matrimony as virgins; their husbands were selected by their fathers, and seldom did the bride get a chance to meet her prospective husband, much less to live with him before nuptials took place.[5] When describing the mishnaic system of women, Neusner made the following statement:

> It is beyond the Mishnah's imagination for a man and a woman to live together without the benefit of a betrothal, a marriage contract and a consummation of marriage. I cannot think of a single rule which takes account of the possibility of cohabitation other than normal, legal procedures.[6]

Neusner's statement summarizes the legal status of the issue that we are discussing, as found in the Mishnah. Even if this rigid view is actually the impression given in these subjective, tendentious and strongly-motivated bodies of data, the Mishnah[7] and the Talmud—and even if people did not exactly conform to the restrictions prescribed by these sources, it seems remarkable, nevertheless, that reference to a previous, highly informal relationship between a man and a woman would actually be made in a marriage contract drawn up between two Jews.

Thus in this second-century CE marriage contract executed by Jews, we encounter a highly unusual statement that the couple had actually cohabited before they were formally married. The following discussion attempts to place this unusual clause in a historical perspective. In order to do so, however, I must first ascertain that, both linguistically and legally, this is the correct reading of the Greek sentence.

---

[4] On the "Greek custom" clause see R. Katzoff, "Papyrus Yadin 18—Legal Commentary," *IEJ* 37 (1987) 239-42; A. Wasserstein, "A Marriage Contract from the Province of Arabia Nova: Notes on Papyrus Yadin 18," *JQR* 80 (1989) 105-30. On the guardian, see now Hannah M. Cotton, "The Guardian (ἐπίτροπος) of a Woman in the Documents from the Judaean Desert," *ZPE* 118 (1996) 267-73. On the dowry and bride price, see M. Satlow, "Reconsidering the Rabbinic *ketubbah* Payment," in S. J. D. Cohen (ed.), *The Jewish Family* (Atlanta 1993) 133-51; Cotton and Yardeni, *Discoveries*, 266-8.

[5] See my *Mine and Yours are Hers: Retrieving Women's History from Rabbinic Literature* (Leiden 1997) 174-83.

[6] J. Neusner, *A History of the Mishnaic Law of Women* 5 (Leiden 1980) 266.

[7] On the Mishnah and the regulation of women's lives, see Judith Romney Wegner, *Chattel or Person: The Status of Women in the Mishnah* (Oxford 1988).

2. σύμβιος

What exactly is the meaning of συμβιόω, the verb used in the document to denote the act of living together? In various documents, this verb signifies married life and the noun derived from it - σύμβιος - simply means "spouse." The verb appears also in another Jewish-Greek marriage document discovered in the Judaean Desert and published some years ago: a remarriage contract, that is, a second marriage contracted by the same couple (Elai son of Simon and Salome daughter of Yohanan Galgoula) after a formal divorce (henceforth *Mur* 115).[8] Sources indicate that remarriage was not an uncommon phenomenon in Jewish society.[9] The document states that Salome had previously been taken by him to wife (προγενομέ[νην] ...σύμβιον), that he had divorced her and now he wished to take her again as his wife "out of need for communal life (σ[υ]νβιώσεος χάριν)."

On the other hand, the more common term for the act of marriage, γαμέω, is absent from Salome Komaise's marriage contract, but appears in *Mur* 115 (εἰ[ς γυναῖ]κα γαμετήν)[10] in *XHev/Se* 69 ([γυναῖκα] γαμετήν)[11] and in *P. Yadin* 18 (γυναῖκαν γαμετὴν πρὸς γάμου),[12] where, conversely, the term σύμβιος and its derivatives are absent.

What then is the semantic difference between the two terms? The lexicons indicate that while the verb συμβιόω describes the ongoing activity of married life, the verb γαμέω denotes the isolated act of taking a wife in marriage.[13] It is therefore not at all surprising that *Mur* 115 would employ the term συμβιόω to describe the couple's previous marriage. Similarly, the use of γαμέω in *P. Yadin* 18 is readily understood; Salampsio is simply taken as a wife. Even in *Mur* 115 γαμέω describes the actual renewed act of taking Salome to wife.

We may, therefore, summarize the evidence and connect it with the Salome Komaise document as follows. The use of the verb συμβιόω indicates an ongoing cohabitation of the couple, which is interrupted by a marriage ceremony in order to make it official. γαμέω is absent because it is unnecessary, since Jesus does not perform a discrete act of taking a wife. We have indeed understood the text correctly. Salome Komaise and Jesus son of

---

[8] R. de Vaux, P. Benoit and J. T. Milik, *Discoveries in the Judaean Desert 2: Les grottes de Muraba'ât* (Oxford 1961) 248.

[9] For example, Herod remarried his first wife, Doris, after the execution of his second wife, Mariamme the Hasmonean (*War* 1.451; *Ant.* 16.85). See also *mGittin* 4:7; *tYevamot* 13:5.

[10] De Vaux et al., *Discoveries*, 248.

[11] Cotton and Yardeni, *Discoveries*, 265.

[12] Lewis, *Greek Papyri*, 78.

[13] LSJ, *s.v.* γαμέω, 337; συμβιόω, 1657; F. Preisigke, *Wörterbuch der griechischen Papyrusurkunden* 1 (Berlin 1925), 282; 2, 508.

Menahem had been living together as a married couple without actually contracting an official marriage. How then should we interpret this information against the historical background of Jewish society in second-century Judaea?

3. Modes of Interpretation

Ancient texts like Salome Komaise's marriage contract paint a picture of ancient Jewish society quite divergent from the conservative impression given by other texts—such as the Mishnah—that many consider normative. Recent and not so recent research into these texts gives rise to two diametrically opposite attitudes: the "apologetic" and the "provocative." Obviously the promoters of the provocative interpretation are the ones who describe the counter-interpretation as apologetic, while the champions of the apologetic view designate the view of their opponents provocative. I do not use either term in a derogatory sense here, although I shall eventually situate myself within the latter.

a. The Apologetic Approach

In the study of texts dealing with women, the apologetic approach is promoted by conservative scholars who set out to demonstrate that the document in question does not really contradict their perception of the ancient world, ancient Christianity, or, as in this case, ancient Judaism. All that needs to be done is to read the document in light of what we "know."[14] It is important for the apologetic Jewish scholar to rest assured that his world view is indeed correct, because it would support his conjecture that Judaism's attitude to women today, which is directly linked to the view of women in rabbinic literature, is in fact the approach always adopted by Jews toward women. It would be highly reassuring for such a scholar to know that since traditional Judaism (as s/he views it) cannot imagine premarital cohabitation, nothing of this nature was ever tolerated or had ever legally existed within Judaism.

This sort of apologetic has already appeared in relation to the Salome Komaise contract. Here are some examples:

(1) *Orphaned Minor*: In his minimal commentary on the document, the editor, Naphtali Lewis, stated:

> Jewish custom is reflected in all probability in the statement that the bridal pair are to live henceforth ... "as also before this time." In Greek papyri in Egypt there are instances of couples living together as man and wife in what is termed as "unwritten marriage" (ἄγραφος γάμος), which was sometimes later converted by a written contract into

---

[14] For an interesting example of this sort see on the Qumranic text *1Qsa* 1.10-1, above chapter 1.

ἔγγραφος γάμος. Close as the parallel may be, however, in [*P. Yadin*] 37 the expression "as also before this time" implies that the bride and groom had been living together since the day of their betrothal, in keeping with the Jewish practice of the time when the bride was both an orphan and a minor.[15]

Lewis' statement betrays a tension between the two interpretations that occurred to him. As a scholar of Egyptian-Hellenistic legal documents,[16] he was inclined to identify this clause with similar legal situations familiar to him from Egyptian papyri. In his legal commentary on the Babatha archive, however, Lewis collaborated with Jewish scholars, who were assigned the task of producing legal commentary on the documents in light of Jewish legal traditions. The commentary is not yet published, but this remark undoubtedly indicates how the scholars involved in this project intend to approach the documents.

Ranon Katzoff has defended the position taken by Lewis in the above passage by stating that according to Jewish law, a man could live with a woman without being officially married to her only if she was a minor whose father was dead, and who had been married off by her mother or brother.[17] Such a marriage would become valid only when the minor girl assumed adulthood and consented to the marriage by refraining from exercising her right of refusal (*mYevamot* 13:2). Katzoff, it appears, inferred from this halakhah that only after this consent would a marriage contract be drawn up. This interpretation seems to me a typical talmudic "pilpul," designed to explain away a clear conflict between law and life by dismissing the case as reflecting a very limited legal situation. This sort of argument occurs frequently in the talmudic text and a specific terminology was developed for it by the talmudic rabbis ("לא קשיא - It is not difficult" i.e. there is no problem here).

In the case of Salome Komaise we can go even further in dismissing Katzoff's argument. Hannah Cotton, who has identified and published the rest of the Salome Komaise archive, states as follows:

We now know a great deal more about Salome Komaise: She was indeed an orphan in 131 [CE, the year the contract was drawn], but not a minor. Already in 127 (if not before) she had been married to Sammouos son of Simon, who represented her in [*XHev/Se*] 63. Yeshu'a son of Menahem is her second husband.[18]

---

[15] Lewis, *Greek Papyri*, 130.

[16] See, e.g., his *Life in Egypt under Roman Rule* (Oxford 1983).

[17] R. Katzoff, "The Age of Marriage of Jewish Girls During the Talmudic Period," in M. A. Friedman (ed.), *Marriage and the Family in Halakha and Jewish Thought* (*Te'uda* 13; Tel Aviv 1997) 9-18. For another example of this kind of interpretation see *idem*, "Polygamy in P. Yadin?" *ZPE* 109 (1995) 128-32.

[18] Cotton and Yardeni, *Discoveries*, 227.

(2) *Marriage Contract and "Ketubbah"*: From a very different quarter and with a different agenda comes the claim that this document should not be studied in the light of Jewish law at all, since it is not really a *ketubbah*, but rather a typical Greek marriage contract.[19] This argument, intended to wrest this and similar documents from the hands of talmudists and place them in those of classicists, suggests that in a confused world where many legal systems operated side by side and some worked better than others, prudent people armed themselves with two documents, each appropriate to a different legal system—the *ketubbah* for the Jewish courts and a contract in Greek for the Roman courts. Such an argument could easily be employed by apologists: Surely Jesus must have written a proper *ketubbah* for Salome Komaise at their actual nuptials, but later, just to be on the safe side, he also composed a Greek marriage contract which stated that the couple had already been married for some time. Salome took this document with her to the cave but carelessly left behind her Hebrew (or more likely Aramaic) *ketubbah*.

This explanation sounds logical. At this point, however, it cannot be corroborated, and circumstantial evidence appears to negate it. In the Judaean Desert both Greek marriage contracts and Aramaic *ketubbot* have in fact been discovered.[20] The Babatha archive, however, seems to me to be the most obvious place to expect a double document situation. Babatha was a very tidy person who treasured her paperwork and preserved it in full, including the Aramaic *ketubbah* from her second marriage;[21] no corresponding Greek marriage contract has been found. This archaeological situation of course, could be a coincidence, and perhaps Babatha never did receive a Greek document from her husband. One may even claim that Babatha's family did not believe in supplementing the Aramaic document with a Greek one. Babatha, however, did preserve the marriage contract of her stepdaughter—this one in Greek. The stepdaughter, like the stepmother, also had only one document, strangely not of the same kind as Babatha's.

It seems to me that there is a much better explanation for the bilingual situation—the time factor. Of the three Aramaic documents preserved in the Judaean desert, the two with their dates intact predate[22] the four dated Greek documents.[23] With the destruction of the Temple, the power of Jewish courts was much curtailed and they became institutions of arbitration rather than effective law-enforcement instruments. It soon became obvious to the holders of the documents that for enforcement of contracts, including marriage

---

[19] This is the case put forward by Wasserstein, "Marriage Contract," 121.

[20] For a complete catalogue, see Hannah M. Cotton "A Canceled Marriage Contract from the Judaean Desert," *JRS* 84 (1994) 65.

[21] Y. Yadin, J. C. Greenfield and Ada Yardeni, "Babatha's Ketubba," *IEJ* 44 (1994) 75-101.

[22] *Mur.* 20 (117 CE); *P. Yadin* 10 (125 CE)

[23] *Mur.* 115 (124 CE); *P. Yadin* 18 (128 CE); *XHev/Se* 69 (130); *XHev/Se* 65 (131 CE).

settlements, the pagan courts were now more reliable, and these courts unfortunately did not usually read Aramaic. The Jews thus resorted to writing Greek marriage documents.

I shall now briefly enumerate and discount some other apologetic explanations that may be advanced for the σύμβιος passage in Salome Komaise's marriage contract.

(3) *"Ketubbah" Written after Marriage*: It may be suggested that Jesus and Salome were married according to Jewish law, but only later wrote down their marriage contract. This notion, however, certainly negates the main thrust of Jewish *ketubbah* legislation:

> Said Rabbi Meir: A man may not keep (ישהא) his wife even one hour without a *ketubbah* (*bBava Qama* 89a).

Further, *aggadah* bears out this approach:

> A betrothed man and woman (ארוס וארוסתו) who were captured by gentiles were married off one to the other. She said to him "Please, do not touch me, since I have no *ketubbah* from you." And he did not touch her until the day he died (*bGittin* 57a).

(4) *Concubinage*: It may be suggested that until the moment when Jesus handed Salome her marriage contract, she was merely his concubine (פלגש) since the rabbinic sources make the distinction:

> What constitutes a wife and what constitutes a concubine (פילגש)? Rabbi Meir says: A wife has a *ketubbah*, a concubine does not have a *ketubbah* (*yKetubbot* 5:2, 29d).

Most scholars believe, however, that concubinage as a legal institution was moribund by the Second Temple period.[24]

(5) *The Putative "Ketubbah"*: According to the Mishnah, if a man does not actually write a *ketubbah*, he is nevertheless obligated to provide for his wife according to a standard set of rules. For example:

> [Even] if he had not written a *ketubbah* for her, [a wife who married as] a virgin collects two hundred *zuz* [on the death of her husband or on divorce] and [one who married as] a widow [collects] one hundred (*mKetubbot* 4:7).

It may be suggested that at first Jesus had thought he need not write a *ketubbah* because, in the event of divorce or death, he would comply with the norms set out by the rabbis, but eventually he came to the conclusion that these were too heavy and he therefore formulated his own marriage contract.

---

[24] See e.g. L. M. Epstein, *Marriage Laws in the Bible and the Talmud* (Cambridge MA 1942) 62-76.

While the amounts cited in rabbinic sources are, as mentioned above, either two hundred *denarii* for a virgin or one hundred for a widow or divorcee, Salome Komaise's contract guarantees the wife only ninety-six *denarii*. The sums stipulated in rabbinic halakhah are minimum amounts and a husband is permitted to pay his widow or divorcee *more*, but certainly not *less*. The sum in Salome's contract thus does not comply with rabbinic dicta.[25]

The apologetic approach has thus produced two interpretations and I have suggested three others, all of which harmonize the σύμβιος clause in the Salome Komaise document with the laws preserved in rabbinic literature. I suppose still other explanations of this sort could be suggested, but I believe I have demonstrated the extent to which these are devised more to preserve the writers' worldview than to decode the meaning of the new source. The victim of this attitude is history. Thus a new approach is required if we are to produce a more credible historical account. This approach can appropriately be named "provocative."

b. The Provocative Approach

The provocative interpretation of passages about women is championed these days by feminist scholars. In her ground-breaking work on women leaders in the ancient synagogue, Bernadette Brooten, after tracing all apologetic explanations of functional titles found for women in synagogue inscriptions from the Greek and Roman world, concluded:

> Rather than trying to fit these inscriptions into our preconceived notions of what women were (or are) and of what Judaism was, would it not be more reasonable to take these in-scriptions as a challenge to our pre-conceptions, as traces of Judaism of which we know very little?[26]

Brooten's book, which suggested the possibility that titles for Jewish women such as ἀρχισυναγωγή (head of synagogue) should be taken at face value, was very provocative when it appeared. Today, after seventeen years, Brooten's book has nearly become a classic, extensively quoted and greatly acclaimed.[27]

The interpretation I wish to suggest for this text, along the same lines, is of a provocative nature. I propose that the text should be taken to mean exactly

---

[25] Both Satlow ("Rabbinic *ketubba*,") and Cotton (Cotton and Yardeni, *Discoveries*, 266-9) have convincingly shown that in any case the sum mentioned in Salome's contract is not a sum the husband will pay his wife if he divorces her, but rather the sum he owes her because she has contributed it to the marriage as dowry.

[26] Bernadette J. Brooten, *Women Leaders in the Ancient Synagogue* (*Brown Judaic Studies* 36; Atlanta 1982) 32.

[27] Thus, Brooten's thesis is tackled alongside the works of such important scholars as Emil Schürer and Jean Juster in Tessa Rajak and D. Noy, "Archsynagogoi: Office, Title and Social Status in the Greco-Jewish Synagogue," *JRS* 83 (1993) 82-4; 87.

what it claims. Some men and women in the Jewish society of second-century Palestine did indeed live together without the benefit of an official marriage. Moreover, this claim can actually be verified from rabbinic sources themselves.

3. Tannaitic Sources

Rabbinic sources, primarily the body of laws that evolved into the Mishnah and other tannaitic corpora, set out to describe the way Judaism should ideally function. These conceptions can hardly be taken as historical descriptions. Legal tannaitic rulings, however, were not created in a vacuum, but composed within a society that functioned in accordance with ancient ancestral customs, various foreign influences and a confusing legal system. Try as they would, the rabbis could not ignore these elements. They could, however bend and mold them to fit into their system. When confronted with a custom or norm that had taken hold in society, they explained it as either an anomalous streak of their halakhah or as a violation of it. Nevertheless, it is exactly these glimpses into practices opposed to the general ethos of the rabbis that should be considered reliable historical matter. Pericopae in rabbinic literature that describe a reality similar to the one emerging from the σύμβιος clause in the marriage contract of Salome Komaise fall into this category. They are garbled and apologetic, indicating that the tendency to explain away did not begin in modern times. Once the apologetics are stripped off, however, we are left with viable information on Jewish social history in the second century CE.

First, the rabbinic legal system recognizes in principle a form of marriage that is instituted through sexual intercourse:

> A wife is acquired in three ways ... by money, by deed or by intercourse (*mQiddushin* 1:1).

This text posits intercourse as a valid effector of marriage—equivalent in all aspects to the writ, which may be interpreted as the marriage contract. Rabbinic literature is later critical of this marriage form (*bQiddushin* 12b), but the relatively old mishnaic tradition presents it as fully legitimate.

Further, rabbinic literature suggests that there were regional differences in the expected relationships between groom and bride prior to nuptials. The Mishnah contains the following statement:

> He who eats at his father-in-law's in Judaea without chaperones (עדים) cannot bring a virginity suit, because he [will be presumed to have been] intimate (מתייחד) with her (*mKetubbot* 1.5).[28]

The issue under discussion here is the accusation of non-virginity that a husband may level against his wife following the wedding night. It is the husband's right to divorce his wife without compensation if he found her not to be a virgin. This tradition maintains that this right was applicable only to Galileans, since Judaean grooms act cavalierly toward their betrothed brides. The tradition here is anonymous, but since it voices criticism of the lax customs of Judaea, it was probably formulated by someone from Galilee. As an outsider who wished to dissociate himself from this practice, the formulator may not even be trying to paint a fair picture of the custom, much less alert us to all its social implications.

The Tosefta also enumerates a number of differences in the matrimonial practices of Judaeans and Galileans:

> Rabbi Judah said: In Judaea, to begin with, they would bring the bride and bridegroom together for one hour before they entered the bridal chamber (חופה),[29] so that he would get accustomed to her (יהא לבו גס בה), and in Galilee they did not do so. In Judaea they would search the bodies (מפשפשין) of the groom and bride one hour before they entered the bridal chamber, and in Galilee they did not do so. In Judaea they would produce two chaperones (שושבינין), one from the house of the groom and one from the house of the bride, and in spite of this they only provide them for marriage (נישואין), and in Galilee they did not do so. In Judaea the two chaperones would sleep where the bride and groom slept but in Galilee they did not do so. Whoever does not follow this custom cannot bring a virginity suit [later] (*tKetubbot* 1:4).[30]

This tradition tells of several customs followed by Judaeans on the wedding night, but not by Galileans. It is recounted by Rabbi Judah bar Elai, whose Galilean-Ushan provenance is well attested. Taken by itself, it may appear to describe stricter measures in Judaea than in Galilee, ultimately making Galileans ineligible to file virginity suits, and contradicting the mishnaic tradition discussed above. However, I believe it should be taken as related to and commenting on the previously discussed mishnah, as its position in the Tosefta indicates. Since that text proves that Judaeans were notorious in their premarital sexual license, if a Judaean husband wished to preserve his right to

---

[28] An interesting interpretation of this mishnah is found in Z. Falk, *Introduction to Jewish Law in the Second Commonwealth* 2 (Leiden 1978) 284. In his opinion the mishnah refers to a poor bridegroom who works for his prospective father-in-law in lieu of the bride price.

[29] On the regional distinction between this concept and the home-taking of the wife (לכנוס), see A. Büchler, "The Induction of the Bride and Bridegroom into the חופה in the First and Second Centuries in Palestine," *Livre d'hommage à la mémoire de Dr. Samuel Poznanski* (Warsaw 1927) 82-132.

[30] For a discussion of this source and parallels in the Talmudim, see A. S. Hershberg, "The Betrothal and Nuptial Practices in the Talmudic Period," *Ha-'Atid* 5 (1923) 95-7 [Hebrew].

file a virginity suit he had to make sure to follow several precautions designed to guard his wife's virginity until entering wedlock. In Galilee, where the unmarried couple was never suspected of misconduct, no such precautions were necessary.

The Babylonian Talmud, on the other hand, understands Rabbi Judah's statement as contradicting the mishnah. Its discussion of his statement begins by positing it against the mishnah, as an indication that the betrothed couple were not routinely intimate before nuptials. At a second stage Judah's statement itself poses exactly the problem I have delineated here; taken by itself, it suggests a stricter convention in Judaea than in Galilee. To counter this difficulty Abbayye suggests emending the text:

> Said Abbayye: [The text should] always ... [be] transmitted: "whoever follows [this custom" instead of "whoever does not follow this custom"] (*bKetubbot* 12a).

This emendation suggests that Abbayye understood the customs of the Judaeans prior to nuptials and described in this statement as the same as the customs described in the mishnah (that is, eating at the father-in-law's house). Rava, Abbayye's traditional adversary, stood behind the integrity of the text and suggested an extended version in order to solve the difficulty:

> Said Rava to him: But it is transmitted "whoever does not follow;" hence said Rava: This is what is intended: "Whoever does not follow Galilean customs in Galilee but follows Judaean customs in Galilee cannot bring a virginity suit" (*bKetubbot* 12a).

Rava also took this statement as describing the same situation as the Mishnah. Both rabbis took it for granted that in Judaea premarital restrictions were *less* severe than in Galilee.[31]

Thus far we established that Galilean rabbis and their followers viewed Judaean matrimonial practices as faulty because the bride and groom were suspected of premarital intimacy. In light of these sources, I shall ultimately claim a Judaean provenance for Salome Komaise's marriage contract.[32] First, however, I wish to discard another possible apologetic solution, which could employ these very same sources in order to weave Salome's marriage back into the Jewish halakhic fabric. This solution would postulate that Salome and Jesus were abiding by the well documented Jewish custom of a prolonged betrothal according to the custom of Judaea.

---

[31] One scholar used these sources differently, see J. Tabori, "Two Wedding Ceremonies: Alcestis and some Jewish Parallels," *Scripta Classica Israelica* 6 (1981-2) 16-22.

[32] In light of this claim I think it is hardly true to maintain, as Hannah Cotton wrote of the previous publication of my paper, that "This radical approach assumes no less than the 'apologetic approach' that, by this time there existed a coherent and operative system of law that had become normative" (Cotton and Yardeni, *Discoveries*, 227-8). All I claim is that the rabbis had to grapple with an existing custom when they formulated their own legal system some 70 years after the documents in question were composed.

5. The Jewish Betrothal Practice

Halakhah maintains that there were two stages in Jewish marriage:[33] the קידושין (literally "consecration") which is followed by a betrothal period (אירוסין) and then the nuptials, in which the husband brings his bride home or under the canopy (חופה). This period, in which the daughter is neither totally under the authority of her father, nor yet controlled by her husband, is one of the most complex from the halakhic point of view.[34] Nevertheless, the rabbis recommended a long betrothal period:

> [The sages] grant a virgin twelve months from [the time] when her [prospective] husband claims her (תבעה בעלה), so that she may maintain (לפרנס) herself (i.e. furnish her trousseau]. And just as they grant [that period] to a woman, so they grant [a similar period of preparation] to the man to maintain himself (*mKetubbot* 5:2).

This period differed from the period following nuptials only in that the betrothed couple was not permitted to have sexual intercourse; in order to insure this, the bride remained under the roof of her father. The benediction that is recited to this day in a Jewish wedding refers to this situation:

> ... and He has forbidden (אסר) us those [merely] betrothed [to us] (ארוסות) but has permitted (התיר) us [only] those with whom we have performed the marriage ceremony (נשואות) (*bKetubbot* 7b).

This custom also explains Joseph's dilemma when, according to the Gospel of Matthew, he discovered that Mary, his betrothed, was pregnant, though he had not yet consummated with her (Matthew 1:18; cf. Luke 1:27).

From the context of *mKetubbot* 1:5 we may infer that the editors of the Mishnah may have understood the situation of the bridegroom at his father-in-law's house as involving a betrothed, but not yet married, couple. Unless chaperones are present at all times, the bride may be suspected of associating with her future husband when the latter spends time at the house of his father-in-law. It is in this halakhic setting that an apologist would seek to locate the Judaean Desert marriage contract.

This very solution, however, creates another halakhic difficulty. The question whether the *ketubbah* was handed to the bride at the time of betrothal or only after the nuptials is by no means trivial. Although this issue is still debated, all agree that there can be no doubt about the case of the abducted Alexandrian women.

---

[33] This is the view of most commentators, but some suggest a tripartite process: שידוכין (matchmaking), אירוסין (betrothal) and נישואין (marriage); see Hershberg, "Betrothal," 75-102.

[34] Neusner, *Mishnaic Law of Women*, 28-42; particularly 37.

Hillel the Elder expounded secular texts (דרש לשון הדיוט). When the Alexandrians betrothed women, someone else would come from the market and abduct her. This case was brought before the rabbis, and they proposed (בקשו) to declare their sons [by the men they ended up marrying] bastards (ממזרים). Hillel the Elder said to [the sons who were branded bastards]: Produce before me your mothers' *ketubbot* (i.e. the marriage contracts they received from their betrothed). These were brought to him. And it was written in it: "When you enter my house [but not before] you shall be my wife according to the law of Moses and Israel (*tKetubbot* 4:9).

This case is dated to the time of Hillel the Elder (ca. 10 BCE). It tells of women who were originally betrothed to one man but ended up marrying another. Their sons avoided being adjudged bastards on the strength of the clause found in the marriage contract the women possessed, which had been given to them at their betrothal. To what extent this tradition describes actual cases is questionable. But even if it is wholly fictitious its formulators assumed that women already possessed marriage contracts during their betrothal period; they may thus be applying to Hillel's time a practice prevalent in their own day. The earliest attestation of the story of the Alexandrian brides is tannaitic. As such it can be viewed as a late contemporary of the Judaean Desert documents. Even if, therefore, the delivery of the *ketubbah* was conceived by the tannaim as taking place at the betrothal ceremony, the Salome Komaise contract, if it assumes a long betrothal, would still contradict tannaitic halakhic rulings, because it was handed to the bride at the end rather than the beginning of this period.[35] Therefore the Judaean Desert document does not fit this halakhic model either.

6. The Palestinian Talmud

Let us now return to the mishnaic text of *Ketubbot* 1:5. The Judaean practice described therein may not necessarily assume a situation of betrothal. In fact it is unknown whether the standard betrothal period decreed by the rabbis was actually practiced by anybody at all. I assume that the Mishnah refers to a period prior to wedlock (נישואין), at which some contact between an engaged couple takes place. This scenario resembles that deducible from the Judaean Desert contract of Salome Komaise, but it is not yet close enough. While the Mishnah voices a suspicion about the likelihood of premarital sexual misconduct, it does not make an outright accusation that, unless precautions

---

[35] See also A. Büchler, *Studies in Jewish History* (Jews College Publications 1; London 1956) 126-59; A. Gulak, "Betrothal Contract and Possessions Acquired Orally According to Talmudic Law," *Tarbiz* 3 (1942) 361-76 [Hebrew]. Although L. M. Epstein (*The Jewish Marriage Contract* [New York 1927] 9-15) agreed that, at the beginning, this was indeed the practice, he maintained that later the customs changed, and the handing over of the *ketubbah* was performed at the time of nuptials. My interpretation may actually suggest the opposite.

are taken, Judaeans will certainly cohabit prior to marriage. Salome Komaise and Jesus, by contrast, casually attest to having actually lived together prior to wedlock, as though this were a normal expected practice.

The commentary of the Palestinian Talmud on this particular mishnah indeed gives the impression that premarital cohabitation in Judaea was more prevalent than the Mishnah cares to admit. Just as an apologetic tendency discerned in the Mishnah pointed to Judaea as the place where premarital cohabitation was normative—whereas in Galilee, the seat of the editors of the Mishnah, this practice was not followed—a new apologetic tendency is now found in the Palestinian Talmud, which sets out to explain and excuse the circumstances that compelled the Judaeans to resort to sex out of wedlock. The excuse here is the horrors of the aftermath of the Bar Kokhba revolt.

Some sources suggest that after the Bar Kokhba revolt the Romans introduced in Palestine the *jus primae noctis*, namely the right of the local governor to deflower all maidens entering wedlock.[36] The Palestinian Talmud refers to this "event" when it deals with the *mishnah* about the husband residing at his father-in-law's house:

> In the beginning [the Romans] decreed a destruction (שמד) in Judaea ... and they decreed that a soldier (איסטרטיוס στρατιώτης) should penetrate (בועל) first. It was then enacted [by the sages] that her husband would come into her (בא עליה) while she was still in her father's house (i.e. during the betrothal period before marriage—*yKetubbot* 1:5, 25c).[37]

This tradition connects the imposition of the *jus primae noctis* with the שמד decrees, which were usually associated with the aftermath of the Bar Kokhba revolt. As a result, the rabbis enacted an emergency measure (תקנה), intended to avert the danger of Jewish maidens' losing their virginity to Roman soldiers and possibly even conceiving by them. In this situation, the prospective couple was actually encouraged to practice sexual intercourse before the marriage ceremony and cohabit while the bride was still in her father's house. The quasi-historical justification for this Judaean custom, namely the *jus primae noctis*, is part of the apologetics of the Galilean rabbis, because in the next sentence the talmudic commentators go on to claim that

---

[36] The date of the alleged event is subject to some controversy. For example S. Krauss ("La fête de Hanoucca," *REJ* 30 [1895] 37-43) dated it to the aftermath of the Jewish revolt in the days of the emperor Trajan (115-7 CE). On the other hand S. Belkin (*Philo and the Oral Law* [Cambridge 1940] 246) saw in it one of the Antiochean decrees (168 BCE). The Bar Kokhba date, championed, among others, by R. Patai ("Jus Primae Noctis," *Studies of the Center for Folklore Research* 4 [1974] 177-80), seems to me, on account of the word שמד usually associated with the Bar Kokhba revolt, to be the interpretation assumed by the rabbis themselves. For a recent historical interpretation which seeks to discover a historical event behind the story, see Vered Noam, "The Seventeenth of Elul in Megillat Taanit," *Zion* 59 (1994) 433-44 [Hebrew].

[37] Cf. also *bKetubbot* 3b. The contents of the Babylonian discourse on the subject are so blurred that they need hardly concern us here.

"although the destruction (שמד) was discontinued, the custom was not" (*ibid.*). This claim means that in Judaea men and women continued to practice premarital cohabitation before nuptials. The Talmud then goes on to state that even "the daughter-in-law of Rabbi Oshaiah entered [the bridal chamber already] pregnant" (*ibid.*). This indicates that these matrimonial practices were followed even in the families of the Judaean rabbis themselves.

This talmudic admission that the custom of cohabitation prior to marriage was difficult to uproot even when the conditions that had brought it about (namely the *jus primae noctis* of the aftermath of the Bar Kokhba revolt) had ceased to exist, also proves that the custom did not arise from those conditions in the first place. Salome Komaise's marriage contract, which is dated to August 131 CE and suggests a similar practice of premarital cohabitation, predates the Hadrianic decrees by four years and thus severs the previously assumed connections between the persecution and the practice.

We have now surveyed another example of rabbinic apologetics—the claim that premarital cohabitation was practiced in Judaea only under the extremely hazardous conditions brought about by the *jus primae noctis* imposed by the Romans in the aftermath of the Bar Kokhba revolt. Yet the Judaean marriage contract of Salome Komaise also describes a premarital cohabitation that predates the Bar Kokhba revolt. This indicates that premarital cohabitation was a local practice particular to and common in Judaea. So, the question must be asked, what was its significance for the men and women who followed it?

7. The Social Implications of Premarital Cohabitation

The social and personal implications of premarital cohabitation in second-century Judaea can also be viewed from either a conservative or a radical stance.

a. The Radical Approach

It may be suggested that premarital cohabitation was a device that allowed the prospective couple to test the ground before actually deciding to pursue a common life together. Such a reconstruction not only constitutes a radical departure from the common view of the traditional Jewish matrimonial customs, but also postulates a society that puts much less value on virginity and paternity. Premarital cohabitation that did not lead to marriage certainly entailed loss of virginity, and in many cases may also have resulted in conception and birth. Insistence on a virgin bride and stress on fatherhood are the pillars of patriarchal society, and in this respect ancient Judaism does not seem to have differed from other patriarchal societies. Some evidence for a lenient approach to these issues, however, can be found in rabbinic literature.

The charge of non-virginity is played down in a series of stories in the Babylonian Talmud (*bKetubbot* 10a). This argument would be supported if one could show that these stories are of Judaean provenance, but unfortunately it is impossible to make such a claim.[38] More promising is the issue of paternity. In a story that describes a case of מיאון—the right of the orphan daughter to reject a husband chosen for her during her minority by her mother or brothers—the Palestinian Talmud tells of a woman who came before the sages with a son on her shoulders and rejected her husband. Despite the fact that the woman had borne a child, the rabbis ruled that the marriage had been invalid and released her from it (*yYevamot* 1:2, 2d; 13:1, 13c). Because the woman was the daughter-in-law of Rabbi Ishmael—a well-known Judaean sage—this story apparently reflects Judaean custom.

b. The Conservative Approach

One can explain premarital cohabitation as a relic of matrimonial customs practiced by an illiterate society; only later was the marriage contract artificially added. This proposal comes close to the Egyptian ἄγραφος γάμος[39] described above in a quotation by Lewis. Thus, although such a marriage was mocked by the rabbis for its casual character, it was really just as strict and binding as that promoted by the rabbis themselves. Perhaps *mQiddushin* 1:1, which describes marriage by intercourse, alludes to these older matrimonial practices that were later discarded. Although for methodological reasons I chose the provocative approach in the interpretation of the sources, with regard to the social implications I lean toward this latter, conservative interpretation.[40]

Excursus: Jus Primae Noctis

In conclusion I wish to address the general historical plausibility of the *jus primae noctis* in Judaea in the aftermath of the Bar Kokhba revolt. This question has been tackled by Raphael Patai,[41] who formulated a remarkable theory. He was well aware of the fact that all medieval literature that evokes

---

[38] Elsewhere I have, in fact, claimed that the provenance of this approach is Babylonian, see my *Mine and Yours*, 191-9. See also Shulamit Valler, *Women and Womanhood in the Stories of the Babylonian Talmud* (Tel Aviv 1993) 41-5 [Hebrew].

[39] See H. J. Wolff, *Written and Unwritten Marriage* (Haverford PA 1939).

[40] My interpretation is, therefore, quite close to that of Cotton, *Discoveries*, 228-9, and I find her attempt to undermine my work on 227-8 quite superfluous.

[41] Patai, "Jus Primae Noctis."

the custom of *jus primae noctis* has been proven folkloristic with no historical basis.[42] On the whole, Patai accepted these conclusions. He argued, however, that a special case can be made for the talmudic sources describing the same sort of custom. He claimed that since all the sources now considered legendary, which depict the practice in Christian medieval Europe, were composed much later than the period they purport to describe, it is acceptable to discard them. In Judaea, by contrast, in the aftermath of the Bar Kokhba revolt, the Romans actually put into practice such a law, as the "reliable" rabbinic sources claim.

As a folklorist, Patai should have known better. If a motif of this sort could have appeared in a sixteenth-century document and upset the entire history of medieval Europe for the next two centuries, the same motif likewise could have cropped up in the fourth- or fifth-century Palestinian Talmud, falsely describing events of the second century.[43] In my opinion, the conclusions of this chapter, which render the *jus primae noctis* narrative of the Palestinian Talmud nothing more than an apology for an inconvenient Judaic custom that is cryptically described in the Mishnah, undermines Patai's claim.[44] From a large repository of folkloristic material circulating worldwide, the *jus primae noctis* was conveniently drawn in order to explain and justify a custom that seemed to undermine the rabbinic view of proper conduct in Jewish society.

---

[42] The myth was first rejected by C. Schmidt, *Jus primae noctis: Eine geschichtliche Untersuchung* (Freiburg 1881). For more recent works upholding this view, see W. D. Howarth, "'Droit du Seigneur': Fact or Fantasy?" *Journal of European Studies* 1 (1971) 291-312; H. F. W. Schmidt-Bleibtreu, *Jus primae noctis: Herrenrecht der ersten Nacht* (Bonn 1988).

[43] The *jus primae noctis* is now an accepted literary motif in folklore dictionaries. See e.g. D. Noy (Neuman), *Motif Index of Talmudic-Midrashic Literature* (Unpublished Ph.D. Thesis, Bloomington IN, 1954) 725.

[44] In this view I join several previous scholars who reached the same conclusions based on different evidence. See I. Levi, "Hanoucca et la jus primae noctis" *REJ* 30 (1898) 220-31, esp. p. 231; and more recently M. D. Herr, "Persecution and Martyrdom in Hadrian's Days," in D. Asheri and I. Schatzman (eds.), *Studies in History* (*Scripta Hierosolymitana* 23; Jerusalem 1972) 101, n. 56.

Chapter Ten

A Divorce Bill?
Notes on Papyrus *XHev/Se* 13*

A wife has no right to divorce her husband in Jewish law—or so claims virtually every textbook on Jewish law. Over the years, of course, scholars have noted exceptions to this categorical assertion.[1] In marriage contracts from Elephantine, for example, the woman's right to divorce equals that of the man.[2] Another example is the Gospel of Mark's logion on divorce, which seems to imply that both men and women, can initiate divorce procedures (Mark 10:11-12). Again, Josephus relates that Salome, King Herod's sister, sent her husband a bill of divorce (*Ant.* 15.259-60). Yet, mainstream scholarship has too often brushed aside these pieces of evidence as a-typical examples, or misunderstandings on the part of a transmitter. The Elephantine community, for example, was described as remote and long out of touch with the center of Jewish life, living a pagan existence and following the legal practices of its neighbors.[3] Mark was described a non-Jewish author, interpreting the actions of Palestinian Jews in light of more familiar Roman legal practices.[4] Salome's actions contravened Jewish law, and succeeded only because of her Roman citizenship.[5]

Until recently, the only extant Jewish divorce bill (*get*) available from the Roman period was a document excavated by a French archaeological team in

---

* I have discussed the document interpreted here with Dr. Ada Yardeni, Prof. Bernadette Brooten of Brandeis University, Prof. Hannah Cotton of the Hebrew University, and Dr. Adiel Schremer of Bar Ilan University. The opinions voiced in this chapter are strictly my own and do not reflect on any of the above.

[1] See the entire volume of *The Jewish Law Annual* 4 (1981). And see also Z. W. Falk, *The Divorce Action by the Wife in Jewish Law* (Jerusalem 1973) [Hebrew].

[2] B. Porten and A. Yardeni, *Textbook of Aramaic Documents from Ancient Egypt 2: Contracts* (Jerusalem 1989) 30-3; 60-3; 78-83.

[3] R. Yaron, *Introduction to the Law of the Aramaic Papyri* (Oxford 1961) 53; 127-8.

[4] E.g. J. Fitzmayer, "The Matthean Divorce Text and some New Palestinian Evidence," *Theological Studies* 37 (1976) 205; E. Lowenstam, "Divorce and Remarriage in the New Testament," *The Jewish Law Annual* 4 (1981) 47-65. See especially p. 60.

[5] E.g. A. M. Rabello, "Divorce of Jews in the Roman Empire," *The Jewish Law Annual* 4 (1981) 92-3.

a cave in Wadi Muraba'at and published by Jozef Milik in 1961.[6] Joseph ben Naksan issued this divorce bill to his wife Miriam barat Jonathan at Masada, perhaps in 72 CE (I shall henceforth refer to this document as in the official publication—*Mur* 19). It confirmed that the Jewish bill of divorce has' undergone very few changes over the last two millennia.

In 1956, however, in an article on work in progress, Milik also claimed that he possessed and would eventually publish another ancient Jewish bill of divorce dated 135 CE, written by a wife to her husband.[7] The Dominican Fathers in Jerusalem procured the document from Bedouins, who claimed to have found it, along with a large group of other documents, in Nahal Se'elim.[8] Milik's statement, surprisingly, aroused little public interest. In 1970, for example, E. Bammel published an article on a wife's right to initiate divorce in Jewish law;[9] Milik's document was not cited. However, in 1982, Milik's note from 1956 caught the attention of the feminist scholar Bernadette Brooten, who wrote a programmatic article about Jewish women's right to divorce in theory and in practice. In her feminist critique of past scholarship Brooten cited Milik as supporting evidence.[10] Brooten's German article has unfortunately had little influence, because it is virtually unknown to English speakers. In any case, she could only speculate on the importance of this text, since the document itself was unavailable.

The Nahal Se'elim divorce bill remained unpublished for forty years. By 1987 it was no longer in Milik's hands. The Se'elim documents, together with similar documents found by Yigael Yadin in Nahal Hever just north of Nahal Se'elim, were in the custody of Jonas Greenfield. Greenfield worked on the documents until his untimely death in 1995. In the course of this period, he spoke extensively about them. In his lectures he mentioned more than once that *XHev/Se* 13, as he designated Milik's unpublished divorce bill, was not a divorce bill at all but a verification that a woman gave her husband to acknowledge receipt of a *get*.

For over forty years this document remained unpublished. Since the death of Greenfield in 1995, however, the document has appeared in three separate publications, thanks to the talent and diligence of the epigraphist Ada

---

[6] In R. de-Vaux, J. T. Milik and P. Benoit, *Discoveries in the Judaean Desert* 2 (Oxford 1961) 104-9.

[7] J. T. Milik, "Le travail d'édition des manuscript du Désert de Juda," *Volume du congres Strasbourg 1956* (*Supplements to VT* 4; Leiden 1956) 21.

[8] For a discussion of the document's *real* provenance see: Hannah M. Cotton and Ada Yardeni, *Discoveries in the Judaean Desert* 27 (Oxford 1997) 1-6.

[9] E. Bammel, "Markus 10 11f. und das jüdische Eherecht," *ZNTW* 61 (1970) 95-101.

[10] Bernadette J. Brooten, "Konnten Frauen im alten Judentum die Scheidung betreiben? Überlegung zu Mk 10, 11-12 und 1Kor 7, 10-11," *Evangelische Theologie* 42 (1982), 65-80, and see also her "Zur Debatte über das Scheidungsrecht der jüdischen Frau," *Evangelische Theologie* 43 (1983) 466-78.

Yardeni.[11] Yardeni (with Greenfield) initially entitled *XHev/Se* 13 "A Ketubbah receipt (שובר)." The body of the text of the first two publications states: "This is a *ketubbah* receipt." A footnote appended to this statement in the initial publication maintains that

> The nature of the document was decided by reading די in line 6, and undermines Milik's opinion that it is a divorce bill (גט) .... Receipts are mentioned several times in the Mishnah and Talmud, see e.g. *mBava Batra* 10:3 "One writes a divorce bill (גט) for a man even when his wife is not with him and a receipt (שובר) for a woman even if her husband is not with her;" *mKetubbot* 9:9 "She says: My divorce bill (גטי) is lost and he says: My receipt (שוברי) is lost;" *mGittin* 8:8 "If the scribe wrote a divorce bill (גט) for the man and a receipt (שובר) for the woman and made a mistake and gave the divorce bill to the woman and the receipt to the man ..." And see also *bGittin* 27a and *bBava Metzia* 13a "If he found women's divorce bills and slaves' release certificates and deeds of gift and receipts (שוברין) he may not return them for fear that they were written and [then the husband] changed his mind [and decided] not to administer them."[12]

However, the word די, which seems crucial to the editor's argument, is also found in a corresponding position in the Masada *get*, so the point of this argument is lost on me.[13] Furthermore, in order to justify the claim that the document is not a divorce bill sent by the wife to the husband, the editor resorted to interpreting lines 1-5a, which are clearly first person feminine, as emanating from the wife, while contending that lines 5b-8, which contain the explicit divorce clause, are spoken by the scribe representing the husband. Then, because of the obvious first person feminine declination, lines 9-10 are, according to this interpretation, again the words of the wife. However, in my view there are no linguistic switches inside the text which justify such an elaborate interpretation, as I will show in my discussion of the text below.

I wrote as much in a note on this document which was published in 1996 in the *Harvard Theological Review*.[14] This article created quite a stir and brought in its wake a number of interesting responses. The most subtle one is Yardeni's third and final publication, which contains several modifications. The title of the document had now been changed to "Waiver of Claims?" The question mark following the name clearly reflects the editor's uncertainty as to the nature of the document.[15] However, reference to my suggestion that it

---

[11] Ada Yardeni, *Nahal Se'elim Documents* (Jerusalem 1995) 55-60 [Hebrew]; *eadem*, with J. M. Greenfield, "A Receipt for a Ketubba," in I. M. Gafni, A. Oppenheimer and D. R. Schwartz (eds.), *The Jews in the Hellenistic-Roman World: Studies in Memory of Menahem Stern* (Jerusalem 1996) 197-208 [Hebrew]; *eadem*, with Cotton, *Discoveries*, 65-70.

[12] Yardeni, *Nahal Se'elim,* 55. The translation is mine.

[13] It was apparently lost on the editors themselves for in the subsequent publication, this sentence has been removed from the footnote; see Yardeni and Greenfield, "Receipt," 197-8, n. 1. But see further on this below.

[14] "Notes and Observations on a Newly Published Divorce Bill," *HTR* 89 (1996) 195-202. And see also my "Notes and Observations: A Correction," *HTR* 90 (1997) 225.

[15] On the provenance of the new suggestion about the nature of the document see below.

was a divorce bill sent by a wife to her husband, which caused the confusion in the first place, is totally absent. My *HTR* article is not cited in the discussion nor in the footnotes, but only in the bibliography of the book.[16] The footnote has also been expanded and is now formulated with less certainty:

> It is not certain that this is a divorce document as Milik believed...; it could be a receipt for a ketubbah. The rejection of Milik's opinion may be supported by two facts: (1) The line mentioning the divorce is not at the beginning of the deed. (2) It is a 'simple' deed with the witnesses' signatures on the front, unlike the deed of divorce from Wadi Muraba'at (*Mur* 19) which is a 'double' deed with signatures at the back.

The two new arguments adduced against the document being a divorce bill are, however, no more convincing than the previous ones. For (1) while it is true that the divorce clause is absent from the head of the document, the editor refrained from mentioning the fact that line 3 of the document is indecipherable, and could have contained such a clause; and (2) the fact that *Mur* 19 is a 'double' document does not prove that divorce documents could not also be produced as 'simple' documents. Certainly no legal commentary at our disposal, rabbinic or otherwise, makes such a claim.

Thus, despite the learned footnote quoted above, which does indeed prove that rabbinic society recognized the existence of the receipt document, Milik's initial judgment that *XHev/Se* 13 is a divorce bill sent by a wife to her husband has not really been rebutted.

The next two responses were more explicit. Adiel Schremer wrote a learned piece on the document claiming that "...in light of the revolutionary character of her hypothesis, one would expect Ilan to show her reading of the document to be the only possible one."[17] He then went on to show that by working really hard, one can read the document differently. Indeed, he perfected Greenfield and Yardeni's argument for identifying the document as a *ketubbah* receipt. The following discussion will address some of the issues Schremer raised in his paper.

From a very different angle comes the critique of Hannah Cotton and Elisha Qimron.[18] These scholars claim that I have misunderstood the nature of the document in question. This piece of papyrus is not a divorce bill. It is a waiver of claims of the wife against her ex-husband. This idea clearly serves as the inspiration for Yardeni's new title to the document. However, Cotton and Qimron agree that this document was written in the wake of a divorce bill, and that the latter was indeed composed by a wife to her husband. In other words, their argument with me is only on the question of form, but not on the

---

[16] Yardeni and Cotton, *Discoveries*, 65-70, and see also p. 331 in the bibliography.

[17] A. Schremer, "Divorce in Papyrus Se'elim 13 Once Again: A Reply to Tal Ilan," *HTR* 91 (1998) 193-202. Quotation from p. 195.

[18] Hannah M. Cotton and E. Qimron, "XHev/Se ar 13 of 134 or 135 C.E.: A Wife's Renunciation of Claims," *JJS* 49 (1998) 108-18.

principle involved. Cotton and Qimron agree that *XHev/Se* 13 proves that in the Jewish society reflected in the Judaean Desert Documents, a wife could divorce her husband. Since from my point of view this is the crux of the argument I will devote less space in my discussion to refuting their claims, and quote their work approvingly when we agree.

I believe that, when viewed together with the *Mur* 19, any reading of *XHev/Se* 13 which denies its substance as a divorce sent by a wife to her husband can only be explained as contemporary apologetics, designed to uphold the traditional view that Jewish women could not divorce their husbands.[19] A traditional text analysis and synopsis of the two texts will amply demonstrate this:

1. Text

XHev/Se 13	*Mur* 19	
בעשרין לסיון שנת תלת לחרת ישראל	באחד למרחשון שנת שת במצדא	1
לשם שמעו[ן] בר כסבה נ[שי]א ישראל		2
[ ].../.[ ]..[ ]ן[ ] לא איתי [לי]	שבק ומתרך מן רעתי דנה אנה {יהוסף	3
אנה שלמצין ברת יהוסף קבשן	בר נ} יהוסף בר נקסן מן [ ]ה יתב במצדא לכי אנתי	4
מן עינגדה עמך אנת אלעזר בר חנינ[ה]	מרים ברת יהונתן [מ]ן הנבלטא יתבא	5
די הוית בעלה מן קדמת דן דן[י]	במצדא די הוית אנתי מן קדם דה די את	6
הוא לך מנה גט שבקין ותרכ[ין]	רשיא בנפשכי למהך ולמהי אנת לכול גבר	7
	יהודי די תצבין וב[ד]ין[ן] להוי לכי מני ספר תרכין	8
[מ]לת מדעה ל[א] איתי לי עמך א[נת]	וגט שבקין בדין [ ]קא יהבנא וכול חריבין	9
אלעזר על צבת כל מדעם וקים עלה	ונזקו ו . . . ן [ ]ע לכי כדן יהי קים	10
אנה שלמצין כול על על כ[ת]ב	ומשלם לרבעין ומז[מן]די תמרין לי אחלף לכי	11
	שטרה כדי חיא	12
	בא[ח]ד למרחש[ון] שנת שת במצדא	13
	שבק ומתרך א[נ]ה מן רעתי יומא דנה	14
	יהוסף בר נ[קסן] לכי אנתי מרים <ברת>	15
	יהונתן [מן ה]נבלטא יתבא	16
	במצדא די ה[וי]ת אנתתי	17
	מן קדמת דנא די אתי רשיא	18
	בנפשכי למ[ה]ך למהי אנתא	19
	לכול גבר יהודי די תצבין	20
	בדין להי לכי מני ס[פ]ר תרכין	21
	וגט שבקין ב[דין כו]ל [ ]ק יהבנה	22
	וכל חר[יבי]ן [ונזקו ו . . .]ן כדן	23
	[יהי קים ו[מש]לם לרבעין ובזמן	24
	[די ת[מרין לי[ן] א[חלף לכי שטרא כדי	25
	[חי]א	26

---

[19] The politics behind this sort of apologetic reading have been amply demonstrated by Bernadette Brooten; see her *Women Leaders in the Ancient Synagogue: Inscriptional Evidence and Background Issues* (*Brown Judaic Studies* 36; Chico CA 1982) 30-2; see above chapter 9, and see also my "On the Provocative Approach Once again: A Response to Adiel Schremer," *HTR* 91 (1998) 203-4.

שלמצין ברת יהוסף על נפשה שאלה כתב	יהוסף בר נק[סן] על נפש[ה]　27
מתת ב[ר] שמעון ממרא	אליעזר [בר] מלכה שהד　28
... בר שמעון עד	יהוסף בר מלכה שהד　29
משבלה בר שמעון עד	אלעזר בר חננה שהד　30

2. Translation

1　On the twentieth of Sivan, year three of the freedom of Israel

On the first of Marheshwan, year six, at Masada[20]

2　In the name of Simon bar Kosbah, the Nasi of Israel

3　[　...　] ... I do not have,

I divorce and release of my own free will, today I

4　I, Shelamzion, daughter of Joseph Qebshan

Joseph, son of Naqsan, from [..]ah, residing on Masada, you

5　from Ein Gedi, with you, you Eleazar son of Hananiah

Miriam, daughter of Jonathan [fro]m Hanablata, residing

6　who had been my husband before this time, that

on Masada, who had been my wife before this time, that you

7

are free on your part to go and become the wife of any

8　this is for you from me a bill of divorce and release

Jewish man that you wish. This is for you from me a writ of release

9　(A word of notice?) I do not have with you

and a bill of divorce. For this I will give back [...]. And all ruined

10　Eleazar concerning a matter of anything. It is confirmed by me

and damaged [...] to you this will remain

11　I Shelamzion all that is written (above)

and I will pay fourfold. And at any time that you ask me, I will replace for you

12

this document as long as I am alive

27　Shelamzion barat Yehosef in person, borrowing the writing of

Joseph, son of Naq[san] for himself

28　Mattat son of Simon (who wrote) what she said[21]

Eliezer, [son of] Malka, witness

---

[20] This text has been previously translated into English only in: Léone J. Archer, *Her Price is Beyond Rubies: The Jewish Woman in Greco-Roman Palestine* (*JSOT Supplement Series* 60; Sheffield 1990) 298-9. In my translation I have consulted her work. The translation of *Papyrus Se'elim* 13 is mine. For it I have relied heavily on Yardeni's translation in *Discoveries* 67and linguistic notes. The final decisions are, however, my own.

[21] On the translation of the last two lines see: Hannah M. Cotton, "Subscriptions and Signatures in the Papyri from the Judaean Desert: The Χειροχρήστης," *Journal of Juristic Papyrology* 25 (1995) 39. See also J. C. Greenfield, "'Because He/She Did Not Know Letters': Remarks on a First Millennium C.E. Legal Expression," *Journal of the Ancient Near Eastern Society* 22 (1993) 39-44, and see particularly p. 40, n. 8.

29	... son of Simon, witness	Joseph, son of Malka, witness
30	Masbala, son of Simon, witness	Eleazar, son of Hanana, witness

3. Commentary

It is important to note one basic difference between the documents—*Mur 19*, as mentioned above, is a 'double' document, that is, the text is reproduced a second time at the bottom. This enables a reconstruction of some of the text missing in one part of the document but present in the other. *XHev/Se* 13 is not a double document. This however, has no bearing on the question of whether it is or it is not a divorce bill.

Lines 1-2: Both documents begin with a date, although that of XHev/Se 13 is more elaborate, taking up two lines. This is because it seems to celebrate Jewish independence under Bar-Kokhba.

Line 3: This line, which is one of two divorce clauses in Mur 19, is badly damaged in XHev/Se 13 and emendation seems hopeless. Cotton and Qimron place much emphasis on the reconstruction of the last three words in the line לא איתי [לי] because these help them reconstruct this document as a waiver of claims rather then the divorce bill itself. I think, however, that the state of the reconstruction being what it is, this emphasis remains rather tentative.

Lines 4-6: Both documents mention the full name of the document's sender, his or her place of residence, the full name of the document's recipient, and his or her place of residence. The only important difference is the reversal of the participants' gender: one recipient is a wife, the other a husband. The terminology used to denote the span of time of the previous marriages is the same (מן קדמת דנא).

The way the scribe wrote the wife's place of residence is important as well. Obviously she came from Ein Gedi (עין גדי), but the scribe altered the final "י" into a "ה" (עינגדה). This seems to be an idiosyncratic preference of his, which has important implications for the decipherment of the rest of the document: in line 6, the word בעלה is translated as "my husband" even though we would have expected בעלי here; in line 7 the word מנה is translated as "from me" even though we would have expected מני here. The translation is based on the idiosyncrasy described above, namely the preference for "ה" instead of a "י" in the end of a word.[22]

For Schremer's reconstruction of the document as a receipt for a divorce bill sent by the wife to the husband, line 6 is especially important. Referring to the editors' emphasis on the word די in this line (mentioned above), he writes "Ilan did not make any effort to explain to the reader Greenfield and Yardeni's argument, and one may wonder whether it was properly understood

---

[22] I am grateful to Ada Yardeni for pointing this out to me. Both Schremer, *ibid.*, 198 and Cotton and Qimron, *ibid.*, 110 refer to this orthographic phenomenon in their articles.

... To my mind the editors referred to the second occurrence of the word די that is at the end of line 6."[23] For Schremer this reconstructed word at the end of the line is of crucial importance because it would serve as the axis on which to hang the switch from wife speaking first person to husband to husband speaking first person to wife. Schremer needs this די in order to add the word אמרת, allowing for such a switch.

There are several arguments against this reconstruction. The first is methodological. There is no certainty at all that a די is even reconstructable at the end of line 6, much less a די אמרת. As Cotton and Qimron put it nicely "Even less to be recommended is the attempt to amend the text so as to reconcile it with the Halakhah by adding ואמרת or די אמרת at the end of line 6 ... Such a quotation does not fit the style of the deed and is without parallel in known documents. Furthermore, the proposed addition of אמרת at the end of line 6 would make this line far too long (even if there is room in the margin) and out of alignment with rest of the lines in the body of the deed, even longer than line 11 which is already part of the subscription."[24]

The second argument is textual. The second די also has its parallel in *Mur* 19, which states די הוית אנתי מן קדם דה די את רשיא בנפשכי למהך ולמהי אנת לכול גבר יהודי דתצבין. Therefore, even if I had misunderstood the editors comment, as Schremer claims, my argument still holds.[25]

Line 7: In *Mur* 19 this line gives permission for the wife to marry any Jew she chooses. Not surprisingly, this clause is altogether absent from *XHev/Se* 13. Because polygyny was permitted, we know that a Jewish man could marry any woman he wished without his wife's permission and without a divorce. My making this assumption does not (as Schremer claims) show that when it suits me I follow Jewish halakhic principles and when it does not I do not.[26] The wife's right to divorce her husband, demonstrated in *XHev/Se* 13, does

---

[23] Schremer, "Reply to Ilan," 195-6.

[24] Cotton and Qimron, "Renunciation of Claims," 116.

[25] Because of the importance Schremer attached to this word at the end of line 6, he seems to have been taken aback when he discovered that the words noting the editors' emphasis on its importance ("The nature of the document was decided by reading די in line 6, and undermines Milik's opinion that it is a divorce bill [גט]" see above) are absent from the second publication of the document in the Stern Memorial volume. In note 8, he wrote "The omission of these words seems to be a mere printing error, for without them the argument lacks any sense" *ibid.*, 195, n. 8. What Schremer did not know, and what I discovered quite by chance is that the omission was intentional. Before his untimely death Prof. Greenfield was kind enough to give me a copy of the manuscript of the document prior to publication. These words were indeed present in the manuscript, but were struck out with a pen, apparently by Greenfield's hand. It seems that the editor himself had ceased to be convinced by this spurious argument.

[26] *Ibid.*, 200, n. 27.

not require a monogamous, Roman-like society and law code, and the Babatha archive itself proves the existence of polygyny.[27]

Line 8: In this line, which is the second divorce clause in the document, *XHev/Se* 13 again follows *Mur* 19 closely. Both documents mention a divorce document in rather similar terms (גט שבקין ותרכין/ספר תרכין וגט שבקין), but they differ on the definition of the recipient: while *Mur* 19 presents the document to a woman (לכי), *XHev/Se* 13 addresses it to a man (לך).[28] Curiously, Schremer totally ignores these clear gender markers—presumably because they upset his argument.

Lines 9-12: The final clauses, although rather poorly preserved both in *Mur* 19 and *XHev/Se* 13, differ substantially in the two documents. This does not, however, indicate that the documents have different purposes. The dissimilarities simply reflect certain essential differences between a divorce issued by a husband and one issued by a wife. The final lines in *Mur* 19 seem to outline the way in which the divorcing husband will meet financial obligations toward his former wife. A divorcing wife, by contrast, has no financial obligation toward her husband. These lines simply constitute a waiver on the wife's part of any financial demands she may have had on her spouse. Whether this indicates that a wife-initiated divorce entailed forfeiture of the woman's marriage settlement is a subject for further research.[29]

4. Conclusion

In light of the foregoing analysis, one should ponder the significance of this new find for Jewish history. One approach is to view this text in its historical milieu, together with the other Judaean Desert legal documents, in which Jewish women and men resort to alternative Hellenistic and Roman legal systems in order to arrange their lives. Was Shelamzion of *XHev/Se* 13 following Roman practice in divorcing her husband? Hannah Cotton has argued that the Greek marriage documents from the Judaean Desert should be viewed as non-Jewish documents issued for Jews in non-Jewish courts.[30] Cotton, however, limited her claim to documents written in Greek and presumably in Roman legal courts under Roman rule. She explicitly stated that her conclusions do not pertain to the Aramaic and Hebrew documents. *XHev/Se* 13, however, while perhaps following Roman law, belies Cotton's

---

[27] As shown by Lewis in his *The Documents from the Bar Kokhba Period in the Cave of the Letters: Greek Papyri* (Jerusalem 1989) 24, and against R. Katzoff, "Polygamy in P. Yadin?" *ZPE* 109 (1995) 128-32.

[28] I am grateful to Ada Yardeni for also pointing this out to me.

[29] And this segment in the document also serves Cotton and Qimron in their claim that it is not a divorce bill, but a waiver of claims.

[30] In Cotton and Yardeni, *Discoveries*, 273-4.

other parameters. It was written in Aramaic and in a completely Jewish court of law, at the time of the Bar Kokhba revolt—the one time during the second century CE when Jews lived under Jewish rule. Thus Cotton's analysis falls short of solving the problem of this document. In their new article on this same document Cotton and Qimron state clearly: "...the objection that [this document does] not represent 'good Jews' but a fringe group or assimilated Jews is bound to be raised ... In view of the opening of *XHev/Se ar* 13 ... we submit that such a claim cannot be accepted."[31]

I would, therefore, suggest that perhaps one should turn the old view of Jewish divorce on its head. Perhaps in ancient Jewish practice women could divorce their husbands, and it is a mere accident of our transmission history that this fact is not sufficiently attested. After all, almost all we know of Jewish legal traditions from the first and second centuries CE and earlier, derives from Pharisaic/rabbinic tradition. Perhaps these writings intentionally distort our picture of other Jewish attitudes to divorce in their time. Consider for example the marriage contracts from Elephantine, which allow for divorce initiated by the wife. Why should one think them unique? They are, after all, the only Jewish marriage contracts extant from the Achaemenid period. And the Elephantine community was not as isolated as some scholars have suggested; its leaders communicated with Temple authorities in Jerusalem.[32] One might likewise consider Mark's description of Jewish divorce. It is true that Mark was probably not Jewish himself, and certainly not a Palestinian Jew. It is, however, striking that the context in which he discusses divorce is an argument with the Pharisees. In Mark 10:2 the Pharisees ask Jesus: "Is it lawful for a man to divorce his wife?" They do not address the question whether a woman may divorce her husband. Jesus' opinion is not relevant to the issue of who may divorce whom, because he denies the right of divorce altogether. But when speaking to his disciples Jesus says: "Whoever divorces his wife and marries another commits adultery against her and if she divorces her husband and marries another, she commits adultery" (Mark 10:11-2). The text thus differentiates between the Pharisees' viewpoint that only the husband may divorce his wife, and Jesus' construction of reality, in which it is possible (though wrong) for both. Finally, while it is true that Josephus maintains that Herod's sister Salome's divorce contravenes Jewish law (*Ant.* 15.259), one should keep in mind that Josephus himself was a Pharisee (*Vita* 12), so it is hardly surprising that his view of Jewish law coincides with theirs. While one can, therefore, interpret Salome's action as that of a Roman citizen rejecting Jewish practice, one could also characterize it as that of a Jew rejecting Pharisaic practice.

---

[31] Cotton and Qimron, *ibid.*, 118.

[32] B. Porten and Ada Yardeni, *Textbook of Aramaic Documents from Ancient Egypt 1: Letters* (Jerusalem 1986), 68-76.

Bibliography

Abrams, Judith Z., *The Women of the Talmud* (Northvale NJ 1995).

Adler, Rachel, "The Virgin in the Brothel and Other Anomalies: Character and Context in the Legend of Beruriah," *Tikkun* 3/6 (1988) 28-32; 102-5.

——, "Feminist Folktales of Justice: Robert Cover as a Resource for the Renewal of Halakhah," *Conservative Judaism* 45/3 (1993) 40-56.

Aharoni, J., "The Caves of Nahal Hever," *Atiqot* 3 (1961) 148-62.

Allegro, J., "The Wiles of the Wicked Woman: A Sapiental Work from Qumran's Fourth Cave," *PEQ* 96 (1964) 53-5.

Alon, Gedalyahu, *Jews, Judaism and the Classical World* (translation I. Abrahams; 2 vols.; Jerusalem 1977).

——, *The Jews in their Land in the Talmudic Age (70-640 CE)* (translation I. Abrahams; 2 vols.; Jerusalem 1984).

Amaru, Betsy H., "Portraits of Biblical Women in Josephus' Antiquities," *JJS* 39 (1988) 143-70.

Angel, J. L., "Ecology and Population in the Eastern Mediterranean," *World Archaeology* 4 (1972) 88-105.

Archer, Léonie, "The 'Evil Women' in Apocryphal and Pseudepigraphical Writings," *Proceedings of the Ninth World Congress of Jewish Studies* A (Jerusalem 1986) 239-246.

——, *Her Price is Beyond Rubies: The Jewish Woman in Greco-Roman Palestine* (*JSOT Supplement Series* 60; Sheffield 1990).

Arensburg, B. and Y. Rak, "Skeletal Remains of an Ancient Jewish Population from French Hill, Jerusalem," *BASOR* 219 (1975) 69-71.

——, with M. S. Goldstein, H. Nathan and Y. Rak, "Skeletal Remains of Jews from the Hellenistic and Roman Periods in Israel (Pathology)," *Bulletins et mémoires de la Société d'anthropologie de Paris* 8 (1981) 11-24.

——, with Anna Belfer-Cohen, "Preliminary Report on the Skeletal Remains from the Ein Gedi Tombs," *Atiqot* 24 (1994) 12*-4*.

Avigad, N., *Beth She'arim* 3 (Jerusalem 1976).

——, *Discovering Jerusalem* (Jerusalem 1980).

——, "On the Identification of Persons Mentioned in Hebrew Epigraphic Sources," *Eretz Israel* 19 (1987) 235-7 [Hebrew].

——, with Y. Yadin (eds.), *A Genesis Apocryphon: A Scroll from the Wilderness of Judaea* (Jerusalem 1956).

——, "Expedition A: Nahal David," *IEJ* 12 (1962) 169-83.

Bagnall, R. S., *Reading Papyri, Writing Ancient History* (London 1995).

——, with B. W. Frier, *The Demography of Roman Egypt* (Cambridge 1994).

Bailey, J. L., "Josephus' Portrayal of the Matriarchs," in L. H. Feldman and G. Hata (eds.), *Josephus, Judaism and Christianity* (Detroit 1987) 154-79.

Bammel, E., "Markus 10, 11f. und das jüdische Eherecht," *ZNTW* 61 (1970) 95-101.

Bar-Adon, P., "Another Settlement of the Judaean Desert Sect at En el-Ghuweir on the Shores of the Dead Sea," *BASOR* 227 (1977) 12-7.

Barthelemy, D., *Discoveries in the Judaean Desert* 1 (Oxford 1955).

Baumgarten, J. M., "On the Testimony of Women in *1QSa*," *JBL* 76 (1957) 266-9.

——, "4Q502, Marriage or Golden Age Ritual?" *JJS* 34 (1983) 125-35.

——, "The Qumran-Essene Restraints on Marriage," in L. H. Schiffman (ed.), *Archaeology and History in the Dead Sea Scrolls: The New York University Conference in Memory of Yigael Yadin* (*JSP Supplement Series* 8; Sheffield 1990) 13-24.

Beall, T. S., *Josephus' Description of the Essenes Illustrated by the Dead Sea Scrolls* (Cambridge 1988).

Belkin, S., *Philo and the Oral Law* (Cambridge 1940).

Bennet-Elder, Linda, *Transformations in the Judith Mythos: A Feminist Critical Analysis* (Unpublished Ph.D. Dissertation; Florida State University 1991).

Ben-Shalom, I., *The School of Shammai and the Zealots' Struggle against Rome* (Jerusalem 1993) 210-21 [Hebrew].

Bentwich, N., *Josephus* (Philadelphia 1914).

Biale, D., *Eros and the Jews: From Biblical Israel to Contemporary America* (New York 1992).

Bickerman, E. J., "The Colophon of the Greek Book of Esther," *JBL* 63 (1944) 346-7.

——, *Four Strange Books of the Bible* (New York 1967).

Blok, Josine H., *The Early Amazons: Modern and Ancient Perspectives on a Persistent Myth* (Leiden 1995).

Boyarin, D., *Carnal Israel: Reading Sex in Talmudic Culture* (Berkeley 1993).

Braud, D. C., "Berenice in Rome," *Historia* 33 (1984) 12-3.

Braun, M., *Griechischer Roman und hellenistische Geschichtsschreibung* (Frankfurt 1934).

——, *History and Romance in Graeco-Oriental Literature* (Oxford 1938).

Brooten, Bernadette J., *Women Leaders in the Ancient Synagogue* (*Brown Judaic Studies* 36; Atlanta 1982).

——, "Konnten Frauen im alten Judentum die Scheidung betreiben? Überlegung zu Mk 10, 11-12 und 1Kor 7, 10-11," *Evangelische Theologie* 42 (1982) 65-80.

——, "Zur Debatte über das Scheidungsrecht der jüdischen Frau," *Evangelische Theologie* 43 (1983) 466-78.

——, "Early Christian Women and their Cultural Context: Issues of Method in Historical Reconstruction," in Adele Yarbro-Collins (ed.), *Feminist Perspectives on Biblical Scholarship* (Chico CA 1985) 65-91.

——, *Love Between Women: Early Christian Responses to Homoeroticism* (Chicago 1996).

Brown, Cheryl-Ann, *No Longer be Silent: First-Century Portraits of Biblical Women* (Louisville KY 1992).

Brown, P., *The Body and Society: Men, Women and Sexual Renunciation in Early Christianity* (New York 1988).

Brüll, N., "Das apokryphische Susanna-Buch," *Jahrbuch für jüdische Geschichte und Literatur* 3 (1877) 1-69.

Brünnow, R., "Reisebericht 1898," *Mitteilungen und Nachrichten des Deutschen Palästina-Vereins* 5 (1899) 23-9; 40-2; 56-61; 81-91; 100-1.

Büchler, A., "The Practice of Halakhah According to Beit Shammai During the Second Temple Period and After the Destruction," *Emlékkönyn Bloch Mózes Tiszteletére (Moses Bloch Festschrift)* (Budapest 1905) 21-30 [Hebrew].

——, "The Induction of the Bride and Bridegroom into the חופה in the First and Second Centuries in Palestine," *Livre d'hommage à la mémoire de Dr. Samuel Poznanski* (Warsaw 1927) 82-132.

——, *Studies in Jewish History* (Jews College Publications 1; London 1956).

Camp, Claudia V., "Understanding a Patriarchy: Women in Second Century Jerusalem Through the Eyes of Ben Sira," in Amy-Jill Levine (ed.), *'Women Like This': New Perspectives on Jewish Women in the Greco-Roman World* (Atlanta 1992) 1-39.

Cansdale, Lena, "Women Members in the *Yahad* According to the Qumran Scrolls," *Proceedings of the Eleventh World Congress of Jewish Studies* A (Jerusalem 1994) 215-22.

Carroll, M. P., "Myth, Methodology and Transformation in the Old Testament: The Stories of Esther, Judith and Susanna," *Studies in Religion* 12 (1983) 301-12.

Cazalles, H., "Notes sur la composition de rouleau d'Esther," in H. Gross and F. Mußner (eds.), *Lex tua veritas: Festschrift für Hubert Junker* (Trier 1961) 18-29.

Clermont-Ganneau, C., "Archaeological and Epigraphical Notes on Palestine," *PEFQS* 35 (1903) 125-31.

Clines, D. J. A., *The Esther Scroll: The Story of the Story* (*JSOT Supplement Series* 30; Sheffield 1984).

Cohen, G. D., *Studies in the Variety of Rabbinic Cultures* (Philadelphia 1991).

Cohen, Naomi G., "The Theological Stratum in the Martha b. Boethus Tradition: An Explication of the Text in *Gittin* 56a," *HTR* 69 (1976) 187-96.

Cohen, S. J. D., "Epigraphical Rabbis," *JQR* 72 (1981-2) 1-17.

——, *Josephus in Galilee and Rome* (Leiden 1979).

——, "Masada: Literary Tradition, Archaeological Remains and the Literary Credibility of Josephus," *JJS* 33 (1982) 385-405.

——, "The Significance of Yavneh: Pharisees, Rabbis, and the End of Jewish Sectarianism," *HUCA* 55 (1984) 27-53.

——, "Parallel Historical Traditions in Josephus and Rabbinic Literature," *Proceedings of the Ninth World Congress of Jewish Studies* 2 (Jerusalem 1986) 7-14.

——, *From the Maccabees to the Mishnah* (Philadelphia 1987).

Colson, F. H., *Philo: With an English Translation* (10 vols.; Cambridge 1941).

Cotton, Hannah M., "The Guardianship of Jesus son of Babatha: Roman and Local Law in the Province of Arabia," *JRS* 83 (1993) 393-420.

——, "A Canceled Marriage Contract from the Judaean Desert (*XHev/Se GR.* 2)," *JRS* 84 (1994) 64-86.

——, with W. E. H. Cockel and F. G. B. Millar, "The Papyrology of the Roman Near East: A Survey," *JRS* 85 (1995) 214-35.

——, "Subscriptions and Signatures in the Papyri from the Judaean Desert: The Χειροχρήστης," *Journal of Juristic Papyrology* 25 (1995) 29-40.

——, "The Guardian (ἐπίτροπος) of a Woman in the Documents from the Judaean Desert," *ZPE* 118 (1996) 267-73.

——, with J. Geiger, *Masada II: The Latin and Greek Documents* (Jerusalem 1989).

——, with Ada Yardeni, *Discoveries in the Judaean Desert* 27 (Oxford 1997).

——, with E. Qimron, "XHev/Se ar 13 of 134 or 135 CE: A Wife's Renunciation of Claims," *JJS* 49 (1998) 108-18.

Crook, J. A., "Titus and Berenice," *American Journal of Philology* 72 (1951) 162-75.

Delamarre, I., *Inscriptionum Graecum* (Berolini 1908).

Dan, Y., "Josephus Flavius and Justus of Tiberias," in U. Rappaport (ed.), *Josephus Flavius: Historian of Eretz Israel in the Hellenistic-Roman Period* (Jerusalem 1982) 57-78.

Davies, P. R. and Joan E. Taylor, "On the Testimony of Women in 1Qsa," *Dead Sea Discoveries* 3 (1996) 223-35.

Destinon, J. von, *Die Quellen des Flavius Josephus* (Kiel 1882).

Destro, Adriana, *The Law of Jealousy: Anthropology of Sotah* (*Brown Judaic Studies* 181; Atlanta 1989).

Dinur, B.-Z., "Historiographical Fragments in Talmudic Literature and their Investigation," *Proceedings of the Fifth World Congress of Jewish Studies* 2 (Jerusalem 1969) 137-46 [Hebrew]

Dittenberger, W., *Orientis Graeci Inscriptiones Selectae* (2 vols.; Lipsiae 1903).

DuBois, Page, *Centaurs and Amazons: Women and the Pre-History of the Great Chain of Being* (Ann Arbor 1991).

Duran, R., "The Martyr: A Synoptic View of the Mother and her Seven Sons," in J. J. Collins and G. W. E. Nickelsburg (eds.), *Ideal Figures in Ancient Judaism: Profiles and Paradigms* (Chico CA 1980) 189-221.

Efal, I. And J. Naveh, *Aramaic Ostraca of the Fourth Century BC from Idumaea* (Jerusalem 1996).

Efron, J., *Studies on the Hasmonean Period* (Leiden 1987).

Eilberg-Schwartz, H., *God's Phallus (and Other Problems for Men and Monotheism)* (Boston 1994).

Eisenman, R. H. and M. Wise, *The Dead Sea Scrolls Uncovered* (Shaftsbury 1992).

Enslin, M .S. (ed.), *The Book of Judith (Jewish Apocryphal Literature* 7; Philadelphia 1972).

Epstein, J. N., "Sifre Zuta: Parah," *Tarbiz* 1 (1940) 52-3 [Hebrew].

——, "On the Mishnah of Rabbi Judah," *Tarbiz* 15 (1944) 1-13 [Hebrew].

Epstein, L. M., *The Jewish Marriage Contract: A Study in the Status of Women in Jewish Law* (New York 1927).

——, *Marriage Laws in the Bible and the Talmud* (Cambridge MA 1942).

Eshel, H., "The Historical Background of the Pesher Interpreting Joshua's Curse on the Rebuilder of Jericho," *RQ* 15 (1991-2) 409-20.

——, with Esther Eshel and Ada Yardeni, "A Qumran Composition Containing Part of Ps. 154 and a Prayer for the Welfare of King Jonathan and his Kingdom," *IEJ* 42 (1992) 216-9.

Falk, Z., *The Divorce Action by the Wife in Jewish Law* (Jerusalem 1973) [Hebrew].

——, *Introduction to Jewish Law of the Second Commonwealth* (2 vols.; Leiden 1978).

Feldman, L. H., "Hellenization in Josephus' Version of Esther," *Transactions and Proceedings of the American Philological Association* 101 (1970) 143-70.

——, *Josephus and Modern Scholarship (1937-80)* (Berlin 1984).

——, "Flavius Josephus Revisited," in W. Haase (ed.), *Aufstieg und Niedergang der römischen Welt* 22.2 (Berlin 1984) 763-862.

——, "Josephus' Portrait of Deborah," in A. Caquot, M. Hadas-Lebel and J. Riand (eds.), *Hellenica et Judaica: Hommage à Valentin Nikiprowetzky* (Leuven 1986) 115-28.

Figueras, P., *Decorated Jewish Ossuaries* (Leiden 1983).

Finkel J., "The Author of the Genesis Apocryphon Knew the Book of Esther," in C. Rabin and Y. Yadin (eds.), *Essays on the Dead Sea Scrolls* (Jerusalem 1961) 163-82 [Hebrew].

Fitzmayer, J., "The Matthean Divorce Text and some New Palestinian Evidence," *Theological Studies* 37 (1976) 197-226.

Finkelstein, L., *The Pharisees: The Sociological Background of their Faith* (2 vols.; Philadelphia 1966).

Flusser, D., "Pharisees, Sadducees and Essenes in Pesher Nahum," in: M. Dorman, S. Safrai and M. Stern, (eds.), *In Memory of Gedaliahu Alon: Essays in Jewish History and Philology* (Tel Aviv 1970) 133-68 [Hebrew].

Fox, M. V., *Character and Ideology in the Book of Esther* (Columbia SC 1991).

Fraade, S., "Ascetical Aspects of Ancient Judaism," in A. Green (ed.), *Jewish Spirituality* 1 (New York 1986) 253-88.

Frey, J. B. *Corpvs Inscriptionvm Ivdaicarvm* (2 vols.; Rome 1936-52).

Froehmer, W., *Les Inscriptions Greques, Musée Impérial du Louvre* (Paris 1865).

Fuchs, Esther, "Status and Role of Female Heroines in the Biblical Narrative," *Mankind Quarterly* 23 (1982) 149-60.

Fuks, A., "Markus Julius Alexander," *Zion* 13 (1944) 10-7 [Hebrew].

Garfinkel, Y., "The Elyakim Na'ar Yokan Seal Impressions: Sixty Years of Confusion in Biblical Archaeological Research," *BA* 53 (1990) 74-9.

Geiger, A., "On the Pharisee Woman in *mSotah* 3:4," *Otzar Nehmad* 2 (1857) 99-101 [Hebrew].

——, *Urschrift und Übersetzung der Bibel in ihrer Abhängigkeit von der inneren Entwicklung des Judenthums* (Breslau 1857).

——, "About the Controversies between the Sadducees and their Followers and the Pharisees and the Difference between the Old and the New Halakhah," *HeHalutz* 6 (1862) 13-30 [Hebrew].

Gera, Deborah, *The Anonymous Tractatus De Mulieribus* (Leiden 1997).

Giangrande, G., "On an Alleged Fragment of Ctesias," *Quadesni Urbinati di cultura classica* 23 (1976) 38.

Glancy, Jennifer A., "The Accused: Susanna and her Readers," in Athalya Brenner (ed.), *A Feminist Companion to Esther, Judith and Susanna* (Sheffield 1995) 287-302.

Glazer, N. N., "Megilat Ta'anit," *Encyclopedia Judaica* 11 (Jerusalem 1971) 1230-1.

Goehring, J. E., "Libertine or Liberated: Women in So-called Libertine Gnostic Communities," in Karen King (ed.), *Images of the Feminine in Gnosticism* (Philadelphia 1988) 329-344.

Goldberg A., "The Eighteen Measures of Bet-Shammai and Bet-Hillel," in A. M. Rabello (ed.), *Studies in Judaism: Jubilee Volume Presented to David Kotlar by his Students, Colleagues and Friends* (Tel Aviv 1975) 216-25 [Hebrew].

Goldstein, J. A., *II Maccabees* (*The Anchor Bible*; New York 1983).

Goodblatt, D., "The Beruriah Traditions," *JJS* 26 (1975) 68-85.

——, "The Talmudic Sources on the Origins of Organized Jewish Education," *Studies in the History of the Jewish People and the Land of Israel* 5 (1980) 89-102 [Hebrew].

Goodman, Martin, *The Ruling Class of Judaea* (Cambridge: Cambridge University Press, 1987).

Graetz, H., *Geschichte der Judäer* 3/2 (Leipzig 1906⁵).

Grant, M., *Herod the Great* (London 1971).

Greenfield, J. C., "Nebuchadnezzar's Campaign in the Book of Judith," *Bulletin of the Israel Exploration Society* 28 (1964) 204-8 [Hebrew].

——, "The Jewish Historical Novella of the Persian Period," in H. Tadmor and I. Efal (eds.), *The World History of the Jewish People: The Persian Period* (Jerusalem 1983) 208-9 [Hebrew].

——, "Ben Sira 42.9-10 and its Talmudic Paraphrase," in P. R. Davies and R. T. White (eds.), *A Tribute to Geza Vermes: Essays on Jewish and Christian Literature and History* (*JSOT Supplement Series* 100; Sheffield 1990) 167-73.

——, "'Because He/She Did Not Know Letters': Remarks on a First Millenium C.E. Legal Expression," *Journal of the Ancient Near Eastern Society* 22 (1993) 39-44.

Grenfell, B. P., A. S. Hunt and D. G. Hogarth, *Fayum Towns and Papyri* (London 1900).

Grintz, Y. M., *Sefer Yehudit* (Jerusalem 1957) [Hebrew].

——, "The Giv'at Hamivtar Inscription: A Historical Interpretation," *Sinai* 75 (1974) 20-3 [Hebrew].

Groag, E., "Julius (Alexander)," *Pauly-Wissowa Real-Encyclopädie der klassischen Altertumswissenschaft* 10/1 (Stuttgart 1917) 151-2.

Guttentag, Marcia and Paul F. Secord, *Too Many Women: The Sex Ratio Question* (Beverly Hills 1983).

Gulak, A., "Betrothal Contract and Possessions Acquired Orally According to Talmudic Law," *Tarbiz* 3 (1942) 361-76 [Hebrew].

Guttman, J., "The Mother and her Seven Sons in Legend and in Books II and IV Maccabees," in M. Schwabe and J. Guttman (eds.), *Johanan Levi Memorial Volume* (Jerusalem 1949) 25-37 [Hebrew].

Haas, N., "Anthropological Observations on the Skeletal Remains from Giv'at ha-Mivtar," *IEJ* 20 (1970) 38-59.

Hachlili, Rachel and Patricia Smith, "The Genealogy of the Goliath Family," *BASOR* 235 (1979) 67-70.

Hacohen Maimon, Y. L., "Rashi," in *idem* (ed.), *Sefer Rashi* (Jerusalem 1956) 108-14 [Hebrew].

Hadas, M., *Aristeas to Philocrates* (*Jewish Apocryphal Literature*; Philadelphia 1951).

Harnack, A. von, *What is Christianity?* (New York 1957).

Harris, W. V., "Child Exposure in the Roman Empire," *JRS* 84 (1994) 1-22.

Hauptman, Judith, "Women's Liberation in the Talmudic Period: An Assessment," *Conservative Judaism* 26/4 (1972) 24-8.

——, "Mishnah *Gittin* as a Pietist Document," *Proceedings of the Tenth World Congress of Jewish Studies* C/1 (Jerusalem 1990) 23-30 [Hebrew].

——, "Maternal Dissent: Women and Procreation in the Mishnah," *Tikkun* 6/6 (1991) 80-1; 94-5.

——, "Pesach: A Liberating Experience for Women," *Masoret* (Winter 1993) 8-9.

——, "Women's Voluntary Performance of Commandments from which They are Exempt," *Proceedings of the Eleventh World Congress of Jewish Studies* C/1 (Jerusalem 1994) 161-8 [Hebrew].

——, *Rereading the Rabbis: A Woman's Voice* (Boulder CO, 1997).

Haussoullier, B., "L'oracle d'Apolon à Claros," *Revue de Philologie* 22 (1898) 260-1.

Hengel, M., *Crucifixion in the Ancient World and the Folly of the Message of the Cross* (Philadelphia 1977).

——, *The Zealots* (Edinburgh 1989).

Henten, J. W. van, "Judith as Alternative Leader: A Reading of Judith 7-13," in Athalya Brenner (ed.), *A Feminist Companion to Esther, Judith and Susanna* (Sheffield 1995) 224-52.

Herr, M. D., "Persecution and Martyrdom in Hadrian's Days," in D. Asheri and I. Schatzman (eds.), *Studies in History* (*Scripta Hierosolymitana* 23; Jerusalem 1972) 85-125.

——, *A History of Eretz Israel: The Roman Period* (10 vols.; Jerusalem 1984) 283-370 [Hebrew].

Hershberg, A. S., "The Betrothal and Nuptial Practices in the Talmudic Period," *Ha-'Atid* 5 (1923) 75-102 [Hebrew].

Herst, R. E., "The Purim Connection," *Union Seminary Review* 28 (1973) 139-45.

Heyob, Sharon K., *The Cult of Isis among Women in the Graeco-Roman World* (Leiden 1975).

Hisdai, Y., "The Origins of the Conflict Between Hasidim and Mitnagdim," in B. Safran (ed.), *Hasidism: Continuity or Innovation?* (*Harvard Judaic Texts and Monographs* 5; Cambridge MA 1988).

Hölscher, G., *Die Quellen des Josephus für die Zeit vom Exil bis zum jüdischen Krieg* (Leipzig 1904).

Hohlwein, N., "Euhemreia du Fayoum," *Journal of Juristic Papyrology* 3 (1949).

Hopkins, K. M., "The Age of Roman Girls at Marriage," *Population Studies* 18 (1964-5) 309-27.

Howarth, W. D., "'Droit du Seigneur': Fact or Fantasy?" *Journal of European Studies* 1 (1971) 291-312.

Hyman, Paula E., *Gender and Assimilation in Modern Jewish History* (Seattle 1995).

Ilan, Tal, *The Names of the Jews in Palestine in the Second Temple and Mishnaic Periods: A Statistical Study* (Unpublished MA Thesis; Jerusalem 1984).

——, "The Greek Names of the Hasmoneans," *JQR* 78 (1987-8) 1-20.

——, "The Names of the Hasmoneans," *Eretz Israel* 19 (1987) 238-41 [Hebrew].

——, "Notes on the Distribution of Women's Names in Palestine in the Second Temple and Mishnaic Period," *JJS* 40 (1989) 187-200.

——, "New Ossuary Inscriptions from Jerusalem," *Scripta Classica Israelica* 11 (1991-2) 149-59.

——, "Queen Salamzion Alexandra and Judas Aristobulus' Widow: Did Jannaeus Alexander Contract a Levirate Marriage?" *JSJ* 24 (1993) 181-90.

——, "Matrona and Rabbi Jose: An Alternative Interpretation," *JSJ* 25 (1994) 18-51.

——, *Jewish Women in Greco-Roman Palestine: An Inquiry into Image and Status (Texte und Studien zum antiken Judentum* 44; Tübingen 1995).

——, "Women Studies and Jewish Studies: When and Where do they Meet?" *JSQ* 3 (1996) 162-73.

——, "The Quest for the Historical Beruriah, Rachel and Imma Shalom," *AJS Review* 22 (1997) 1-17.

——, *Mine and Yours are Hers: Retrieving Women's History from Rabbinic Literature* (Leiden 1997).

——, "King David, King Herod and Nicolaus of Damascus," *JSQ* 5 (1998) 195-240.

——, "In the Footsteps of Jesus: Jewish Women in a Jewish Movement," in Ingrid R. Kitzberger (ed.), *Transformative Encounters: Jesus and Women Re-viewed* (Leiden, in press).

——, with Jonathan Price, "Seven Problems in Josephus' *Bellum Judiacum*," *JQR* 84 (1993-4) 189-208.

Israeli Academy of Language, *The Historical Dictionary of the Hebrew Language: The Book of Ben Sira: Text, Concordance and an Analysis of the Vocabulary* (Jerusalem 1973).

Jacobs, M., *Die Institution des jüdischen Patriarchen (Texte und Studien zum antiken Judentum* 52; Tübingen 1995).

Jalabert L. and R. Monterde, *Inscriptions Grecques et Latines de la Syrie II: Chalcidique et Antiochene* (Paris 1939).

——, with C. Mondesert, *Inscriptions Grecques et Latines de la Syrie IV: Laodicée Apamene* (Paris 1955).

Jones, A. H. M., *The Herods of Judaea* (Oxford 1938).

Jones, B. W., "Two Misconceptions about the Book of Esther," *CBQ* 39 (1977) 171-81.

Jordan, Ruth, *Berenice* (London 1974).

Katzoff, R., "Papyrus Yadin 18—Legal Commentary," *IEJ* 37 (1987) 239-42.

——, "Polygamy in P. Yadin?" *ZPE* 109 (1995) 128-32.

——, "The Age of Marriage of Jewish Girls During the Talmudic Period," in M. A. Friedman (ed.), *Marriage and the Family in Halakha and Jewish Thought (Te'uda* 13; Tel Aviv 1997) 9-18 [Hebrew].

Kenyon, F. G., *Greek Papyri in the British Museum* 3 (London 1907) 61-8.

Keuls, Eva C., *The Reign of the Phallus: Sexual Politics in Classical Athens* (New York 1985).

Klausner, J. "Queen Salome Alexandra," in A. Schalit (ed.), *The World History of the Jewish People: The Hellenistic Age* (London 1972) 242-54.

Klawiter, F. C., "The Role of Martyrdom and Persecution in Developing the Priestly Authority of Women in Early Christianity: The Case of Montanism," *Church History* 49 (1980) 251-61.

Klein, S., *Jüdisch-palästinisches Corpus Inscriptionum* (Wien-Berlin 1920).

Kloner, A., *The Necropolis of Jerusalem in the Second Temple Period* (Unpublished Ph.D. Thesis, Hebrew University; Jerusalem 1980) [Hebrew].

———, "A Burial Cave of the Second Temple Period at Giv'at Hamivtar, Jerusalem," in A. Oppenheimer, U. Rappaport and M. Stern (eds.), *Jerusalem in the Second Temple Period: Abraham Schalit Memorial Volume* (Jerusalem 1980) 191-224 [Hebrew].

———, "A Tomb with Inscribed Ossuaries in East Talpiyot, Jerusalem," *Atiqot* 29 (1996) 15-22.

Kraemer, Ross S., "A New Inscription from Malta and the Question of Women Elders in Diaspora Jewish Communities," *HTR* 78 (1985) 431-8.

———, "Hellenistic Jewish Women: The Epigraphic Evidence," *SBL Seminary Papers* 24 (1986) 183-200.

———, "Non Literary Evidence for Jewish Women in Rome and Egypt," *Helios* 13 (1987) 85-101.

———, "Monastic Jewish Women in Greco-Roman Egypt: Philo on the Therapeutrides," *Signs: Journal of Women in Culture and Society* 14 (1989) 342-70.

———, "Jewish Women in the Diaspora World of Late Antiquity," in Judith R. Baskin (ed.), *Jewish Women in Historical Perspective* (Detroit 1991) 43-67.

———, "Women's Authorship of Jewish and Christian Literature in the Greco-Roman Period," in Amy-Jill Levine (ed.), *'Women Like This': New perspectives on Jewish Women in the Greco-Roman World* (Atlanta 1991) 221-42

———, *Her Share of the Blessings: Women's Religions among Pagans, Jews and Christians in the Greco-Roman World* (Oxford 1992).

Krauss, S., "La fête de Hanoucca," *REJ* 30 (1895) 37-43.

Kugel, J. L., *In Potiphar's House: The Interpretive Life of Biblical Texts* (Cambridge MA 1990).

Kutscher, Y., *Hebrew and Aramaic Studies* (Jerusalem 1977) [Hebrew].

LaCocque, A., *The Feminine Unconventional: Four Subversive Figures in Israel's Tradition* (Minneapolis 1990).

Laffey, Alice L., *An Introduction to the Old Testament: A Feminist Perspective* (Philadelphia 1988).

Laquer, R., *Der jüdische Historiker Flavius Josephus* (Gießen 1920).

Lebram, J. C. H., "Purimfest und Estherbuch," *VT* 22 (1972) 208-22.

Levi, I., "Hanoucca et la jus primae noctis" *REJ* 30 (1898) 220-31.

———, "Le martyre de sept Macchabees dans la Pesikta Rabbati," *REJ* 54 (1907) 138-41.

Levine, Amy-Jill, "Diaspora as Metaphor: Bodies and Boundaries in the Book of Tobit," in J. A. Overman and R. S. MacLennan (eds.), *Diaspora Jews and Judaism: Essays in Honor of and in Dialogue with A. Thomas Kraabel* (Atlanta 1992) 105-17.

———, "'Hemmed in on Every Side': Jews and Women in the Book of Susanna," in Athalya Brenner (ed.), *A Feminist Companion to Esther, Judith and Susanna* (Sheffield 1995) 303-23.

———, "Sacrifice and Salvation: Otherness and Domestication in the Book of Judith," in Athalya Brenner (ed.), *A Feminist Companion to Esther, Judith and Susanna* (Sheffield 1995) 208-23.

Levine, L. I., "The Jewish Patriarch (Nasi) in the Third Century," in W. Haase (ed.), *Aufstieg und Niedergang der römischen Welt* 2.19.2 (Berlin 1979) 649-88.

———, *The Rabbinic Class of Roman Palestine in Late Antiquity* (Jerusalem 1985).

Levison, J., "Is Eve to Blame? A Contextual Analysis of Sirach 25:24," *CBQ* 47 (1985) 617-23.

Lewis, N., *Life in Egypt under Roman Rule* (Oxford 1983).

———, *The Documents from the Bar Kokhba Period in the Cave of the Letters: Greek Papyri* (Jerusalem 1989).

Licht, J. (ed.), *The Rule Scroll* (Jerusalem 1965) [Hebrew].

——, "The Wiles of the Wicked Woman," in B. Uffenheimer (ed.), *Bible and Jewish History: Studies in Bible and Jewish History Dedicated to the Memory of Jacob Liver* (Tel Aviv 1971) 289-96 [Hebrew].

——, "The Book of Judith as a Work of Literature," in M. Z. Kaddari, A. Saltman and M. Schwarcz (eds.), *Baruch Kurzweil Memorial Volume* (Ramat Gan 1975) 169-83 [Hebrew].

Lidzbarski, M., *Handbuch der nordsemitischen Epigraphik* 1 (Weimar 1898).

Lieberman, S., *Tosefeth Rishonim* (4 vols.; Jerusalem 1939) [Hebrew].

——, "Sin and its Punishment: A Study in Jewish and Christian Visions of Hell," in S. Lieberman, S. Zeitlin, S. Spiegel and A. Marx (eds.), *Louis Ginzberg Jubilee Volume* (Hebrew volume; Philadelphia 1945) 249-70 [Hebrew].

Littman, E. and D. Magie, *Syria: Publications of the Princeton University Archaeological Expedition to Syria in 1904-5 and 1909, Division III: Greek and Latin Inscriptions* (Leiden 1921).

Lowenstam, E., "Divorce and Remarriage in the New Testament," *The Jewish Law Annual* 4 (1981) 47-65.

Lubitch, Rivkah, "A Feminist Look at Esther," *Judaism* 42 (1993) 438-46.

Macurdy, Grace H., *Hellenistic Queens* (Baltimore 1932).

——, *Vassal Queens and Some Contemporary Women in the Roman Empire* (Baltimore 1937).

Madden, F. W., *History of Jewish Coinage* (London 1864; republished New York 1967).

Margaliot, M., "On the Antiquity of Seder Eliyahu," in M. D. Kassuto, J. Klausner and J. Guttman (eds.), *Sefer Asaf* (Jerusalem 1973) 370-90 [Hebrew].

Mason, S., *Flavius Josephus on the Pharisees: A Composition-Critical Study* (Leiden 1991).

Mattila, Sharon L., "Wisdom, Sense Perception, Nature and Philo's Gender Gradient," *HTR* 89 (1996) 103-29.

Mazar, B., *Beth She'arim* 1 (Jerusalem 1973).

Meir, Ofra, "The Story as a Hermeneutic Device," *AJS Review* 7-8 (1981-2) 231-62.

Merkelbach R. and J. Nolle, *Die Inschriften von Ephesos* 6 (Bonn 1980).

Meshorer, Y., *Jewish Coins of the Second Temple Period* (Tel Aviv 1967).

——, *City Coins of Eretz Israel and the Decapolis in the Roman Period* (Jerusalem 1985).

Metzger, B. M., *An Introduction to the Apocrypha* (New York 1957).

Meyer, P. M. *Griechische Papyrusurkunden der Hamburger Staats- und Universitäts-bibliothek* 1 (Leipzig-Berlin 1911).

Meyers, Carol, *Discovering Eve: Ancient Israelite Women in Context* (Oxford 1988).

Michel, O. and O. Bauernfeind, *De Bello Judaico* (München 1959).

Milik, J. T., "Une Lettre de Simon Bar Kokheba," *RB* 60 (1953) 277-82.

——, "Le travail d'édition des manuscript du Désert de Juda," *Volume du congres Strasbourg 1956* (*Supplements to VT* 4; Leiden 1956) 17-26.

——, "La Patrie de Tobie," *RB* 73 (1966) 522-30.

——, "Daniel et Susanne à Qumrân?" in J. Dore, P. Gerlot and M. Carrez (eds.), *De la Tôrah au Messie: Mélanges Henri Cazelles* (Paris 1981) 337-59.

——, "Les modèles Araméens du livre d'Esther dans la grotte 4 de Qumrân," *RQ* 15 (1991-2) 321-99.

Mireaux, E., *La reine Bérénice* (Paris 1951).

Mood, A. M., F. A. Graybill and D. C. Boes, *Introduction to the Theory of Statistics* (1974).

Moore, C. A., *Esther: Introduction, Translation and Notes* (*The Anchor Bible*; New York 1971).

——, "On the Origins of the LXX Additions to the Book of Esther," *JBL* 92 (1973) 382-93.

——, *Daniel, Esther and Jeremiah—The Additions: A New Translation with Introduction and Commentary* (*The Anchor Bible*; New York 1977).

———, *Judith: A New Translation with Introduction and Commentary* (*The Anchor Bible*; New York 1985).

Moore, G. F., *Judaism in the First Centuries of the Christian Era* (3 vols.; Cambridge 1964).

Müller, C. and T., *Fragmenta Historicorum Graecum* (Paris 1928).

Nathan, H., "The Skeletal Material from Nahal Hever," *Atiqot* 3 (1961) 165-75 [Hebrew].

Naveh, J., "An Aramaic Tomb Inscription Written in Paleo-Hebrew Script," *IEJ* 23 (1973) 82-91.

Niehoff, Maren, *The Figure of Joseph in Post-Biblical Jewish Literature* (Leiden 1992).

Neusner, J., *Rabbinic Traditions about the Pharisees Before 70* (3 vols.; Leiden 1971).

———, *From Politics to Piety: The Emergence of Pharisaic Judaism* (Engelwood Cliffs NJ 1973).

———, *A History of the Mishnaic Law of Women* (5 vols.; Leiden 1988).

———, *In Search of Talmudic Biography: The Problem of the Attributed Saying* (*Brown Judaic Studies* 70; Chico CA 1984).

———, *Reading and Believing: Ancient Judaism and Contemporary Gullibility* (*Brown Judaic Studies* 113; Atlanta 1986).

———, "Josphus' Pharisees: A Complete Repetoire," in L. H. Feldman and G. Hata (eds.), *Josephus, Judaism and Christianity* (Detroit 1987) 274-92.

Nickelsburg, G. W., *Resurrection, Immortality and Eternal Life in Intertestamental Judaism* (Cambridge MA 1972).

Niditch, Susan, "Esther: Folklore, Wisdom, Feminism and Authority," in Athalya Brenner (ed.), *A Feminist Companion to Esther, Judith and Susanna* (Sheffield 1995) 26-46.

Noam, Vered, "The Seventeenth of Elul in Megillat Taanit," *Zion* 59 (1994) 433-44 (Hebrew).

Noy (Neuman), D., *Motif Index of Talmudic-Midrashic Literature* (Unpublished Ph.D. Thesis, Bloomington IN, 1954).

Oesterley, W. O. E., *An Introduction to the Books of the Apocrypha* (New York 1935).

Otto, W., "Herodes," in *Pauly-Wissowa Real-Encyclopädie der Klassischen Altertumswissenschaft,* Supplementband 2 (Stuttgart 1913) 1-200.

Pape, W., *Wörterbuch der griechischen Eigennamen* (2 vols.; Braunschweig 1863-1870).

Patai R., "Jus Primae Noctis," *Studies of the Center for Folklore Research* 4 (1974) 177-80.

Paton, L. B., *International Critical Commentary: Esther* (Edinburgh 1908).

Perowne, S., *The Life and Times of Herod the Great* (London 1960).

Peskowitz, Miriam, "Spinning Tales: On Reading Gender and Otherness in Tannaitic Texts," in J. L. Silberstein and R. L. Cohn (eds.), *The Other in Jewish Thought and History: Construction of Jewish Culture and Identity* (New York 1994) 91-119.

———, "The Gendering of Burial; the Burial of Gender: Notes from Roman Period Archaeology," *JSQ* 4 (1997) 105-24.

Pfeifer, R. H., *History of New Testament Times with an Introduction to the Apocrypha* (New York 1949).

Philipson, D., *The Reform Movement in Judaism* (Cincinnati 1907).

Polotzky, H. J., "The Greek Papyri from the Cave of the Letters," *IEJ* 12 (1962) 258-62.

Pomeroy, Sarah B., *Goddesses, Whores, Wives and Slaves* (New York 1975).

———, "Infanticide in Hellenistic Greece," in Averil Cameron and Amélie Kuhrt (eds.), *Images of Women in Antiquity* (Detroit 1985) 207-22.

Porten, B. and A. Yardeni, *Textbook of Aramaic Documents from Ancient Egypt 1: Letters* (Jerusalem 1986).

———, *Textbook of Aramaic Documents from Ancient Egypt 2: Contracts* (Jerusalem 1989).

Preisigke, F., *Wörterbuch der griechischen Papyrusurkunden* (2 vols.; Berlin 1925).

Price, J. J., "The Enigma of Philip ben Jakimos," *Historia* 40 (1991) 77-94.

Prusak, J., "Women, Seductive Siren and the Source of Sin? Pseudepigraphical Myth and Christian Origin," in Rosemary R. Ruether (ed.), *Religion and Sexism: Images of Women in the Jewish Christian Traditions* (New York 1974) 89-116.

Rabello, A. M., "Divorce of Jews in the Roman Empire," *The Jewish Law Annual* 4 (1981) 79-102.

Rabinowitz, L. I., "Talmud, Jerusalem," in *Encyclopedia Judaica* 15 (Jerusalem 1971) 774.

Radday, Y. T., "Esther with Humour," in Y. T. Radday and Athalya Brenner (eds.), *On Humour and the Comic in the Hebrew Bible* (*JSOT Supplement Series* 23; Sheffield 1990) 295-313.

Rahmani, L. Y., *A Catalogue of Jewish Ossuaries in the Collections of the State of Israel* (Jerusalem 1994).

Rajak, Tessa, "Moses in Ethiopia: Legend and Literature," *JJS* 29 (1978) 111-22.

———, *Josephus: The Historian and his Society* (London 1983).

———, "Josephus and Justus of Tiberias," in L. H. Feldman and G. Hata (eds.), *Josephus, Judaism and Christianity* (Detroit 1987) 81-94.

———, with D. Noy, "Archisynagogoi: Office, Title and Social Status in the Greco-Jewish Synagogue," *JRS* 83 (1993) 75-93.

Rak, Y., B. Arensburg and H. Nathan, "Evidence of Violence on Human Bones in Israel, First and Third Century," *PEQ* 108 (1976) 55-8.

Rawson, Beryl, "From 'Daily Life' to 'Demography'," in R. Hawley and B. Levick (eds.), *Women in Antiquity: New Assessments* (London 1995) 1-20.

Reich, R., "The 'Boundary of Gezer' Inscriptions Again," *IEJ* 40 (1990) 44-6.

Reifenberg, A., *Ancient Hebrew Art* (New York 1950).

Reimann, O., "Inscriptions Greques provenant du recueil Cyriaque d'Anacone," *Bulletin de correspondence hellènique* 1 (1877).

Reinhartz, Adele, "Philo on Infanticide," *The Studia Philonica Annual* 4 (1992) 42-58.

Renan, M., "Nouvelles observations d'épigraphie hébraïque," *Journal Asiatique* 6 (Serie 6; 1865) 550-60.

———, "Note additionalle à la page 81," *Mémoires de l'Institute Impérial de France: Académie des Inscriptions et Belle Lettres* 26 (1870) 559-60.

Rey-Coquais, J. P., *Inscriptions Greques et Latines de la Syrie VI: Ba'albek et Beqa'* (Paris 1967).

Richardson, N. H., "Some Notes on 1QSa," *JBL* 76 (1957) 108-22.

Rivkin, Ellis, "Defining the Pharisees: The Tannaitic Sources," *HUCA* 40-41 (1970) 205-49.

———, *A Hidden Revolution: The Pharisees' Search for the Kingdom Within* (Nashville 1978).

Rogers, P. M., "Titus, Berenice and Mucianus," *Historia* 29 (1980) 86-95.

Rosenfeld, B. Z., "The 'Boundary of Gezer' Inscriptions and the History of Gezer at the End of the Second Temple Period," *IEJ* 38 (1988) 235-45.

Rosenthal, E. S., "The Giv'at ha-Mivtar Inscription," *IEJ* 23 (1973) 72-81.

Rosenthal, L. A., "Die Josephgeschichte mit den Büchern Esther und Daniel verglichen," *ZATW* 15 (1895) 278-84.

Rostovzeff, M. (P. M. Fraser, ed.), *The Social and Economic History of the Roman Empire* (Oxford 1957).

Roth, C., *A Short History of the Jewish People* (London 1969).

Roussel, P. "Nicanor d'Alexandrie et la porte du temple de Jerusalem," *REG* 37 (1924) 79-82.

Runnalls, Donna, "Moses' Ethiopian Campaign," *JSJ* 14 (1983) 135-56.

Safrai, S., "Beit She'arim in Talmudic Literature," *Eretz Israel* 5 (1958) 206-12 [Hebrew].

———, "Was There a Women's Gallery in the Synagogue of Antiquity?" *Tarbiz* 32 (1963) 329-38 [Hebrew].

———, "Torah Learned Women in the Mishnaic and Talmudic Period," *Mahanaim* 98 (1965) 58-9 [Hebrew].

——, "Eleazar of Modi'in," *Encyclopedia Judaica* 6 (Jerusalem 1971) 603.

——, "The Tales of the Sages in Palestinian Tradition and the Babylonian Talmud," in: J. Heinemann and D. Noy (eds.), *Studies in Aggadah and Folk-Literature* (*Scripta Hierosolymitana* 22; Jerusalem 1971) 209-32.

——, "The Synagogues South of Mt. Judah," *Immanuel* 3 (1973-4) 48-50.

——, "The Era of the Mishnah and Talmud (70-640)," in H. H. Ben-Sasson (ed.), *A History of the Jewish People* (Cambridge MA 1976) 307-82.

——, "The Role of Women in the Temple," *The Jerusalem Perspective* (July/August 1989) 5-6.

——, "The Place of Women in First Century Synagogues," *The Jerusalem Perspective* [September/October 1993] 3-6; 14.

——, *In Times of Temple and Mishnah: Studies in Jewish History* (2 vols; Jerusalem 1994) [Hebrew].

Saldarini, A. J., *Pharisees, Scribes and Sadducees* (Edinburgh 1989).

Sanders, E. P., *Judaism: Practice and Belief 63 BCE-66 CE* (London 1992).

Sanders, James A., "The Dead Sea Scrolls: A Quarter Century of Study," *BA* 36 (1973) 110-48.

Satlow, M. L., *Tasting the Dish: Rabbinic Rhetorics of Sexuality* (*Brown Judaic Studies* 303; Atlanta 1995).

——, "Reconsidering the Rabbinic *ketubbah* Payment," in S. J. D. Cohen (ed.), *The Jewish Family* (*Brown Judaic Studies* 289; Atlanta 1993) 133-51.

——, "'They Abused Him Like a Woman': Homoeroticism, Gender Blurring, and the Rabbis in Late Antiquity," *Journal of the History of Sexuality* 5 (1994) 1-25.

——, "'Texts of Terror': Rabbinic Texts, Speech Acts and the Control of Mores," *AJS Review* 21 (1996) 273-97.

Schäfer, P., *Der Bar-Kokhba-Aufstand: Studien zum zweiten jüdischen Krieg gegen Rom* (*Texte und Studien zum antiken Judentum* 1; Tübingen 1981).

——, "Der vorrabbinische Pharisäismus," in M. Hengel and U. Heckel (eds.), *Paulus und das antike Judentum: Tübingen-Durham-Symposium in Gedenken an den 50. Todestag Adolf Schlatters (Mai 1938)* (Tübingen 1988) 125-75.

Schalit, A. *König Herodes: Der Mann und sein Werk* (Berlin 1969).

Schechter, S., "The Quotations from Ecclesiasticus in Rabbinic Literature," *JQR* (O.S.) 3 (1891) 682-706.

Schiffman, L. H., "The Conversion of the Royal House of Adiabene in Josephus and Rabbinic Sources," in L. H. Feldman and G. Hata (eds.), *Josephus, Judaism and Christianity* (Detroit 1987) 293-312.

——, "Laws Pertaining to Women in the Temple Scroll," in Devorah Dimant and U. Rappaport (eds.), *The Dead Sea Scrolls: Forty Years of Research* (Leiden 1992) 210-28.

Schmidt, C., *Jus primae noctis: Eine geschichtliche Untersuchung* (Freiburg 1881).

Schmidt-Bleibtreu, H. F. W., *Jus primae noctis: Herrenrecht der ersten Nacht* (Bonn 1988).

Schneider, B., "Esther Revised According to the Maccabees," *Liber Annus* 13 (1962-3) 190-218.

Schottroff, Luise, "Frauen in der Nachfolge Jesu in neutestamentlicher Zeit," in W. Schottroff and W. Stegemann (eds.), *Traditionen der Befreiung* 2: *Frauen in der Bibel* (München 1980) 91-133.

Schremer, A., "Divorce in Papyrus Se'elim 13 Once Again: A Reply to Tal Ilan," *HTR* 91 (1998) 193-202.

Schuller, Eileen M., "Women of the Exodus in Biblical Retellings of the Second Temple Period," in Peggy L. Day (ed.), *Gender and Difference in Ancient Israel* (Minneapolis 1989) 178-94.

——, "Women in the Dead Sea Scrolls," in M. O. Wise, N. Golb, J. J. Collins and D. G. Pardee (eds.), *Methods of Investigation of the Dead Sea Scrolls and the Khirbet of Qumran Site: Present Realities and Future Prospects (Annals of the New York Academy of Science* 722; New York 1993) 115-31.

Schürer, E., G. Vermes, F. Millar and M. Black, *The History of the Jewish People in the Age of Jesus Christ (175 BC-AD 135)* (3 vols.; Edinburgh 1979).

Schüssler-Fiorenza, Elisabeth, *In Memory of Her: A Feminist Theological Reconstruction of Christian Beginnings* (New York 1982).

—— (ed.), *Searching the Scripture* (2 vols; New York 1994).

Schwabe, M., "Notes on the History of Tiberias: An Epigraphical Study," in M. Schwabe and J. Guttman (eds.), *In Memoriam Iohannis Lewy* (Jerusalem 1949) 200-51.

——, with B. Lifschitz, *Beth She'arim* 2 (Jerusalem 1974).

Schwartz, A., *Die Erleichterungen der Schammaiten und die Erschwerungen der Hilleliten: Ein Beitrag zur Entwicklungsgeschichte der Halachah* (Wien 1893).

Schwartz, D. R., "Κατὰ τοῦτον τὸν καιρὸν: Josephus' Source on Agrippa II," *JQR* 72 (1981-2) 241-68.

——, "Josephus and Nicolaus on the Pharisees," *JSJ* 14 (1983) 157-71.

——, "Herod in Jewish Sources," in M. Naor (ed.), *King Herod and his Age (Idan* 5; Jerusalem 1985) 38-42 [Hebrew].

——, *Agrippa I: The Last King of Judaea (Texte und Studien zum antiken Judentum* 23; Tübingen 1990).

——, "Law and Truth: On Qumran-Sadducean and Rabbinic Views of Law," in Devorah Dimant and U. Rappaport (eds.), *The Dead Sea Scrolls: Forty Years of Research* (Leiden 1992) 229-40.

——, *Studies in the Jewish Background of Christianity (Wissenschaftliche Untersuchungen zum Neuen Testament* 60; Tübingen 1992).

——, "Josephus on Hyrcanus II," in F. Parente and J. Sievers (eds.), *Josephus and the History of the Greco-Roman Period* (Leiden 1994) 210-32.

——, "Hillel and Scripture: From Authority to Exegesis," in J. H. Charlesworth and L. L. Johns (eds.), *Hillel and Jesus* (Minneapolis 1997) 335-62.

Schwartz, J., "Once More on the 'Boundary of Gezer' Inscriptions and the History of Gezer and Lydda at the End of the Second Temple Period," *IEJ* 38 (1988) 47-57.

——, "Once More on the Nicanor Gate," *HUCA* 62 (1991) 245-83.

Schwartz, S., *Josephus and Judaean Politics* (Leiden 1990).

——, "Review of S. Mason, *Flavius Josephus on the Pharisees: A Composition-Critical Study*," *AJS Review* 19 (1994) 86-7.

Segal, A. F., *The Other Judaisms of Late Antiquity (Brown Judaic Studies* 127; Atlanta 1987).

Segal, M. Z., *The Complete Book of Ben Sira* (Jerusalem 1972) 37-42 [Hebrew].

Seligman, J. with J. Zais and H. Stark, "Late Hellenistic and Byzantine Burial Caves at Giv'at Sharet, Bet Shemesh," *Atiqot* 29 (1996) 43-62.

Shaw, B. D., "The Age of Roman Girls at Marriage," *JRS* 77 (1987) 30-46.

Shinan, A., "Moses and the Ethiopian Woman: Sources of a Story in the Chronicles of Moses," in J. Heinemann and S. Werses (eds.), *Studies in Hebrew Narrative Art (Scripta Hierosolymitana* 27; Jerusalem 1978) 69-72.

Sievers, J., "The Role of Women in the Hasmonean Dynasty," in L. H. Feldman and G. Hata (eds.), *Josephus, Bible and History* (Detroit 1988) 132-46.

Skehan, P. W., "The Biblical Scrolls from Qumran and the Text of the Old Testament," *BA* 28 (1965) 87-100.

Sly, Dorothy, *Philo's Perceptions of Women (Brown Judaic Studies* 209; Atlanta 1990).

Smallwood, Edith Mary, *The Jews Under Roman Rule: From Pompey to Diocletian* (Leiden 1976).

Smith, M., "Palestinian Judaism in the First Century," in M. Davis (ed.), *Israel: Its Role in Civilization* (New York 1956) 67-81.

Smith, Patricia, "The Human Skeletal Remains from the Abba Cave," *IEJ* 27 (1977) 122-3.

——, with J. Zias, "Skeletal Remains from the Late Hellenistic French Hill Tomb," *IEJ* 30 (1980) 109-15.

——, with Elizabeth Bornemann and J. Zias, "The Skeletal Remains," in E. M. Meyers, J. F. Strange and Carol L. Meyers (eds.), *Excavations at Ancient Meiron, Upper Galilee, Israel 1971-2* (Cambridge MA 1981) 110-8.

Sonne, I., "The Schools of Shammai and Hillel seen from Within," in S. Lieberman, S. Zeitlin, S. Spiegel and A. Marx (eds.), *Louis Ginzberg Jubilee Volume* (English volume; New York 1945) 275-91.

Sperber, D., *Roman Palestine 200-400: Money and Prices* (Ramat Gan 1991).

Steckoll, S. H., "Preliminary Excavation Report in the Qumran Cemetery," *RQ* 6 (1968) 323-36.

Stegemann, H., "The Qumran Essenes: Local Members of the Main Jewish Union in Late Second Temple Times," in J. T. Barrera and L. V. Montaner (eds.), *The Madrid Qumran Congress* 1 (Leiden 1992) 83-166.

Stern, M., "Aspects of Jewish Society: The Priesthood and Other Classes," in: S. Safrai and M. Stern (eds.), *The Jewish People in the First Century* 2 (*Compendia Rerum Iudaicarum ad Novum Testamentum* Section One; Philadelphia 1976) 531-630.

——, "Sicarii and Zealots," in M. Avi-Yonah and Z. Baras (eds.), *The World History of the Jewish People: Society and Religion in the Second Temple Period* (Jerusalem 1977) 263-301.

——, *Studies in Jewish History: The Second Temple Period* (Jerusalem 1991) 402-7 [Hebrew].

——, *Greek and Latin Authors on Jews and Judaism* (3 vols.; Jerusalem 1976-84).

Stiehl, Ruth, "Das Buch Esther," *Wiener Zeitschrift für die Kunde des Morgenlandes* 53 (1956) 4-22.

Swedlund, A. C. and G. J. Armelagos, "Paleodemographic Studies," in *Demographic Anthropology* (Dubuque IA 1976) 33-55.

Swidler, L. J., "Beruriah: Her Word Became Law," *Lilith* 3 (1977) 9-12.

——, *Biblical Affirmations of Women* (Philadelphia 1979).

Tabori, J., "Two Wedding Ceremonies: Alcestis and some Jewish Parallels," *Scripta Classica Israelica* 6 (1981-2) 16-22.

Talmon S., "'Wisdom' in the Book of Esther," *VT* 13 (1963) 419-55.

——, "Fragments of Scrolls from Masada," *Eretz Israel* 20 (1989) 278-86 [Hebrew].

——, "Was the Book of Esther Known at Qumran?" *Dead Sea Discoveries* 2 (1995) 249-67.

Tcherikover, V. A., A. Fuks and M. Stern (eds.), *Corpus Papyrorum Judaicarum* (3 vols.; Cambridge MA 1960-4).

Thackery, H. St. J., *Josephus: The Man and the Historian* (New York 1929).

Tiktin, S. A., *Darstellung des Sachverhältnisses in seiner hiesigen Rabbinatsangelegenheit* (Breslau 1842).

Thompson, S. K., *Sampling* (New York 1992).

Torrey, C. C., "The Older Book of Esther," *HTR* 37 (1944) 1-40.

Tov, E., "The Lucanic Text of the Canonical and Apocryphal Sections of Esther: A Rewritten Biblical Book," *Textus* 10 (1982) 1-25.

Trenchard, C. W., *Ben Sira's View of Women: A Literary Analysis* (*Brown Judaic Studies* 38; Chico CA 1983).

Tyrrel, W. B., *Amazons: A Study of Athenian Mythmaking* (Baltimore 1984).

Tzaferis, V., "Jewish Tombs at and Near Giv'at ha-Mivtar," *IEJ* 20 (1970) 18-32.

——, "The 'Abba' Burial Cave in Jerusalem," *Atiqot* 7 (1977; Hebrew Series) 61-4 [Hebrew].

Urman, D., "Jewish Inscriptions from Dabura in the Golan," *IEJ* 22 (1972) 16-23.

——, "Jewish Inscriptions of the Mishnah and Talmud Period from Qazrin in the Golan," *Tarbiz* 53 (1984) 513-45 [Hebrew].

Valler, Shulamit, *Women and Womanhood in the Stories of the Babylonian Talmud* (Tel Aviv 1993) [Hebrew].

Vaux, R. de, "Fouille au Khirbet Qumrân: Rapport Préliminaire," *RB* 60 (1953) 83-106.

——, "Fouilles de Khirbet Qumrân," *RB* 63 (1956) 533-77.

——, *Archaeology and the Dead Sea Scrolls* (Oxford 1973).

——, with J. T. Milik and P. Benoit, *Discoveries in the Judaean Desert* 2 (Oxford 1961).

Vermes, G., "Sectarian Matrimonial Halakhah in the Damascus Rule," *JJS* 25 (1974) 197-202.

——, *The Dead Sea Scrolls in English* (London 1987).

Viereck, P., *Ägyptische Urkunden aus den Königlichen Museen zu Berlin: Griechische Urkunden* 1 (Berlin, 1895).

Visotzky, Burton, "Most Tender and Fairest of Women: A Study in the Transmission of Aggadah," *HTR* 76 (1983) 403-18.

Wacholder, B.-Z., *Nicolaus of Damascus* (*University of California Publications in History*; Berkeley 1962).

——, with M. G. Abegg, *A Preliminary Edition of the Unpublished Dead Sea Scrolls* (3 vols.; Washington DC 1995).

Waddington, W. H., *Inscriptions Grecques et Latines de la Syrie* (Paris 1870).

——, "Aux Fastes de la province d'Asie," *Bulletin de correspondance hellènique* 6 (1882) 289-91.

Wasserstein, A., "A Marriage Contract from the Province of Arabia Nova: Notes on Papyrus Yadin 18," *JQR* 80 (1989) 105-30.

Weber, M., *Ancient Judaism* (Glencoe IL 1952).

Wegner, Judith Romney, *Chattel or Person: The Status of Women in the Mishnah* (Oxford 1988).

Weigand, T., *Die Inschriften* in A. Rehm (ed.), *Didyma, 2 Teil* (Berlin 1958).

Wiener, M., *Abraham Geiger and Liberal Judaism: The Challenge of the Nineteenth Century* (translation E.J. Schlochauer; Philadelphia 1962).

Weiss, M., "The Authenticity of the Explicit Discussions in Bet Shammai-Bet Hillel Discussion," *Sidra: A Journal for the Study of Rabbinic Literature* 4 (1988) 53-66 [Hebrew].

Weiss-Rosemarine, Trude, "Josephus' 'Eleazar Speech' and Historical Credibility," *Proceedings of the Sixth World Congress of Jewish Studies* 1 (Jerusalem 1973) 417-27.

White, Sidnie-Ann, "Esther: A Feminine Model for Jewish Diaspora," in Peggy L. Day (ed.), *Gender and Difference in Ancient Israel* (Minneapolis 1989) 161-77.

Wilcken, U., "Berenike," *Pauly-Wissowa Real-Encyclopädie der klassischen Altertumswissenschaft* 3/1 (Stuttgart 1897) 282-7.

Wills, L. M., *The Jews in the Courts of Foreign Kings* (*Harvard Dissertations in Religion* 26; Minneapolis 1990).

——, *The Jewish Novel in the Ancient World* (Ithaca 1995).

Wire, Antoinette C., *The Corinthian Women Prophets: A Reconstruction through Paul's Rhetoric* (Minneapolis 1990).

Wolff, H. J., *Written and Unwritten Marriage* (Haverford PA 1939).

Wyler, Bea, "Esther: The Incomplete Emancipation of a Queen," in Athalya Brenner (ed.), *A Feminist Companion to Esther, Judith and Susanna* (Sheffield 1995) 111-35.

Yadin, Y., "Expedition D," *IEJ* 11 (1961) 36-52.

——, "The Excavation at Masada: 1963/4 Preliminary Report," *IEJ* 15 (1965) 1-154.

——, *Masada: Herod's Fortress and the Zealots' Last Stand* (London 1966).

———, *Bar Kokhba: Rediscovery of the Legendary Hero of the Second Jewish Revolt against Rome* (Jerusalem 1971).

———, with J. Naveh, *Masada 1: The Aramaic and Hebrew Ostraca and Jar Inscriptions from Masada* (Jerusalem 1989).

———, with J. C. Greenfield and Ada Yardeni, "Babatha's Ketubba," *IEJ* 44 (1994) 75-101.

Yardeni, Ada, *Nahal Se'elim Documents* (Jerusalem 1995) [Hebrew].

———, with J. M. Greenfield, "A Receipt for a Ketubba," in I. M. Gafni, A. Oppenheimer and D. R. Schwartz (eds.), *The Jews in the Hellenistic-Roman World: Studies in Memory of Menahem Stern* (Jerusalem 1996) 197-208 [Hebrew].

Yaron, R., *Introduction to the Law of the Aramaic Papyri* (Oxford 1961).

Yasif, E., *The Tales of Ben Sira in the Middle Ages: A Critical Text and Literary Studies*, (Jerusalem 1984) [Hebrew].

Young, Robin D., "'The Woman with the Soul of Abraham': Traditions about the Mother of the Maccabean Martyrs," in Amy-Jill Levine (ed.), *'Women Like This': New Perspectives on Jewish Women in the Greco-Roman World* (Atlanta 1991) 67-81.

Zias, J., "Anthropological Evidence of Interpersonal Violence in First Century A.D. Jerusalem," *Current Anthropology* 24 (1983) 233.

———, "Human Skeletal Remains from the 'Caiaphas' Tomb," *Atiqot* 21 (1992 - English Series) 78-80.

———, "Human Skeletal Remains from the Mount Scopus Tomb," *Atiqot* 21 (1992 - English Series) 97-103.

———, "Canabis Sativa (Hashish) as an Effective Medication in Antiquity: The Anthropological Evidence," in S. Campbell and A. Green (eds.), *The Archaeology of the Dead in the Ancient Near East* (Oxford 1995) 232-4.

———, "Anthropological Analysis of Human Skeletal Remains," in G. Avni and Z. Greenhut (eds.), *The Akeldama Tombs* (*IAA Reports* 1; Jerusalem 1996) 117-20.

Zeitlin, S., "Studies in Tannaitic Jurisprudence: Intention as a Legal Principle," *Journal for Jewish Lore and Philosophy* 1 (1919) 297-311.

———, "Queen Salome and King Jannaeus Alexander: A Chapter in the History of the Second Jewish Commonwealth," *JQR* 51 (1960-1) 1-33.

———, "Zealots and Sicarii," *JBL* 81 (1962) 395-8.

———, "Herod: A Malevolent Maniac," *JQR* 54 (1963-4) 1-27.

———, "The Books of Esther and Judith: A Parallel," in M. S. Enslin (ed.), *The Book of Judith* (*Jewish Apocryphal Literature* 7; Philadelphia 1972) 1-37.

———, *The Rise and Fall of the Judaean State* (3 vols.; Philadelphia 1978).

Zimmerman, F., *The Book of Tobit* (*Jewish Apocryphal Literature*; New York 1958).

Index of Sources

The Hebrew Bible

The New Testament

Josephus

Apocrypha and Pseudepigrapha

Tobit
1:1-2   139-40

Susanna
1   139
56-7   146

Aristeas
250   132

Esdras
4.14-32   125

Ancient Authors

Philo
Special Laws
3.118-9   204

Hypothetica
11.14   38

De Vita Contemplativa 38

Homer
Iliad
3.189   130, n. 4
6.186   130, n. 4

Aeschilus
Prometheus
723   130, n. 4

Suppliant Maidens
287   130, n. 4

Eumenides
628   130, n. 4
685-90   130, n. 4

Euripides
Madness of Hercules
408-17   130, n. 4

Ion
1145   130, n. 4

Aristophanes
Lysistrata
676   130, n. 4
Herodotus
4.110-7   130, n. 4

Xenophon

Anabasis
4.4.16   130, n. 4

Plato
De Republica
5.454E-457C   128

Laws
7.804E-805A   128
7.805E-806 C   129, n. 2
7.806B   130, n. 4

Menexenus
9B 7.806 B   130, n. 4

Aristotle
Politics
1.5.1260a   128
2.6.1269b   129
5.9.1313b   128

Diodorus Sycalus
2.44-6   130
3.52-5   130
3.55.3   130; 131
17.77.1-4   129
40.3   203

Strabo
Geographia
11.5.3   130-1
11.5.4   129

Pausanias
Description of Greece
8.16.5   223

Livy
36.2   129
36.7   129

Rabbinic Literature

Dead Sea Documents

Index of Authors

Index of Persons

Index of Subjects

adultery/adulteress 56; 69-70; 105; 110; 115; 143; 148; 160; 165; 165; 167; 173; 262

Alexandria 54, n. 25; 120, n. 89; 131; 204; 221; 222; 225; 226; 233; 246-7

Amazons 129-32

Babatha archive 7; 217; 223; 232; 235; 245; 239; 261

Babylonia 43; 137; 162; 170; 171; 173; 182; 183; 188-9; 190

Be fruitful and multiply 59; 60

Beit Hillel and Beit Shammai 4-5; 43-81

Beit Shammai see Beit Hillel

betrothal 27; 46-50; 59; 236; 239; 241; 244; 245; 245-7

chastity 52; 70; 146; 148; 170; 173; 193

child 58; 64; 147; 205; 206; 208; 250
— birth/bearing 160; 202; 207; 211-2
— exposure 203-4
— hood 205
— less 29; 56
— mortality 7; 198; 199-202
— raising/rearing 3; 34; 203-4
— skeletons 205
— welfare 61

children 15; 49; 57; 78; 91; 97; 105; 107; 116; 187; 196; 198; 199; 201; 201; 203; 205; 206; 214

Christianity 4; 11; 31-7; 44; 81, n. 78; 176; 196; 210; 222, n. 26; 225, n. 42; 238; 251

conversion 25-6; 67; 70; (100); 116; (117); 196

Day of Atonement 18; 31, n. 59; 69

Dead Sea 227; Sect/Scrolls 4; 17; 23, n. 42; 31, n. 59; 38-42; 72; 140-1; 155; 157, n. 10; 197; 198; 201; 205-6; 214; 220, n. 15

Diaspora 12-3; 38; 139

divorce 7; 34; 39; 50-2; 57; 59; 92; 116; 163; 166; 169; 196; 237; 241; 244; 253-62

Egypt/ian 34, n. 68; 38; 131-2; 133; 135; 147; 196; 211; 211; 218; 219; 223-33; 239; 250

Ein Gedi 198; 201-2; 207; 214; 223; 225; 227; 235; 257-8; 259

elder(s) 68; 76; 121; 125; 132; 145; 149; 149; 187; 228; 247
— women 40

Essenes 38; 39; 41; 140; 205-6

Fourth Philosophy see Zealots

Idumaeans 1; 28; 74; 115

incest 57-9; 62; 93; 95-6

inheritance 54-5; 63, n. 40
— women's 32; 72-3; 204; 226

jealousy 79; 105
— of women 34; 95-6; 97; 119; 120

Jerusalem/ites 21; 27-8; 30; 67; 74; 78; 86, n. 5; 93, n. 30; 94; 106; 132; 135; 137; 139; 153; 178; 195; 198; 199-201; 209, n. 43; 212; 221; 222; 254; 262

Judaean Desert 197; 198; 217; 223; 235; 237; 240; 241; 247; 247; 257; 261

ketubbah 29; 36-7; 54-5; 236; 240-2; 246; 255

levir/levirate 29; 48; 49; 53; 56-59; 72, n. 59

love 57; 75; 102; 127
— between men and women 105; 104; 111; 113; 114; 166

lover/s 93; 111-2; 137, n. 29; 165

maidservant see slave

marriage 7; 8; 20; 23; 27; 29; 39-41; 45; 46-63; 70-1; 72, n. 59; 73; 86; 88; 92; 94-6; 105; 109; 111; 115; 116-21; 131; 151; 160; 162; 166; 196; 212; 219; 225; 227; 229; 235-42; 259; 259; 260

martyr/martyrdom 5; 76-7; 143; 177-8; 190